MW01515795

MODERN PROBLEMS, ANCIENT PERSPECTIVES

FROM HUNTERS AND FARMERS

TO

HUNTED AND FARMED

Copyright © 2015 by Vernon Molloy

All rights reserved. No part of this publication may be reproduced, stored in or introduced into a retrieval system, or transmitted, in any form, or by any means (electronic, mechanical, photocopying, recording, or otherwise) without the prior written permission of the copyright owner and publisher of this book.

Table of Contents

Modern Problems, Ancient Perspectives

Vernon Molloy

Foreword

The alternative to realism sketched below proposes a way of thinking in which the 'world thing' is replaced with the 'world event'. Dissolving things into underlying parcels of events changes everything we understand while leaving understandings more or less intact. This can be great fun. It also means that political and economic problems can be seen in new ways. I know this flimsy sketch will not persuade anyone to abandon the idea that the world is an actual place full of actual things but I hope it is persuasive enough that you take an alternative story for a test drive. What is this possibility? We presently think 'the world' was brought into existence by some event such as the Big Bang or Divine Creation. We see ourselves living in the aftermath of this stupendous event. However — especially if one is religious — this means the world is little more than a set of problems to be overcome, a trysting place and a vast examination hall. On this account — subscribed to by realists and theists alike — each of us awoke one day and found ourselves in circumstances that had to be negotiated whether we liked it or not. For most theists, these difficulties amount to a preamble to a supernatural existence wherein there are no material things and — if we make a passing grade — we get to exist eternally at some spiritual analogue of physical perfection. On the other hand, for those who fail to pass muster, what happens next involves Hell-fire and damnation!

No matter what the outcome, there are neither children nor old people in this story. Since they have not reached the age of reason, children cannot be praised nor blamed, rewarded or punished. They have no place in an eternity predicated upon praising or blaming. Old people seem verboten as well, perhaps because they do not have the stamina to appreciate the ecstasies of Heaven or the torments of being burned alive. (These difficulties are managed by having the deceased enter Heaven or Hell at their most vigorous age.)

If a person is not religious the prognosis is almost as bleak: a short, troubled life, then oblivion.

Modern Problems, Ancient Perspectives

In the following I stand this story on its head. Events have pride of place and notions of things and entities (including persons) are useful but chimerical imaginings in the minds of beings like you and I.

I like the word *being*. The word says all that needs to be said. I think it says all that can be said.

As well I hope to interest you in a way of thinking about male-female relationships sketched in *Axioms of Subordination*.

- A discussion of *The Nature of Consciousness* follows.
- *Concrete Problems* proposes that most human beings do not develop as far cognitively as Jean Piaget proposed.
- *Truth Tables* examines the fallacy of dividing the world into realms: self, possessions (stuff) and everything remaining.
- *Why the Music Stopped* explores connections between the music industry and breadlines.
- *The Perception of Time in Cities* was written more than twenty years ago. The essay contains early versions of several ideas discussed below. They have apparently been ruminating away and contributing to this project.

The point is, my awareness had nothing to do with *creating* or *expressing* these notions. Insofar as you and I understand ourselves as the sum total of our conscious episodes, we must also understand ourselves as narratives based on nothing more than being the first beneficiaries of event occurring within the collections of events bearing our names.

Vernon Molloy

School Bus Days

I recall my first year as a high school student at Madoc, Ontario in 1956.

Not much about the school comes to mind, but I remember bus trips from the family farm — ten miles as the crow flies, perhaps fifteen as the bus meandered up and down side roads picking up and disgorging students.

I do not recall how I came to occupy the seat behind the driver, but I remember that it fell to me to operate the door letting students on or off.

I assume the driver appreciated this. At least, he did not put me in my place. 'Helping out' was *de rigeur* in rural circumstances when much had to be accomplished manually.

I have no recollection of how the other students regarded my efforts. To my knowledge they didn't object although I am sure snickering was involved.

Unfortunately, the help I began offering my fellow passengers later on — to assist them through doors that had opened for me — was not the help they had in mind. The further my 'helping out' project evolved, the more exciting the doors I imagined myself opening for them, the more resistance I encountered.

The more resistance, the more voluminous and strident my overtures became.

You see where this is going. My acquaintances started defending themselves. Invitations were rarely extended a second time. "Come on in!" waves transformed into "Keep on going!" gesticulations.

This has been the story of my life. I am not complaining. I am having a wonderful time. Appearances notwithstanding, I remain young enough to be disappointed at how few conversations I am able to provoke.

There is much to talk about.

Modern Problems, Ancient Perspectives

As well, talking about what is going on is the only chance you and I have of extricating ourselves from the fate the world's clever and beautiful people have in mind for us.

Unfortunately, most of my conversations – and most conversations I observe others having – involve little more than pissing contests. The goal is to emerge with whatever collection of understandings, responsibilities and prerogatives one had at the outset intact. If a 'gotcha' moment moment can be scored along the way, victory is declared!

I have come to understand why this is so. The problem has nothing to do with arrogance, hubris or the conversational deficits of interlocutors. These are the names we give to difficulties that have been, as William Butler Yeats warned in *The Coming*, slouching towards Bethlehem for ten thousand years.

This book attempts to describe these problems and sketch a few possible solutions. Most days I am not optimistic about how this will turn out, but my 'door opening' habit started early.

I started out opening school bus doors so my classmates could get on a contraption promising to transport us to a bright future.

I am ending up suggesting why we might wish to get off the machinations that resulted before they transport us into oblivion.

This has an ironic symmetry, or at least a soupçon of poetic justice.

Vernon Molloy

Why The World Seems So Real

**Bancroft, Ontario
1920: my mother's
childhood home**

**Coe Hill, Ontario 1920: my father's
childhood home**

I have good news.

Modern Problems, Ancient Perspectives

The world is more interesting than we think.

Human beings are more interesting as well. We are not afterthoughts carved out of creation by God Herself. Nor are we stolid entities distilled out of molecules by Darwinian evolution.

Every creature is an event that coalesces, catches fire for a time and then fades into new arrangements.

If you doubt this, a moment's introspection discovers many challenges to common sense and realism.

For example, you and I are only aware of a few of the events constituting our lives.

Another challenge is that, unless we talk to one another, we have no idea of what is going on in one another's lives - and a correspondingly impoverished sense of an actual world.

Finally, no matter how robust our sense of objects and events come to be, objects and events do not exist in real time relationships with us. Awarenesses are images of past events. They involve vanished states of affairs. Sometimes these intervals are measured in picoseconds, sometimes longer. The sunshine we are enjoying came into existence 8 minutes before it reached us. Light from Alpha Centauri - the closest star to our solar system - started our way 4.5 years ago.

We are good at remembering experiences but have no recollection of intervals separating them. Our memories hang together seamlessly. My life resumes every morning more or less where it left off when I went to sleep.

This sets the stage for realism (the idea of an actual, external world), and for the narratives we think of as our lives. (I owe this understanding to Derek Parfit: *Reasons and Persons*, Oxford Paperbacks, 1984.)

Because we talk about our private experiences – and sometimes organize projects based on these conversations – we eagerly agree that they reflect an actual world and what is going on in it.

I hope to persuade you that this cannot be true. Conscious episodes are generated by neural events in creatures like you and I. These events integrate memories with local events with a view to predicting what will happen if we do, or fail to do, something.

These proceedings are best understood in terms of Stimulus-Response networks. Conscious episodes occur within the stretched out hyphen spaces (-) separating Stimulus from Response that human beings are capable of.

As far as we know, the ability to improve responses by interposing conscious episodes distinguishes human beings from other forms of life. However there is no reason to assume that this capacity does not occur in other creatures. Consciousness is not a divinely-endowed faculty human beings have and other creatures lack. Consciousness is a straightforward evolution of the stimulus-response capabilities defining life. The fact that conscious episodes look and feel like something is a computationally economical way of embodying 'organic significances' so that best responses occur automatically.

My arguments supporting this proposition will all be simple. Sophisticated individuals might wish to cleanse their palate by considering the reality described by quantum physicists.

The most relevant idea is that observations are necessary to resolve probabilities into actualities. The following is from http://en.wikipedia.org/wiki/Quantum_mechanics

> According to one interpretation, as the result of a measurement the wave function containing the probability information for a system collapses from a given initial state to a particular eigenstate.
>
> ... The basic idea is that when a quantum system interacts with a measuring apparatus, their respective wave—functions become entangled (http://en.wikipedia.org/wiki/Quantum_Entanglement), so that the original quantum system ceases to exist as an independent entity.

I think this means that quantum resolutions only benefit observers who happen to be 'in the room' and enjoying simultaneous experiences they get to talk about.

These conversations, based upon simultaneously-resolved quantum events, become the ground of realism and common sense.

Each person makes observations resolving probabilities into notions of coherent, enduring objects and entities. When enough human beings do this simultaneously and invent ways to discuss and record their impressions, languages and cultures emerge and, eventually, notions of an actual world.

If one of these persons happens to be an Einstein, he or she then spend time insisting that the God responsible for the universe would not have included dice playing at the heart of his/her creation.

To consider realism (the claim that we live in an independently existing actual world) from another vantage point, the 2013 Nobel committee recognized that the Higgs Boson and associated Higgs field were responsible for *massive* particles. Because of Higgs Bosons, some events no longer proceed at the speed of light. Without such differentiation, you and I would not exist because nothing would clump together sufficiently to be noticed, much less evolve into creatures capable of noticing.

In other words, the private worlds and conscious episodes we think of as our lives are tips of unfathomable events. Everything going on, including conscious episodes, are best understood as sub-events of the *Big Bang* event said to have occurred (but really only started) fourteen billion years ago.

In the meantime, until we get this sorted out, *seeing is believing*. Although human beings occasionally acknowledge that appearances can be deceptive, we have not grasped that images and sensations are more or less elaborate predictions of what the future might hold.

Notions and images of dogs, cats, trees and people are individuals' best guesses of what would happen if we reached out and touched the events signified.

The ensuing idea that images are glimpses of an actual world full of things, entities and events are wonderfully useful but also wonderfully dangerous conceits.

The most important mischief involves the ways objects and thoughs seem complete and perfect. They seem complete and perfect because the processes generating them generate just enough consciousness to contain them – with never an inch nor a millimetre to spare.

Like mythical Cadillacs, images, concepts, thoughts... come 'factory—equipped' with perfectly-sized parking spaces.

This is also why empty, bored, unfulfilled... consciousness is never an issue. Experiences of unease, anxiety or inadequacy..., can always be tracked back to a hormonal event, a failed project or some commercial blandishment.

- Recommendations that life—styles could do with a bit of improving occur all day every day. In 2012, more than $500 billion was spent on advertising.

- According to Charles Dickens' *A Christmas Carol,* a bit of undigested beef could be involved.

The point is, our factory setting is that every idea, every image, every conclusion... seems perfect. How could it be otherwise? The function of ideas, images, conclusions... is to improve responses. Timeliness is all-important. The notion that ideas, images, conclusions... are guesses that could always do with a bit of improvement never crosses our minds. Indeed, until communities, languages and cultures emerged, such notions would have been wool-gathering distractions interfering with fast, effective responses.

This explains why we are willing to gossip endlessly about non-issues: the weather, the antics of public figures or the prospects of drug—addled athletes rather than critiquing one another's conclusions or beliefs. We believe the world is fixed, immutable and *external.*

The idea that each of us is hosting a private distillation of what is going on never occurs to us.

Modern Problems, Ancient Perspectives

In the grip of this picture, only the inebriated or ideologically-driven regularly attempt to persuade bystanders of the brilliance of their take on the world.

Surprisingly, for reasons discussed further along, such proselytizers find converts, fans and followers more often than might be expected. The resulting troops, cohorts, fans and fanatics populate history books. These followers can often be put to profitable work – or deputized to overwhelm or kill other ideologues' followers.

I propose a more interesting — and I think more survivable — way of thinking about what is going on:

- *Each person dreams a world into existence and then imagines herself inhabiting it.*
- *You have your world. I have mine. There are as many imaginary worlds as there are people.*
- *There is no corresponding actual world, although corresponding processes are real.*

Why do these imaginary worlds seem so real? Why do we treat one another badly? The answers are intertwined.

The idea of an external world catalyses notions of self—hood; which makes conceits about mutually conscious individuals plausible.

The relationship between persons and the world is a "chicken or egg first?" issue. Both have to be present before either can be identified.

Ironically, without consciousness and notions of self-hood, human beings would exist in selfless relationships with one another and the world.

The downside is that we would not notice or enjoy this Zen state because conscious episodes would be few and far between.

This belief in an actual world nurtures good and bad possibilities. The idea of an actual shared world depends upon creatures like you and I comparing experiences and "talking up a storm". This idea of an actual world is therefore created by interlocutors concluding that they are 'referring to' a fully-fledged external world.

More than a million human beings are now indulging in a *second* collective fantasy: they are conceiving and inhabiting another virtual world called *Second Life.*[1]

We take up such possibilities: gambling, the vicarious lives of sports fans and pornography consumers, lust to get to heaven... , like ducks to water.

With regard to *First Life* claims, investigations into the processes responsible for conscious episodes are slowly dissolving common-sense claims and realist ontologies.

- As far as we know, only human beings have the capacity to retain and reflect upon memories. Other creatures depend upon reflexes, conditioned responses, speed, strength, vision... to achieve survival and reproduction.
- When memories and reflections occur in communities, they spawn languages, cultures, hunting trips, ball games and talk about an actual world.
- As far as we know, only human beings have the cognitive resources necessary to organize experiences into notions of selves, events and a world containing them.
- As far as we know, only human beings conjure

---

[1] Second Life users (also called Residents) create virtual representations of themselves, called avatars and are able to interact with other avatars, places or objects. They can explore the world (known as the grid), meet other residents, socialize, participate in individual and group activities, build, create, shop and trade virtual property and services with one another. It is a platform that principally features 3D-based user-generated content. Second Life also has its own virtual currency, the Linden Dollar, which is exchangeable with real world currency.
http://en.wikipedia.org/wiki/Second_Life

16

themselves into existence as persons living in
and travelling across an actual world.

These proceedings not only grant human beings a central role
in internal theatres, they guarantee that other species are
understood as less important. The logic is simple. They do not
regard themselves the way we regard ourselves. They inhabit
an eternal present without notions of *here* and *now* and *there*
and *then.*

Since they do not know that they exist, they have nothing to
lose.

This is convenient I because it means that you and I can farm
them, slaughter them or make them into pets.

We do not have to worry about them worrying about what is
happening Only human beings worry about tomorrows. Only
human concoct supernatural fantasies to wriggle away from
the prospect of death.

Aside from being blatantly self-serving, such arguments
overlook important problems with 'actual world' stories.

- Human beings have been elevating a few of the
  events constituting their existence into 'organic entity'
  and 'thing' status.

- Human beings have only a brief time to experience
  what is going on

- Survival demands that we pay particular attention to
  local events.

- Other attention-determining factors include whether
  we have some hunting, farming, petting... project in
  mind.

A more reasonable view is that, whenever we see birds flying
or squirrels making impossible leaps, we are glimpsing tiny
portiosn of an unfathomably complex reality.

Worlds conjured up on the basis on such glimpses, worlds
populated with similarly truncated notions of persons and

objects..., are useful the way it is useful to throw dust in the air to see which way the wind is blowing.

No matter how valuable, the resulting information should not be confused with what is going on.

A Bit of History

At some point I began to understand that I had a name. Thinking back I can almost see myself swimming into view. But whose view? This is what we have to think about.

As this understanding - probably better described as a premonition - took root, I became aware not only of being alive but of *myself* being alive.

Eventually this feeling took centre stage - although I have never gotten a good look at myself. The best I can manage are glimpses in mirrors and out of the corner of my eye. In any event I became the principal character (and only audience) in my inner theatre. In today's jargon I became my own graphical interface, my own GUI!

However – and I think this is true of everyone – I prefer to think about these proceedings differently. I prefer to believe that I enjoy magisterial relationships with the objects and events populating my conscious experiences. Obvious candidates include *my body* - but *my* house, car, job, family, religion and nation are high on the list.

In this story, everything and everyone else becomes a world to be travelled or a resource to be plundered.

I am told that the being having these experiences and claiming these resources became identifiable August 22, 1942. This is usually referred to as *being born*.

My fortune is that I was judiciously encouraged. My family and community, comprised of similarly named events, had enough resources that they could afford to have children, but not so much that these children were prevented from prospering.

Armed with images of foetuses floating in amniotic sacs, pro-lifers insist that *human beings* commence nine months earlier than birthdays suggest.

This is an excellent observation but the analysis leaves off too soon. Why stop at conception? Why is every person not

19

foreshadowed when their parents met?... or when their parents in turn were imagined and conceived a generation earlier?

Conversations about 'conception days', 'birthdays', 'death days'... attempt to parcel up proceedings that have neither beginnings nor endings.

After a few decades of immortality fantasies, I started doing stuff to retain my status: bicycle, run, eat well, drink more than I should, bicycle, do push ups... . So far, so good... although the equilibrium between *catabolism* and *anabolism* — between *building up* and *tearing down* — feels increasingly precarious.

When not muttering to myself or importuning strangers, I operate a tree farm near Belleville, Ontario. This has something to do with having been raised on the same farm when the principal crop involved children. I also read Ralph Waldo Emerson and Henry David Thoreau when a world very like the world they were describing existed outside my door.

(For an audio rendering of *Walden* chapter 1: http://mirror.csclub.uwaterloo.ca/gutenberg/2/6/2/8/26289/o gg/26289—01.ogg.

If this whets your interest: http://www.gutenberg.org/files/26289/26289—index.html)

For such reasons – and an apparently insatiable curiosity about what is going on – my life has been seized with philosophical issues. The need to survive economically also led me to question common-sense claims underpinning political and economic proceedings. I eventually realized that the most dangerous claim is the notion that human beings enjoy free will as a birthright — that we are souls or persons inhabiting bodies.

Ironically, the secular version of the incarnated soul story is equally worrisome. The idea that human beings represent an extraordinary evolutionary achievement sanctions equally facile claims of entitlement. In short, whether 'Divinely Ordained' or 'ordained divinely', the notion that human beings are special helps explain why we are now convening the biggest destruction of life since a comet eliminated the dinosaurs 65 million years ago.

Since there are no safe places on sinking ships, this conceit threatens our well-being as well. Global warming, environmental contamination, resource-depletion issues... are already causing misery and turmoil.

In most discussions these issues are traced to population growth, industrialization or moral decay. The truth is more complicated, but we might have seen it coming had we not been distracting ourselves and one another with fairy tales:

1. Modern economies require endless growth to avoid collapse.
2. Endless growth is impossible in a small world.
3. If a proportion of human needs were met by way of self-reliant communities, spontaneous efficiencies would reduce environmental burdens.
4. In such communities 'progress and development' would be invested in preserving rather than exploiting resources.
5. The resulting durable devices and small systems would assist 'emerging populations' far better than the antics of multinationals and the politics of globalization.

In the meantime, the only 'good news' is bad news for most of us. Increasingly intelligent machines and systems mean that wealth is flowing to an ever smaller proportion of human beings, to military and corporate adventures; and to entertainments designed to distract the rest of us from what is going on.

Every new technology, every improvement in institutional and manufacturing efficiency... means products and services can be produced with fewer people earning a *living wage*. The resulting collapse of the *supply:demand* equation has been destabilizing economies for decades.

This only makes sense if the wealthy are moving to a different model. (See http://news.bbc.co.uk/2/hi/programmes/newsnight/9382745.s

tm)

The idea that the world economy is winding down should not surprise anyone. Since the wealthy now own everything of value, they have no further need for profit. Beyond maintaining the status quo, common sense and self-interest recommends that they expand the proportion of human beings on $2.00 a day lifestyles. The proportion is presently around fifty per cent.

Something like eighty per cent could be achieved this century! How else can human beings' environmental footprint become sustainable?

This is not a conspiracy theory. There is no need to think about the wealthy conspiring to bring about environmental harm reduction in draconian fashion. Winding the global economy down will occur without anyone having to make a phone call or organize a meeting. The need is implicit in weather reports, global warming statistics and common sense.

People rarely become wealthy by being stupid. They have well-grounded suspicions regarding what you and I hope to get up to. They know we hope to live the American Dream. Indeed, this is the fantasy they have been using to control us since the Industrial Revolution.

The wealthy and powerful people also know that the rest of us will put up with almost anything if 'necessary changes' occur slowly enough.

Finally, the changes needed to 'save the world' are already baked into political institutions and economic machinations. All that is needed is for the present crop of beneficiaries do nothing to prevent these regressive proceedings from continuing.

If time permits, if poll results become alarming, crocodile tears, hand-wringing and expressions of alarm and consternation about unemployment and poverty are useful palliative measures.

To glimpse an alternative to this prospect, non-wealthy

populations need to think about themselves in new ways. We need to recognize that persons do not exist because Divine Creation, evolution — or, a recent hypothesis, harnessing fire to cook food — yielded creatures with big brains.

In *The Origins of Consciousness in the Breakdown of the Bi— Cameral mind*, (1976,2000: Houghton Mifflin/Mariner Books) Julian Jaynes proposed that self-awareness emerged when genetic endowments combined with cultural resources — something he thinks first occurred roughly 3000 years ago, between the times the Greek poet Homer penned *The Iliad* and *The Odyssey*.

However and whenever it happened, a threshold was crossed recently. Although beings just like you and I have existed for at least 250,000 years, self-aware persons only became reliable possibilities recently.

Rather than assume that self-awareness, personhood and consciousness are birthrights, we need to figure out how conscious episodes became a reliable feature of human existence. We need to do everything we can to keep these achievements alive.

The ideas in this book are my contribution. They are based on a way of thinking about reality introduced by the Greek philosopher Heraclitus (circa 500 B.C.) and developed in Alfred North Whitehead's 1927 Gifford Lectures and his book *Process and Reality*.

Briefly, process metaphysics sees the world as an event, not as a container stuffed with things undergoing change. Within this context, consciousness ebbs and flows as 'local events' we refer to as persons.

Linking rich consciousness with a fragile balance of cultural activities, community life and self-sufficiency underscores the importance of getting 'things' right.

Vernon Molloy

A Bit More History

In 1729, two years after *Gulliver's Travels* was published, Irish writer Jonathan Swift published *A Modest Proposal*. This famous essay featured a suggestion for poor families seeking to improve their prospects: "a young healthy child well nursed is at a year old a most delicious, nourishing, and wholesome food, whether stewed, roasted, baked, or boiled...".

In the 18th century, terrible poverty in Ireland made the idea of raising children for wealthy tables plausible in the hands of a satirist of Swift's talent. After all, such children would be well fed for a year or more, rather than starving from the moment of birth. Even so, Swift's suggestion was so outrageous that he did not anticipate being attacked for being in earnest. He was however — which must have both delighted and horrified him.

Swift's send up continues to be an excellent description of the way human beings treat one another. Wealthy individuals and wealthy nations continue to exploit human beings, so long as they can be identified as alien or inferior.

A historically documented, and now scientifically established, fact is that when individuals become wealthy and powerful, claims of a corresponding special status soon follow. This means that wealth soon comes to be seen as nothing more than an individual's due. No one worries that, by definition, wealth and power can only be for the few — and that this inevitable resulting arrogance automatically reduces the non—wealthy to morally-defensible targets.

More often than not, the rest of us agree with this grim calculus. If we make any rejoinder it is to sell our souls — and anything else we can get our hands on — in attempts to join the wealthy at the top.

To be sure, things have changed, but not in ways to be proud of. Three hundred years of *progress* and *development* since Mr. Swift ruffled aristocratic feathers mean that today's movers and shakers can reach out and touch people on the other side of the world. Indeed, they have contrived ways to include future generations in their clutches.

I have come to understand that there is only one way to avoid this prospect. Unfortunately, the solution involves our favourite fantasy — the notion that human beings automatically become persons a few months or years after birth.

This conceit has been exacerbating greed and arrogance on one hand; and recommending apathy and despair on the other.

How could these proceedings be repaired? We must recognize that we are not little Gods charging about the world in bodies we possess and control like riders on horses. Instead we must recognize that we are events. Like thunderstorms, cats, trees and stones... we emerge and remain identifiable for a few hours, days, years — even, for a few persons, centuries.

Shakespeare, Darwin, Christ, Newton, Einstein... continue to inform events even though they no longer enjoy identifiable centres, even though their *sturm und drang* has passed, even though they are no longer *alive* in the sense of being their own beneficiaries.

Another issue is that talk about persons, animals, objects and 'current events' involves claims that are in no way guaranteed even when human beings are involved. Persons, languages, rich inner lives... require communities of mutually-aware beings. Squirrels and earthworms cannot have the conversations required to become persons. They do not suffer anxieties, endure dreads or savour moments because they are not, and cannot become, self—aware the way human beings often do.

When such communities emerge — as far as we know they have always been *human* communities — some events swim into view as persons and others as lesser creatures. Events left over become stones, houses, atoms and, eventually, Higgs' Bosons.

This brings up an important point. No matter how many imaginary worlds exist, no matter how many conscious beings inhabit these worlds, talk about entities, objects, persons and morality only occurs if awarenesses are communicated among entities in mutually beneficial ways. If I shout: "Watch out for the car!" and this prevents you from being run over, you and I are likely to conclude that we share an actual, independently-existing external world.

We are also likely to have a favourable feeling about one another and perhaps come to include one another's well-being in our presentiments.

This useful fiction has been leveraged into *realism* — the idea of an actual world populated with moral and rational agents. Ironically the resulting arrogance, potential for ownership claims and sense of insularity has also been spawning sophisticated technologies, shallow relationships and devastated communities. In short we are sawing off the limb we depend upon.

This matters a great deal. Without locally funded well-being, we will not be able to sustain the idea of *The World* as an exquisitely balanced event. We will be less and less able to imagine one another or our future selves and include these imagined entities in our calculations and projections. This is important because your and my future selves and our present relationships are logically and ontologically identical. If I do not care what happens to you today then I cannot be concerned about will happen to me tomorrow. The ramifications of what each of us get up to today will inevitably participate in both of our futures.

If we run this story backwards, every life can be understood as an unimaginably complicated manifestation of converging historical events. In this story, personhood and personal efficacy (claims of being able to *choose* or *will*) reflect historical events. Whenever such events are named and attain personhood status, our expectations, anticipations, forebodings... about these persons reflect our intuition that these converging influences will continue to manifest themselves in the guise of what so-called individuals get up to.

What is exciting is that these converging influences can set up complicated, richly-endowed events with inscrutable, internal proceedings that can result in novel, creative, unpredictable outcomes.

This is what we mean when we talk about persons.

If this is true, the global inequities now writhing into existence should worry us for a more subtle reason. After thousands of years of incrementally growing awareness, understanding and mutual concern, 'progress and development successes' appear to be collapsing the likelihood that human beings occasionally enjoy internally-sourced conscious episodes.

If so, logic suggests that our capacity to demonstrate moral and rational behaviour will decline in lock step.

Vernon Molloy

From Farmers to Farmed

How The *Ivanhoe Molloys* Went Wrong

In the following I use my family, hereafter the *Ivanhoe Molloys, to* exemplify a psychological/economic relationship that has not been much thought about. The *Ivanhoe Molloys* also serve as a metaphor for the idea of poor people.

More often than not, people are poor because well—endowed, clever or entrenched populations regard them as resources that can — and perhaps should — be capitalized upon.

What is surprising is that so many poor people seem to agree.

The story of the *Ivanhoe Molloys* also summarizes the emergence of the modern world. As I hope to demonstrate, exploitative relationships are not cast in stone. They have a more interesting genesis than greed or avarice.

I think this possible genesis suggests a solution.

Unfortunately, the solution requires more from the poor and soon-to-be-poor populations than we have ever demonstrated. Fortunately, the solution requires a good deal less than we have been handing over.

The third millennium had barely begun when Canadians learned that child prostitution had taken root in their once innocent land. Unspeakable transactions are occurring not only in cities but in small or remote communities we thought well beyond the reach of organized crime.

Because these problems seem to be springing up in remote places 'of their own volition', some are worried that something about the way we live might be involved.

Tom Cohen's article in the *London Free Press*, April 2000 provided a clue about as to what this something might be. Mr. Cohen reported that 60,000 Canadian children run away from home every year. Half end up selling sexual favours to survive. More recently (October 5, 2013), Jennifer Quinn and Robert Cribb's *Toronto Star* article: "An on-line creation: middle-class hooking", warned that the prostitutes involved "could be from a suburban family being sold through the Internet... . They could be your daughter".

Commentators, grief counsellors and soothsayers have been rushing in to reassure Canadians that nothing is wrong with youngsters' moral fibre — although the same cannot be said of their clients! The problem and explanation they identify is that poverty has been increasing for decades, even in 1st world nations. In other words, the *force majeure* driving child prostitution is grim economic necessity. In turn, this reflects equity failures, employments shortfalls, failures to produce enough goods and services or, more likely, some combination of such factors.

Pundits and soothsayers are also agreed that these shortfalls can usually be traced to corporate or political incompetence – with corrupt politicians and greedy captains of industry accounting for the rest. Their conclusion? The *Industrial Revolution* project: to have ever more people become wealthier and wealthier, is the solution.

Progress and development is the only game in town.

In other words, until progress and development agendas mature and the results are equitably distributed, some children will be forced to sell sexual favours to survive. The solution involves more investment in industry and commerce and paying more attention to integrity and due process. This was the article of faith recommended by American President John Kennedy in the 1960s: a rising world GNP will eventually lift even sorry boats.

Prostitution

Child prostitution is one of the most disturbing entries on the list of 21st century problems. Canadians often shake their heads over news of 3rd and 4th world children forced into the sex trade because of poverty. How could such transactions be occurring in Canada?

Even if we are not as wealthy on average as we were fifty years ago, we are still better off than most people in the world.

In the following I propose that poverty has little to do with child prostitution here, although it is doubtlessly involved elsewhere. Child prostitution should be regarded as the tip of an iceberg of harms visited upon young and old alike. These harms can be traced to the witches' brew of urbanization, specialization and globalization called *progress and development*. The reality is that, in spite of smart phones and high definition TV, honest-to-God poverty is on the increase, especially when quality of life issues are factored in. However poverty's consequences are not restricted to soup kitchens and an increasing population of working poor Canadians. Further harms can be traced to *perceived inequities* both within and among nations. These harms demoralize adults and children alike. This demoralization exacerbates malnutrition and health issues and — no small irony — perpetuates the control corporations and governments have over customers and citizens. Their agendas rarely include public well-being — even though this is the claimed focus of business plans and political platforms.

In other words, poverty is not the only cause of childhood prostitution; and in 1st world nations may not be the most important. An equally important factor involves the *perception that one is poor.*

Thinking about poverty this way illuminates why rhetorical flourishes and political projects often make matters worse. Drawing attention to equity issues and then failing to do anything about them reminds people that they are in a bad way and that repair is probably impossible!

Modern Problems, Ancient Perspectives

To provide some background I am going to describe my family's experience of poverty and subsequent "Doing pretty well thank you!" narrative.

Born in 1942, I was the first of seven children on a 100 acre farm near Ivanhoe, twenty miles north of Belleville, Ontario. We farmed with horses and eventually a small tractor, raising cows, pigs and chickens and growing hay and grain to feed them.

We had a wonderful time.

One after the other however, we realized that we were poorer than our neighbours – and poorer still with respect to the life-style opportunities advertised in magazines and on display in store windows in Madoc, Stirling and Belleville!

Fortunately we were unaware of these shortfalls during our childhood. We passed our days – I recall that they seemed to stretch ahead endlessly! — pursuing activities available to children in the country. We fished and hunted. We played tag, hockey and baseball with friends and occasionally with our parents. By watching and helping in the house and fields, by participating in threshing and cutting wood bees, we gained a sense of what would be required of us as adults. We learned that being warm had to do with cutting and stacking wood. We learned that being fed involved looking after animals, picking berries and pulling weeds.

These lessons proceeded without school teachers or trips to zoos. No one organized presentations or contrived `teaching moments'. No examinations were sat, no certificates issued — save the stern reminders recalcitrant wood stoves or weeds were (and still are!) capable of delivering.

I remain so convinced of the value of such experiences that I cannot stop recommending them. You will not be surprised to hear that these efforts are not well received. I rarely get second invitations. Indeed, now that my reputation is established, I don't get out much at all.

What I find unsettling about this has little to do with my sparse social life. My brothers and sisters all became adults prepared to move heaven and earth so their children would experience as little as possible of the events that made them the people they are.

- This is not hard to understand. The life-style the I*vanhoe Molloys* regarded as natural and acceptable would cause alarm today. Children's Aid might have to get involved, and perhaps even the SPCA. Even adjusted for inflation, the income required to escape poverty today is far greater than our family managed the best year we ever had.

- Fortunately, we are not comparing apples and apples. Like every generation before them, the *Ivanhoe Molloys* produced a good deal of the food, fuel and entertainment they needed. They did so with sweat equity, ingenuity and stubbornness. Indeed, we thought we were well situated. After all we had more to work with than any generation before us. We had access to raw material. We possessed or knew of devices and technologies that could be used to promote personal and community self—sufficiency. Chain saws, welding machines, cheap electricity, cheese factories, community markets... were everywhere. We had a telephone! Granted, most phones were 'party—line' but no one complained. We could contact one another whenever we liked — and we could keep a covert ear on what our neighbours were on about. This early version of Facebook satisfied our prurient curiosity — while leaving most of the day free for other adventures!

- In short, the *Ivanhoe Molloys* were *empowered.* Our immune systems were robust for the reason pet owners, diarists and supervisors score better than underlings and specialists. Such benefits are difficult to measure. They so not appear in business plans or balance sheets. One fact is not in dispute however. Like rural people everywhere, the *Ivanhoe Molloys* were responsible for a significant proportion of our own well—being. We had some of the resources and skills needed to look after ourselves.

Modern Problems, Ancient Perspectives

- Among many benefits of this now vanished resourcefulness, we felt good about ourselves and one another. After all we were working to improve or at least secure our mutual well—being. Life does not get any better.

- The *Ivanhoe Molloys* had another advantage. Our circumstances and the devices we farmed with were virtually identical to those our parents' and grandparents had used thirty and sixty years earlier. The difference was that we lived against a backdrop of better-off contemporaries and more sophisticated farming equipment. In other words, we had something to compare ourselves to. Because of this benchmark, the *Ivanhoe Molloys* compressed two generations of economic and cultural development into one experience — two lifetimes for the price of one!

- Of course this meant that we experienced more pressure to 'get ahead' than our parents and grandparents had. This seemed manageable however. Commercialism was in its infancy and globalization and multinationals had not been heard of. Certainly my friends and schoolmates seemed to get the balance right. I do not recall anyone complaining about life—style deficits. No one talked about running away to get a bit of respect. (It's true that they had the *Ivanhoe Molloys* for a benchmark. Perhaps our shortfalls contributed to their sense of well—being!)

- At the same time none of us were living in the stone age. Magazines and television programs were full of advertisements. There were articles about space exploration, jet cars and even three—dimensional television. In fact, in our imagination, we were as much on the cutting edge of 'progress and development' as children today.

- The difference is that, not only did I have to go outside to pee, I could do so without anyone paying the slightest attention.

Vernon Molloy

- Until the modern era and flush toilets, reminders that we are not supernatural beings were part of daily life. Outdoor urinals and the gritty business of subsistence work prevented advertisements from infecting us with the notions of entitlement and cynicism common among even grade school children today.
  You see where this is headed. Progress and development is now occurring at such a pace that children no longer get a 'spring season' wherein their lives and options seem adequate. In today's constantly improving world, children do not get even a few years of untroubled life of the sort the Ivanhoe Molloys, their parents, grandparents and schoolmates enjoyed.

Ordinary People

There was nothing special about the *Ivanhoe Molloys*. As it is turning out however, there was something unusual about our circumstance. We had ordinary needs for food, warmth, security and entertainment. The difference was that some of these needs could be satisfied locally. This meant that our parents were less worried about employment prospects or political events. The vagaries of the stock market was never discussed. Our problems were close to hand and we had the ways and means to solve at least some of them.

Another quiet benefit we enjoyed is that these opportunities for subsistence activities occurred locally and spontaneously. Their *authenticity* was not diminished by having been contrived by institutions, pedagogues or parents. Chores were dictated by natural events including but not limited to wood stoves and animals in the barn. Of course institutions, authority figures, movie stars, sports icons... were part of our lives – but they did not occupy us all day every day.

Today, with televisions, computers, internet chat rooms, MSN... few children have spontaneously-occurring, appropriate responsibilities. Those that do occur have almost always been contrived by institutions or authority figures.

In the *Ivanhoe Molloys'* world, tendencies to be petulant, demanding or rebellious were defused because, most of the time, there were no persons or institutions to blame for what clearly needed doing.

Urban children have lost something else that I think bears upon the child prostitution issue. It is no longer necessary to not have food, shelter or companionship to feel hard done by. No matter where they live – including in 3rd world nations, northern communities or wealthy communities – youngsters struggle with commercially-induced notions of what their bodies should look like and their life-styles consist of.

Morning, noon and night they compare their circumstances with fantasies brandished by television, movies and the music

35

Vernon Molloy

industry.

More often than not, they come up a dollar short.

Unusual Times

Even in the 1950's and 1960's, our sense of well-being was endangered. 'Progress and development' was becoming a conflagration that would consume the lives of hundreds of millions of people in the guise of improving them. Homes and life-styles were increasingly well-appointed, technologically accomplished and expensive.

In spite of our parents' efforts, the *Ivanhoe Molloys* remained behind the curve. We were progressing, but not as rapidly as our neighbours. Electricity arrived at the farm in 1956. Television and the Ed Sullivan show replaced *The Lone Ranger* and *Fibber McGee and Molly* on the radio.

Thus, even though we were making strides in terms of creature comforts, as we moved into adolescence we each realized that our lives left much to be desired.

In one sense, this did not matter. We had had a wonderful childhood and nothing could take that away. However feelings of *relative poverty* can be devastating no matter when they occur. The economic successes the *Ivanhoe Molloys* subsequently enjoyed are due to a robust work ethic and habit of self—sufficiency. At the same time, I think our modest adult accomplishments relate to deep running feelings of inadequacy. We recognized that our family's circumstances were inadequate — and concluded that these *shortfalls* reflected personal *shortcomings*.

I remember being embarrassed because it took me so many years to recognize that I should be embarrassed.

I think this explains why the *Ivanhoe Molloys* never dreamed big — although we had stamina and self-discipline to spare. A little more arrogance, a little more hubris — or perhaps a better appreciation of the value of our circumstances — and we might have amounted to something!

Vernon Molloy

City Life

As the years passed, the *Ivanhoe Molloys* moved on to various cities: Kingston, Aurora, Brampton, Cooksville.... Cities were where jobs and a good life could be had. Along with excitement and opportunities, careers needed 'establishing', RRSPs needed purchasing and pension plans setting up. Quietly and insidiously, we settled into weekly cycles: five days working, two day weekends, an apparently inexhaustible number of such cycles awaiting us. The seasons disappeared from our consciousness or were viewed through weekly interstices.

Before we knew it we were counting the years until we could retire to *heaven on earth,* to the period referred to as the *golden years*.

Just in case this was not enough inducement, urbanization promised that necessities would always be nearby: shopping malls, hospitals, police departments and funeral parlours.

To be sure, a few recidivists (a broader community than the *Ivanhoe Molloys,* but a fringe population nonetheless) embraced urban values reluctantly. In fact – something I once took comfort in – some *Ivanhoe Molloys* included a few acres, a garden, a barn big enough for a riding horse... in their plans.

Unfortunately, neither cows, chickens nor subsisting communities were retained! Recreational horses could be countenanced more readily than utilitarian cows!

We were, after all, getting ahead. We had moved beyond the need for subsistence activities. The proof was that we could afford useless animals and toy barns.

In fairness – even if cows or chickens had been thought of – by —laws, health regulations and surly neighbours would have been problematic. God knows what would happen if people drank unpasteurized milk or consumed underground economy eggs!

(Actually God and I both know what might happen — something resembling the *Ivanhoe Molloys!* I have come to realize that this is not enough to hang even one hat upon –

38

but hope springs eternal!)

As urbanization proceeded, corporate and political agendas focused upon obstructing subsistence activities. These activities were regarded as 'quack grass', as noxious weeds that needed to be prevented from rooting up now that the fields had been cleared and resplendent urban barns stood waiting.

Although this is rarely talked about, I think one of the worries keeping the world's people-farmers awake at night is that independent individuals — I once dreamed of the *Ivanhoe Molloys* in such terms — might start exploring non-corporate uses for devices and technologies.

This could lead to wild-life quotients and communities expanding in unpredictable and unprofitable ways. Against this prospect, commercials and life-style magazines have been warning us about the hazards of unsanitary kitchens, of grannies selling cookies at farmers' markets and the dangers of unpasteurized milk.

These warnings exist cheek-to-jowl with advice about creature comfort enhancements, domestic conveniences and entertainment options. If time remains, *desirable* orgasmic quotients are pondered and useful techniques recommended.

Just in case this is not enough to convince populations that urban life is wonderful, new products continue to pop up. Shoppers and consumers are now advised on how to deal with obesity, diabetes and skeletal deformities caused by a lack of activity and sunshine-related vitamin D. Young and old alike must be trained to recognize elder and sexual abuse and protect against INTERNET scams. Grief counsellors stand at the ready in case something untoward happens. A few days ago (January, 2014) I learned on the CBC that happiness is a teachable skill soon to be included in lesson plans.

What does this have to do with child prostitution? I always thought the *Ivanhoe Molloys* had an important advantage. We were poorer in comforts and conveniences than our neighbours but we had an advantage they lacked. We had the opportunity and incentive to become self-reliant being 'sort of poor' in rural circumstances afforded.

Vernon Molloy

When the realization that we were relatively poor occurred to us one by one, it had the nature of a thunderclap. Of course, we were not poor at all! We just happened to be a generation behind our neighbours in terms of farming practices and conveniences.

This meant that the *Ivanhoe Molloys* crammed two lifetimes into one experience.

This crash course should have alerted us that 'progress and development' was proceeding rapidly. This should have caused us to wonder whether it might not be proceeding too rapidly. Our classmates did not have this advantage. They had been born into 'better circumstances' and were well positioned to habituate to ongoing improvements without noticing what remarkable transformations were occurring.

When the *Ivanhoe Molloys* passed into adolescence our lifestyle deficits became unmistakable and we had to run hard to make up lost ground.

However, even with this 'heads up' advantage, we did not ask whether all this progress and development was all it was made out to be. I think this failure to say: "Hold on here! Let's think about this!" is one of the reasons we did not value our 'original circumstances' enough to insist upon their retention.

What happened instead was that we too became infected. We too came to understand that, no matter how luxurious, our circumstances were not commensurate with our status as human beings. We could not wait to transcend subsistence activities, unseemly self-reliance, the security of neighbours helping one another.... We embraced urban occupations and perilous incomes as if they made sense.

Even if we never became good at conning people, we lost sight of the distinction between making and taking a living.

More importantly, we failed to retain wholesome circumstances for our own children. We regarded these failures as proof that we were getting it right, that we were 'getting ahead'! As insular and myopic as any bred-in-the bone urbanite, we learned to coddle a few children, relatives, pets, friends... and call it enough.

The most worrisome thing I know is that the *Ivanhoe Molloys* failed to understand the toxic nature of the Faustian bargain they were embracing.

With our 'heads up' advantage yielding so little, what are the chances that enough people will be able to resist the siren call of 'more, more, better, better' driving us over a cliff?

If not us, who? If not now, when?

Vernon Molloy

Deeper Harms

In 2000, Canadians were horrified to learn that some children were being co-opted into the sex trade. We did not understand that this was the tip of an iceberg of harm. Parents have been sanctioning governments and commercial institutions to pursue activities compromising the well-being of children for decades. The associated decline of family and community life is one of the reasons so many young 'leave home' when puberty arrives. The idea of 'home' has been truncated, abbreviated, evacuated... of meaningful activities and possibilities to the point that leaving becomes a relatively trivial decision.

So constituted, and in the grip of commercially-inculcated expectations as well, some perceived slight, some unrequited 'consumer need'..., can be enough to prompt the young to take their chances on the streets.

Here they can count upon being targeted by pimps, dealers, thieves and other traffickers in misery. The obvious thread running through the resulting delinquency, depression, suicide and sexual abuse... involve unrequited life-style expectations. The deeper story involves the situational factors that make such disappointments inevitable.

Indeed, urban populations are experiencing a perfect storm. The commercial and political activities promoting life-style improvements have been simultaneously outsourcing and automating the productions satisfying them. The result is that there are fewer and fewer employments capable of financing expectations now regarded as matters of life and death.

The irony is that millions of children in the developing nations would risk their lives to gain opportunities available to Canada's poorest families.

The lesson is that the perception of poverty is:

- more or less independent of the economic status of families;
- a by-product of commercial agendas.

Modern Problems, Ancient Perspectives

To make matters worse, obsession with life—style issues has led western populations into an insatiable sense of entitlement and an unwillingness to delay gratification. We vote for endlessly growing economies and conservative politics every time we pull our wallets out. The results include western workers competing with desperate workers in emerging nations for the dwindling supply of money in unemployed and poorly employed 1st world pockets.

There is no doubt that our children, and certainly our children's children, will endure poverty far worse than anything the *Ivanhoe Molloys* experienced.

These consequences were all implicit in the *Ivanhoe Molloys'* narrative. We were content with our lives until we learned that `better things' were possible. Fortunately our childhood was over by the time this occurred. Today, whether rich or poor, every child is continuously instructed that something is missing in their circumstances and that a trip to the Mall is required to set things right.

Unhappily, no matter how many such trips are made, progress and development is now proceeding so rapidly that new gadgets are immediately regarded as obsolete and unsatisfactory. People raised in such circumstances have contempt for what has been `accomplished' on their behalf. They are dismissive of unprecedented accommodations and entertainments because the next best new thing is only a month away. They are contemptuous because they have never experienced the hunger or cold that was the original motivation for value-creating work. They may have never seen sustained, disciplined effort. The work parents perform occurs elsewhere; and parents are the only adults children have non-institutional contact with. With neither personal nor observational experience of what goes into the creation of goods or services, young people have no idea what it costs someone somewhere to provide the comforts, conveniences and entertainments they dismiss as trivial, as nothing more than their due.

As well – and for good reason – young people are dismayed by the adult lives they know about. Their perfectly defensible instinct is to repudiate any such fate for themselves. Unhappily they are poorly equipped to manage risks or responsibilities. Their life-skills are restricted to making demands, negotiating better deals and occasionally *breaking things*. When these antics no longer achieve satisfactory outcomes, their only recourse is to *leave home* — perhaps seeking legal advice along the way.

All of this is to the amazement and consternation of parents who cannot understand why the comforts they have struggled to provide – `far better' than anything they experienced – have not been sufficient.

Rural Lessons

Proponents of urbanization, occupational specialization, progress and development... overlook an important truth. Moral and prudential lessons are best acquired by way of a childhood spent in the context of self-subsisting families and communities. This was the way human beings lived until perhaps 100 years ago.

To be sure, hunting, gathering and agrarian forms of life also leave much to be desired. The work is constant, hard and occasionally perilous — but the elements of wholesome living are embedded in such experiences. We should have kept what was excellent and set about improving the rest. We should have kept babies, childhood and communities safe. We should have recycled bath-waters and pursued progress and development incrementally and cautiously.

Instead 1st worlders rushed to cities where they contrived to live as far away from nature as possible, on tiny portions of the world and on one another's backs.

These days, if anyone worries about global warming, resource depletion environmental degradation, bio—diversity..., such episodes are short—lived. Such problems seem impossibly large because we have become impossibly small. We perform specialized tasks that must be integrated with similarly minute undertakings to form complicated productions beyond anyone's understanding. We acknowledge no responsibilities beyond a few prescribed duties and post descriptions. We certainly have no sense of personal responsibility to assess whether what we are getting up to is useful or even survivable.

Under such circumstances, business as usual is the only possibility. Democracies become stratagems transferring responsibility from beneficiaries to victims; from urban farmers to *de facto* animals in urban barns. Under such circumstances we do not ask whether the occasional problem we do ponder – perhaps with David Suzuki's help or the latest report from the International Panel on Climate Change (IPCC) – are not another face of the child prostitution issue.

Vernon Molloy

Both reflect the loss of thoughtful relationships with the natural world and one another.

- A great deal of what is necessary for well-being and conservation once occurred spontaneously in communities and families. No one had to contrive `teaching moments'. They were built into what was going on.

- Subsistence living is rigorous and demanding. With the encouragement of corporations and politicians, we have decided that this is something children can do without.

- Our lives are given over to earning money to obtain a stream of immediately obsolete devices and frivolous services.

- The rationale has been to shield children from the experiences that caused their parents to become the persons they are.

This can all be summed up in a single question: What became of the circumstances that once allowed human beings an unhurried childhood, a few wonderful years when everything seemed right?

All that remains of that bright world is that we now spend our lives fretting about what we have not yet purchased; working like horses and spending like asses to put matters right.

Why This Matters

I will conclude with another advantage the *Ivanhoe Molloys* enjoyed but made little use of. Two elements were involved: (1) We experienced the rigours and demands of subsistence living. 2) We had endless opportunities to observe wild animals and their domesticated cousins in barns.

These experiences and contrasts should have been grist for our mills! We saw wild animals 'making a living' by investing physical and instinctual assets in activities determining whether they survived or perished, reproduced or vanished.

We saw that 100% of the value of these activities came to animals 'doing the work'. When wild animals are involved, no useful distinction can be drawn between *producing* and *consuming*. Value flows seamlessly: hunting or grazing becomes digesting and living. We think about wild animals in terms of early birds getting worms and squirrels gathering nuts because we talk about ourselves this way.

We never see wild animals *working*.

Domesticated animals are another matter: a workhorse is a familiar concept. (We sometimes imagine ourselves behaving like one.) Another reason work talk makes no sense when wild animals are concerned is that understanding is not improved by using terms like *working* or *consuming* There is no need to talk about value passing from a *working wild animal* to a *consuming wild animal*. Wild animals lead fully integrated lives. They are consummate masters of subsistence living.

On the surface animals in barns live similarly. The hens in the *Ivanhoe Molloys'* barn passed their days scratching for seeds and clucking over successes. Our cattle ate grass or hay during daylight hours and passed their evenings chewing cuds to complete its complicated digestion. These were value-adding activities from our point of view. Of course, we also believe that animals do not have points of view. If we ever discovered that animals are capable of points of view we would have more trouble treating them as assets. (I hope we would have more trouble. Perhaps we would just give them the right to vote, now that we know that democracy and enfranchisement do not threaten hierarchy and hegemony!)

The point is that the idea of *animals working* only makes sense in the context of farmers and barns. Their lives have been arranged so that the value of their activities flows to owners.

In the same way, pets can be seen as working animals. Their work involves purring, barking, looking cute or, if the animal is a boa constrictor, lurking in a cage. Pets generate complex benefits for owners. Along with companionship and unqualified love, pets allow owners to imagine themselves to be compassionate, empathic nature loving individuals – bolstering innocent bystander claims as commerce and industry consumes everything in sight and obliterates a dozen species every day.

I recently realized that there was another dimension to pet ownership. Human beings like to think of themselves as intellectually and spiritually superior to other creatures. But what if this prowess has cultural components accumulated painstakingly over thousands of years? What if it is a group accomplishment and not an individual endowment? This is not quite as ego-satisfying as having souls incarnated by God. This is not the same as belonging to a species who happened to catch the evolutionary brass ring. So what pets allow us to do is share our cultural and economic achievements with other creatures, as a way of testing whether they have been artificially held back from becoming persons.

Anthropomorphic talk aside, the results are in. Two hundred million dogs and cats in North America, supported to the tune of $40 billion per year... prove it. Not one sonnet, scientific nugget or interesting yodel has been produced. Therefore there is no need to rethink feed lots, slaughter houses or the already defensible manly harvesting of wild animals.

To return to the issue at hand: much of the value the *Ivanhoe Molloys'* animals achieved was confiscated from them and there was nothing they could do about it. We harvested as many eggs and as much milk as possible.

Modern Problems, Ancient Perspectives

When young and especially hungry I remember keeping a close eye on likely hens until they favoured me with an ovulation!

In return, we provided our animals with enough food and shelter to keep them productive. This was tough love however. They were sometimes required to hand over everything. To their surprise and consternation, I introduced any number of chickens to the chopping block. When a cow was no longer productive, or some purchase was necessary, a trip to the local sales barn or abattoir was the order of business.

In other words, this time spent observing the relative fates of wild and domestic animals should have underscored the value of subsistence life-styles for the Ivanhoe Molloys.

Granted, our animals got food and shelter without the effort wild animals had to invest. They enjoyed security from weasels and coyotes. Wild animals must fend for themselves on all these fronts. The benefit is that they live beyond the purview of farmers. They never do a lick of work!

They could still be harvested of course. Hunting seasons abound. Factory trawlers continue prowling the world's oceans scooping up species they would have disdained a half-century ago when cod, salmon, tuna... seemed inexhaustible.

Whenever wild creatures are netted or shot, their lives are transformed into value – accounting entries in business plans guaranteeing more of the same next year.

Now that a majority of human beings are urbanized and specialized, what we get up to is best understood as mutual farming. We live in ways wherein we are either people farmers and herd animals. Like the cows, chickens and crops of simpler times, we have become *domesticated populations.* The gathering of milk, eggs, hay, grain... have been replaced by corporations harvesting profits from 'outlets' in shopping centres, malls and, increasingly, on-line. Farming has always been a perilous undertaking. In modern circumstances crop failures consist of business losses, bankruptcies, recessions and depressions. Whenever these contretemps occur we anxiously consult farmers' almanacs written by Adam Smith, John Keynes, Galbraith.... The idea that things go awry because we have been up to no good never crosses our minds.

Another lesson the *Ivanhoe Molloys* should have noticed is that we were not nearly as accomplished about subsistence activities as wild animals. Even with 'locally, organically grown' eggs, milk and meat as a resource, we had to supplement our 'life style' needs with paid employments. My father worked as an auto mechanic, log cutter and milk-truck driver whenever he was not working on the farm. This was heavy lifting. He was well-aware that a good deal of the value of his work was harvested by owners of the garages employing him. He was well-aware that if we could have become more productive, more efficient, better-capitalized... on the farm we could have ramped up our subsistence activities and avoided the need to hire ourselves out.

In spite of these cautionary, homely examples all of the *Ivanhoe Molloys* went on to lives centred upon pulling out wallets to purchase everything needed. We spent the rest of our time struggling to replenish the contents of these wallets.

The need to pull out wallets dramatizes the difference between wild and domesticated lives. The cattle, chickens and horses of our childhood paid dearly for their accommodations. They were *working animals*. They had become resources for the *Ivanhoe Molloys*.

This was true even though they got shelter and food without much effort. This was true even though their lives superficially resembled those enjoyed by deer, rabbits, birds, squirrels and woodchucks.

There you have it. In every way possible, the *Ivanhoe Molloys* experienced the importance of subsistence activities. What did we do with this information? One might have hoped we would have recognized its importance for individual, family and community well-being. Unhappily, rather than valuing, retaining and enlarging this core of resourcefulness, we saw the need for subsistence activities as an embarrassment. They felt like proof that we were not smart or industrious enough to get clear of the need to feed, warm and entertain ourselves.

As a consequence, instead of expanding our capacity to be self-sustaining by purchasing or inventing labour-saving devices and community economies, we migrated to whatever city offered the best deal.

And what bargains we struck! Before we took up residence in urban stalls, we had been a little bit wild, a little bit free.

This wildness was our most important asset and we could not wait to discard it. We forgot that self-subsisting individuals are more or less immune to being harvested by corporations, ideologues, politicians, i.e., by people-farmers whose names became more familiar to us than our own.

In short, had the *Ivanhoe Molloys* paid more attention to the fate of animals in barns, we might have seen the value of retaining and enlarging self-subsisting activities. We might have figured out, or at least worried about, ways to approximate the freedoms enjoyed by the birds, woodchucks and foxes we had glimpsed along fence-lines and in fields.

Urban Seductions

In spite of unusual advantages of circumstance and experience, the *Ivanhoe Molloys* did none of this. Pondering this led me to appreciate the seductions persuading poor and soon-to-be-poor populations to give up subsistence activities. We too embraced progress and development, dismissing self-sufficiency as a primitive way of life. We too failed to insist that new technologies, new resource-extraction stratagems, new efficiencies... included net benefits for ordinary lives, communities and subsistence activities in business plans.

We ignored our own treatment of farm animals and trusted that powerful individuals and corporations would not treat us similarly, that they would include our well-being in their calculations because we were, after all, all human.

Vernon Molloy

This naiveté overlooked not only the obvious benefits of harvesting wealth from domesticated creatures but our own psychological experiences. Admittedly, all the Ivanhoe Molloys were harvesting were eggs and milk but the principle is the same — we understood ourselves as *entitled.* We never questioned our sense of superiority.

The anecdotal, scientific and historical evidence about the ubiquitousness of this sense of entitlement is overwhelming. These are not moral failings however and we would do well to stop thinking in such terms. Human beings are hard-wired so that whenever they find themselves in positions of wealth and power, they conclude that they deserve everything they can get their hands on. In primal circumstances, being on top or in front often meant being at greater risk and so a few perquisites made it worthwhile. Individuals supplying these benefits got something in return – they got an improved chance to survive!

I remember a lovely song with the lyrics: "Those were the days my friends. We thought they would never end."

Those days are gone my friends.

In other words, no matter how well intentioned they may be at the outset, successful politicians and business tycoons soon come to regard citizens and customers the way I regarded the chickens whose eggs I was confiscating and whose neck I would soon introduce to the chopping block. They were resources and property.

The fact that I organized their affairs, provided them with security, accommodation and food only added to my right to do as I pleased with them. I was, after all, a higher form of life. My status as a *human* being meant that I deserved everything they had. My sole obligation was to refrain from egregious cruelty. This slippery notion did not prevent the *Ivanhoe Molloys* from voting for factory farms, factory trawlers and genetic modifications when we became even more exalted, even more deserving, urbanites.

There was nothing exceptional about the *Ivanhoe Molloys.* The noteworthy elements in our lives were circumstantial. Our advantages included mild poverty, subsistence possibilities and a nearby community of slightly better-off people. These circumstances allowed us to measure how rapidly things were changing. We had been born on a farm where workhorses, walking ploughs, grain binders and pitchforks were part of daily life. These activities were eminently acceptable because they were identical to those our parents and even our grandparents had grown up with. Unlike our parents and grandparents however, our's was an era of mechanization and labour-saving devices.

I remember talk about what this 'progressing and developing' was costing in terms of community life. There a vague premonition that 'the neighbourhood' was dissolving because there was less need to thresh grain or cut firewood by way of community work bees.

For the most part however the future seemed bright. Probably no one found 'progress and development' more seductive than the *Ivanhoe Molloys*. Since our dependence upon subsistence activities was greater than most of the people we knew, escaping from the need to get food and wood into the house and look after animals with manual labour was often on our minds.

We should have been more careful about what we were wishing for. The tractors and implements that promised relief from hard physical work were expensive to obtain and operate. These realities encouraged economies of scale: the cost of purchasing and operating tractors rationalized larger farms, which called for still larger tractors.

In less than half a century the reorganization of rural life was a *fait accompli*. Small farms were abandoned or amalgamated. The proportion of Canadians involved in agricultural activities shrank from 65% in 1930 to less than 3% in 2013. Farms become vast, hydroponic-like factories, many now computerized. Crop inputs are trucked in as fuel, fertilizer, herbicides and pesticides. The sons and daughters of my generation and the one following migrated to cities where factories, offices and employment opportunities abounded. Their work ethic, initiative and self—reliance is still talked about. Unfortunately this resource dried up along with the small farms, large families, rural cheese factories and one—room schools that made them possible.

These days most of the work in rural Ontario is automated, accomplished with enormous machineries or performed by foreign workers 'allowed in temporarily' because the sons and daughters of urban Canadians are unwilling or incapable of lending an hand.

In terms of living in ways wherein local needs are looked after locally, a culture of subsistence activities and community-based self-reliance has vanished.

This has been a huge mistake. Many economic, environmental and social problems can be traced to failures to retain and expand autonomy and self-reliance in ordinary lives. The *Ivanhoe Molloys* had some of this going on. As a proportion or daily needs, our parents and grandparents had even more. Why was this wildness, this cultural resource... not valued? Why were the circumstances that made a healthy proportion of economic autonomy possible not retained?

This is a problem no nation has solved.

I think one reason for this failure is that subsistence activities emerge out of necessity. This origin rarely participates in consciousness eposides except as a set of problems to be solved and is therefore rarely understood as seminal and worth retaining.

This is part of a more general issue: the circumstances and generations causing problems rarely hang around long enough to participate in solutions. Certainly the value of legacy infrastructure, socialization practices, naturally occurring 'teaching moments'... are rarely included in business plans or lists of best practices. Although tiny, the *Ivanhoe Molloy* story is a useful metaphor for what has been going on since the Industrial Revolution. Like everyone else, we behaved like body-builders who, after attaining strength through sustained effort, decided to 'progress and develop' beyond the need for the barbells and disciplined efforts that made us the people we were.

No More Barbells

The *Ivanhoe Molloys* did not recognize the importance of subsistence activities. We could not wait to extricate ourselves from the circumstances that made us possible by making us necessary. Rather than enlarging and refining self sustaining technologies and practices for our own benefit and as an alternative for our children to consider, we migrated to cities. Although we did not think about it, we were moving from circumstances wherein we enjoyed a measure of control over our lives into circumstances where everything would be controlled from outside.

In other words, we allowed ourselves to be domesticated. In no time we found ourselves in basement apartments or in high—rise buildings. Our lives soon became indistinguishable from the lives of the animals we had once farmed and harvested. We found jobs so we could purchase foodstuffs, life-style products and entertainments. For the first time survival depended upon the *effluents of our affluence* being flushed away or otherwise tidied out of sight by sewage systems, garbage trucks, recycling trucks and community composting facilities. No more backyard privvies. No more peeing outside.

The *Ivanhoe Molloys* failed to notice another important change. When we moved to town and secured employment, the value of our work began to be harvested by analogues what we had been doing: making off with milk, eggs, and occasionally the entire carcasses of farm animals.

The *Ivanhoe Molloys* became the *Urban Molloys.* We were no longer wild in any interesting way although we sometimes imagined ourselves behaving badly. The truth is we had become caricatures of our former selves. We were the subdued, corralled assets of politicians and corporations providing employment opportunities, consumables and orchestrating our lives in increasingly detailed ways. Our producing and consuming activities were no longer 'locally integrated' the way they are in wild animals — or in human beings to the extent that they engage in subsistence activities.

Vernon Molloy

To put this another way, urbanized human beings are split into producing and consuming functions. In cities nothing that is produced is immediately consumed the way it is with wild animals, subsisting human beings and communities. Urban dwellers are at war within and among themselves. When we work we strive to get as much money for as little effort as possible. When we shop, we try to get as much product for as little money as possible.

Commercial, political, institutional... interests lost no time setting up camp in these target-rich zones. Writ large, the failures of the *Ivanhoe Molloys* to resist urbanization, specialization, the loss of wildness... set the stage for the modern world.

To be sure, assembly line productions, occupational specialization and economies of scale can be wonderfully productive. What have not been factored into the cost: benefit analyses municipal politicians brandish are the efficiencies and small-footprints inherent in subsistence activities. Wild animals do this best of all. It costs them nothing to transfer goods and services from production to consumption. Advertising costs are similarly avoided because there is no need to transfer information from workers to shoppers. In today's world, every product and every service has a dollar value. Work done outside of the *commercial-industrial-taxation* complex becomes seditious, *underground economy* activities. Snitch lines already exist in Canada and global free trade agreements are already targeting backyard carrots as illegal imports.

As soon as individuals are organized into producing and consuming functions, as soon as all value-adding activities are monetized and accounted for, the value of work must travel through complicated networks before consuming is possible. This is an arduous journey, with many spoons dipping out the best bits along the way.

At journey's end, not much value remains for domesticated populations; just enough to keep them alive, productive and mollified.

Modern Problems, Ancient Perspectives

The global advertising market reached $495 bil-lion this year, up +3.8% on 2011. The US remains the largest market with $153 billion in advertising revenues. Japan, China, Germany and the UK complete the top five.[2]

Along with round-the-clock promotions and profit-taking chicaneries, the costs of infrastructure, transportation, regulation, supervision, surveillance and advertising have to be included before the net benefit of urbanization, specialization and industrialization can be calculated.

I think that if this calculation was fairly performed, 'progress and development' might no longer seem the logical or only course. Indeed, the social, moral and psychological consequences of the loss of local subsistence activities are probably incalculable.

This does not mean that they are not being measured by what is going on.

----

[2] http://news.magnaglobal.com/article_display.cfm?article_id=1666

Vernon Molloy

From Farmers to Farmed

Another factor accelerating the rush to urban life is that the benefits of subsistence activities are difficult to quantify. The most important is that the value of subsistence activities and local economies flows only to individuals, families or communities doing the work. What could be more wholesome? In the urban alternative, an increasing proportion of the value of work performed goes to individuals, corporations and governments organizing and supervising what people get up to. This is a self-perpetrating cycle. The loss of subsistence activities means that more and more ordinary requirements must be organized, capitalized, delivered, taxed and monitored. Put another way, urban populations no longer need to be thought of as persons because they no longer think of themselves as persons. Instead they understand themselves and one another as leaders and followers and *producers* or *consumers*. Such half-persons were never seen in the world until perhaps fifty years ago.

This is the darkest consequence of urbanization and specialization. The integration of producing and consuming activities under the overarching consciousness generated by subsistence activities is the best way, perhaps the only way, human beings have of 'keeping an eye' on what is really going on. In short, a healthy proportion of subsistence activity is the *sine qua non* of person-hood. What does it mean to be a person? I have no idea of what constitutes a person because my not having any idea is part of the requirement! However but I do have some sense of how to identify human beings who are not persons. For example people in the grip of leader/follower arrangements, people subsumed under military or religious hierarchies, people whose conduct can be predicted with dreadful certainty... do not make the cut. The reason is transcendental. If history consisted entirely of such individuals there would not be much history to speak of, an oral tradition, rich cultural resources. There is a simple test I think we all use: when you come across a person you have no idea of what they will say or contribute to what happens next but you have a good feeling about it. When you come across a leader or a follower, a worker or a consumer... you know exactly what is in store for you.

In fairness, much of what is going on is defensible. Economies of scale, new technologies, capitalization options flowing from monetization and banking systems are often beneficial — even after the value of the displaced subsistence activities is subtracted. (We rarely do this of course!) You and I have been enjoying advantages that only became possible when the *Industrial Revolution* got up to speed.

What we have not worried about is that the notion of 'progress and development' is especially irresistible to half-persons, i.e., to individuals who regard themselves alternately as workers or consumers depending upon the time of day. Konrad Lorenz thought that man was *"the missing link between apes and human beings".* The man he had in mind was not a *worker* or a *shopper* whose *human being* quotient has been compromised. A culture populated with workers and consumers, who never think of themselves as whole persons, is a dangerous place. All kinds of mischief can root up that would never be tolerated in economies populated with fully-fledged human beings.

To take a familiar example: new versions of computers, smart-phones, automobiles... are now eagerly awaited events. Corporations failing to satisfy consumers' perennial *Christmas morning* expectations risk being overwhelmed by adroit competitors. Like children disenchanted with a toy after an hour, our lust for more, better, faster... has led to engineered obsolescence, automobiles that rust out in a decade, around the clock promotions and a constant turnover of retailers as malls, big box stores and now INTERNET retailers compete for consumers' wallets. Consumers are not regarded as people by corporations, they are resources to be exploited in much the way Garret Hardin described in his 1968 paper "The Tragedy of the Commons"[3] .

• *As a rational being, each herdsman seeks to maximize*

---

[3]"The Tragedy of the Commons". *Science* 162 (3859): 1243–1248. 1968.

his gain. Explicitly or implicitly, more or less consciously, he asks, "What is the utility to me of adding one more animal to my herd?" This utility has one negative and one positive component.

- *The positive component is a function of the increment of one animal. Since the herdsman receives all the proceeds from the sale of the additional animal, the positive utility is nearly + 1.*

- *The negative component is a function of the additional overgrazing created by one more animal. Since, however, the effects of overgrazing are shared by all the herdsmen, the negative utility for any particular decision-making herdsman is only a fraction of - 1.*

- *Adding together the component partial utilities, the rational herdsman concludes that the only sensible course... is to add another animal to his herd. ...But this is the conclusion reached by each and every rational herdsman sharing a commons. Therein is the tragedy. Each man is locked into a system that compels him to increase his herd without limit — in in a world that is limited. Ruin is the destination toward which all men rush, each pursuing his own best interest in a society that believes in the freedom of the commons.*

- *Freedom in a commons brings ruin to all.*

The energy and resources consumed by corporations as they jockey to exploit consumers are a covert cost of the loss of subsistence living. These expenditures can also be understood as processes transferring value from impoverished populations to conspicuous consumers. It is one thing to live well. It is morally and rationally indefensible to spend billions of dollars($500 billion in 2012) crowing about the joys awaiting consumers as soon as they acquire this or that new product.

Closer to home, progress and development are having toxic consequences for employees as well. Labour saving and labour simplifying technologies are improving in lock step with the sophistication of goods and services. These efficiencies are shouldering workers aside or downgrading wages so that they remain commensurate with shrinking responsibilities.

How can responsibilities be shrinking as products become more sophisticated? The answer is that more and more intelligence is being incorporated in production machineries and software. This is why outsourcing has become the mainstay of the global economy. Information technology means (1) that the number of workers involved per unit of production is diminishing; and (2) remaining workers are easily replaceable cogs without bargaining power.

In other words, urban populations are ignoring not one but two elephants in their increasingly crowded barns. (1) The *benefits* of progress and development are *progressive.* This is why statistics report an increasingly small percentage of increasingly wealthy individuals. (2) Progress and development's *consequences* are *regressive.* Occasional successes notwithstanding, most human beings are becoming poorer in terms of wages commanded and certainly in terms of subsistence possibilities. To be sure, leisure and entertainment options exist that were undreamed of a century, often even a decade, ago. These are poor substitutes for the lives human beings once enjoyed. No matter how many televisions sets one has access to, vicarious experiences are ignoble. In 2014 Canadian youngsters were reported as spending eleven hours a day in front of some sort of electronic screen — television, computer, smart phone, video game console... .

When these proceedings have gone as far as they can, the world will be owned by a small percentage of human beings. The rest of us will no longer have jobs worth speaking of or the skills, resources and tools allowing us to survive more than a few days on our own. Even if we re-acquired or re-invented the homely skills and resources our parents and grandparents took for granted, there will be few opportunities to put them into play.

Everywhere we might look, everything will be owned by someone else.

Vernon Molloy

What's Next?

In addition to equity, employment and political issues, both developed and emerging nations appear to be experiencing self-inflicted Armageddon. Worries about global warming, the end of fossil fuel, potable water, anything resembling civilized behaviour... are in the air.

Like the post-Armageddon Millennium yearned for by Jehovah's Witnesses, the winners of today's economic Ponzi schemes hope to ride the world's economic horses into the promised land.

Although never spoken of publicly, the wealthy may be hoping that the end game has begun. The consensus is that the environmental clock is ticking. In the absence of profound changes in what human beings get up to, some combination of climate change, resource depletion or nuclear calamity is threatening to close everybody's account. Many of these threats are beyond comprehension. However there seems to be a growing (if not yet fully conscious) recognition that global consumption must be downsized to secure a future wherein having a fat bank account counts for something.

For the first time there is reason to believe this might be possible. Two centuries of profit taking have spawned wonderful technologies, information systems and a global economy. With these resources in hand, the wealthy can imagine a future free of the need to farm cattle, chickens and unseemly creatures like you and I.

Moving On

Enough of nostalgia! A central paradox of urban life[4] involves the unexpected consequences of progress and development. These consequence have not gone unnoticed but they have not been given their due. Bleak self-estimations are inevitable in cultures obsessed with more, better, faster... forms of life. A declining sense of personal competence is the inevitable corollary of growing dependence upon machineries, professionals and 'outsourcing' to satisfy wants, needs and life-style expectations.

If the resulting life-styles are out of reach for a growing proportion of human beings, these circumstances are progressively demoralizing for most and increasingly satisfactory for the few. This has little to do with hedonism – we can only wear one pair of pants or go on one trip at a time. Wealth's central pleasure requires the nearby, visible existence of lot's of poor people.

Even when individuals are doing well, feelings of apathy and resignation, a sense of 'settling down and settling for', a collapse into fandom, fanaticism and ideological commitments... are common responses to economic turmoil and political confusion.

What is also troubling is that these consequences render populations vulnerable to further encroachments. In *Walden* (1854) Henry David Thoreau observed that the *"The mass of men lead lives of quiet desperation...."* The desperation Thoreau had in mind involved the manual labour required in rural America. Such drudgery has been reduced although it remains a fact of life for 3rd world sweat shops and factories. Some have suggested that workers in emerging nations may

---

[4]Modern human beings thought of the world as increasingly organized and rational, and imagined this progress continuing forever. Post modern thought is less optimistic. Fredrich Nietzsche's "God is dead!" school of thought is an excellent example. Human beings have moved into a state of understanding where God is no longer relevant because belief in orderliness and eternal progress is no longer possible. Whatever else God may be for believers, He (or She) was the benchmark of orderliness: a tidy point from which creation ensued.

be worse off than the slaves owned by North Americans and Europeans. Since no one 'owns' sweat shop employees, they can be impoverished and ignored with no one the wiser and without *de facto* slave owners incurring financial risk.

As well, a growing proportion of industrial activities, toxic by-products and terrible working conditions... have been safely removed from sensibilities of western consumers. Few 1st worlders willingly spend time in abattoirs or butcher shops unless they have a particular cut in mind or want to make sure that they are getting value. Although visible poverty is a prerequisite for feeling wealthy, one of the subtler attractions of urban life is that it eliminates the need to observe manual labour.

The details of sausage making no longer obstruct breakfast pleasures. We do not want to know anything about the lives of the animals that live and die for our benefit.

Knowledge of other forms of life is restricted to Zoo trips and watching Davis Suzuki's *The Nature of Things* and *National Geographic* programs.

Of course there are 250 million pets in North America. The emotional energy and financial support these animals enjoy is legendary. They are frequently loved to death! Pet ownership is not only healthy for owners, it provides them with opportunities to burnish their moral credentials before tucking into steaks and life-style embellishments.

After all, pet owners point out, they are providing similar enjoyments to their beloved animals. So what if the delicacies pets consume come from chickens, pigs and cattle? So what if the animals petted vs. animals slaughtered lottery operates in mysterious ways? So what if the world is being gutted and the lives of future generations are being compromised in the bargain?

Look how well we are treating Fluffy the Cat and Jake the Dog!

Rocket Ride

As the wealthy ramp up efforts to secure assets and avert environmental catastrophe (these are overlapping projects!) it is useful to put the prospects of the 'remaindered rest of us' in context.

Human beings have always recognized that being bright, comely or strong was a good idea. Such individuals often enjoy splendid lives. They are encouraged, applauded and supported by the rest of us. They prosper in part because we enjoy success stories and still hope to come across one of our own. Evidence that a few people are succeeding is so reassuring that we fail to recognize that such successes now depend upon the rest of us experiencing shortfalls. This is not an entirely new problem of course. However, during the centuries when most of our lives proceeded outside of aristocrats' control, some of the pleasures and value of our work often remained with us. Now that we are urbanized, specialized and domesticated, the relationship between wealth and power for a few and general immolation is approaching 1:1.

Therefore, although we can dream as much as we like, logic tells us that for the first time we should really anticipate what Thomas Hobbes described as a "nasty, brutish and short" life.

In spite of this logic and the historical record, and even though the horizon is darkening after a century wherein universal prosperity seemed possible if not plausible, the usual person's understanding that something is rotten in Denmark seems further removed than ever.

Why should this be so? Part of the answer is that it is still possible to believe progress and development will save us all. After all, new individuals appear on wealthy lists every year. A significant proportion of human beings still retain middle classe perches. Some even have a plan they think will allow them to continue doing so for another few decades. In *The Waiting Game* [5] Charlie Gillis observed that Canada's baby boomers expect a large a transfusion of cash and assets as soon as their parents die.

> *... for many Boomers, the money can't come soon enough. Half of home-owners in their 50s still have mortgage debts, and one in two Canadians tell pollsters that they expect to retire before they have paid off their homes. ...The average person aged 56-65 is carrying $27000.00 in consumer debt, such as credit cards and car loans. They are going to need cash to maintain their standard of living... and their desperation is starting to show.*

These people are unwittingly authenticating urbanization, specialization and the American Dream. Crass schemes, petty torments, hurrying Mon and Dad to their eternal reward... are best understood as overhead costs of the political and economic Ponzi schemes we think of as progress and development.

In the meantime, the entertainment and sports "industries" allow billions to imagine that they are leading worthwhile lives. They get to participate voyeuristically and vicariously in beautiful lives. They glory in the accomplishments of a few athletes.

In North America two hundred million dogs and cats allow pet owners opportunities to lord it over lesser creatures in a parody of the way they are treated by overlords.

We understand well enough where these value we experience come from. We reward individuals for making themselves available for our delectation, titillation and scorn. The wealth/poverty divide is made acceptable by publishing salacious, intimate details about the lives of movie stars and professional athletes. We dine upon upon the travails of

---

[5]Macleans: March 16, 2015

people such as Canada's Conrad Black and Toronto Mayor Rob Ford.

Hundreds of millions depend upon such titillation, voyeurism and *de facto* pornography to make their lives worth living. (In 2014 I sometimes caught myself looking for gossip about Rob Ford to get my day started.)

What we do not notice is that these solutions prepare us for more of the same.

The way things are going the middle class has be eliminated for mankind to survive. We should probably be glad that the process is underway. The reason the middle class has to be eliminated, and the reason its elimination is now possible, is rooted in rich/poor relations. Although the poor have always done everything asked of them, they were never been able to elevate the gifted and fortunate to their manifest destiny.

The Industrial Revolution solved this short-coming . As the *Ivanhoe Molloys'* demonstrated, folk-ways, self-sufficient individuals and communities become ashes in our mouths as soon as city lights appeared on the horizon.

Add a sprinkle of grain along the ramps to promise land and we were there for you!

Actually not much grain was required. We could not wait to be herded into cities, factories and shopping centres. Cities promised a bit of heaven on earth. They promised sanctuary, over-arching wombs for domestic wombs.

Why is this worth thinking about? The economies of developed nations can be thought of as three-stage rockets. As we know, the function of lower and middle stages is to propel *payloads* into orbit. Once this is accomplished, spent stages must be discarded lest they bring the whole contraption down.

The parallels with post industrial revolution economies are striking. As the 3rd Millennium gets underway, economic and political dislocations signal that the middle class is collapsing.

Middle and lower-class populations face problems today they have never had to deal with before. The technologies and global economy made possible by industrial-strength profit-taking have spawned a global super-nation whose de facto citizens are the world's wealthy.

All that remains is to disentangle themselves from the spent populations that propelled them into ascendency.

There is no need to despair however! Hobby farmers often keep excellent horses in splendid barns. In the same way the wealthy will keep fine specimens from our ranks for entertainment and riding purposes!

As regards the rest of us — you and I and everyone we know — the story is simple. Now that we have *progressed and developed* beyond the need for subsistence activities, now that we have moved into urban barns and become dependent and hapless, we can be managed, harvested, obsoleted, discarded... as circumstances require.

The fact that the middle class is shrinking in the nations that gave it birth tells the rest of us all we need to know.

As well as spawning machineries, multinational corporations and the global economy, middle class expectations distracted the *Ivanhoe Molloys* from the need to retain and develop self-sufficiency. The promises of entrepreneurs, corporations and politicians effortlessly swamped the real possibility that we could have retained elements of self-sufficiency, family and community life in urban circumstances.

This failure, this spiritual sickness, has become a global epidemic. We are demoralized, paralysed, spent.... We have been divided and conquered, not only among but within ourselves.

Now that the work most of us are capable of has been obsoleted, outsourced, down-sourced or automated, the middle class itself can be eliminated. Even this has been automated. There is no need for anyone to dirty their hands with indictable activities. The processes and financial instruments delivering wealth up the rich-poor ladder have been baked into legislations, best practices and market-sanctioned corporations.[6]

The remaining problem - the possibility that even demoralized middle class populations might not embrace their fate quietly - has spawned an unprecedented political phenomenon. For the first time in history rulers and the wealthy class are recommending that populations everywhere demand that their nations become duly-constituted, properly-functioning democracies.

The political arrangement that used to keep the wealthy awake worrying about what would happen when populations got the vote now helps them sleep.

The reason is simple. Populations whose lives depend upon the status quo for employment, food, shelter, security... can be trusted with a vote. In such circumstances democracy becomes a stratagem transferring responsibility for what is going on to the victims of what is going on.

In addition, robust, properly-conducted democracies insulate the wealthy from malcontents and secure their property – the only property there is – from revolutionary antics.

---

[6]A familiar example involves percentage-based remuneration adjustments favoured by unionized workplaces – and by managers 'modestly' applying the same factor to their own salaries.

The resulting ballooning of wages drives top earners ever further from bottom earners, destroying workplace equities and setting the stage for more labour unrest.

To the extent that unrest is successful and percentage-based repairs are achieved, the problem worsens.

A related example involves 'bracket creep': as wages increase in ways more or less offset by inflation, marginal tax rates migrate upward without any requirement to argue for or defend new taxations.

Why Advertise?

In the interval after progress and development turned upon the middle-class – my sense is that this started around 1970 – products continued to pour from the world's factories.

Even if the ambition was to reduce the world's GNP to sustainable levels, this had to be accomplished in ways that appear to be driven by market forces. Economic activities must continue being promoted as a way of demonstrating that governments and wealhy interest groups are not actively shuttering the middle class. Businesses must continue to urge shoppers to pull out wallets and credit cards to keep the dream alive. Politicians must continue to announce infrastructure, technological and educational investments promising a brighter future.

The sky cannot be falling. Everyone says so!

Apologists and soothsayers recommending more of the same count upon no one pointing out that just such investments spawned the technologies now degrading, downsizing and outsourcing the employments that made the middle class possible.

The world has a tiger by the tail. The faster we swing economies around the angrier the animal becomes.

We have a pretty good idea that as soon as we stop it's game over. (Think: recession, depression, World War 3....)

Accordingly, more progress and development and more vigorous promotions always seem to be called for.

As well, the EU's problems with Greece in the summer of 2015 illustrated, more and longer productivity from fewer employees, pension claw backs and higher taxes are on the table whenever sufficiently dire problems arise.

The more expensive promotions and infrastructure investments become, the more rigorously workforces must be rationalized to compete in the global economy. The more productive employees become the more economies decline. Lots of people have to earn lots of money to buy the products automated machines and Third World populations are capable of producing. Automated machines and Third World workers meaning shrinking wages everywhere.

The rest of the story is that, even if we could somehow get past this predicament, keeping the global economy ball in the air is not an option either.

As many have pointed out, we cannot keep expanding populations and life-styles.

We will either figure this out proactively or Mother Nature will clean up the mess.

In the meantime, no one worries that the micro-economic solutions politicians and economists profer make no sense. Consumers imagine that businesses pay for the advertising clamouring for their attention. Business men and women know better even if they never say so. They know that overhead expenses are transferred to consumers when goods and services are purchased. Business people may even recognize that frivolous overhead costs reduce consumers' capacity to purchase.

However this is the way business is conducted. Consumers expect to be pitched products and services. They are not in the habit of researching and making purchasing decisions independently. Any business voluntarily reducing advertising expenses with a view to lowering prices and reducing its environmental footprint would disappear in modern retailing's cacophony and hyperbole.

It is also interesting to ask whether this expensive promoting of products and services might not be an element in the 'wind the middle class down' project. As automation and globalization undermine ordinary incomes there is an apparent need to do more advertising. The associated costs further erode purchasing power – a feedback loop that helps get the green job done even as it demonstrates apparently sincere efforts to resuscitates economies.

On the surface advertising activities have pollution and resource depletion costs that seem to contradict the possibility that a covert green agenda is in play. However. from a Malthusian perspective, such costs are green. Any activity wasting money – including military initiatives, greed, commercial waste... keeps purchasing power out of consumers' hands and – in terms of aggregate environmental footprint – is better than any alternative.

Let's be honest: if more money had come our way we would have had larger families or grander life-style expectations. Either consequence is unsustainable. There are already too many human beings living too high on the hog.

Advertising offers political benefits as well. Advertising reassures citizens that all is well. Advertising reminds customers that they are important. In an era of globalization, multinational corporations and unimaginable inequities, diminishing advertising activities might very well cause consumers to wonder whether they really are in charge!

Advertising also introduces new products and services to consumers who could not otherwise 'decide' to purchase or recommend them: "A taste of heaven has just arrived at a store near you! It is already marked down so there is no need to wait for a sale!"

This is one of the few defensible uses of advertising, but it scarcely explains why another picture of a pound of hamburger is a good idea.

To summarize, the direct and indirect costs of promotional activities are worth thinking about. They deplete resources and pollute. Promotional activities *diminish* the quantity of goods and services consumers are able to purchase.

These issues can be organized under two headings. The first is that advertising costs are regressively distributed. They reduce the purchasing power of the poor more than middle class or wealthy individuals. The objection that poor people do not pay embedded advertising costs because they do not purchase much overlooks the point. People are frequently poor because the value of their work has been stolen by colonizers, imperialists, multinationals and global trade agreements.

In western nations those who have nothing are often referred to as homeless. There is a far larger population of poor people however. They are living in slums or on the garbage/refuse piles surrounding many cities, especially in the emerging world.

> *Late in 2003 the United Nations reported that one billion people—approximately one third of the world's urban dwellers and a sixth of all humanity, live in slums. And it predicted that within 30 years that figure would have doubled to two billion—a third of the current world population.[7]*

---

[7]https://www.wsws.org/en/articles/2004/02/slum-f17.html

also:
UN Habitat states that the number of people living in slum conditions is now estimated at 863 million, in contrast to 760 million in 2000 and 650 million in 1990.
https://www.cordaid.org/en/news/un-habitat-number-slum-dwellers-grows-863-million/

I can think of a fate worse than homelessness or slum living – the horror of life in the miasmic North Korean culture sometimes referred to as the hermit kingdom. What is interesting – and faintly hopeful – is that Kim Jong-un and his remarkable lineage are not responsible for what is going on. The adoring crowds depicted in this picture are not responsible either. They and Kim Jong-un have been transmogrifying one another into caricatures.

It is often said that business assets include customers' good will. Modern corporations have an asset they never talk about. In the two hundred years since the industrial revolution began, corporations and governments have converted the entire population into a resource not unlike the asset talked about in Garret Hardin's "The Tragedy of the Commons"[8] – and have been making similarly profligate use of it.

This asset has two elements: (1) urban populations' need to purchase everything required to live combined with (2) their need to find work to finance these purchases. Like the commons in Hardin's essay, these elements exist in the public domain. , They are regarded as equally available to any corporation or entrepreneur who wishes to go into business.

---

[8] http://www2.geog.ucl.ac.uk/~mdisney/teaching/tutorials/hardin_1968.pdf

Modern Problems, Ancient Perspectives

Indeed, now that subsistence activities have vanished, these elements and this asset now *constitute* the public domain! Just like the intemperate farmers Mr. Hardin talked about in his essay, corporations, businessmen and politicians spend time calculating whether to set up another industry or retail outlet, another metaphorical cow to graze upon apparently limitless expanse of consumers' grass.

However there is one important difference however between this commons and the one Mr. Hardin had in mind. Urbanized human beings not only need to purchase goods and services to live, they need to earn enough to purchase these goods and services.

Manufacturing and retailing corporations have been whipsawing these complementary needs into calls for more progress and development, more efficient workplaces, economies of scale, automation and outsourcing.

This is where the second shoe descends. If overheads are regressively distributed in that embedded costs of production, distribution and promotion represent a bigger proportion of low incomes than high, the profits earned by commercial enterprises go disproportionately to the wealthy.

There are two reasons for this. The first is that high income earners have more disposable income after personal operating expenses. The poor must spend all or almost all of their money on necessities. Having disposable income allows investments in properties, businesses and stock markets. Over time these differences compound and have much to do with the existence of rich and poor people at any point in time.

When this factor is added to other accounting practices – i.e., percentage-based wage adjustments in union contracts – an inexorable undermining of equity can be seen working tirelessly so that working tirelessly avails us not at all.

Many commercial practices are necessary and defensible but promotional activities are not on the list. Although touted as economic stimulant, promotional activities also depress wages, working condition and sales volumes[9] . The fact that advertising sometimes causes consumers to 'choose' different products is irrelevant. The costs of frivolous promotions and vacuous competitions with competitors diminish the public's purchasing power, sales volumes and the number and wages of people producing goods and services.

Equally importantly, the apparent need to advertise diverts attention from resource depletion and conservation issues. If advertising was not a daily distraction, consumers would more likely think about the durability and longevity of products and life-cycle environmental costs. For decades products have been engineered to have short or medium term lifespans as part of corporations' business plans. The reflected costs of this strategy environmentally and in terms of ordinary well-being are incalculable.

What is urgently needed are low cost ways to mediate production and consumption activities without attempting to control them for the benefit of manufacturers, retailers and governments. Why not let naturally-occurring wants and needs determine what is produced? What would be wrong with letting word of mouth and reputations for product excellence and durability motivate sales? What a pleasant, dignified world that would be! Products would be valued for their utility, durability, longevity and recyclability.

All of these possibilities are given short shrift when workers and consumers are regarded as assets and billions of *their dollars* are spent to determine which 'big player' will have access to their wallets.

This is not to suggest that the wealthy are actively or consciously conspiring against the poor. Although inequities are occasionally talked about in such terms, a more useful explanation is possible. Poverty is better understood as reflecting lower and middle class failures to retain a core of subsistence activities in personal and community lives. Inequities and poverty also reflect failures to hang onto the value of wages earned when individuals move to or are born

---

[9]This is another example of the *fallacy of composition.*

into cities and take up 'gainful employment'.

In short, failures to retain subsistence activities, failures to remain a little bit wild... are the reasons the poor are increasingly with us. We should have recognized that promises made to coax, lure, seduce... us from communities and subsistence lifestyles were promises we would end up paying for.

Because 'progress and development' occurs gradually, over years not weeks, urban populations rarely notice that their work experiences have less and less resemblance to products consumed at night, on weekends or upon retirement. Because of this separation of work experiences from products and services consumed, commercial, regulatory, financial and promotional agencies seem necessary features of modern life. Since products never appear before human eyes until the last moment of their creation, inspection, quality control functions have to be built into manufacturing and distribution chains to protect end-users.

In such ways, politicians and corporations have done the apparently impossible. They have divided persons into two awarenesses. We are workers by day and shoppers by night. Our conscious lives are similarly partitioned. Each of the resulting half-wits regards its complement as if it lived on a separate continent rather than inhabiting the same body!

You can test this. Ask yourself: How often does your worker-self ponder how its conduct will impact your shopper-half? How often does your bargain chasing, Wall Mart frequenting shopper-half worry about domestic jobs or community vigour while filling shopping carts? The fact that these questions rarely occur tells us something important. Urbanization not only means the loss of subsistence possibilities but the loss of person-hood. If this sounds a bit much, surely the concept of a person includes a being surveying all of the activities comprising its life. Surely the idea of a person includes the expectation that producing and consuming activities will be optimized in the light they shed upon one another.

This failure to lead integrated *producer + consumer = person* lives, more than any other failure over the last century, has had devastating consequences. To the extent that an overarching interest in maximizing the utility and efficiency producing and consuming activities is not occurring, workers and consumers can be inveigled into activities that do not have whole persons in mind.

Unhappily this does not mean that the world's non-urbanized populations are still enjoying subsistence activities. If so they would be invaluable because they would have habits and understandings the rest of us could take up as we are thrown off of the bus.

The fact is, non-urbanized populations have been displaced and psychologically traumatized by urban economic and political machinations. In addition they are distracted by the glow of city life. Infected with *life-style disease,* they are no longer content with traditional lives. Canada's aboriginal communities struggle with alcoholism, drugs, gasoline sniffing and high suicide rates. Their old ways of life are withering in the light of distant cities and new ways of life are forever out of their reach.

They are out of reach for city dwellers as well but we are acclimatizing nicely! That is the difference between being on the outside looking in and being an insider looking nowhere.

Even when this is not true, one has to grow up in a time and a place and experience ways and means of living for one's circumstance to feel natural and sufficient. If cultural inheritances bleed away for any reason, for example immigration or the promiscuous of smart technologies, that life is likely to feel disjointed the way second languages are always less fluent and spontaneous than mother tongues.

This may be why a surprising number of handsome, lovely, well-to-do young people from 1st world nations are heading east to join terrorist organizations.

There is every reason to believe that these problems will get worse. According to the Global Health Observatory[10]

> *...urban growth peaked in the 1950s, with a population expansion of more than 3% per year. Today, the number of urban residents is growing by nearly 60 million every year. The global urban population is expected to grow roughly 1.5% per year, between 2025-2030. By the middle of the 21st century, the urban population will almost double, increasing from approximately 3.4 billion in 2009 to 6.4 billion in 2050.*

The fantasy of escaping the rigours or subsistence living explains why politicians and corporations had an easy time developing cities, establishing multinationals and concocting trade agreements locking domestic populations into life and death struggles. Governments and corporations rarely encounter persons asking after the true costs of progress and development. The questions half-witted producers or consumers ask can usually be handled by pointing a finger at whatever function happens to not be in the room. If a shopper-person has an issue, the solution involves pointing at greedy unions. If a worker-person asks a question, the answer involves consumer-driven *Realpolitik* – the need for world-class efficiencies is why his or her job had to go.

When politicians and corporate leaders tout life style and security issues they are typically appealing to their *consumer half-wit* constituency. Conservatives and Republicans can be understood as provoking *worker-half wits* into throwing *Tea Parties*.

These are the reasons the consequences of multinational corporations and trade agreements for whole persons rarely cross anyone's mind. Such questions are the provenance of people who recognize the importance of subsistence activities for well-being, whether subsistence activities are understood in context of individual, community or national self-sufficiency.

---

[10]http://www.who.int/gho/urban_health/situation_trends/urban_population_growth_text/en/

Vernon Molloy

To be sure, when pink slips start arriving because jobs have been outsourced or automated to placate 'value—conscious' consumers, squeals and cackling will likely occur.

The *Ivanhoe Molloys* heard such episodes in our good old days, when life stretched ahead of us; when McNuggets had not been heard of and chickens had to be introduced to the chopping block.

Unfortunately the squeals of outrage we have been getting up since, our demonstrations and letter writing campaigns..., have the same outcome our hens' cackling had. A day or a week later we too will have settled back into our stalls — assuming we still have stalls to call our own.

Wildness Quotient

The outstanding faults of the economic society in which we live are its failure to provide for full employment and its arbitrary and inequitable distribution of wealth and incomes.

John Maynard Keynes, 1936.

It is useful to summarize why retrieving or inventing subsistence activities will determine the fate of persons, communities and 'middle ground' possibilities.

- It is impossible to steal the fruits of subsistence activities while they are occurring – although, as hunters and the *Ivanhoe Molloys* can attest, it is possible to harvest the fruits of such activities after they have concluded.

- In terms of conservation, sustainability and equity, subsistence activities mean the value of work takes the shortest possible path from production to consumption. Wild animals do not worry about profit-taking or other forms of thievery. No portion of the value they generate is diverted into infrastructures, governments and promotional activities.

- This is important to think about for another reason. Human beings' ecological footprint is not entirely due to the sum total of our life-styles. A good deal has to do with the way we do business. Billions of advertising dollars are spent putting our consuming halves in touch with our producing halves.

- There is no need for subsistence activities to become 100%. (Indeed this is neither possible not desirable.) However it is clear that, when subsistence activities approach 0%, all hell breaks loose.

- Subsistence cultures are necessary for human well-being but they are not *necessary and sufficient.* Many important goods and services could not be achieved by individual or community productions. Sophisticated medicines, products and manufacturing technologies improve well-being. These developments and resources also create subsistence possibilities that could not have been achieved any other way. YouTube is a wonderful resource for DIY types. Social media and public databases provide ways to organize consumers into groups and do collective bargaining on their own behalf, reduce virulent promotional activities and provide new ways to discipline corporations and governments. Such databases could also link workers and consumers into local economies and achieve an independent layer of community-centred goods and services.

- Enlarging subsistence activities in these ways would invigorate central economies. New products and services would emerge catering to local activities. Central economies would evolve synergistic relationships with individuals and communities. Local economies are regarded as subversive for the same reasons underground economies are thought of as weeds to be exterminated. The reality is, if nations are going to embrace *globalization,* they must simultaneously practice *localization.* More generally, if human beings are going to survive multinationals and global trade agreements, they must achieve a corresponding growth in local economies and communities so that each functions as a countervail to the other.

- Anecdotes, biblical references, the "power corrupts" rule... remind us that wealth and power invariably enlarge notions of entitlement. If we get beyond scapegoating one another we soon see that arrogance and hubris are spawned by wealth instead of the other way around. This generates an ironic paradox:

- Failures to retain and enlarge subsistence activities increases profit-taking opportunities.
- These opportunities increase both the number and

proportion of wealthy individuals.
- The more wealthy individuals there are the more likely it is that governments will legislate in their favour and against subsistence forms of life.
- The further down this road we travel, the more rich/poor inequities seem just what God or Mother Nature had in mind to both parties to the relationship.
- In short, mankind's historical failures to retain subsistence activities, and expand them as cultural resources accumulated, set the stage for power and wealth for a few and poverty for everyone else. Although marginalized populations seek explanations for their difficulties by pointing to greedy, corrupt individuals, the truth is that these individuals are spawned by their own failures to hang onto the value of their work.
- These consequences are setting the stage for further harms. Cities with millions of people are tempting targets for multinational corporations, aggressive nations and terrorists. Every citizen knows what it feels like to be part of a greedy nation; even if these feelings are only expressed patriotically or as jubilation should one's team wins *Olympic Gold*. Informed and alarmed by our own greed and cupidity, we understand why standing armies are needed to protect us from external and internal threats.
- Each such army rationalizes the need for armies in other nations. All of these costs and consequences can be tracked back to subsistence failures and the misappropriations of cultural resources.
- If human beings had not crowded into cities, if we had remained spread out and somewhat self-sufficient, the money needed to protect ourselves from one another would have been smaller.[11]
- World military expenditure in 2012 is estimated at $1.756 trillion.
- This corresponds to 2.5 per cent of world gross

---

[11]   http://www.globalissues.org/article/75/world-military-spending

domestic product (GDP), or approximately $249 for each person in the world;

- With regards to advertising, global costs reached $495bn in 2012, up 3.8% over 2011 (*Magna Global Advertising Forecast 2013*). These expenditures reflect corporate competition. They are also sanctioned by the apparent need to inform consumers about products. This is necessary because products bear little resemblance to the bits and pieces we get to work on — or because they are produced off-shore.

- Nations, corporations and institutions continue to emerge and grow larger because human beings keep handing over more and more needs and responsibilities to be organized and harvested. We are told that if we do so we will receive enough income to purchase what we 'really, really want'. We are told that it is far better to leave the production of goods and services to professionals and corporations.

- Every year we depend upon an increasingly small percentage of human beings for everything needed. The rest of the story is that the wealth and power this confers on this small population means that they are increasingly indifferent to our fate.

- You and I know what this feels like. When was the last time you thought about the workers in distant factories producing the articles and services you depend upon? For that matter, when did the working poor around the corner last cross your mind?

- Even if we experience an occasional empathic episode, even if we occasionally pay attention to poverty, homelessness, food banks, crime statistics and child prostitution... we are still oblivious to an iceberg of harm. Being poor in urban circumstances is far worse than being poor in rural communities where subsistence activities remained possible. Few people today have skills relevant to any of their needs. (They often have few skills of any description!) More and more of the poor and elderly lack families and communities. The urban young must make do with chat—rooms, Facebook and Play Stations. The only mercy they are experiencing is that they have no inkling of what these facile, vacuous entertainments are costing them.

- Now that every conscious episodes comes from some external source of stimuli, now that everything of value has become someone else's property, poverty and despair are truly linked. This unprecedented, toxic circumstance can be expressed in terms of our lost wildness. This important notion deserves a name. I propose *Wildness Quotient* or *WQ*. No societies' WQ can be 100% – if only because this would preclude the idea of *society*. It is equally clear that a society's WQ must not be 0% — if only because this precludes the idea of *human being*.

- Indeed, as WQ quotients approach 0%, more and more human beings are being identified as economic liabilities. As value adding work is automated or outsourced, it is already costing more to keep many of us fed, entertained and supervised than we are generating. Sooner or later these calculations will begin to inform public policy.

- Have you noticed how often *euthanasia* and *assisted suicide* is in the news these days?

None of this should distract us from a simple truth. People are increasingly poor in spite of wonderful machineries drawing down the planet's resources. The explanation is the same today as it has always been. People have never been good at hanging onto the value of their work. This value has always been vacuumed away from individuals, families and communities by governments and corporations. As the resulting wealth accumulates, a good deal has been re-invested in people-replacing technologies. These investments are paying handsome dividends. When not replaced outright, employments are being simplified and wages clawed back.

This is the process that has poor and middle class populations by the throat.

Vernon Molloy

What Do You Think?

Corporations and nations are usually thought of as the progeny of politicians, visionaries, captains of industry... harnessing more or less willing citizens, workers, consumers, soldiers... into projects achieving transformative results. Some of these results are excellent – and some, as Germany's leaders and followers demonstrated during the Second World War, terrifying.

Nations, corporations, institutions, sports teams... are also understood as quasi-creatures; albeit of such a primitive sort that they do not threaten human beings' hegemony. This is the claim that human beings are not only moral and rational agents, but the *only* moral and rational agents on the planet.

We have had similar problems in the past. We talk about God as omniscient and omnipotent. We also talk about ourselves as agents making choices and putting them into play. How can this claim be squared with the idea of God as omniscient and omnipotent? One traditional answer is that God gave human beings free will but, being omniscient, knows what choices we will make and therefore sanctioned them ahead of time. Another explanation, also favoured by St. Augustine[12] , was that free will meant we could be held accountable but our will was not sufficiently robust to threaten God's hegemony.

We use the same twisty logic thinking and talking about nations, corporations and institutions. We speak of them getting up to stuff, of being responsible for large events: for example, Germany and Japan were responsible for the Second

---

[12]The Catholic Church considers Augustine's teaching to be consistent with free will.[127] He often said that any can be saved if they wish.[127] While God knows who will and won't be saved, with no possibility for the latter. ...This knowledge represents God's perfect knowledge of how humans will freely choose their destinies.[127]
http://en.wikipedia.org/wiki/Augustine_of_Hippo

Vernon Molloy

World War. However this sense of corporate or national agency is never so robust that it threatens our hegemony!

The word *organization* is apt in this discussion because these *virtual organisms* have much in common with organic life. Corporations and nations reflect complex arrangements of human beings, who are in turn composed of complex arrangements of cellular and sub-cellular processes. There are differences of course. Corporations and nations organize cells and organs: producers, consumers and voters... in primitive ways.

Indeed, because they are so clumsily designed, nations and corporations can also be thought of as cancers living upon the resources - human and otherwise - they have overtaken. This is where the story of *Ivanhoe Molloys* is again instructive. As long as human beings' *Wildness Quotient* was not 0%, as long as it was between 20% and 30% perhaps, nations and corporations emerged but only occasionally became malignant. Unless one really believes that the wars of the 20th century can be blamed upon a few hundred or a few thousand villains, a more plausible explanation is required.

I propose that wars occur when ordinary human beings are so disposed, so constituted, so alien to one another, so partitioned into workers and consumers... that their conscious episodes are no longer capacious enough to constrain monstrous activities. Thus when we see wars and other dreadful events, we are almost always seeing armies sanctioned, financed and constituted by worker-persons or shopper-persons attacking one another under the tutelage of overseers hoping to extract still more wealth and power.

In all of these proceedings, the decline of complete-person conscious episodes, driven by the loss of wildness, families, communities, subsistence activities..., provides fertile ground for Nazi consciousness, Fascist consciousness, Communist/Capitalist consciousness, Christian/Islam consciousness... to root up.

Friedrich Nietzsche expressed this a similar view in terms of the stupidity of followers but I think the problem is more alarming. Stupidity could be repaired and Nietzsche doubtlessly hoped that his insights might have salutary consequences. Many have had such dreams: Noam Chomsky, Al Gore, David Suzuki.... Unfortunately, when human beings' capacity for consciousness has been co-opted into ideologies, corporations and nations, there is little reason for optimism.

> As long as a man knows very well the strength and weaknesses of his teaching, his art, his religion, its power is still slight. The pupil and apostle who, blinded by the authority of the master and by the piety he feels toward him, pays no attention to the weaknesses of a teaching, a religion, and soon usually has for that reason more power than the master. The influence of a man has never yet grown great without his blind pupils. To help a perception to achieve victory often means merely to unite it with stupidity so intimately that the weight of the latter also enforces the victory of the former.[13]

The take away is that, until the 21st century, corporations and nations have been constrained by the naturally-occurring autonomy or wildness of citizens. A WQ of 20% — 30% seems to have been enough to keep them from destroying everything.

The challenge is to now repair the WQ of most people so that survival again becomes possible. This will be difficult and time is running out.

While we are at it, we have nothing to lose by aiming for a *wildness quotient* so robust that the corporate monsters we unwittingly constitute become beasts of burden instead of the other way around.

I think a 50% proportion of personal and community subsistence activities would do the job. What do you think?

---

[13] from *Nietzsche's Human, all too Human, s.122, R.J. Hollingdale transl.*

Foreword

January 27, 2014: American folk singer Pete Seeger died at age 94. After reading the lyrics of one of his songs I realized that they expressed something I have been struggling to articulate.

The path through flowers, husbands, soldiers, graveyards and back to flowers is evocative — and the role of women even more so.

I do not imagine that Mr. Seeger intended anything like what I have in mind but his lyrics lend themselves to that interpretation.

Let me hasten to say that I am not lumbering women with responsibility for what human beings get up to. My suggestion is that women are not innocent bystanders, even if the torments they experience at male hands are heart-rending.

> *Where have all the flowers gone, long time passing?*
> *Where have all the flowers gone, long time ago?*
> *Where have all the flowers gone?*
> *Young girls have picked them everyone.*
> *Oh, when will they ever learn?*
> *Oh, when will they ever learn?*
>
> *Where have all the young girls gone, long time passing?*
> *Where have all the young girls gone, long time ago?*
> *Where have all the young girls gone?*
> *Gone for husbands everyone.*
> *Oh, when will they ever learn?*
> *Oh, when will they ever learn?*
>
> *Where have all the husbands gone, long time passing?*
> *Where have all the husbands gone, long time ago?*
> *Where have all the husbands gone?*

Vernon Molloy

Gone for soldiers everyone
Oh, when will they ever learn?
Oh, when will they ever learn?

Where have all the soldiers gone, long time
passing?
Where have all the soldiers gone, long time ago?
Where have all the soldiers gone?
Gone to graveyards, everyone.
Oh, when will they ever learn?
Oh, when will they ever learn?

Where have all the graveyards gone, long time
passing?
Where have all the graveyards gone, long time
ago?
Where have all the graveyards gone?
Gone to flowers, everyone.
Oh, when will they ever learn?
Oh, when will they ever learn?

Where have all the flowers gone, long time
passing?
Where have all the flowers gone, long time ago?
Where have all the flowers gone?
Young girls have picked them everyone.
Oh, when will they ever learn?
Oh, when will they ever learn?

Axioms of Subordination

The most important realization I have ever had — the one I most hope to share with you — is that consciousness does not do the work human beings have been claiming.

Equally importantly, relationships among men and women are not restricted to those described and celebrated in cultural activities, daily events and casual conversations. For at least 10,000 years, stuff going on below the surface has been driving *civilization* and, more recently, *progress and development*.

Modern Problems, Ancient Perspectives

Briefly:

1. Rather than a faculty deciding upon or supervising cognitive activities, conscious episodes occur when memories, experiences, personal priorities and local events combine to generate imaginary arenas wherein *apparent choices* occur before being 'acted upon'. Although these proceedings sometimes involve consciousness, their outcomes are never *achieved*, *willed* or *chosen* by consciousness. Blackboards and chalk, paper and pencils..., facilitate cognitive events in similar ways. We do not understand this. We believe that consciousness actually does stuff in terms of understanding and choosing and that this capacity is what sets human beings apart from other forms of life. The truth is, consciousness is a straightforward evolution of cognitive abilities: reflexes, conditioned responses... possessed by all forms of life.

2. Closer to home, unwittingly Faustian contracts have been defining domestic relationships for at least 10,000 years. These contracts have been spawning sophisticated projects and economies. The results are often splendid, but they are also harming an increasing proportion of human beings and other forms of life. Species are vanishing by the dozens if not hundreds every day and many are worried that the planet could become uninhabitable within the foreseeable future.

3. These contracts harness men to domestic projects, corporations and governments, even as they exempt women from responsibility for events 'outside of homes'. This disenfranchises half of the population when all hands are needed to deal with the consequences of what we have been getting up to.

4. Finally, consciousness functions as an organ of communication among non-conscious proceedings within individuals and communities. In conjunction with (2), this sets the stage for individuals, corporations and nations to capitalize upon the

Vernon Molloy

'progress and development' initiatives implicit in (3).

In the following these notions are sketched in more detail. My approach is reductionist in that I take issue with common sense ideas regarded as indubitably true. Nothing in what follows is a new discovery. My ambition is to find simpler explanation for what we get up to than the stories we have been telling.

The most important simplification involves the nature and function of consciousness. The second clarification applies this model to political and economic consequences.

The good news is that rethinking consciousness in this way opens up interesting possibilities. If we are in political and environmental hot water because we have been getting stuff wrong, repairing these errors could be therapeutic!

In the meantime, since this *magic bullet* will require time to pervade our dark reaches, I suggest a number of repairs to local circumstances.

This is probably unnecessary. I think these remedies, and many others, will automatically occur to anyone persevering to the bottom of these arguments.

Background

The woman at the centre of the following discussion is an amalgam of women I have had the fortune to spend time with.

To this imaginary woman, I have news! A breakthrough has occurred in my understanding. This insight seems traceable to conversations and experiences we have shared, conversations and experiences which never seem to include items from my bucket-list.

I realize this because I have always had bucket-list items to contribute.

This does not seem to be the case with most men; perhaps because they are amazed to have been given tasks to perform and shelter from the storm.

I too am grateful. Even so I have a bad feeling about where this is headed. Although the following is addressed to this imaginary woman, I have my family, friends and community in mind as well. I haven't been able to provoke non-domestic conversations or projects with you either.

It would not surprise me if many of you have been having similar difficulties but have been too polite to complain.

Vernon Molloy

Men and Women

Many problems can be traced to the demands of domestic responsibilities throughout history and around the world. Whether rich or poor, individuals or families are always seeking to improve quality of life and security measures. The problem is, no matter how much is achieved, each level is soon perceived as inadequate.

This is why, in spite of unprecedented production and resource-extracting technologies, poverty is tormenting an increasing proportion of human beings.

If men and women spent more time thinking about what politicians and corporations were getting up to, if we spent less time feathering our nests, we would have already figured out how to hang on to the value our work and clever machines create.

We have instead been allowing much, if not most, of this value to be siphoned into military expenditures, frivolous commercial activities and wealthy accounts.

There is evidence that the wealthy of the world are no longer content with simply farming domesticated populations. Perhaps they have read their Robert Malthus and are worried about the inevitable resource depletion implicit in exponentially rising populations and life-styles. Perhaps they have seen Al Gore's *An Inconvenient Truth* and been worrying about already existing environmental footprints.

What solutions might have occurred to them? The captains of industry have certainly been investing some of the wealth they have been extracting from *hoi polloi* barns in research and development. Automated production machineries and software programs have been rendering traditional skills obsolete for decades.

It is also true that commerce is no longer restricted to supplying basic commodities and servicing needs like changing tires and hauling garbage. Subsistence activities:

94

socializing, educating, health practices, moral and sexual cautions... have been institutionalized, capitalized upon and automated. Software programs now help soldiers assess whether they are suffering post traumatic stress syndrome (PTSD).

Such achievements illuminate why unemployment, marginal employment, part-time employment, contract work, hospitality work, prostitution... now define career paths for an increasing proportion of youngsters, and for oldsters finding themselves unemployed.

The logic that is never talked about is that new technologies may generate new employment opportunities, but these opportunities rarely compensate for employments obsoleted or automated out of existence. If there was no bottom line advantage for corporations and businesses progress and development would not occur. The advantages of new devices flow up economic ladders – they are *progressively distributed*; costs and consequences go the other way – they are *regressively distributed*.

Globalization, centralization, specialization... have rendered billions dependent upon the acumen and integrity of a small proportion of human beings. Fifty million, perhaps five hundred million, regard themselves as being in charge of what is going on. The rest of us seem content to let them think so.

No matter how many leaders you think there are, that number is shrinking as economic and political practices continue concentrating wealth and power in their hands.

One factor camouflaging these proceedings is that plenty of us get up to low-grade mischief. Some of us look like villains in commercial and military events. Even when happily ensconced in domestic arrangements men hunt, fish and play testosterone-addled games. They watch others playing games with equal fervour. In addition, many men have a penchant for getting lost and discovering new places/ideas — which they drag home hoping for a pat on the head or something more delightful.

Vernon Molloy

This mischief is small potatoes compared to the real harm we have been getting up to: the unbidden consequences of our responsible, law-abiding lives. The value-generating activities underwriting economic growth, infrastructure projects and armies can always be tracked back to what men and women get up to domestically.

In these proceedings women define what is required. Men move heaven and earth to make it so.

Of course this is not what we think is going on. There is perpetual talk about the need for perpetual progress, development and economic growth. The problems Mr. Malthus warned about: resource depletion, environmental problems, glass ceilings, chauvinism, inequality... are ignored or gossiped about as if they were facts of life similar to winters, sickness and mortality.

Even when substantive discussions occur, regarding anthropogenic change for example, a simple truth is never on the table. The projects driving economies are conceived, sanctioned and supervised by wives and mothers. These projects — which include security-achieving political and military activities and 'progress and development' initiatives — have become so ingrained, so habitual, so automatic... that they rarely enter anyone's consciousness.

Men do not think about these matters unless laughing at themselves.

As far as I can tell, women do not think about these matters at all. Comfort and security agendas are so wholesome and life-affirming that they cannot be questioned and nothing else is worth talking about.

The resulting dynamos of activity (presently 3 billion male/female value-breeding pairs) are the principal resource and stock-in-trade of leaders, corporations and politicians for centuries. The resulting industrialization, commercialization, economic globalization... is now threatening everything. As the 3rd Millennium begins, the next generation's prospect is

96

bleaker than its parents for the first time in history. Insatiable interest in progress and development, the lust to transform homes into virtual wombs with everything trucked in from somewhere and flushed anywhere, is unsurvivable. In first world nations life-style excesses, climate controlled comfort, grief counsellors, crossing guards and all day every day entertainments... are making us fat, sick, surly and impoverished. In 2013

> seventy per cent of Americans were obese. Globally, the percentage of adults who were overweight or obese - classed as having a body mass index greater than 25 (http://www.bbc.co.uk/health/tools/bmi_calculator/bm i.shtml) - grew from 23% to 34% between 1980 and 2008.[14]

It is important to understand that these consequences have nothing to do with what women or men get up to as individuals. Human beings would not have survived if women's instincts had been less robust.

Left to their own devices men are equally harmless in anthropogenic change terms. They are genetically important but otherwise ancillary to reproduction.

Things started going awry when men and women began combining their previously disconnected physiological and cognitive assets into pair-bonds and nascent cultural resources.

We have a sense of when this occurred. Because of naturally-occurring constraints and population controls the *biosphere* was balanced and sustainable until perhaps 10,000 years ago. To be sure, life was doubtlessly even more difficult than that described in Thomas Hobbes' 1651 *Leviathan* as "nasty, brutish, and short". This began to change when domestic contracts harnessed men and women into breeding pairs, families, communities... and, eventually, economic dynamos. These arrangements spawned the agrarian revolution,

---

[14]http://www.bbc.co.uk/news/health-25576400

governments, corporations, technologies and military activities to defend (or expand) nations of homes.

Until family-based economies emerged, no other species has ever dominated the planet. No other species has come close to deserving the epithet *anthropogenic!*

In short, until the link between sex and procreation became part of human consciousness, things were going along famously — if treading lightly upon the world counts for anything. During this epoch (more than 90% of *Homo sapiens sapiens'* time on earth), males' contribution consisted of squabbling with one another and improving the gene pool any way they could think of. This included exterminating or side-lining males with marginal reflexes, strength and energy. Men still have this instinct, as demonstrated by their inexhaustible interest in activities where the goal is lift heavy objects, hit things as hard as possible and score into nets — metaphors, symbols and icons whose significance is instantly clear to every testosterone-addled male.

This sorting out controlled human populations. Intuition suggests that complementary adaptations would have occurred among women. For example, there is (inconclusive) evidence that menstrual cycles in close-knit communities adjust until they are synchronized. The proposed mechanism involves pheromones shortening or lengthening cycles until everyone lines up.

If this turns out to be true, this synchronicity would have complemented the 'fitness selecting' quarrelsome men were achieving. Synchronized menstrual cycles placed women in competition for males with the stamina to survive and find their way to whatever passed for home. In other words, menstrual synchronicity maximized the benefit of sorting males into winner and losers. All else being equal, 'survivor males' would gravitate to attractive women.

At the same time, menstrual synchronicity is not critical to this argument. Even if an alpha woman happened to not be fertile at opportune moments, her fitness, attractiveness, perpetual state of oestrus... would still distract suitors from inferior possibilities.

Modern Problems, Ancient Perspectives

The need to compete for a small population of survivor males also explains another feature of modern life. After domestic concerns are in order women often turn attention to 'improving' their appearance. (Some reverse this order of business, although this is frowned upon by the sisterhood.) The reproductive benefits of comfort and security are self-evident. In the context of a limited supply of men, perpetual oestrus + attractiveness would have been a naturally-occurring population controlling factor, even as it selected for fitness — a naturally occurring eugenics program!

In the primal world, not every woman would become pregnant because the limited supply of surviving men would have been co-opted by superior women. Cosmetics, hair salons, fashion magazines, cooking shows, romance therapists... reflect this ancient reality. Women continue to compete with one another with a view to conceiving the best children possible.

Of course, as agrarian, settled, civilized... ways of life emerged, this fitness achieving, population controlling dynamic changed. Most men survived long enough to reproduce and most women were disposed to help them do so. A process selecting for genetic excellence and constrained populations was turned on its head. Men traded their wild lives for domestic bliss. Women traded their excellent lives for drudgery and misogyny. Children — the reason for all of the fuss — took every opportunity to join their fathers and explore lifelong infantilism.

When the technologies making the modern world possible — which can also be traced to men harnessing their hunting ingenuity to domestic matters — matured sufficiently to extract fossil fuels and invent combustion engines, the *Industrial Revolution* smashed into the world like a comet.

Vernon Molloy

Nurturing Nations

Nations and corporations are among the unintended consequences of the mutually-subordinating relationships men and women have been entering into for thousands of years. Men subordinate themselves to gain reproductive options and securities. Women subordinate themselves to enhance the prospects of their children no matter what this costs them personally, no matter what it costs other people's children, global resources and world security. In other words, nations and corporations came into existence when reproductive instincts married men's existential anxieties with women's need to nurture. Corporate greed, political malfeasance and criminal behaviours are therefore minor players in human beings' troubled history. Greed and malfeasance would have had little traction if the mutual, male/female subordinations had not corraled men and women into becoming factory and cannon fodder.

In micro-economic terms there is profit to be made selling nest-feathering products, fashions and cosmetics to women. Marketing to men is simpler still. They are always interested in new trucks and tools, always looking for opportunities to do some vicarious living through the exploits of their favourite teams. Men love such distractions, tools and toy weapons because they whisper of primal days when they got up to stuff without anyone caring, when they got up to stuff without being told to do so.

There is still more profit to be made if manufacturing trucks and guns can be automated or outsourced — although the problem of finding customers when more and more people are unemployed or marginally employed remains unsolved.

This may, of course, be no problem at all. As already suggested, the globalization of poverty may be just what the wealthy have in the back of their minds. What other 'green

100

plan' has a hope of reducing environmental footprints quickly enough and sufficiently to save the world?

Save the world for whom you ask? The answer is as plain as the noses on our faces. The world must be saved for the bright, beautiful and strong. It must be saved for the top ten per cent or something like seven hundred million.

This could be rounded up to one billion if green technologies come on stream fast enough.

In the meantime, regardless of whether the global claw-back is led from the top or steered from the bottom, regardless of whether plans are consciously entertained or put into play by deploying unindictable failures to act, people like Noam Chomsky, Henry David Thoreau, the Club of Rome, Rachel Carson, Margaret Thatcher, perhaps even Mrs. Stephen Harper... have been sounding the alarm about out-of-control growth for decades. Their protestations do not seem to have made an iota of difference — although it is possible things would be worse had they not been occurring.

What is more important is that nothing has been said about where these problems are coming from. Perhaps we cannot see what is going on because it is going on everywhere. Human beings are engineered to look for explanations standing out against the background of domestic affairs and reproductive agendas. What happens when the explanation *involves* domestic affairs and reproductive agendas?

To be sure, there are more user-friendly explanations for why warnings, statistics and dire portents are falling on deaf ears. The most optimistic is that men have been putting aside their misgivings because they are being given exciting domestic work to do. If women instinctively focus upon domestic issues, men may be similarly disposed to think about broader issues. Big-picture understandings would have helped on the hunt and remembering how to 'get back home' would also have been useful. When men entered into domestic contracts to 'help out' in return for promises of monogamy and a chance at reproductive success, big picture understandings, which could have led to worrying about the dark side of progress and development, may have been set aside as part of the quid pro quo.

If so, men could quickly become useful if men and women ever got around to discussing shopping list issues with sustainability and wholesomeness in mind.

Unfortunately it seems more likely that neither big nor small worries cross the typical male mind. My intuition is that the first time men experienced purposefulness and identity was when mutually subordinating reproductive arrangements emerged. When this became part of the human experience men piggy-backed their minuscule ambitions and fragile egos upon woman's instinctive certainty that comfort and security mattered and that no amount was too much.

If so this could explain why Robert Malthus, Henry Thoreau, Rachel Carson, David Suzuki, Noam Chomsky and all the Cassandras of history have been crying out in vain. The world looks the way it does because countless millions of women (presently three billion) have been struggling to make their circumstances as womb-like as possible — and an equal number of men have been 'helping out' with every fibre of their being.

They have been helping out with all of their might because doing so is better than the existentially-fraught alternative.

However domestic projects came to be, they have been inexhaustible wealth-creating engines for ambitious. clever human beings. The mutually subordinating contracts entered into by men and women have been delivering generation after generation to factories and shopping centres. Women could be depended upon to attempt to raise their children in the safest, most comfortable circumstance possible. If men knew what was good for them they helped out and did not ask why.

Equally importantly these contracts guaranteed that neither men nor women 'wasted time' worrying about what was going on beyond homes and communities. This has continued to be the case even when what was going on was ruinous.

As well, until recently, human beings lacked the population

numbers and technologies to do significant harm. The world could safely be regarded as a limitless resource and garbage dump. Every generation inherited a more or less level playing field. Even though there have always been rich and poor people, almost everyone possessed the skills and resources needed to pursue subsistence activities. When local resources were used up or polluted, new regions were always waiting to be discovered and colonized — usually to the consternation of Aboriginals who had already 'discovered themselves' and thought nothing further was needed.

For 21st century populations, few possibilities remain for those who are not well-educated, well-to-do or meet stringent immigration criteria. Thus, even if a new continent should suddenly turn up, urban populations have become so specialized that it is hard to imagine migrating anywhere and running the risk of landing in circumstances demanding subsistence skills and Inner Directed attitudes.

Even so, escape fantasies still occur. Millions of lottery tickets are sold every day. An even more outlandish response to the mess we have made involves migrating to another planet. Rather than repairing problems where we live, in ways that might benefit our future selves and our children and grandchildren, a surprising number of us dream of boarding yet another contraption and getting out of Dodge.

The following is from the Mars One website:

> Mars One will establish a permanent human settlement on Mars. Crews of four will depart every two years, starting in 2024. Our first unmanned mission will be launched in 2018. Participate in this mission to Mars through our crowd-funding campaign.[15]

This is pretty ominous stuff. Focusing 'like lasers' upon domestic projects means that we never ask whether we might not have achieved an optimum balance between progress and wholesomeness a decade or a century ago. Women rarely look at the mess they and their consorts have been making. Men are oblivious to their own sickly, obese, demanding children

[15]http://www.mars-one.com/mission

Vernon Molloy

— and contemptuous of the populations 'over there' they exploit and torment to achieve such results.

City Life

Another reason we might wish to rethink progress and development is that herding human beings into cities is turning out to be a bad idea.

> *The world is undergoing the largest wave of urban growth in history. In 2008, for the first time in history, more than half of the world's population will be living in towns and cities. By 2030 this number will swell to almost 5 billion, with urban growth concentrated in Africa and Asia. While mega-cities have captured much public attention, most of the new growth will occur in smaller towns and cities, which have fewer resources to respond to the magnitude of the change.*[16]

Corralled and dependent urban populations are more readily sorted into producers and consumers, leaders and followers, rich and poor than hunter-gatherers or the inner-directed cowboys described in David Pressman's *The Lonely Crowd* published in 1950. Even today such people can be occasionally identified in urban settings although they are clearly an endangered species. Mr. Riesman referred to such individuals as *inner-directed recidivists*.

I think this means that circumstances calling for Inner Directed behaviours tend to be lonely and stressful – like being in solitary confinement or stranded on an island. Most men are willing, if not anxious, to trade such astringent pleasures for nicely-appointed nests — especially if they get to kick up carefully-monitored fusses from time to time.

On the other hand, for reasons examined further along, I think women are instinctively Inner Directed and do not find this the least bit stressful. Women are so centred and comfortable that they have no trouble lending assurance and direction to men taken on as projects and instrumentalities.

---

[16]http://www.unfpa.org/pds/urbanization.htm

They are even willing to accommodate adolescent antics. Women may even enjoy the quiet moments associated with hunting and fishing seasons; perhaps to reconsider bargains struck; perhaps to entertain new tenders.

As regards urbanization and specialization, these fraught, dangerous forms of life are congruent with domestic priorities. The more crossing guards, the more flashing lights on school buses, the more detailed and intrusive governments and corporations... the more life seems sanitized, comfortable and secure.

The simplest way to understand these proceedings is to think of homes as extended wombs. It seems incontrovertible that homes are mandated, designed, supervised and maintained by women. On the other hand, for the most part, homes are constructed by men and serviced with male-designed infrastructure and utilities: water, energy, sewage systems, transportation... systems.

The purpose of homes is to provide warm, secure shelters for neonates, real or imagined, human or otherwise. Cities can be thought of as large external wombs for dense collections of private external wombs. Necessities are transported into cities. By-products are trucked and flushed away.

Cities are womb-like in another way. Because every place is becoming like every other place, because experiences are increasingly restricted to virtual reality technologies like the internet and smart phones, the need to actually live in place A instead of place B, or to travel between A and B, the need to have conversations or experiences with nearby people... is receding.

The Industrial Revolution achieved these remarkable transformations in less than three hundred years. Along the way a small proportion of human beings became wealthy indeed. The rest of us sorted ourselves into middle and lower class populations.

The Industrial Revolution then morphed into the *Digital Age* and began making everyone except the wealthy very poor indeed.

The irony is that the Industrial Revolution owes its existence to a threshold population of Inner Directeds — the characteriological type least likely to thrive in urban circumstances. The United State's present political and economic prowess owes a great deal to the Inner Directeds frontier life and subsistence activities had been spawning until David Riesman drew attention to their decline in the 1950s.

Americans still regard themselves as exceptional because of the achievements of these Inner Directeds. Americans continue to speak about themselves in manifest destiny terms, although evidence of extraordinary will or competence is almost entirely historical.

With a seventy per cent obesity rating in 2014 and an economy staggering under frightening levels of public and private debt, the United States is well down the road to economic and political self-immolation. The best a population drifting into narcissism, Other Directedness and self-idolatrization can hope for is sardonic attention. The chances are good that these characteristics will instead be perceived as weaknesses inviting attacks.

Such problems are not restricted to the USA. First World nations are all pursuing economically perilous behaviours. If nations pursue circumstances wherein domestic populations have less and less value-adding work to perform, these nations will inevitably go bankrupt. This day can be put off by going into debt, dumping one-time resources into moribund markets – think Canada's oil (tar) sands – and by stealing value from third world workers.

Western nations are also engaging in an ironic form of self-administered genocide. The statistics tell the story: us white westerners are not reproducing sufficiently to maintain our numbers. This means that we are not only importing life-style products but people to enjoy them!

Vernon Molloy

I am being a bit facetious. The reason immigration policies (and possibly the Syrian refugee crisis in 2015) have become part of western business plans is that economies must grow or collapse. As far as I know, there are no economic models or historical examples of steady-state economies. What would a steady-state economy look like?

My sense is that *progress and development* would be replaced with *regress and development*.

This would be an exciting change. A consciously-abetted steady-state economy would invest in technologies to achieve goods and services decided upon by consumers and groups of consumers rather than by politicians and corporate executives examining entrails behind closed doors.

In the meantime so many percentage-driven financial calculations, remuneration packages and taxations have been baked into business models that economies must either grow or collapse.

This is why corporations continue to grind out products and services promising to make us attractive, comfortable and secure. The fact that their productions have already made us poor, obese and full of chemicals with important names is simply irrelevant.

An important element in these proceedings is that men regard themselves are always on probation. They think that they have to continuously demonstrate domestic and reproductive credentials by extracting still more value from nature and transferring still more wealth from remote populations.

The rest of story is equally familiar. Women disavow responsibility for anything and everything that goes on outside of their homes, while completely controlling everything occurring inside. When not 'at work' an equal myopia characterizes men. They have little interest in domestic affairs but instinctively patrol 'their property'; wherein their 'bit of heaven' is situated.

Modern Problems, Ancient Perspectives

These proceedings are unfortunate for a final reason. Instead of seeing themselves as well-positioned to insist upon wholesome, economies, women regard themselves as innocent bystanders or victims of misogyny. Like the rogue male myth, there is plenty of abuse to fund this stereotype. However the reality is that most men are not rogues and most women are not victims. Most men can't wait to subordinate themselves to the woman of their dreams. Most women regard domestic terrorism as an inalienable, non-negotiable right.

This is not hyperbole: by definition, a terrorist is anyone resorting to sanctions or the threat of sanctions to get what he or she wants.

This is true whether what is wanted involves instinctively-sourced shopping lists or demands from Bible-Belt or Bomb-Belt brigades.

More Background

These suggestions — I agree they are not fully-articulated or well defended — depend upon intuitive links between what most of us get up to day-by-day and the state of the world.

On a personal note,I have been dabbling in subsistence activities all of my life. Some of these projects have been tolerated by the women who have graced my life, rather the way a precocious chimpanzee would be indulged.

I too am capable of useful work if closely supervised.

For the most part my vagaries and unwelcome suggestions about what we should also get up to domestically have only succeeded in dissolving relationships with a succession of remarkable women.

One after another they put up with me, sometimes for years. Perhaps a masochistic streak is commoner than we think. Perhaps I am perceived as potentially useful in case something untoward happens. (Women pursue relationships with convicts in case they come across someone who needs exterminating.)

I think the more likely explanation is that I have the status of a Shi Tzu dog. Without intending to, I have learned the hapless, bedraggled trick. If I demonstrate that I need nurturing and direction, I seem to know that I will be tolerated longer than I deserve.

Unfortunately, understanding this only makes me more anxious. I worry about what my presence has cost women in my life. I think about what I am not getting up to because of what I am getting up to. I also keep attempting to find the right argument or illustration to get even one of my items onto the domestic agenda.

I regret to report that this has failed completely.

Vernon Molloy

On the subject of failure, when I bring up the fact that I have been unable to interest anyone in the delights of process metaphysics or the tactical advantages of team shopping, the suggestion is sometimes made that I have 'presentation problems'. My sentences are lumbered with big words, my arguments are convoluted.

More importantly I am reminded that I have yet to demonstrate what even one of my schemes would look like in action.

Even though I hear these observations with dismay, even though I know my score has been reckoned and my page turned, I hear myself making lame responses. I point out that problems big enough to warrant talking about are boiling out of the of dozens, hundreds, thousands... of lives. Such difficulties cannot be solved by persons acting alone. Discussions, consensus, co-ordinate, collective responses... are required.

My modest ambition has been to provoke discussions and raise the possibility of such responses. (Surely it is clear that I would be an eager participant in any such project!)

In the face of decades of failure, I continue to repair arguments already repaired a dozen times. I hear myself muttering that luminous possibilities should expect rough treatment. An ironic impasse! The worse the prospect, the less people want to talk about what is coming over the horizon. The worse things get, the less willing I am to talk about anything else.

My sharpest disappointment is that my friends, relatives and intimates have not had the patience or interest to hear me out sufficiently to either got excited along with me or repair my confusions. If someone I knew came to me with a story about what they thought was going on and what might be done about it, I would not sleep until I understood what they meant — even if it involved learning another language!

Even though I understand that nothing personal is involved, these proceedings feel like contemptuous dismissal.

Feelings of Contempt

"Aha!" the woman of my dreams says. "Feelings of contempt never once crossed my mind!"

I have come to understand that you are right about this. My suggestions are handled the way unsavoury information, or information contradicting some point of view, are almost always handled. Unwelcome notions and contradictory information are deflected into cognitive trash bins and never make it into consciousness. This is why you are genuinely surprised whenever I suggest that you would not put up with such treatment if you were on the receiving end.

As far as you are aware, contempt has never been involved in our proceedings because conscious dismissals were rarely part of your experience. From my point of view repudiations have been occurring. You are not aware of them because they were orchestrated by deep-running cognitive events outside of your conscious episodes.

Of course, being dismissed reflexively is the worst possible fate a would-be conversationalist can experience. 'Conscious decisions' to hit delete buttons are more manageable than automatically deflections by spam filters. Conscious decisions mean that issues, possibilities, persons... are still actively generating awareness screens. Until spam filters become mature and automated, good presentations can sometimes overturn 'conscious decisions' to delete.

Granted, in my case, this is only theoretical.

I bring this up for a reason. What is more significant than another bout of self-pity by another geriatric fool is the realization that non-conscious dismissals, priorities, prejudices, bigotries... are happening in all of us all of the time. I think this means that most of the stuff people get up to does not originate in or involve consciousness. The sources of what people value, are interested in, will countenance in conversations... only occasionally involve or require conscious episodes in their genesis. When consciousness is involved it functions as a lens through which problematic or novel issues are viewed or illuminated. When this viewing is sustained – and this seems to be a singularly human ability – conscious episodes amount to metaphorical blackboards upon which conversations are written and projects are planned, instantiated and supervised.

I remember owning a bicycle when I was in public school. The bicycle had a generator powered by the back wheel. This generator supported a small headlamp illuminating a few meters of the path ahead – but only if one was travelling at a good rate of speed!

This illumination was better than nothing, but not by much! The seductive predicament is clear. The temptation is to go faster and faster because this allows one to see further. The problem is that the dangers associated with going faster and faster overwhelms the advantages of enlarged awareness.

I think this captures the risks of insouciant *progress and development*. The consequences of faster, better, stronger... are divergent and regressive. The advantages of faster, better, stronger... are convergent and progressive.

This formula also captures what is going on in conscious episodes. Conscious episodes are generated by activities 'down below'. They function to illuminate a way forward. The analogy captures the idea that consciousness is a result of stuff going on and not their cause. It also captures the sense that the function of consciousness is to facilitate or enable resolutions, choices, responses... by illuminating possible paths. These illuminations, these insights, are what we have in mind when we talk about being 'subjects of experience', of having souls and being persons.

I have been conducting a 'thought experiment' that seems to demonstrate why this explanation sheds light upon unhappy

113

world events. I have been asking what people thought Hitler would answer if asked whether he harboured any prejudice against Jews. A surprising number agree that Hitler would have denied any such feelings! They also agree that – had Hitler been hooked up to a lie detector device – his denial would have registered as truthful!

This is my intuition as well. If you agree, you must also concur that Hitler was not aware that he was a bigot. Hitler had no consciousness of making choices leading to bigotry. Every lie detector test along his trajectory would have found him innocent.

In other words, the horror Mr. Hitler became evolved outside of his consciousness. To be sure, Hitler was doubtlessly aware of some of the machinations actualizing the projects fulminating within him. Many projects were *deputized* to individuals whose loathsome conduct became almost as well-known as Hitler's[17] . Doubtlessly practical details were resolved during conscious episodes in those individuals put Buchenwald and Auschwitz into operation; and perhaps during their trials at Nuremberg.

If toxic behaviours manage to root up, they sometimes spawn monstrous growths. Conscious episodes along the way, awarenesses of successes or failures (don't even think about what counts as success for such beings!), filter down to become part of their respective archipelagos. We all possess or — more accurately — are possessed by such repositories. These are the mechanisms spawning the projects, intentions, choices... that make up our lives, the cognitive proceedings sometimes generating conscious episodes but always manifesting as values, prejudices, notions of entitlement, identity, patriotism and xenophobia.

This tells us something. The world is rife with conversations, criminal investigations, public enquiries... trying to determine who is responsible for this or that state of affairs, this or that event. What is the purpose of all of this forensic work?

---

[17]http://en.wikipedia.org/wiki/List_of_Nazi_Party_leaders_and_officials

Modern Problems, Ancient Perspectives

Lots of people have observed that scapegoating — ascribing responsibility for the conduct of the many upon a few — is demoralizing and disenfranchising. I think this is correct, but that we are overlooking a deeper harm. The assumption that makes scapegoating plausible depends upon the claim that questions about "who is responsible" can be resolved by investigating the contents of an individual's consciousness.

A saviour, a Dear Leader... who passed his or her life in a coma would be an unsatisfactory scapegoat! How could we blame what must be deflected and accounted for upon such creatures? How could we absolve ourselves?

Yet the Hitler thought experiment suggests that what occurs in consciousness has little to do with what human beings get up to. A more plausible account sees consciousness functioning as a mouse whisker probing unknown spaces, a shark fin tracing its owners' path, a periscope taking a look around.

Even this reduced account postulates consciousness as *doing something*. As argued below, consciousness is not active in any way whatsoever. At the same time, consciousness is not passive for the reason a blackboard or a piece of paper could be said to *receive* impressions. More importantly, what occurs next is often informed, sharpened, focussed... by what has gone on during conscious episodes. So consciousness can be thought of as both a repository and a medium passing 'organic information' from past to future.

This storing and passing of information has many consequences including the subjective experiences you and i think of as *the present* , the *actual world* and, of course, one another.

Vernon Molloy

Consciousness's Modest Role

the great majority of men... work gradually at eclipsing their ethical and ethical-religious comprehension, which would lead them out into decisions and conclusions that their lower nature does not much care for.

Soren Kierkegaard

Quite a few people have suggested that I spend too much time fussing about consciousness. This puzzles me because conscious episodes are all we have to talk about. How can it not be interesting to think about what might be going on and the reasons conscious episodes occur? There are many questions in philosophical literature: what is the relationship between consciousness and its contents? Which comes first? Or – as I propose – are contents and consciousness not like chickens and eggs constantly creating and shading into one another?

Another introspective observation I have made - and assume that the same holds true for others - is that thoughts and conclusions either flow from previous thoughts, from awarenesses traceable to *external* events and conversations — or pop up unbidden the way creative people frequently describe.

This spontaneity is the principal reason I think we have been getting consciousness wrong – an error that has been having toxic consequences. A great deal turns upon what function consciousness is 'performing' – indeed upon whether consciousness is *doing* anything at all in the sense of being intrinsically *active* instead of being a *passive*.

After accepting the view that consciousness is the seat of agency and personhood for decades I came to understand that this could not be true and that consciousness is not able to act upon or engage with its contents. Like our passive awareness of sounds, sights and feelings, conscious episodes are generated by cognitive events and not the other way around.

This modest self-evident claim replaces the notion of consciousness as active or efficacious in and of itself. We presently believe that consciousness brings something to the party that does not exist when human beings are too young to be 'fully conscious' or, as Catholics say, to have reached the *age of reason.* or when we are sleeping, drugged or knocked out.

We believe that consciousness differentiates human beings from other forms of life and does so by transforming *animal behaviour* into *human conduct*. Thus Kierkegaard's comment assumes, implies, accepts... that consciousness can choose to "work gradually at eclipsing... comprehensions".

Why consciousness would not simply obliterate problematic comprehensions instead of grinding them down is not clear. What is clear is that the 'eclipsing' Kierkegaard speaks of involves claims that it occurs *ex nihilo,* that it cannot be tracked back to previous causes, including previous decisions of the person whose decision it is.

Free will and *choosing* talk depend upon the claim that consciousness judges and interprets its own contents; which is like saying that rulers can measure themselves, see whether they fall long or short and then make necessary adjustments! This is what it means to speak of individuals performing (or not performing) acts for which they can be praised or blamed. The litmus test is whether individuals are conscious, 'in possession of their faculties' and have the time to form a premeditated intention. Thus, a guilty mind (intention to perform some criminal act) must exist prior to the act being performed: *mens rea* before or during *actus reus*.[18] Although rarely stated so explicitly, a similar analysis applies to apportioning praise, rewards and financial outcomes.

In spite of depending upon a clearly false claim in a

---

[18]For an interesting discussion:
http://en.wikipedia.org/wiki/Concurrence

Vernon Molloy

straightforward way, free will talk is surprisingly flexible and difficult to challenge. For example it accommodates increasingly detailed explanations regarding the genesis of human activities. To be sure there is a premonition that everything human beings get up to will eventually be explained behaviouristically. Until this happens we simply keep moving our special status claim so that it is always outside the sphere of behaviours that have chemical or hormonal explanations.

Alternatively we acknowledge that these explanations could eventually explain everything we get up to, but insist that nothing turns on this. We say: "Yes, but look at *what* we get up to!"; then carry on as if agency and morality talk made as much sense as it did thousands of years ago when supernatural entities were as thick on the ground as thieves.

The irony is that human beings can become persons: i.e., autonomous moral and rational creatures, as soon as we stop insisting that we already are. The recipe is as simple and homely as the nose on our face. The most important ingredient involves recognizing that personhood is not a guaranteed birthright. The second is that, while personhood is possible, it must be achieved.

Persons are like gardens. Persons must be grown.

What is a person? This is impossible to say because as soon as a definition is struck the next person we come across may have become so by clambering over it. However it is possible to make some headway by saying what persons are not. For example the Hitlers and Kim Jong-uns of history, and their goose-stepping buffoons, are not persons in any interesting sense of the word. The chanting, gesticulating, genuflecting congregations in churches and Walmart stores are not persons either. The chances of coming across persons is higher in refugee camps than in the platoons responsible for refugee camps

----

The business of growing persons is important and will be discussed further along. In the meantime a bit of house-cleaning is in order.

Modern Problems, Ancient Perspectives

If human beings had not begun the process of understanding themselves by claiming that consciousness is active and efficacious, I think we would have evolved a more useful view of ourselves and one another. I think we would have a different sense of the world. For example, the phenomenal world we experience (full of private images and imagined proceedings) would not have automatically translated into 'common sense' claims involving an actually-existing external world that individuals *inhabit*. As soon as what is going on is understood in such partitioned ways a great deal of confusion and divisiveness is baked into everything that follows. Realism is one possible explanation of the phenomenal world. There are many possible stories and perhaps realism would not be the one almost all human beings have settled upon had it not been presented as axiomatically self-evident.

For example, if elements, objects, entities, events... are understood as private images in subjective lives, there is no reason to talk about things as more than figures of speech summarizing and conveying information. Thus it is convenient – perhaps too convenient – to organize populations under quasi-object headings: liberals, conservatives, protestants, catholics, rich, poor, communists, capitalists....

These shorthand measures allow stump speeches and harangues to proceed without reinventing ideological wheels. They mean that robust entreaties, vigorous disputes, bar room brawls and military adventures need not waste time reviewing and reiterating what the fuss is all about.

As well, thinking about what is going on in terms of things, entities, persons... has survival value. One of the reasons the digital age and internet is expanding so astonishingly is that programmers and users find graphical user interfaces computationally liberating. [19] What is interesting to think about is that we have seen this before. Thinking about real-life experiences in terms of objects, entities and persons is advantageous for the same reason *graphical user interfaces*

[19]https://hbr.org/2015/04/were-all-terrible-at-understanding-each-other

(and *second life avatars)* are seductive. GUIs eliminate the need for terminal screens and complicated command strings. The consciousness model I have been recommending proposes that things, entities, persons... are best understood as Graphical User Interfaces (GUIs) greatly reducing computational burdens and response times.

This suggests that reflexes and conditioned responses evolved into a capacity for conscious episodes. Conscious episodes are conditioned responses stretched out until they encompass seconds, minutes, hours... instead of microseconds. This suggests that the capacity for conscious experiences is an emergent phenomenon and not a supernatural or Darwinian endowment.

Along with mischiefs touched on below, the claim that consciousness is a choice-generating engine sets the stage for the most amazing scapegoating ploy possible. By regarding consciousness as an indictable or praiseworthy source of decisions, we identify an inscrutable aspect of our own being as responsible for what we get up to.

To be sure, we often find that we must resort to multiple villains when scapegoating becomes implausible with just one face to blame. In this way the moral responsibility of millions of Germans for Second World War events was transferred to twenty three war criminals tried at Nuremberg. There was not twenty four because Hitler had killed himself — a fact that improved the scapegoating ploy because self-condemning, self-punishing villains are able to shoulder enormous responsibility. Not surprisingly cultures around the world do everything they can to encourage such behaviour.

Scapegoating was also what Freud was on about when he developed a model 'spreading responsibility' for human behaviour among id, ego and superego. This absolved persons from culpability in a curious way even as it allowed Dr. Freud to take credit for his remarkable insights!

This is also what Descartes had in mind with his awkward account of mental (supernatural, spiritual) substances interacting with the material world by way of pineal glands.

Modern Problems, Ancient Perspectives

The culturally-embedded practice of scapegoating is what lawyers have in mind upon when they argue for or against Murder in the First Degree. If responsibility for heinous behaviour cannot be vested in persons by virtue of *mens rea* talk then responsibility must flow through to generative circumstances.

In this story the German nation would have been far less able to shake off responsibility for the Second World War by offering up a handful of miscreant individuals.

The fact that these individuals were malignant caricatures made the scapegoating trope all the more effective.

A more plausible story is that the conscious episodes referred to by lawyers are the tips of cognitive icebergs. We see such icebergs forming all the time. No matter how desperate their circumstance, children and adolescents are intensely alive, interested and curious. They have not yet been rendered into individuals *whose minds are made up* by internal spam filters deflecting, dissolving, dismissing... information streaming in from whatever world they happen to live in.

(I refer, of course, to the world before television, smart phones and the INTERNET rendered privately-sourced conscious episodes quaint remnants from a now archaic inner-directed, self-subsisting era.)

Cognitive filters diminish the need to pay attention to recurring events, problems and individuals. This was excellent so long as we were living in circumstances where novel individuals and problems kept turning up. Unfortunately, urban life — the de facto womb within which more and more human beings find themselves — contains few problems that cannot be solved with flicking switches, flushing toilets or calling 911.

As a consequence human beings are enjoying fewer and fewer conscious moments. This is why time seems to go faster as one gets ages. Fewer events requiring conscious episodes mean fewer memories.

In fairness, banality offers an ironic benefit. A disengaged, myopic life tests the quality of economic and political circumstances. If urbanites can survive without paying attention to what is going on, then what is going on must be wholesome. The downside is that we may not notice much about our excellent lives, and what kind of an excellent life is that?

As well, should mischief become unmistakeable, alarms will sound but perhaps too late for for canaries. Even this can be useful. If enough people come to grief because communities and corporations are infected with toxic elements or proceedings, legislations are sometimes enacted to protect future populations. The tobacco industry provides an example. Harms suffered by smokers eventually led to constraints upon advertising and no-smoking bans.

These are murky waters however. Such repairs can themselves become toxic. Legislation, surveillance, interdiction... sanction — and sometimes demand — myopia and dependence on the part of the usual person. The resulting circumstance — each element well-intentioned — can itself diminish the incidence of conscious episodes.

In fully-developed nanny states, people may be alive and healthy but they risk not being aware of much that is going on, of not being alive in any interesting sense.

In such a world, only flawed, insecure individuals have a natural defence against falling into trivial lives. The bright, gifted and well-educated are especially at risk. You might want to ask yourself how your own life is going — although, for reasons already discussed, it is hard to take such measurements.

No worries. I have three *external* examples:

1   The Alan Gummo group — an email list I am glad to belong to and whose postings I read with interest — are all excellent people. For the most part they are closing upon their best before date — or, like me, looking back at it. With the assistance of Facebook, email and digital cameras, they pass their time sharing memories of road trips, musical adventures and anecdotes from days gone by. These accounts

are seasoned with delightful, sardonic observations about what is going on.

2   The second example is larger: the *Die Off* group moderated by the indefatigable Jay Hanson. Several hundred strong, this congregation contemplates the consequences of running out of cheap oil. They spend time thinking about what this will look like — and where one might best flee to. (Mr. Hanson opted for Hawaii some time ago.) When not so engaged, Die Off members discuss the intractable greed, myopia and stupidity of politicians, corporations and the chattering classes. Even Die Offers are regularly scolded for straying off topic or neglecting reading lists.

3   North America's baby boomers are making their final appearance. An unprecedented proportion of old people are wandering around clutching shopping lists, golf carts, fishing poles and vacation brochures.... If they are worried it is not about what is going on but whether they will outlive their assets. Quite a few spend time trying to outwit their children and grandchildren seized with the same question.

What is common across these examples is how few of us consider our own complicity in problems we identify — or wonder whether we should do more than wave hands and point fingers! The people in the examples above are as well-informed and articulate as any population the world has seen.

Many claim to have seen dreadful straws in the wind!

Mystery solved! What we get up to, what we talk about, which vacation we will take... does not originate in consciousness but boils up from below. Our conscious episodes reflect the melding of prejudices, bigotries, values, folk-ways, ethnic identities, personal anxieties and local events. These episodes facilitate, integrate and, in a thousand ways, make sustained, sophisticated responses possible. Conscious episodes are also the *sine qua non* of long-term projects and vacation trips. They constantly add to and refine spam filters so that future conscious episodes remain unfettered and agile, our consciences untroubled and serene.

After all, who knows when we might be required to sit for a lie detector test; or be rigorously questioned by a concerned friend?

Of course, for almost all of human history, freeing up our capacity for conscious episodes so we can better attend to what is 'going on locally' is just what the doctor ordered. The problem is, these adaptations assume something that is no longer true. They assume that human beings are not themselves the problem! But we have become our own nemesis - a source of cumulative, incremental trouble that we are cunningly engineered to overlook. We can no longer afford to ignore the consequences of what we are getting up to. The problem is, these are the last things on our minds for a simple, fatal reason. What we are getting up to instantly becomes the retina upon which events are seen.

In addition, information to help us think and talk about big picture issues now exists in such abundance that we have a false sense of well-being. The fact that all this information is instantly available is wonderfully reassuring. And if we happen to have a point of view requiring a Google search (which I think really means *Go ogle*) a flood of corroborating data is instantly available.

In addition to the heavy lifting accomplished by scapegoating, two aspects of urban life help us concoct sophisticated ways to deflect responsibility. News rushes at us day and night; most with a twelve hour shelf life and a "if it bleeds it leads" flavour. This frenetic attention to minutia encourages the belief that there must be well-informed people somewhere deciding that these are the issues we need to focus upon.

The reality is that the media is trying to appeal to a public with more and more entertainment options and ever shorter attention spans. This means that what is being put out is making the problem worse — a *chicken or egg first* process in reverse.

124

Modern Problems, Ancient Perspectives

These mutually-reinforcing relationships are 'achieving' something unprecedented. They are diminishing the likelihood that urbanized, specialized individuals will pay 'conscious attention' to anything at all.

In addition we glimpse see how each such dismissal adds a new filter to those protecting individuals from *wasting conscious episodes* upon already dealt with matters. When these filters add to existing bigotries, the narrow focus of specialized individuals and the repetitive nature of urban life, it is not surprising that vigorous conversations and useful responses rarely occur.

There is no reason to believe that we have plumbed to the bottom of this well. Spam filters also amount to self-fulfilling prophecies. As events requiring conscious attention become familiar they are assimilated into the unseen archipelago we all harbour. These repositories meld with current events, cultural repositories, physiological and hormonal determinants... and form increasingly focused, increasingly detailed filters.

This has three results:

1   In urban circumstances less and less of what is going on warrants attention.

2   As we specialize, the proportion of information that seems incomprehensible increases and the proportion that warrants attention decreases.

3   In the way convicts and the citizens of authoritarian regimes adjust their dreams of what better days would look like, spam filters constantly adjust ideas of what is possible and desirable so that feelings of equanimity and security remain possible.

On a personal level, my intimates, family and friends now seem to have spam filters successfully identifying and deflecting every one of my overtures so their capacity for conscious episodes is not wasted. Nothing I can think of warrants attention.

If such dismissals are occurring in other lives — and I have no reason to believe my experiences are unusual — mutual disengagement may be an unindicted epidemic infecting urban relationships.

None of this would matter if we were, as we have been imagining, moral and rational agents with God-like abilities to make and act upon choices. On the other hand, if we are only occasionally conscious, and if consciousness is nothing more than an interval during which cognitive events interpose between stimuli and responses, a dark picture emerges. Consciousness remains important but in a different way. Consciousness becomes a facilitator, a mediator, a convenor of undertakings which have themselves never been *consciously reviewed* or *consciously discussed*.

Conscious episodes are important for another reason. They make subjectivity possible. Conscious episodes are how we know that we are alive. They are the channels through which we communicate. The problem is, the conscious episodes that make communication and subjectivity possible are neither guaranteed to occur nor to keep occurring.

If we were the little Gods we imagine ourselves to be, if we enjoyed consciousness and agent-hood as a birthright, we could perhaps afford to be cavalier. We are not such however. This is why it matters a great deal that we have been systematically eliminating consciousness-generating occasions and calling it *progress and development*. Like a person perched on a limb and sawing vigorously, we are not even looking to see which side of the cut we are on.

In other words, human beings appear are engaging in a novel kind of genocide. We are transforming from occasionally self-aware persons into zombies where every conscious experience is externally sourced.

Like body-builders who cannot go past mirrors without taking an admiring look, we think: "Just think of what I could do…!" And then: "…If I could just think of what I could do!"

Larger Spheres

There is another reason rethinking consciousness could improve our prospects and those of creatures crossing our paths. If we are not Little Gods then our conscious episodes flow from two processes.

- The first involves the evolutionary and reproductive events spawning consciousness-capable creatures.

- The second involves the cultural resources and communities fashioning persons out of raw human beings.

These threads combine to produce individuals who then interact with relevant events. What does relevant mean? The factors determining whether a person is male or female, Caucasian, oriental or Negro, rich or poor, American, Chinese or Russian or ... constitute backdrops against which lives play out.

The factors combine to produce the conscious episodes we think of as our lives. The resulting conceits overlook that this capacity is an emergent phenomenon involving incremental improvements to the adroitness and scope of responses across phyla and species and millions of years.

The resulting capacity for conscious episodes subsidize other useful functions, but these benefits are mostly collateral or unintended. For example, strings of conscious episodes automatically achieve the points of view we think of as ourselves and one another.

A little later, when we begin to experience points of view experiencing themselves, sensations of temporal depth become possible; vantage points emerged that greatly improved our capacity to make predictions and mount sophisticated, long-range projects.

These advantages also seduced human beings into ironic traps. We have been sorting ourselves into leaders and followers and having at one another for thousands of years.

Vernon Molloy

More recently, we appear to be 'progressing and developing' in ways eliminating the need for internally-funded conscious episodes.

We have, in a literal sense, been contriving ways to not only feed and water ourselves with machineries and trade-pacts, we have taken to outsourcing the need to be self-aware! How could this be possible? The answer includes hubris, myopia and arrogance. We think of ourselves as self-sufficient Gods immune to existential degradation.

This folly is worrisome for secular reasons as well. To the extent that human beings' conscious episodes are externally sourced, individuals' time, energy *and capacity for consciousness* becomes available to nations, corporations and religious institutions.

We have been seeing the results for centuries. Ideology and fanaticism are not new problems but there have never been so many organizations vacuuming individuals into corporate and institutional machinations. This is why what is going on can be increasingly understood in terms of what corporations and nations are getting up to: war games, economic trysts, recessions, trade pacts....

Another way of saying the same thing is to suggest that the proportion of unconscious proceedings governing the activities and conversations of friends, families and intimates is increasing. These increases pave the way for, and hence foreshadow, new levels of ideology, patriotism and bigotry.

Our fragmented, disjointed, co-opted... lives are coalescing into large and small undertakings without anyone being aware of the frightful nature of what is being convened. In the 20th century military conflicts claimed 160 million lives. In the summer of 2012, Syria collapsed into domestic violence. More than 20,000 Syrians killed one another in less than two years. These protagonists, unable to cease and desist 'of their own volition', could only beseech the United Nations to force them to stop killing one another.

The inability of citizens and customers to restrain themselves even when their lives and the lives of their families and communities are on the table is not just a temporary characteristic of this or that confrontation. We drift from one predicament to the next in part because we are indifferent to or unaware of what is going. We are indifferent and unaware in part because we blithely believe we can choose a different path whenever we decide to do so. Dismissive of straws in the wind because of this conceit, we bide our time, even though our houses are on fire and our ships are sinking.

Finally, these predicaments rationalize the conceits that allowed them to boil up in the first place. We explain why we do not exercise free will and repair problems: some problems are too large for even Godlike individuals to fix.

More importantly, Godlike individuals rarely work together. That would not be Godlike!

Vernon Molloy

Emergent Forms of Life

The falling off of internally-sourced conscious episodes that characterizes urban life signals a corresponding diminution of anything resembling volition or agenthood. This reduction of the number of human beings whose behaviour cannot be predicted – i.e., who fail the *persons* litmus test – correlates with the growth of institutional, corporate and government control over the homely details of what we get up to.

This is not all we might wish to think about. Nations, corporations and institutions have agendas that go well beyond the wishes of voters, workers or consumers. These organizations are often spoken of as if they were creatures with volitions and agendas. To be sure, we express such notions metaphorically, perhaps as a hedge against accusations of childish anthropomorphism. Even so, corporations have always had the legal status of persons, and this status is being fleshed out. As well corporations, institutions and nations are immortal. They can grow to any size and develop organs of assimilation and defence.[20]

The issue of corporate intentionality is complicated because the activities of nations and corporations flow from the activities of the citizens, employees, customers... who constitute or compose their being. What is overlooked in our estimation that corporations are composed of such activities and nothing more is that organized proceedings have *emergent* properties. They enjoy outcomes greater than or different from the outcomes one would expect adding up the intentions of constituent parts. These outcomes then participate in knock-on events. Since these events could not, or need not, have been part of the intentions of employees, customers or citizens, it seems fair to say that they *belong* to the *organization.*

---

[20]http://www.npr.org/2014/07/28/335288388/when-did-companies-become-people-excavating-the-legal-evolution

130

Vernon Molloy

An excellent example of an emergent property notices that hydrogen (a flammable gas) combines with oxygen (necessary for combustion) and forms H_2O water – a compound whose properties are not readily predicted by examining its components, yet one that is exceptionally good at putting out fires!

This homely example demonstrates an important characteristic of emergent phenomena. They cannot be predicted by examining the central tendencies, wishes, votes... of the atoms, cells, networks of cells, citizens... constituting creatures, corporations, or nations.

This means that your and my economic and political participation in corporations and nations is prior to and constitutive of political and economic outcomes. Therefore we are in no position to 'control' outcomes by assessing and then choosing courses of actions. We are instead like the proverbial donkey trying to reach a bit of hay dangling from a pole attached to its back.

More importantly, even if we achieve a 'dangling hay' workaround, we could not 'manage' the events this altered state of affairs would spawn. We have no way of knowing what they will consist of until they have been experienced.

This is a simple way of understanding our predicament and a transcendental way of refuting free will and agency claims.

To some extent we already understand ourselves in emergent terms. We recognize that our existence depends upon synergies among millions or billions of body parts, cells, gut bacteria... and we know that what we get up to could not be anticipated by summing the agendas of our cellular components.

The question is not whether corporations and nations are under human control but whether they are more usefully understood as forms of life rising out of the same sort of emergent possibilities our own conscious episodes depend upon.

If so, and to the extent that these conscious episodes depend upon 'outside events', urbanization, specialization and globalization suggests another problem. Corporations and nations may be taking advantage of these dependencies to gain further sway – and become even more autonomous in the process.

Already billions of conscious episodes occur every day in movie theatres, hockey arenas and on television screens. Our lives are increasingly 'cloud based'. Our capacity to have conscious episodes – which sets the stage for amazing achievements, understandings and great harms - is being co-opted by corporations and nations. Our ability to function autonomously is being bartered away for the conveniences and pleasures of having our lives *organized* - of having needs and wants met without the need for *conscious episodes*.

This outsourcing and automating of circumstances invoking conscious episodes and evoking a sense of being alive seems surprising at first glance. I have come to understand that being conscious is like being in a house with a smoke detector sounding. Our desire is to find out what is wrong so we can resume whatever somnolent state we were in before the alarm sounded. We also do whatever it takes so that the alarm will not sound again. Modern technologies amplifies this inclination thousand times.

Certainly episodic consciousness is not the halcyon life we enjoyed while in our respective wombs. This is not how we understand Heaven either. Heaven is thought of as an eternal, blissful, serene contemplation of the Divine - an unending delightful slumber with never a pulse of alarm or requirement to pay attention.

On the other hand, if our supernatural destiny involves that other place, we have been warned to expect an eternity of conscious episodes as we sizzle endlessly on (or in) God's Divine Spit.

In other words, conscious episodes appear to be something human beings avoid as often as possible and as soon as possible. Circumstances requiring conscious episodes signal

132

that something out of the ordinary is occurring. Now that pretty much everything has been organized, secured, battened down... 'something out of the ordinary' is almost always bad news.

Whether corporations are regarded as emergent life forms or not, the falling off of internally-sourced conscious episodes means that when urbanized, specialized individuals conspire ('breathe together') beneficial or destructive events can occur without anyone noticing. Hitler's megalomania did not infect his countrymen because they consciously considered his arguments and consciously voted for him. What occurred was that the German population's consciousness-capable minds became a medium of communication automatically and unconsciously orchestrating their similarly constituted internal archipelagos.

With Hitler as focal point and vector of infection, conscious episodes networked Germans harbouring bigotry, anti-Semitism and master race conceits into a living, breathing organization. The Second World War erupted with Germany and then Japan as fulminating epicentres.

The problem has not gone away.

> Anti-Semitism in Europe increased significantly in recent years. At the same time it should be noted that many European countries have comprehensive reporting systems that record incidents more completely than is possible in other countries. Because of this significant difference in reporting systems, it is not possible to make direct comparisons between countries or geographic regions. Beginning in 2000, verbal attacks directed against Jews increased while incidents of vandalism (e.g. graffiti, fire bombings of Jewish schools, desecration of synagogues and cemeteries) surged. Physical assaults including beatings, stabbings and other violence against Jews in Europe increased markedly, in a number of cases resulting in serious injury and even death. Also troubling is a bias that spills over into anti-Semitism in some of the left-of-centre press and among some

intellectuals.[21]

How can this behaviour be recurring after causing so much torment and receiving so much condemnation? I suggest that when consciousness is displaced from its natural role of gluing local events and human beings into persons it can become a medium of communication among unconscious archipelagos - which doubtlessly contain cesspools of primal characteristics. This creates the possibility of your and my unconscious nature 'communicating' and forming unconscious alliances. When these alliances become corporations, nations and armies, they develop momentum and intentionality distinct from the character of constituent workers or citizens.

We have seen the devastation such organisms or quasi-organisms are capable of but have not taken the examples to heart. I suggest that this is because we believe corporations and nations rise out of the conscious choices of citizens and workers. We believe they come into existence innocently and are thereafter guided by 'invisible hands' in marketplaces and governments.

We admire democratic forms of government because we believe that conscious agents voting is the only legitimate source of political power, the only path to public well-being.

What if none of this is true? Few of my conversational gambits seem to provoke conscious responses among people I regularly come across - although I am sometimes seem interesting to new acquaintances. Since there is nothing special about me I infer that most conversations most of the time reflect a few events that manage to that evade the spam filters we have all been building up.

In other words, filters and deflectors are determining whether conscious episodes occur and what their content will be.

Most of the time this makes excellent sense. By automating responses, habituation, conditioned reflexes and spam filters

---

[21]http://www.state.gov/j/drl/rls/40258.htm

free up conscious episodes to deal with novel circumstances.

Since I propose that consciousness is an elaboration of stimulus-response and conditioned response networks, it follows that spam filters determine what conscious episodes contain, and indeed whether they occur at all. Unfortunately (for Cassandras and wretches like me) these machineries also deflect tedious or alarming information. Psychologists speak of *permissible cognitive dissonance* — an expression covertly retaining the claim that consciousness actively engages information getting past prejudices, stereotypes, and cultural predispositions.

With the help of family, friends and intimates — I could not believe you would all dismiss me if I was actually crossing your minds — the non-conscious origin of *what we become aware of* eventually became clear.

I call the mechanisms involved *spam filters.*

Vernon Molloy

Spam Filters

There is much to think about. How do spam filters come into existence? Can they be modified? If so, how? How do spam filters relate to moral and ethical problems? These are important issues because internal archipelagos consisting of experiences, memories, cultural resources and spam filters, orchestrate the conscious episodes we think of as our lives. They generate the thoughts, intentions and conversations we think of as ourselves and one another.

What is also interesting is that spam filters are implicated in what we *do not think of* and *do not get up to.* We would not be able to drive cars, play instruments, read books or carry on conversations without such attention-freeing resources and functions. Nervous systems are designed so that repetitive stimuli are soon ignored. This has a dark side however. Prejudices, racisms, bigotries... have been described as coping mechanisms simplifying the blizzard of information human beings must deal with. All else being equal, new events are more likely to trigger conscious episodes than familiar; but interest and attention only lasts long enough to 'judge' whether the event represents a threat or an opportunity and to then mediate responses.

This suggests that, in circumstances where the environment changes little from day to day while information grows exponentially in the background, spam filters, bigotries, prejudices, automatically declined conversational gambits... increasingly determine the quantity and content of subjective experiences. An explosion of information is occurring. The internet makes this information effortlessly available by providing a bottomless resource of spreadsheets, databases, search engines, on-line calculators.... A consequence many already worry about involves what happens when the need to remember facts or perform calculations *in one's head* disappears. What if retaining information and performing calculations is an important source of conscious episodes? If so, information technologies and the internet may be outsourcing the need for conscious episodes and what's the fun of that?

These gadgets and electronic miracles are also tools for politicians, ideologues and corporations engaged in surveillance, data mining and co-opting individuals into supra-human activities. They have become a resource for pushing public buttons and an important source of distraction and entertainment. These distractions and dependencies mean the public is more likely to put up with encroachments they would otherwise find intolerable. There has been excited talk about the way social media help organize demonstrations, rallies and protests. There has been hopeful talk that the INTERNET is loosening the hold corporations and governments have on the truth. This is well and good. On the other hand, there is so much chattering, tweeting and texting going on that we barely look up while walking down stairs or crossing highways. When one lives in a sea of information it is almost as if there was no information at all. Certainly there is no easy way to test whether information or news we have Googled is true. This function used to be carried out, albeit imperfectly, by reputable, identifiable sources that could be critiqued, criticized and possibly sued.

Perhaps more importantly, social media provide unprecedented opportunities to confuse saying something with doing something. Political and economic problems can spin out of control even as millions of individuals generate 'bit storms' of remonstration and adjuration.

One reason for these harms is the common-sense view that consciousness is a special faculty that does something in and of itself. Activities purporting to elevate or raise consciousness seem intrinsically valuable. Individuals, artists and musicians involved in 'consciousness raising' activities are praised or blamed because we all think they are *actually doing something*. There is a small element of truth in this. Conversations can have valuable results. Indeed conversations must initiate and orchestrate projects that could arise in no other way. However such conversations can also replace projects if consciousness-raising is seen as an undertaking in and of itself.

Vernon Molloy

The internet makes this confusion so satisfying and so plausible that nattering on has become an epidemic. The twitter-verse is alive with sounds and furies signifying nothing.

The objects, subjects, targets... of much of this excitement: the leaders of corporations and nations, the beneficiaries of regressive practices, are able to sleep soundly because social media is relieving public anxiety or outrage. They know that tweets are useless from the point of view of victims and harmless from the point of view of villains whose undertakings might otherwise face more potent sanctions and interdictions.

Certainly, as the quantity and complexity of information increase, we seem to be retreating from the dream of becoming *Renaissance People.* We focus upon small arenas of knowledge or competence. We see ourselves necessarily and legitimately wrought into institutions and corporations as *functions.* We are okay with this because we believe that our underlying conscious faculty continues undeterred and unabated no matter what our circumstances consist of and what activities they command us to do.

After all: are we not moral and rational agents enjoying free will as a birthright? Are we not junior Gods prancing around the world the one True Big God gave us to use, come Hell or high water?

So persuaded, with further life style enhancements already on route from China, we are not worried that our ability to have conscious episodes is becoming the resource of corporations and nations. The most intimate aspects of our lives now weld us by the dozens, hundreds, thousands... into institution, corporations, nations and ad hoc teams pursuing projects with non-human purposes and inhuman consequences. Do these arrangements, these institutions, corporations and nations... have intentions and agendas of their own? We often speak as if this is so.

I think we should stop pretending that such talk is

138

metaphorical. The nations and corporations ploughing up and down the world are not under human control.

The hegemonic relationships involved run the other way.

In the end it may not matter whether national and corporate projects reflect the aggregated intentions of managers, shareholders, employees and customers or whether corporations are virtual entities distilling out of synergistic relationships among citizens, employees and customers. It may not matter because, if corporations and nations have autonomous existence and agendas, these agendas are informed by the ambitions of individuals in crows nests or at ships' helms.

These ambitions are informed by the hubris and arrogance that comes from inhabiting such perches.

In other words, the intentions of corporations and nations and the intentions of wealthy populations may be abetting one another in chicken/egg fashion. Our acceptance of this state of our affairs reflects the view that persons are moral and rational agents surveying realms legitimately carved out of an actual world.

In the end - this is what I think - it makes sense to regard corporations, nations and important individuals as mutually-enabling elements in stratagems that have people like you and I in their cross-hairs as resources and targets

What is not in doubt is how these synergies and stratagems have been playing out in our lives.

We would have been more difficult to control and harvest had we understood conscious episodes as fragile achievements that make remarkable lives possible and allow you and I to glimpse ourselves and one another.

The Progress Myth

A factor compounding these difficulties has nothing to do with whether what is going on can be parsed into agents, persons and corporations and resolved into causal relationships.

This factor involves the rate at which the world is 'progressing and developing'. More than forty years ago, *Future Shock* author Alvin Toffler observed that the rate of technological change was causing 'stress and disorientation'. Information overload was leading people to distance themselves from one another and avoid news about what was going on.

Ironically the technologies responsible for this need were the technologies employed to accomplish it.

This is even more evident today. Everywhere one looks people are finding increasingly sophisticated ways to ignore who and where they are and who they are with.

They often do this by phoning or texting someone whose principal attraction may be that they are somewhere else.

This could be nothing more than an annoying or humorous characteristic of today's young people. However an important harm may also be occurring. When significant technological or cultural changes occur within an individual's lifetime, the perceived relevance of parent, grandparents, communities, cultural resources... is diminished.

Stories about strategies, joys and horrors - even evocative tales of growing up experiences - are likely to be dismissed as archaic and irrelevant by sophisticated 'persons in a hurry'.

This insouciance encourages still more 'progress and development'. We see little reason to not proceed as rapidly as possible, to not "drill baby, drill!"..., because we are increasingly oblivious to what is being traded away.

This could explain why comfort, convenience and

technological prowess trumps other considerations. Global sports events, Google Glasses, three-dimensional movies, high resolution media... already allow billions to lead vicarious lives watching sports teams, mixed martial artists and beautiful people.

Closer to home, technologies already allow fans, spectators and gamers to communicate with computers, Game Boys, X boxes and media players... using gestures and eye movements. Brain wave control and communications systems – telepathy and telekinesis – are on the drawing boards or already here.

The result is an increasing proportion of human beings living in literal wombs in urban barns. We do not notice because our conscious episodes are externally inculcated. We are becoming the "brains in a vat" philosophy students use to think about epistemological problems and ontological issues.

Now that we have come this far, nothing prevents these dependencies from enlarging further until all of our conscious episodes are organized, institutionalized and monetized by the alien forms of life: the nat ions and corporations constituted out of and battening upon our lives.

Without gadgets turned on and our selves plugged in, our sense of being alive is already fragile. You can test this. The next time you get a chance, interrupt someone's ear bud reverie and ask for their time of day. Watch their eyes as they disengage from whatever they were enjoying. Watch how they hurry you along so they can get back to wherever they were doing.

An alarming proportion of urban populations' conscious episodes has already been outsourced. In every way corporations and governments have been able to contrive, human beings' need to be delivered from the womb to the world so they could become fully-fledged persons has been transmogrified into commercial opportunities and government mandates.

Vernon Molloy

Although we continue to be born in old fashioned ways, not much else of natural and community life remains intact.

This is sometimes a good thing but one consequence of today's technological accomplishments should give us pause. Our capacity to generate conscious episodes without corporate input and media-driven stimuli, our capacity to generate a sense of self, our capacity to be our own person, is being obliterated.

Democracy and Fascism

Citizens in democracies choose new leaders all the time. This is, after all, the purpose of enfranchisement and elections. Yet nothing much seems to change. There is a deepening sense of inevitability. Fringe politicians circle citadels but rarely garner enough support to gain a seat. In Canada, comfortably ensconced Liberals and Conservatives bicker endlessly over municipal problems while NDP and Green Party politicians struggle to inject equity and sustainability issues into conversations.

What is not often recognized is that urbanized populations are congenitally unable to consider real changes to 'present circumstances'. [22] Lacking extended families, communities and subsistence options they have little choice except to vote for anyone promising to enhance security and employment/consuming opportunities. I think this is why 1st world populations have been embracing conservatism and, in some cases, fascism. When things are going poorly the urge to find people to blame rises up. Anti-Semitism is in the news in England, Europe and even in Germany and Israel's prospects seem increasingly fraught. *Homeland Security* measures are now part of daily life for Americans and anyone visiting the USA. In North America and Europe immigration policies systematically discriminate against the sorts of people who originally 'settled the Americas'. We want the best, the brightest, the wealthiest.... We like the looks of such people (when they are not wearing hi jabs). Perhaps we understand (without consciously articulating the realization) that syphoning 'the best people' away from 3rd world nations perpetuates the economic difficulties allowing 1st world nation to harvest value from poorly-paid workers.

Economic globalization places every worker in competition, forces wages and working conditions everywhere to a global common denominator and transfers responsibility for domestic problems to *global Realpolitik.*

The resulting economic and political paralysis is the worm at

---

[22]Even so, on May 5, 2015, Canada's province of Alberta elected a majority NDP government, ending 44 years of progressive conservative control.

the heart of arguments for democracy. What does it gain populations to achieve the right to vote when their only realistic choice is the status quo?

In other words, urban populations are suffering from *de facto* fascism. Dictators have been replaced with dictatorial circumstances and feelings of *force majeure.*

In such circumstances, the benefits of democracy become regressive. Elections absolve leaders of responsibility for decisions taken. Democracies transform citizens into indefatigable workers and consumers because they encourage dreams of ownership, participation and possibility.

Democratic capitalism means wealth and power with no strings attached – a reality borne out by equity statistics. Democratic capitalism means a better-funded 'industrial-military complex' than authoritarian governments have been able to achieve. The impotence of command economies is arguably why the USSR collapsed and the cold war ended. This may be the reason Vladimir Putin is attempting to reconstitute the USSR in 2014: first Crimea, then the Ukraine, then... who knows? Now that a shiny new wealth-generating engine has been added to their economy a reinvigorated Russia could soon be strutting the world along with the USA and China.

Of course, democratic forms of governance are better than their alternatives. This should not cause anyone to overlook that democracy's advantages go mostly to the well-to-do. For most human beings democracy's benefits remain hypothetical. There is no doubt that democratic procedures could yield wholesome outcomes and policies. The fact that politicians and corporations are now promoting democracy means that they are no longer worried about this happening.

There is another reason democracies have become the flavour of the day. Democratic populations are creative and productive. They have also demonstrated that they are not good at hanging onto the wealth.

 The results can be sketched:

REPRESENTATIVE DEMOCRACY vs FASCISM
IN URBAN CIRCUMSTANCES

Scenario One

REPRESENTATIVE DEMOCRACY

Urban citizens/voters ⟻ (sorted into: Liberal, Conservative, NDP, Green... factions) ⟻ Election Events ⟻ Industrial/Commercial Rendering Factories ⟻ A Pauper's Grave for most ⟻ Many wealthy/powerful people

Scenario Two

FASCISM

Urban Citizens ⟻ Faux Election Events ⟻ Industrial/Commercial Rendering Factories ⟻ A Pauper's Grave for most ⟻ A few wealthy/powerful people

Specialization

The technologies driving this state of affairs require increasing levels of worker specialization. Consumers must also become sophisticated about what smart phones, laptops, GPS devices, induction ovens... are capable of. This does not mean that individuals are becoming sophisticated in wholesome ways. When value-adding skills are 'reverse engineered' they can be automated or outsourced to factories and call centres with software packages and videos guiding naïve workers every step of the way.

The downside is that tiny skills command tiny wages. This has led to a paradox: the capacity of individuals to earn enough money to purchase goods and services is diminishing even as the variety of goods and services increases.

Shallow sophistication come with its own risks. Familiarity with smart phones means becoming addicted to powerful applications able to recognize, remember, interpret, organize and motivate our lives.

An alarming proportion of young men in Japan are reported to have taken on a "mole like existence" characterized by a lack of interest in relationships with women:

> A survey by the Ministry of Health, Labour and Welfare in 2010 found 36% of Japanese males aged 16 to 19 had no interest in sex - a figure that had doubled in the space of two years.

Some of these young men are choosing virtual women, establishing avatars and arranging for the resulting virtual couples to spend time together. The girlfriends reside in a Nintendo computer game called Love Plus (http://www.bbc.co.uk/news/magazine-24614830). The boyfriends provide the pockets and batteries needed to keep lovers in close proximity and charged up.

Specialists

By definition specialists perform focused activities that must be coordinated with other activities to yield goods or services. There is great potential in this arrangement. Specialists often become highly competent and a world boasting such competencies can be harnessed to almost any task.

However, although lots of tasks become imaginable and potentially doable, projects will only occur if there is a reasonable chance of profit for individuals or corporations organizing specialists into productive activities.

This state of affairs is problematic in and of itself. Specialists tend to not do much by way of organizing or linking up with one another and taking on projects spontaneously. Specialists tend to identify themselves as resources. They see their function and responsibility in terms of making themselves available for whatever projects conveners, organizers, visionaries... have in mind. Welders will weld up whatever is put in front of them. Carpenters will build whatever structure contractors and blueprints dictate.

What is equally interesting is that the availability of specialists and technological resources encourages organizers and entrepreneurs to dream up projects they would not otherwise have thought of.

What is not much thought about is that the projects these coalitions undertake will be projects generating wealth and power for organizers, managers and investors. In other words, in circumstances with a large proportion of specialists, who never get up to anything unless they have been hired, economic activities will be limited to those whose benefits can be regressively distributed.

Indeed, as we are seeing, these projects tend to be regressive in other ways. They collectively nurture technologies and political developments such as global trading arrangements that lead to increasingly simple employments, automation and outsourcing.

147

Specialists provide a further benefit to hegemonic relationships. They can be counted on to not ask awkward questions. Indeed specialists tend to have little interest in, or even awareness of, overarching issues. Even when concerns arise there is little or no sense of responsibility or competence to evaluate whether projects should be pursued.

This means almost any initiative can occur if a profit-promising business plan can be constructed. In urbanized, specialized circumstances no one outside of interest groups (Save the Whales, ...Old Growth Forests, ...the Children, ...the Planet) will question whether projects are relevant, wholesome or even survivable.

Should worries pop up even so, specialists have a fall-back argument — not an argument exactly, but an article of faith. Seized with the idea that we are Little Gods (wellsprings of moral and rational decisions that require no further explanation) we believe that mankind is collectively pondering, for example, sustainability issues. Accordingly, we believe that the sum total of human consciousness could repair the world problems if enough of us chose to do so! This is a wonderfully seductive fantasy. So persuaded we each get to rationalize the emergence of increasingly toxic circumstances in ways that avoid notions of personal responsibility. We get to do nothing and claim that we are respecting one another's right to choose.

On this model, we could find ourselves marching like Lemmings towards a cliff edge with no one demurring. Everyone remains silent, each hoping that other people elect to not do stupid stuff and we survive another day.

What a remarkable predicament! We live according to a story that encourages us to not even attempt to avert disasters staring us in the face. We reassure ourselves by noting that human beings must be collectively making perverse moral or rational choices and that this is what the results look like.

As we lay back to resume our slumbers we sagely conclude

that God (or Darwinian selection) will doubtlessly sort out all this good and evil stuff and see that justice is done.

There are two engines powering these proceedings. The first is the belief that consciousness has the traction and efficacy common sense and cultural activities have been claiming. The second is that individuals must be conscious before they can be held accountable. The problem with this story – as the thought experiment about the Hitler lie detector test illustrated – is that what we happen to be aware of from time to time may have little to do with the values and prejudices stewing within us, generating behaviour and occasional conscious episodes.

To the extent that this is true the question of whether consciousness has Godlike efficaciousness, whether it is a *cause* or *consequence* of cognitive events, becomes moot. If consciousness is a consequence conscious episodes are still factors in further episodes.

This is not what we think and not what we have been claiming however. If the claim that consciously-mediated proceedings — conversations, essays, rhetorical flourishes — set the stage for consciousness to *make decisions* is false, many common sense notions will have to be rethought. This could be wonderfully clarifying. Such an investigation could, for example, illuminate why Al Gore's *An Inconvenient Truth* remains an irrelevant truth.

Moreover, once this confusion is cleared away, we would see ourselves and one another in new ways. What we get up to, what we value, what we are prepared to discuss... rises out of non-conscious events. These outcomes may involve conscious episodes but only is the sense that consciousness *facilitates* or *enables realizing* and is sometimes involved in *actualizing* unconscious proceedings[23] .

---

[23]To *realize* something is to fish information out of the stream of being and give it form, substance and possibly a name. *Actualizing* involves making a response informed by these 'internal' cognitive events so that the stream of being proceeds in ways informed by what has been going on within creatures like you and I. This altered event thereafter

Vernon Molloy

In other words, rather than a faculty making choices and then choosing whether to put the results into play, consciousness and conscious episodes would be understood as blackboards upon which histories write futures.

---

is available for further *realizations* by the same person or by other persons.

150

Marginal Conclusions

Time to tie some of these notions together:

- Even though I have come to know better, my failures to engage family, friends and acquaintances in conversations and projects continue to feel like conscious repudiation.

- On the bright side, thinking about these failures in ways that do not involve scapegoating my family and friends has spawned understandings that would not have otherwise occurred.

- Since I knew I could not be the reason – given the provocative brilliance of my overtures – I had to look for other explanations!

- This led to a startling hypothesis: What if conversational gambits are often trashed, deflected, spam filtered... before they reach anyone's consciousness?

- This would explain a great deal of what has been going on in both public and private lives.

I have also come to understand that it is not only the passage of time that ages human beings. When we live in homogeneous surroundings, when we perform repetitive tasks day after day, something dreadful occurs. Human beings evolved to live in challenging, fluid circumstances. In such circumstances, reflexes, conditioned responses and automatically-generated spam filters are just what the doctor ordered. There is no reason to be interested in circumstances that have been successfully negotiated. Until recently, human beings needed to keep their big brains freed up so they could address new problems and survive long enough to reproduce.

But what if new circumstances and problems are not presenting themselves in obvious ways? What if we live in

Vernon Molloy

cities and perform repetitive duties year after year? What if we become specialists with a built-in rationale for avoiding responsibilities beyond being an excellent specialist?

The problem is clear: human beings are constituted so that familiar events can be safely ignored. As urbanization and development proceed the incidence of novel experiences and associated need for conscious episodes decline. The danger is clear. The number and seriousness of background threats, the incidence of slow-moving exploitations and extortions, can increase and increase and hardly anyone will notice.

No matter how old we are when this dreadful somnolence overtakes us — it appears to be occurring sooner and sooner — its victims have *ceased* living to all intents and purposes. They can hardly be distinguished from actually dead people using the only measuring tool that matters. (1) What such people say and do can be predicted more or less perfectly; (2) they appear untroubled by pesky conscious moments; (3) if you interrupt their reverie they will be startled or annoyed and do whatever it takes to get past you so they can resume not doing whatever they were not doing.

Note to self: I see that coming to understand conscious episodes as *results* and not as *causes* has not prevented my 'social failures' from keeping me awake at night. Perhaps this demonstrates how little influence conscious episodes have over subsequent conscious episodes even within persons. In other words, if my internal communications to my own future selves are being ignored, how could I have expected more from my friends, family and intimates?

With this caution in mind – that you should not expect much to come of them – here are a few more understandings that have occurred to me:

- If I had been similarly dismissive of the people dismissing me, I would not have had the rich life I have enjoyed. On the other hand I would have less to regret: I would have fewer friends, and fewer understandings to fail to share with them.

152

Modern Problems, Ancient Perspectives

- It may be that most people share a "nobody blows the whistle on anybody" understanding too subtle for me to grasp. A simpler possibility is that human beings do not 'consciously choose' what they will discuss. Conversations — conscious episodes in general — reflect the automatically occurring unconscious activities of spam filters accepting or rejecting overtures and possibilities. There are other elements involved of course, including the state of one's digestion.

- Cognitive events that survive this inbound/outbound filtering boil up as thoughts, words, inclinations, actions and conscious experiences. These episodes are how we become aware of ourselves, other people and the world. They are how we know that we are alive

- Conscious episodes have nothing to do with the moral or rational content of activities. Instead of authoring, assessing or choosing thoughts and inclinations... conscious episodes facilitate projects spawned by non-conscious proceedings. Everywhere we look we see individuals born into cultures and moulded into corresponding 'isms': Catholics spawn more Catholics, Americans more Americans, Muslims more Muslims.... Wherever and whenever children occur, they eagerly absorb the world around them until a private world builds up within. Each of these toy worlds is unique because each replicates the experiences composing individual narratives. Sooner or later these internalizations coalesce into vantage points with imaginary selves at their core.

- Like tiny suns these toy worlds eventually achieve a critical mass of information. They then 'heat up' and begin to resist further *informing*. Sooner or later these core selves become bright enough to believe that they have seen all there is to see; not noticing that their vision extends precisely to the boundaries of their understanding.

- When this occurs, human beings become dead to

further intents, purposes and experiences as surely as if they were dead in fact. This is the mechanism responsible for ideology, dogmatism, bigotry, arrogance and indolence.

- The fantasy that consciousness is the pullulating source of moral agency and responsibility encourages us to overlook that consciousness-evoking circumstances are being replaced with homogeneous banalities, multimedia blandishments and sports events.

- As we learn to rely upon search engines and the INTERNET, our capacity to achieve consciousness out of internal resources diminishes. We become promiscuous about what counts as acceptable. A flickering inner life is alarming no matter how well appointed our houses or well-hydrated our complexions. Our immune systems sag. We vote the conservative ticket. We tether ourselves to Blackberries, iPads, sports arenas and television. We scan the horizon for the next new technology or Dear Leader.

In the public domain, the notion of consciousness as agent has been shaping politics and economies for centuries. With this inner-agent/Little God fiction as a resource, corporations and politicians have little difficulty deflecting public attention from the inequalities they have been baking into business plans and legislations. Ever since Adam Smith wrote *The Wealth of Nations,* talk about "invisible hands", "rational consumers" and other sacred cows have deflected attention from the inherently, implacably regressive nature of marketplace proceedings.

More ominously, now that they have gotten over their fright about what 'the vote' might mean, the wealthy are becoming enamoured of democratic forms of governance. They have come to understand that consumers are not rational and self-interested. They have come to understand that urbanized, dependent democratic populations are manageable because they can only really vote for more of the same.

In addition they have come to value democratic forms of governance because

- democratic nations are revolution proof;

- populations enjoying democracy work harder because they believe prosperity will occur as soon as the rising tide gets around to their boats;

- democracies transfer responsibility for economic machinations from beneficiaries to victims.

The notion of consciousness as agent also lets nations and corporations off the hook. Inequities, pollution, resource depletion... are understood as reflecting voters' and consumers' historical *conscious* choices. At the same time, the public recognizes that presidents and chief executive officers are needed if sustained, complicated projects can be undertaken and so rewards and responsibilities can be appropriately apportioned.

This makes sense because we understand our own lives in just such terms. We think that our conscious faculty 'heads up' the organs, cells and neurological resources comprising 'our bodies'.

I hope I have made a case that this cannot be true. Whether they occur in presidents, workers or consumers, conscious episodes do not make choices. The most that can be said is that they facilitate proceedings. The incidental fact that conscious episodes set the stage for persons to be understood as choice engines allowing them to be blamed or praised is an unexpected bonus. With this story in hand, and with properly democratic nations in place, the victims of economic and political shenanigans inherit the blame for what is going on while praise and wealth flow to perpetrators.

This analysis of consciousness suggests that anyone hoping to repair materialism, childhood obesity, war-warmongering, climate change... will have to find ways to influence what is going on that do not depend upon, or at least do not begin and end with, consciousness-raising projects.

Vernon Molloy

Finally, after detaining you for so long, I fear that I must leave you with very little. My only suggestion comes from experience. I grew up poor and homely to boot on a small Ontario farm. (Fortunately, I was not too homely to boot!) With few alternatives, I read everything I could get my hands on. Even today everything I come across gets stuffed into my cognitive basement where it mixes with whatever is already there.

I have only vague notions of what's already down there. I have no idea of what is going on as all this stuff digests itself. (Freud spoke of a 'dream factory' in this context.) I have no idea of what will come out of my mouth until some event triggers an insight, a sense of possibility, an urge to buttonhole a bystander — a next sentence in a conversation!

The thing I have noticed is that information stuffed in today — even something as simple as a new word — can often be discerned in ideas announcing themselves a moment, day or week later. What an incentive to stuff stuff in! Benefits include an inner life occasionally capable of conscious episodes without prodding by commercials, sports heroes or fanatics.

I think it is intuitively clear that self-authoring, self-subsisting individuals would have would less interest in acquiring or polishing possessions. They know they are alive without consulting mirrors, the state of their wallets, acquiring new gadgets or the opinions of Facebook friends. Self-sufficient and self-directing, they would be less available to be wrought into corporations and nations and better-equipped to scrutinize what they get up to.

In other words, stuffing stuff in - which really means being open to *informing* - may be human beings' only way to influence what we think about and what we get up to.

As well - again I have only a sense that this makes sense - understanding consciousness as *result* and not as *cause* would make us more thoughtful. We would be less inclined to promote notions into ideologies just because they seem perfect and complete. We would be more likely to share ideas and not simply defend whatever collection we got lumbered with before spam filters reduced us to fanatics, ideologues and conservatives.

There is a final benefit to understanding consciousness as consequence and not as cause. The projects, corporations, notions and nations boiling from our basements would no longer be able to represent themselves as embodying decisions made by the conscious faculties of God-like human beings.

Finally (I saved the best for last) understanding conscious episodes as rewards in a life well spent would encourage conversations. Whenever such conversations have occurred in my experience – every once in a while and almost always unexpectedly — they have been wonderful. They put men and women in touch with one another.

We know a great deal about what mutually-subordinating human beings are capable of. We have glimpsed the negotiations transforming women into domestic terrorists and their significant others into hapless tools. History tells us what happens when these 'breeding pairs' are seized and capitalized upon by clever and unscrupulous individuals.

What we do not know is what could be accomplished if the Faustian contracts binding men and women into economic dynamos were renegotiated.

The possibility is exhilarating. As soon as ill-conceived reproductive agendas are identified as the principal reason human beings have been doing so much harm, men and women might start talking to one another.

Vernon Molloy

The Problem

As the woman of my dreams knows, I have been attempting to have conversations with her and other people about domestic issues. The problem is, whenever I suggest that men have little or nothing to say about what gets included in domestic priorities, the conversation is pretty much dead in the water.

If time permits, you remind me that you, in fact women in general, spend far more energy upon domestic tasks than I – even though we equally beneficiaries. I agree entirely. Indeed I will stipulate that I enjoy benefits that are such a natural expression of your generous nature that they never cross your mind.

What concerns me is that we never entertain notions I have about what we should also be doing.

In other words, if you do not initiate a domestic project, it does not occur. More importantly – unless the initiator is female – no project is conscionable.

This is worth thinking about because it seems such an accurate description of male-female relationships.

In the following I suggest how this came to pass and why many problems can be tracked back to it.

Some may already be objecting:if male/female relationships usually involve subordinated men, why are men everywhere said to be in control of economies and governments — and everywhere abusing this power?

A simple answer is possible. Every nation, every ethnic group, every tribe... contains a small proportion of individuals whose lives, accomplishments and behaviours define those nations, groups and tribes. There is a logical problem with this that is worth thinking about. Thus, the stereotypical human male leaves much to be desired. Moreover, stereotypes offer plausible explanations for what human beings get up to, including misogyny. Everything makes sense until we remember an awkward fact. Every stereotype exists in a

158

context and this context forms the backdrop against which the stereotype stands out. Thus, before they can be noticed, tall people require average-sized people to *stand out against*.

Ironically therefore, most human beings are the opposite of the stereotypes defining the populations they collectively constitute.

Therefore, with regard to male/female relationships, I propose two clarifying *axioms of subordination*. The first is that economies, technologies, standing armies... are rooted in female values and reproductive relationships constructed upon them.

How could it be otherwise? Women embody powerful instincts to conceive, comfort and nurture children. These instincts made it possible for human beings to survive thousands of difficult centuries. Moreover, until recently, it was impossible to do too much nurturing. All that women could manage, with their hearts and bodies on the line, was barely enough to keep their big-brained, bobble-headed children alive until puberty sent them on their own desperate missions.

So what happened? Ten thousand years ago — after perhaps one hundred and fifty thousand years of 'occasional involvement' in reproducing activities — men became seriously interested in what was going on domestically. They did not become equal players of course but a new item was added to their bucket lists. Prior to this, men passed their days getting lost in the jungle, playing war games and variously sorting out who would father next generations.

Something happened that caused men to make themselves available for domestic projects.

This availability, this new resource, greatly expanded the ability of women — especially attractive women — to improve their circumstances. I think the change occurred when men realized that sexual activities were more than recreational opportunities – that men were essential for children to be born.

This was a realization of enormous importance. For the first time men glimpsed a way to extricate themselves from the grim prospect of mortality and death — a prospect their daily adventures, competitions and perilous lifestyles kept front and centre in their minds.

Death need not be the end. They too could live on through children.

Women have always had this solace. They also have the advantage of knowing whether they have had a child.

Men have no such comfort or guarantee, and no real way of achieving either.

They could try however. The contracts that ensued stipulated that men could keep turning up at camp-fires as long as they did not turn up empty handed. Indeed, as men gained reproductive toeholds, negotiations defining male-female relationships became increasingly onerous. Over time they transformed matriarchal to patriarchal cultures, invented chastity belts, the cash surrender value of virginity and a thousand forms of misogyny.

For their part, women promised to be faithful and pretended to subordinate themselves in return for help with warmth, comfort and security projects. They did this because, as far as they are concerned, the only thing in life that matters is providing newborns with the most comfortable external womb possible, increasing their chances in a harsh world.

Not a bad plan and not a bad bargain. Almost all of us would not be here otherwise.

Although this never crossed anyone's mind, these contracts contained signing bonuses for both men and women. Women got to transfer responsibility for what would soon be going on to the men actualizing the industrial and commercial projects they were covertly sanctioning. (Part of my dangerous research involved suggesting to women that deflecting responsibility was the reason they were willing to assume husbands' surnames.)

These contracts marked the beginning of agrarian forms of life,the cash surrender value of pulchritude and an insatiable interest in 'progress and development'. Why insatiable? No level of creature comfort, no cave, cabin, house, mansion... is as good as the accommodation children enjoyed in the womb. To make amends for the fact of birth women instinctively do everything they can to make the nearby world as womb-like as possible. When men offered to help out in exchange for promises of fidelity, the modern world stirred into life. As William Yeats predicted in *The Second Coming*...

> *That twenty centuries of stony sleep*
> *Were vexed to nightmare by a rocking cradle,*
> *And what rough beast, its hour come round at last,*
> *Slouches towards Bethlehem to be born?*

There was a bonus for men as well. When they realized that they too would get to enjoy womb-like domesticity, perpetual adolescence became possible. Hunting, fishing and squabbling activities, that had previously been matters of life and death, could now could be indulged or not depending upon the weather and the contents of job jars.

In short, by corralling a divine women, men gain a sense of purpose, a sense of identity and and a glimpse of immortality. Not only that, they get to live in extended wombs constructed according to plans drawn up, or at least vetted, by the women of their dreams.

Men think that they achieve heaven by entering into such arrangements. Women are more realistic, which explains why they fuss endlessly about marriages and births and generally convene as many celebratory opportunities as possible. Women sense how much they will have to sacrifice for their children. They know deep down that moving from public to covert matriarchy has been disastrous for them as individuals and persons.

No matter! It's all about the babies!

Such expectations also explain why women settle for, and sometimes seem to prefer, infantile men. Women have always done the heavy lifting involved in bearing and raising children. Against this backdrop any assistance is better than none; and unquestioning assistance is best of all.

Vernon Molloy

Since men cannot be trusted with domestic or child-rearing responsibilities, and they certainly cannot be trusted to decide what these responsibilities should consist of, there really is nothing to discuss.

However negotiated, these arrangements have us by the throat: "You have your orders sir! If you want to be assured that any child I have is your child, impress me: Kill something or somebody! Dig something up! Make the world a proper place to bring a child into!"

The projects boiling out of this Faustian bargain give every evidence of being unsurvivable. The world is heating up and running out of resources. Populations are sorting into factions armed with fearsome weapons and non-negotiable agendas. None of this seems to matter to most of us most of the time. Men and women continue to focus "like lasers" upon homes, children, pets and an ever smaller circle of friends. If time and energy remain, we count the days until weekends, holidays, birthdays... sometimes death, offers respite.

What Consciousness Does

After gnawing at the question of what consciousness does for years I have come to a simple understanding. Simple is good because discussions typically assume that consciousness actively does stuff and then worry whether an individual was conscious and compos mentis when 'an act' was performed. What if consciousness was present when 'the act' occurred but has no decision-making function? What if the function of consciousness is to be a facilitator, perhaps akin to a blackboard, wherein decisions are resolved by processes melding unconscious and external events?

If so consciousness is serving as a matrix or medium within which complicated, sustained resolutions proceed, acting as a kind of glue linking cognitive events together so they can generate coherent responses and probably so they can be recalled as coherent events and participate in future meldings.

The most important difference is that we would no longer be able to blame or praise individuals because they were conscious when an act was initiated. This would change the notion of agent so that it became a way of referencing entire beings or narratives rather than conscious episodes. Excellent and creative beings or narratives could still be celebrated and encouraged. Indeed, we would have even more reason to celebrate excellent narratives among all the narratives that have been named and compiled into population counts. We would understand conduct as rising coming from entire beings and not from free will choices whose excellence (or malignancy) we have no reason to expect to continue.

On the same analysis, our attitude towards malignancy would no longer be compromised by worrying whether a particular act reflected a free will choices or a bred-in-the-bone disorder. Interdiction could begin at once. We might even investigate antecedents with a view to figuring out how to prevent problems.

163

Vernon Molloy

When consciousness is understood as efficacious agent, no such response is possible. All we can do is lay hold of and lock black box recorders away.

Consciousness occurs because human beings have a robust capacity to generate representations of experiences. These representations almost always spawn some version of *realism:* the claim that an external world exists, full of rabbits and rocks and the elements rabbits and rocks are composed of.

You and I acknowledge that we are similarly constituted. Even so we think of ourselves as inhabiting, possessing and blithely running around within the world spawning us.

The alternative is that no such world exist; although events giving rise to these conceits are certainly occurring.

This modest explanation solves the many difficulties of common sense/realism accounts by *dissolving* them.

You ask: why does the phenomenal world seem so real, tangible and external? Why does any other proposition seem so absurd? The answer begins by noting that you and I have experiences. Since experiences often include other human beings we eventually figured out how to talk about what seems to be going on. These conversations compared and fact-checked our image-laden inner lives and spawned second and third-order abstractions.

As these conversations convened and co-ordinated increasingly sophisticated projects, the results led to increasingly detailed inner lives in participants.

Each such rendering consists of unique collections of imaginary entities, objects and events. Each rendering supports an infinite number of resolutions; and each sets the stage for further conversations and subjectivities, narratives and point sources of creativity.

There are many reasons why this capacity evolved. The original involves testing possible responses in 'thought experiments' before putting 'skin in the game'.

Modern Problems, Ancient Perspectives

Another feature of these proceedings is that thought experiments occur spontaneously. There is no person within orchestrating what is going on; and there is no need to postulate a material world underwriting the inclinations, images, projects... populating imaginations. When you and I think about persons, entities and objects, when we talk about moral and rational agency, only imaginary entities and proceedings are in our minds. These entities rise up spontaneously the way gestalts are automatically perceived within ambiguous stimuli. We have all enjoyed images where foregrounds and backgrounds switch spontaneously and we see different images including, in this case, one vase or two faces.

Almost all of the images populating conscious experiences are not ambiguous in this way and are never observed 'switching around'. This is useful and reassuring but not ontologically significant. The contents of common-sense and realism reflect stuff going on in brains, not corresponding objects and entities *out there*! (There are, of course, corresponding events. We distil their tendencies or vectors into image-predictions and sometimes name the results.) Thus, to *realize* something is to experience it coalescing until something 'still enough' to be an image occurs. This image generates *and then occupies* a conscious episode. The resulting insights are talked about, used to plan projects and underwrite claims of an actual world.

Aiding and abetting realism and common sense interpretations of what is going on is the claim that consciousness is the cognitive engine responsible for choosing, volitions and intentionality. Of course we have this the wrong way around. Awareness and self-awareness emerge as brains mature and experiences accumulate. Self-awareness provides a locus around which a growing body of information attaches and organizes itself. Self-awareness makes it possible to test candidate responses in thought experiments.

As well, self awareness sets the stage for projects requiring an hour or a month's attention.

Vernon Molloy

In other species this capacity exists minimally or not at all. Orientation is accomplished spontaneously among, for example, flocks of geese and bee colonies. These creatures are doubtlessly aware of what is going on but they are not aware of being aware! There is no need for self-awareness and temporal depth because every creature other than human creatures exist in exquisite harmony with local events. When you and I observe what they are getting up to, we are seeing tiny portions of the Big Event hurrying by.

Primitive versions of this sort of information can be gained by throwing handfuls of sand into the wind to gain a sense of how it is blowing.

Biologist Richard Dawkins talks about extended phenotypes. He proposes that we should think of beaver dams as beaver's extended phenotypes. Beaver dams are, after all, reliable signals that beavering is occurring well beyond beaver bodies. Dawkins suggests that beaver dams are guided into existence by beaver genotypes, in a watered down version of the way genotypes guide phenotypes into existence.

In a non-realist world view - without conveniently partitioned objects and entities - Dawkins' idea easily extends to support the idea that cities, Box Stores, smart phones... could be thought of as extended human phenotypes.

It follows that, since dams, houses, cities... are community projects, the recurring relationships making them possible could also be thought of as extended phenotypes. Realism and common sense considers persons, entities and objects from the top down or after the fact as *fait accompli*.

They are more readily understood from the bottom up or as *emergent processes*.

There is no need to imagine beaver dams enjoying awareness. Consciousness occurs in creatures like you and I because we are not particularly good at immediately useful activities. What we have by way of compensation are enhanced response capabilities leveraging conscious episodes.

The point is, consciousness has important functions, but

166

these functions do not include the claim we have been basing our special status talk upon. Our cognitive lives are energized by the same chemical and electrical events every creature depends upon.

The thing that differentiates human beings involves our large brains and the activities this capaciousness makes possible. These activities include remarkably detailed memories or representations of experiences. What is not often noted is that these memories are vivacious in ways proportional to the alacrity of experiences that caused them to be *informed.*

A memory of a thrown ball is not a collection of static representations describing a ball-in-flight but a representation of an active event. This vitality combines with similarly active representations in other memories. Thus notions of balls-in-flight automatically combine with notions of brittle windows to yield 'shards-of-glass' resolutions.

The point - which cannot be overemphasized - is that consciousness does not actively combine notions of balls and glass windows and come up with shattered window predictions. These representations, these memories, meld together 'of their own volition'. They sometimes generate feelings of alarm or excitement that something calamitous is about to occur. Sometimes this sense of alarm is enough to prevent a ball from being thrown. Talk about the inherently active nature of consciousness, which common sense leverages into moral and rational agency talk, is unnecessary. Conceptual events are best understood as manifesting the lively nature of dispositions laid down by experiences. These representations capture an active world. It is this represented liveliness that fuels cognitive events, rather than some putative agent or *a priori* being acting freely and generating volitions or acts of will out of nothing.

This story has the advantage of being parsimonious and modest. There is no need to think of consciousness as evaluating, retrieving orchestrating... the representations that go into conscious moments. Representations or memories 'attend to' their own invoking, evoking and combining automatically. In most cases this occurs outside of consciousness, which capacity is thereby left available to mediate unusual situations.

The point is that consciousness, self-consciousness, subjectivity... exist along a continuum of adaptations including reflexes, conditioned responses and habituation. Birds fly up when possibilities or dangers hove into view. Human beings take conscious flight in the same ways for the same reasons.

A central function of consciousness involves linking the 'idea-of-oneself' with complex cognitive events. These experiences flesh out the sense we have of our selves, other entities and objects. Such experiences deepen and amplify awareness and the sense of being at the centre of streaming events. In this way we become aware of being aware - of being alive and knowing it. This is a seminal achievement. Almost everything we regard as singularly human would be impossible without it. The problem arises when consciousness and self-consciousness is identified with the self that is always at the centre of experience. Jacques Lacan referred to this sense of self as the hole at the centre of awareness. The trap is that sense of self is always present whenever we are aware of problems being sorted out.

The 'incidental fact' that it is always present because it is being generated by these sorting out activities is not part of this awareness! This ubiquitousness has tricked us into believing that consciousness is somehow orchestrating cognitive events, that it is somehow *doing* work. Au contraire! Consciousness is necessary for self-consciousness. Self-consciousness makes orientation, focus and long-term projects possible. Self consciousness anchors cognitive events and external activities whose semantic content and scope transcend immediate moments.

This allows human beings to make deep and subtle use of experiences. This allows human beings to undertake projects reaching around the world and into the future.

Traditional models of memories and cognition have struggled to explain how individuals are able to 'access' memories.

168

Modern Problems, Ancient Perspectives

Before I can retrieve a 'correct memory', I must know what I am looking for. A second set of memories, or at least a set of programmable filters, must therefore exist in the 'agent' part of the brain. Before a search could begin there would have to be some way of knowing when and if it had succeeded.

If other words, no action could begin because every consciously-mediated, consciously initiated, consciously terminated... cognitive event involves an infinite regression.

As well, claims that consciousness act in agent-like fashion while storing and retrieving memories impose compounding storage problems. Whatever the physiological basis of memories turns out to be, coding, associating and retrieving memories become comprehensible only when the processes involved are understood as self-initiating, self-tending and automatically concluding.

Once such an autonomous process is in place it is not hard to see cognitive events generating conscious episodes that function as focal points for complicated resolutions and sustained responses. Conscious episodes can also be seen mediating among physiological states, local events (hunger, opportunity, danger...) and relevant memories. As these elements invoke one another insights flash up. These insights are imbued with the flavour of memories elicited by local events, and so our subjective lives look and feel as real as real can be.

On this account, 'acts of recollection' do not involve or require agents acting or consciousness doing anything. In straightforward ways, memories, sentences words, verbal and non-verbal responses... simply appear in consciousness. To be sure, we sometimes find ourselves attempting to remember an event or a name if they fail to turn up automatically.

These 'efforts' are best understood as proprioceptive strategies enabling dispositional meldings to 'have another go at it'. As often as not, trying to remember is counter-productive. The memory remains on the "tip of one's tongue", perhaps to emerge later when 'efforts to remember' cease.

Mnemonic memory tricks have the same function and probably reflect a predisposition to remember stories and

Vernon Molloy

accounts strung together with rhythms or melodies. Our interest in music hearkens back to an era when cultural repositories involved oral tradition resources. I cannot recite the alphabet without invoking a bit of doggerel from grade school, or remember how many days there in the months. I can do sums in my head because I learned the times tables a long ago. This homely skill amazes cashiers these days; and brings them to a standstill if I find the right change after giving over a bill and they have entered its value into the cash register.

I hardly ever do this for fun.

Memories as Dispositions

Even though we know that the organization of the brain is made up of a gazillion decision centers, that neural activities going on at one level of organization are inexplicable at another level, and that as with the Internet, there seems to be no boss, the puzzle for humans remains. The lingering conviction that we humans have a "self" making all the decisions about our actions is not dampened. It is a powerful and overwhelming illusion that is almost impossible to shake. [24] [25]

Michael Gazzaniga

If we consider the notion of memories and mental images as non-physical entities located in private "spaces", puzzling questions arise. Do memories and images exist *un-had:* i.e., do they exist when they are not participating in conscious episodes? Can two persons experience identical images? Do images have "rear" surfaces which are not being experienced? What are images made of? What is the connection between the space images seem to occupy and real space? Are there laws for private space?

---

[24]Gazzaniga, Michael S., Who's in Charge?: Free Will and theScience of the Brain, (HarperCollins: Kindle Edition. 2011-11-15) p. 75.

[25]The past forty years of research have shown that the human brain has billions of neurons organized into local, specialized circuits for specific functions, known as modules. For instance, in the human brain, an example of different circuits running in parallel and processing different inputs was demonstrated by a neuroimaging study done by Mark Raichle, Steve Petersen, and Mike Posner. One part of the brain reacts when you hear words, another particular part of the brain reacts to seeing words, still another area reacts while speaking words, and they can all be going at the same time.
Gazzaniga, Michael S., Who's in Charge?: Free Will and the Science of the Brain. HarperCollins: Kindle Edit(2011-11-15).(p. 33)

171

My proposal avoids these questions. Claims and requirements vis-a-vis cognitive proceedings are unaffected by the possibility that we store no memories at all but instead synthesize them as required. Just as we are said to have reflexes, habits, conditioned responses, dispositions to act... without thinking of them as existing in particular locations in our brains, we acquire dispositions to have "memory-experiences" that do not reside in particular locations.

Thus, for the same reason we do not ask: "Where is a stream of water located?", memories do not exist until they are called for. They emerge progressively in step-wise fashion, each step achieved by conditioned-response networks, multiplied, multiplexed and gated in complex ways.

A benefit of the memories as dispositions model is that limitless memories could arise from finite sets of elements. Memory-experiences involve patterns of association, with individual 'components' reused endlessly. This effortlessly accomplishes another feature the common sense/realist view has difficulty with. Memories are not snapshots, or even a series of snapshots coming rapidly enough to give the illusion of continuity. Memories flow because they are laid down by flowing experiences.

A further difficulty confronting traditional memory theories involves the matter of storing representations. How could any top-down or outside-in program accomplish this? In addition, a constant (and presumably increasing) expenditure of energy would seem necessary to maintain stored representations.

These difficulties are eliminated if memories understood as generated as required. Memory experiences occur the the way water rushes down channels scored by 'original' rains; recreating original events again and again.

This is how the Grand Canyon came into existence. This explains cultural resources and events and perhaps why wars and rumours of wars continue grinding and obliterating lives.

On the dispositional model, memories and conscious episodes are triggered by local events, conversations, dreams or internal ruminations. When their course is run, memories accomplish their own automatic flushing or concluding, a requirement traditional accounts ignore. In the disposition model, memories are neural storms that rise up and fade away on their own recognizance.

In the absence of some such explanation, mechanisms to initiate, sustain and suitably terminate memories would be necessary.

The common sense/realist model poses other difficult questions: would recollected memories be 'replaced' at their original address when individuals are finished using them? Alternatively, are memoires copied from templates that remain in secure locations? If this is not the case, what mechanism keeps memory stalls available until memorizers are done with them?

Finally, common sense stories about human memory require mechanisms able to view, analyse and respond to retrieved images and understandings. These tasks are thought to involve consciousness functioning as a critical faculty judging, assessing, deciding, willing, acting....

We see that this claim of efficaciousness does not explain anything, any more than talking about God as the Prime Mover responsible for the universe does explains anything.

Self-enabling Dispositions

An important advantage of regarding memories as self-enabling dispositions involves the effortless way this model explains the flowing nature of experience. There is no need for additional cognitive functions to account for a central characteristic of subjective lives and conscious episodes.

The same explanation illuminates our ability to see figures in ambiguous shapes - including the dreadful creatures sometimes seen lurking behind bushes and along fence lines. The notion of self-enabling dispositions also explains the trope phenomenon. To repeat the example from the previous section, tropes are often found in psychology textbooks. They feature ambiguous figure - ground images that switch before our eyes; or, more leisurely, images that emerge out of ambiguous stimuli: Rorschach ink blot responses, faces in clouds, the man in the moon... .

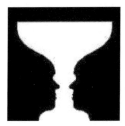

As well as being interesting in their own right, tropes provide a way of thinking about conscious episodes. (Similar events doubtlessly generate the points of view "before our eyes" expressions refer to.) In the realist model, meaning occurs when individuals distil or reify (elevate to "thing' status ') ideas of objects, entities and events out of recurring patterns of stimuli.

According to realists objects and entities actually exist in an external world and are perceived directly by creatures with eyes to see. Quasi-objects such as hurricanes, tornadoes or

Vernon Molloy

storms are referred to metaphorically as when we say "The tornado touched down..." or "The storm is over."

On this account, the inner worlds of individuals more or less adequately reflect what is going on externally. Responses to events are compiled, adjudicated and controlled by conscious faculties. This is why persons who are asleep or drugged are deemed incapable of choosing or controlling themselves and cannot be praised or blamed for what they get up to.

On the alternative proposed here, this sequence is turned on its head. Image-laden experiences occur. Each person distils an imaginary landscape out of these experiences and divides this landscape into *inner* and *outer*. Each person is automatically positioned at the centre of this inner realm and sees herself travelling across an imagined world in an imagined body.

The fact that real events subsidize these useful fantasies does not mean that they are also true. There are no corresponding artefacts 'out there', no perfect horses or trees in Platonic Realms, no noumenal horses or trees as Immanuel Kant proposed. Put another way, there is no division between *inner* and *outer* - no matter how useful this partitioning has been. There are no partitions between you and I either. We are like waves on lakes that only appear to be individually approaching shore. Our wind may be up for the moment, but we will wind up soon enough, our vaunted truths collapsing back into the water.

In the meantime, we occasionally glimpse what is going on. Watching squirrels and birds... wild animals in general is like being in a glass-bottom boat. This vantage point (which consists entirely of the fact that we are each vantage points!) allows us to voyeuristically watch other creatures going about their lives naturally, spontaneously, without self-consciousness getting in their way.

Another glimpse into what is going on occurs during intervals when figure-ground relationships are reversing. (Further along I give an example that works so well that it counts as a *moving picture!)*

If these glimpses are too brief to serve any purpose, processes bridging across chicken, egg, chicken, egg... events expand enough to encapsulate a sufficiently large over-arching event that can be contemplated at leisure. At least they do for me – as well as affording opportunities to contemplate the consternation of realists trying to figure out which event came first and caused the second.

Not only do we have only occasional glimpses into what is going on, we have no idea what these glimpses look like to one another. Our lives consist of irreducibly private vantage points.[26] Realists acknowledge serious epistemological difficulties between what we think is true and what is the case. On their understanding, the task of truth seekers, scientists and persons of good will is to bring these elements as close together as possible. The problem is, this task cannot be completed and, until it is completed, we have no (non-utilitarian) way of judging whether any step way is right or wrong.

Part of the problem confronting realists and common sense advocates is that the truth is neither out there nor within us. Just as the fallacious "chicken or egg first" question warns, there is no truth of the matter because there is no matter to speak of.

In the final analysis, all I am entitled to say is that the world is occurring and that images are predictions about what will happen next.

---

[26]Ludwig Wittgenstein talked about experiences as analogous to possessing a beetle in a matchbox we cannot show to anyone, only describe.

The Single Memory Myth

A simple thought experiment, can be performed from the comfort of your chair.

I propose that it is impossible to form an image of any object or entity, be it a rock, a bumble-bee or a bird, without seeing this object in the context of a tree, a flower or the ground. Even if the object is extracted from any recognizable context it still must be viewed within a nimbus of awareness; and this special circumstance depends upon the object having previously acquired *meaning* in context-rich circumstances.

For identical reasons the notion of a (single) memory laid down as a discrete entity, which could then be recalled, remembered or apprehended and then restored to a database of memories, is incoherent.

In real-life perceptions and experiences tend to include more and more of what is going on. Habituation, peripheral vision, peripheral hearing... constantly suggest new events to focus upon.

The subjective lives of human beings are rich because memories automatically elicit and evoke one another, generating conscious episodes, dreams or fugue states, depending upon the time of day, the quality of companions and (a recent addition) the presence of smart phones.

This is why the pragmatics of remembering offers no difficulty for the dispositional model. We remember ourselves, the world and the people we have experienced. These recollections occur spontaneously because the dispositions involved automatically elicit one another.

This may be all that can be said: the concatenating of dispositional elements generates conscious episodes. These episodes stitch themselves together into notions of selves, objects and an actual world.[27]

---

[27]The 'sophistication process' is relentless. The brain is

Vernon Molloy

The engine driving these proceedings is human beings' capacity to experience ourselves experiencing; and to keep doing this until we understand ourselves not only spatially but temporally – as a thing occupying space and enduring across time.

This accomplished, we concluded that these experiences demonstrate that we are persons inhabiting the world. Our growing expertise is taken as proof that we are becoming increasingly educated and wise about the world we live in.

The reality is that we do not 'live in' the world — even if 'live in' is understood in Heraclitus' modest "cannot step in same river twice" terms.

We are not inhabiting whatever is going on for a simple reason. We are tiny results of whatever is going on.

---

constantly being rewired. Sometimes this is good news...
http://www.thestar.com/news/world/2014/04/07/how_the_int
ernet_may_be_changing_the_way_we_read.html

Cyclopean Perception

Consciousness has been described as the most provocative and mysterious aspect of human life.[28] Consciousness is idolatrized as the faculty distinguishing human beings from other forms of life.

In the dispositional model this 'hard problem' is replaced with a straightforward emergent explanation, and this invitation to hubris evaporates. The capacity of have conscious episodes is an evolution of stimulus — response capabilities. The luminous, sensuous nature of consciousness comes from mapping layer-upon-layer of mutually-invoking dispositions in the capacious human brain. This achieves the possibility of complex, nuanced simulations of experiences triggered by current events 'with a view' to improving survivability.

These proceedings are often of considerable duration and can themselves participate in further responses.

Psychology books feature diagrams locating sense modalities on the cortex of the brain, and similar diagrams depicting depicting motor responses. These mappings roughly locate 'input' and 'output' functions.[29]

Bela Julesz has provided a way of thinking about these mappings. Julesz speaks of "Cyclopean perception" — the fact that we perceive the world as unified, seamless and whole.

Julesz' example is vision based on "peripheral" information from two retinas, but which requires an internal "retina" for the formation of images. (The same process doubtlessly occurs in other forms of life but only human beings have the neural resources to reflect upon and talk about what the results 'look like'.)

There is evidence that meaning in visual art, music, poetry and linguistic expression... is similarly "Cyclopean". The dispositional model invites a similar explanation of subjectivity. Conscious episodes occur when organic inputs

---

[28]http://consc.net/papers/facing.html
[29]http://en.wikipedia.org/wiki/Cortical_map

and cognitive events activate cognitive "retinas". The procedures wherein data is gathered are features of body and the central nervous system architecture. The brain communicates internally in ways analogous to optical retina events melding into an internal Cyclopean retina.

Like conscious episodes, Cyclopean retinas can be thought of as coalescing and disappearing on the fly. They participate in forming new dispositional elements from internal cognitive events. Alternatively, conscious episodes can be thought of as "topological spaces". In either case the result is the same. A self-initiating, self-guiding, unconscious engine is the source of the thinking, musing and day-dreaming we think of as our lives.

When these proceedings go well we speak of ingenuity, creativity and, occasionally, genius.

Of course such proceedings can also participate in tragic outcomes and dreadful pages in history books.

There is another danger: the quality and quantity of conscious episodes is not guaranteed just because an individual is alive. Our capacity for subjectively rich lives reflects our inherited cognitive machinery, our DNA. Whether and to what extent this capacity is utilized depends upon cultural and economic resources and individual narratives.

On this cultural front, wonderful examinations of dangers and possibilities continue to be produced and made available to billions of human beings. Libraries, universities, documentaries, internet resources, TED[30] talks... do their best to bring both good news and ominous portents to public attention.

Even so, an increasing number of people are worried that human beings may be failing the survivability test[31] . Although the issues I have been talking about may seem oblique to such worries, confusion about the nature and function of

---

[30]https://www.ted.com/
[31]http://guymcpherson.com/2011/09/couchsurfing-with-my-soapbox/

consciousness is an unindicted factor in many problems.

We are convinced that consciousness is a magical faculty. We believe that human beings are point sources of choices and wilful acts transcending determinism and causality. By regarding ourselves as Little Gods, we set the stage for giving ourselves undue respect and everyone else undue censure. We think we can use this 'divine status' to evade or veto the warnings, wisdom and understandings contained in cultural resources.

If problems and moral issues wriggle past these obstacles and generate conscious worries, we satisfy any sense that we 'should do something' by bringing this or that issue to public attention.

If we feel strongly about some calamity, we may even walk, run or bicycle from A to B to 'raise awareness and money for repairs.

The problem is that such responses encourage more of the same. The results: more talking, choosing, willing... have nothing to do with solving problems. 'Consciousness-raising projects' that lead to more consciousness-raising make no useful difference.

Indeed, since they represent days, months, years... spent adjuring one another to do better, they represent actual, ameliorative possibilities not taken up.

This is not what God or Mother Nature had in mind when big brains were evolving. Understandings, insights, 'thought experiments'... are useful if and only if they improve responses. When events are proceeding naturally, i.e., when human beings are not distracted by God stories and God-like conceits, the outcomes of thought experiments occurred automatically at appropriate 'real world' interstices.

There is another problem. Big picture insights or understandings... cannot engage large, abstract issues because such issues have no real world existence. Big understandings are only useful if translated into actionable understandings and *thoughtful* responses. The adage: "think globally, act locally" says it all.

Part of the difficulty is that big ideas are so manifestly important (at least to the subjectivities giving birth to them!) that their achievements feel like ends in themselves.

Hence a great irony: ideas that could do the most good if put into play are the ideas least likely to see the light of day.

Does this mean that consciousness has only belated observer or unwitting saboteur status? The answer is no to both.

Consciousness is a straightforward evolution of nervous system mechanisms common to all forms of life. These mechanisims include conditioned responses, habituation and gestalts. The capacity for conscious episodes and self-awareness generates remarkable possibilities. However these possibilities do not transform human beings into Little Gods.

We need to get over ourselves.

A familiar caution could help us climb down from our high horses: "If wishes were horses, beggars would ride."

Getting our feet back on the ground could have another benefit. Insights are valuable if they lead to useful responses by individuals whose insights they are. If insights are instead invested in conversations, adjurations, promulgations preachings... they are useless and often dangerous. The capacity to have insights evolved to improve responses to dangers and opportunities.

A moment too late can be as fatal as a year.

String Theory

Abstract
A few difficulties confronting anyone claiming
free will because they regard themselves as Divinely incarnated souls or as evolution's finest
flower.

Persons claiming that human beings make choices usually
think this is nothing more than common sense and that
nothing more needs to be said.

To be sure, we understand that some choices fail to be
executed, but always because something unexpected got in
the way or an accident or some other new factor interrupted
putting the choice into play.

As well, we regularly change our minds; using free will a
second or even a third time.

Unless something like this happens however, 'choices' exist as
accomplishments of the persons whose choices they are.
Indeed, even being countermanded does not alter the fact
that a choice existed for a time. Every choice becomes an
eternal fact. Perhaps the most dramatic consequence is
spoken of in Christian terms: being an angel and therefore an
almost perfect being, Satan's choice to set up a dark kingdom
in opposition to God cannot be undone even if he were to
wish it so. In fact, he cannot wish it so because of his own
perfect, complete nature. As a consequence Satan must
continue to do all he can to prosecute our undoing with every
strategm he can devise.

Given that human beings now number almost seven billion,
each making hundreds if not thousands of choices every day,
the number of eternal facts being generated defies
comprehension.

In spite of this profusion, in spite of the fact that even
challenged human beings make choices from an early age, we
also believe that no other creature has this capability –
although we acknowledge that choice-capable beings may
exist elsewhere in the universe.

Vernon Molloy

The consequences of these remarkable claims lie all around us, and nowhere more clearly than in the way we regard and treat other creatures. Human beings harvest other forms of life for any purpose whatsoever: making them into pets, beasts of burden or consuming them directly.

As long as 'undue cruelty' is avoided, these practices are morally acceptable. We claim this prerogative because they are incapable of making choices. The logic is straightforward. Unable to choose to not be harvested, farmed, petrified... other creatures have no relevant feelings or thoughts – no terrors, no feelings of boredom or repugnance about their fate and so their fate is not a moral issue.

Thus, if even one human being 'pardons' and rescues one turkey at Thanksgiving, the supererogatory quality of human beings' morality and empathy is underscored.

This capacity to feel is at the heart of cultural events and hegemonic claims. This is why CBC Radio's Anna-Marie Tremonte (a brusque, take no prisoners woman) spends so much time examining her guests' emotional responses to events that befall them, and scarcely any time to consider other consequences.

The capacity to feel – and the consciousness required to know that one is feeling – is what we think sets human beings apart from other creatures. This is why grief counsellors rush to children whose classmates have been murdered by megalomaniacs, committed suicide or gotten themselves run over while texting.

The claim that only human beings have feelings defines and sanctions almost all cultural practices. The idea that other forms of life are incapable of forming conscious 'intents and purposes'... permits human beings to do whatever we like. Worms wriggling on hooks, embryos terminated before the end of the second trimester, animals in factory farms... are discounted according to this logic. People with unusual skin colour, cultural practices or sexual orientation are at risk because of this logic.

Modern Problems, Ancient Perspectives

The argument is that the capacity to have feelings implies a consciousness deep enough to contain a self with ideas of personal history and destiny.

"If you're happy and you know it clap your hands!" sets the stage for talk about persons, agency, choices and culpability. It also diminishes the likelihood that we will have much to clap about, audiences, sports fans and Kim Jong-un's terrified acolytes notwithstanding.

In the following I suggest a few more reasons this self-deification is fallacious and sketch an understanding that could be put in its place.

If we think about what must be involved putting choices into play, it is s obvious that more is needed than awareness of a desirable or fearful outcome. 'Eternal fact' status notwithstanding, choices must be pushed into the world if they are to count – or even be noticed by anyone other than their author. This is true whether the world is thought of as a seamless event (my preference) or as a thicket of objects, entities and causes bringing objects and entities into and out of existence.

What would such pushing consist of? To gain a sense of this, it is useful to compare choices with strings. Choices have logical connections with individuals whose choices they are. Strings can be thought of in the same way. Like strings, choices do not have sufficient rigidity to make headway. As soon as we imagine them extended beyond the beings giving rise to them, 'outside events' begin to participate in what is occurring.

In other words, whether free will achievements of incarnated souls or the fruits of physiological, psychological and experiential proceedings, choices only have traction within persons giving rise to them.

We walk, talk, move our arms... according to desires arising from internal events, or because of internally-mediated responses to external events.

Thinking about these proceedings in terms of strings is instructive. Strings cannot be pushed. On the other hand, a grapple on the end of a rope (a big string!) allows me to haul a stick close enough to get my hands on it and transform it into a 'corporeal extension'. This extends my arm and enlarges the sphere wherein my choices have consequences.

Now my choices can range over a wider sphere and now my sense of being a choosing person is enlarged!

In similar ways, a musician's instrument becomes an extension of his or her being, as does a backhoe in an expert's hands. The intentions of musicians and backhoe operators extend through their instruments. Now comes the important part! These instruments, these extensions... become one of the factors and elements generating choices. Anyone in possession of a new tool finds themselves inventing and then 'choosing' to undertake projects the tool makes possibly or more readily accomplished. Learning a new word or concept similarly enlarges the scope of possible choices.

In other words, a person choosing is a figure of speech referring to the present state of the always changing resources and experiences human beings have been anthropomorphizing into persons and free will talk.

This process works the other way as well. As we age and decline our sphere of possible choices, our sense of what is possible, shrinks. This is doubtlessly a blessing. It would be terrible to be locked in an old body full of doomed youthful choices.

What is interesting is that this means that choices reflect what is intrinsically possible to human beings at various stages of their lives. This sense of intrinsic possibility can be extended by means with sticks, back-hoes, violins and – to take a modern example – deep-ocean drilling rigs and nuclear weapons. If human choices do not reflect some God-given soul or evolutionary achievement but the present size of sticks in our hands then what we are getting up to is a function of what we have been getting up to and there is nothing to call a halt save some ghastly Malthusian outcome.

Modern Problems, Ancient Perspectives

There is another reason the notion of 'persons choosing' is incoherent.

Logically, everything persons are aware of is stale-dated. There are several reasons for this. The most important is that an event must have occurred, or at least gotten underway, before awareness is possible. In addition, time is required for information to travel to a person, and still more time for this information to be processed into contents of awareness.

More than eight minutes is required for light to travel to the earth from the sun. During this interval, human beings cannot know whether the sun has winked out or gone nova.

Similarly, if you and I are three meters or three kilometres apart, our awareness of one another proportionately lags the events constituting our being. You may object that the intervals involved are so small that they can be ignored. However, no matter how small, intervals matter when thinking what can reasonably be said about intentions, persons, free will and choices.

Time for a summary. Each of us harbours a personally-imagined world full of imaginary selves and over-arching expectations involving these selves. These imaginations reflect ongoing efforts to anticipate what will happen based on news that is never real time but always more or less out-of-date.

Based on such information, premonitions, expectations and predictions occur. Within constraints imposed by bodies (sometimes amplified and extended with sticks, violins and backhoes), hopefully-useful responses occur. I see a rabbit. I throw a rock towards where I expect the rabbit to be when the rock gets there.

This modest vantage point is a far cry from the story we have been telling ourselves about the world as a suitable home for magisterial human beings with a Divine capacity to understand, choose and act.

Finally let's consider what could be salvaged from these

fantasies. Let's consider what would be gained if we discarded them and became less arrogant by doing so.

The first fruit is the modest realization that a capacity for robust premonitions and predictions is the only feature separating human beings from other forms of life.

In this story, the images you and I have of one another are graphical user interfaces (GUIs). These images are user-friendly place-holders for the complex unseen events comprising our respective beings.

The 'actual world' can be similarly explained. When we see trees through the windows of houses, these trees and houses seem part of an actual world. The snowflakes, raindrops and rabbits seen through these windows and crossing these lawns are understood respectively as ephemeral events and lesser beings passing through our world.

The Nature of Evil

There is surprisingly little evidence that well-intentioned politicians and moral teachers have made much difference in the course of history. Of course, we cannot wind the clock back to see how things would have gone without the influence of Jesus Christ, St. Augustine, Henry Thoreau or, as a place-holder for modest contributors, Dr. David Suzuki.

Would human beings have been more or less destructive in the absence of history's moral beacons?

On the other hand, it is hard to imagine how we could have survived had we been more violent. Therefore, if these moral beacons have been deflecting or mitigating bad behaviour, human survival until now may be due to them.

On the other hand, since human beings survived for thousands of years without cultural resources, churches and the institutions that made St. Augustine and Dr. Suzuki possible, the answer is not clear.

I think this means that the question of evil must be thought about obliquely and intuitively.

I propose that we consider the possibility that moral beacons have been doing more harm than good. Human beings have invested millions of man-years over the centuries adjuring one another to put things right. These individuals could have, and I think should have, put their own shoulders to obstinate, stuck, broken... wheels instead.

Indeed, if moralisers want to communicate a thought or make a point, what's wrong with "actions speak louder than words"? Not only is there no evidence that moralisers have been making a good difference, they have arguably been encouraging others to satisfy their insights by raising alarms, ringing bells and pointing fingers.

Vernon Molloy

My own hope is that repairing the way we think about consciousness diminishes 'incarnated agent' notions and returns *actualizing* and *instantiating* insights to be our first order of business.

This conclusion about the importance of actual responses can be reached another way. History is full of stories about evil men and wretched machinations. These stories encourage a simplistic, dangerously disenfranchising view of human affairs. To take an example everyone is familiar with, when Hitler and his colleagues were indicted at Nuremberg they became scapegoats for millions of Germans. No matter how monstrous Hitler may have been, he was one person. He could not have held such sway unless there had been corresponding dispositions within the German population.

A better way to understand his career is to see the Germans of his era as suffused with complementary malignant dispositions. More importantly, they must have been so constituted before Hitler came upon the scene. Hitler's role was to be the *necessary* that achieved *sufficiency*. When Hitler added himself to the mix - it does not matter for this argument whether he 'chose' to do so or was driven by genetics and experience - all hell broke loose.

This also seems to be a useful way to think about what is going on today. Evil is not vested in a few people while everyone else gets absolved. Like false *chickens or eggs first?* questions, the Second World War did not occur because of either Hitler or the German population. The cause was the *German Event.* The elements of this event – Hitler and the German population – had complementary relationships.

Each are necessary for the other to show up.

This story locates the problem of evil across societies - and reminds us that the backdrop of evil is as close by and homely as you and I.

No nation, no culture, no epoch... can prevent megalomaniacs from occurring. However human beings might be able to achieve cultural and economic countervails diminishing the likelihood that 'remaindered' populations will lend their lives to their ambitions.

This also makes sense from an evolutionary point of view. There is no reason to hope that most of us will ever be interested in large issues or abstract notions. For almost all of history individuals lumbered with such notions would have been culled because they were not paying enough attention to what was going on around them to survive let alone reproduce.

At least this was the case until cultural resources, technologies and agrarian economies provided big idea people with vantage points from which they could trick the rest of us into handing over some of the value of our work. Sometimes this quid pro quo involved eternal bliss or punishment talk, sometimes it involved virgins. Mostly it involved opportunities to lord it over others: to enslave, look down upon, torment, put to death... as opportunities and needs dictated.

In other words, Hitlers are best understood as signalling the presence of malignant dispositions within populations. They are like the or malignant growths on unhealthy bodies.

The last thing we should do is ignore what such people are telling us about the nature and location of evil.

Vernon Molloy

Concrete Problems

The model of cognition proposed by Swiss psychologist Jean Piaget during the 1920's speaks of four stages of cognitive competence. The final is *Formal Operations* – the capacity to think about problems and possibilities in overarching ways that go beyond immediate needs and wants, digestive tract issues and local events. Piaget thought

> *the growth of knowledge is a progressive con-struction of logically embedded structures su-perseding one another by a process of inclusion of lower, less powerful logical means into higher and more powerful ones up to adulthood. Therefore, children's logic and modes of thin-king are initially entirely different from those of adults.*

What is interesting is the way this model illuminates historical events and economic and political problems. This occurred to me reading a paper for a cultural psychology course more years ago than I care to think about. According to this paper (whose reference I have unfortunately misplaced) aboriginal do not typically demonstrate *Formal Operations*, but always achieve *Concrete Operations*. That is, they are wonderfully good at solving day-by-day problems, but not much interested in what might be going on over the hill or more than a day or two in the future.

Others have made similar observations:

> *Some psychologists believe that only 30% of the population reach formal operations. This is the one stage were Piaget seems to have over-esti-mated rather than under-estimated the ability of the child. Dasen argues that some cultures don't develop formal operational thought at all.[32]*

> *Bradmetz (1999), in a longitudinal study showed that out of 62 children tested at the age of 15,*

[32] *http://psychology4a.com/develop3.htm*

192

on a series of Piagetian tasks, only one had reached formal thought![33]

This seems a fair description. Most of us fail to exhibit four Piagetian modalities. This has been observed in both anthropological research and modern settings. In a study of supermarket shoppers Capon and Kuhn (1982) found that most could not apply the Formal Operations skill of proportional reasoning to calculate best buys. They concluded that Formal Operations "appears to be the only stage in Piaget's sequence that is not attained universally".

Why would Piaget have thought so highly of human beings? Could he have been indulging intra-species anthropomorphism? What if most human beings simply regurgitate ideas without having much understanding of what they mean? Homilies, guiding principles and heuristics come to mind: a stitch in time saves nine; do unto others as you would have them treat you; loose lips sink ships....

If maxims represent widely and deeply understood truths (typical of Formal Operations populations), there would be no need for them.

Thus an important question arises: do most human beings really proceed beyond Concrete Operational understandings? What if only a small proportion of human beings, say twenty per cent, perceive deeper patterns and implications?

The economic and political implications would be enormous. If most of us are Concrete Operationals and nothing but we are sitting ducks for those thinking in big-picture ways. We may be useful at solving problems presented by circumstances, predicaments or examinations, but have no capacity to transform the context of these questions into further questions.

If so, most of us are vulnerable to being manipulated and exploited by our big-picture Formal Operations cousins. They can 'hide in plain sight', their agendas safely beyond ordinary awareness and meaningful response.

---

[33] *http://psychology4a.com/develop2.htm*

Vernon Molloy

On this account, politicians, megalomaniacs, executives... are not cunning, greedy bastards. They are taking advantage of situations, resources and people in ways reflecting their cognitive endowments *and those of target populations*. As was said of Isaac Newton, when he won a mathematical contest against the equally gifted Leibniz, "A lion is known by its claw".

Fortunately, not all Formal Operations individuals rush to take advantage of others. History is full of *Cassandras* and *Chicken Littles* trying to point out issues and dangers that are apparently obvious to them and yet somehow escape most people's attention.

These efforts almost always come to naught. If Piaget was wrong about everyone completing all four stages of cognitive development, the Cassandra problem may flow from the fact that the ability to understand and respond to non-local issues is beyond the capacity of perhaps eighty per cent of human beings.

To be sure, events occasionally cause Concrete Operations people to look beyond immediate circumstances. In the weeks (but not the months) following Indonesia's December 26, 2004 tsunami disaster, the global response was heartening. However, even as this generosity was reported and applauded, commentators – including Canada's Stephen Lewis – grumbled that South Africa's AIDS-riddled population would have benefited enormously had even a small percentage of such help been coming their way.

An abbreviated (three stage) Piagetian model suggests (1) that such failures are not moral issues; and (2) they may be bred in our bones. Responses to disasters are short-lived because sustained attention to non-local issues requires "biologically secondary abilities" that are simply not available. Concrete Operationals relapse into personal concerns and current events because "biologically primary" activities are human beings' 'factory settings'.

To take another example, now that HIV/AIDS has been around for decades, the plight of beleaguered nations like Africa no longer registers on on the world's empathic radar screens. In addition, AIDS, Hepatitis C, STD's, life-style diseases... are often regarded as self-inflicted 'behaving carelessly' harms. This understanding allows bystanders to excuse themselves from responsibility.

At the same time international relief efforts have elements appealing to Concrete Operational and capable of motivating and sustaining large responses. Natural disasters, political crises, terrorists attacks... could happen anywhere at any time. Our sense of living in a secure community is bolstered if our nation participates in global responses.

For the most part, when fires or floods have been dealt with, intruders repelled – or difficulties have prevailed long enough that they become 'part of the furniture' – Concrete Operationals return to business as usual. Surviving soldiers spend little time thinking about causes of conflict or repairing the social, economic or spiritual deficits that lead to war. Exceptions include Canada's Romeo Dallaire and the afore-mentioned Stephen Lewis. Mr. Dallaire spent years struggling to repair the political and moral failures implicated in the Rwanda massacres. Mr. Lewis has been equally tireless with respect to global failures to respond to Africa's AIDS crisis.

Lewis and Dallaire fail to grasp that some large difficulties may not be repairable. They may reflect institutional, corporate and national activities emerging out of a naturally-occurring lopsided proportion of Concrete and Formal Operationals. This proportion sets the stage for megalomaniacs and dictators to brandish their respective cohorts of Concrete Operationals and set them upon one another.

I will not belabour this point with a list of events and names - every day's news brings fresh examples.

The circumscribed understanding of Concrete Operationals can also be seen in their inability to attend to their own well-being, if doing so involves delaying gratification for more than a few minutes. South Africans pursue dangerous sexual practices in spite of overwhelming evidence that their lives are on the line.

Vernon Molloy

For Concrete Operational males, sexual urges are more than enough to overrule worries about AIDS and STDS. For women, cultural expectations, economic constraints and concern for children further erode their ability to protect themselves.

An abbreviated (three not four stage) Piagetian landscape also explains why appeals for the modest sums needed to defuse Africa's AIDS crisis now fall upon deaf ears. The same model illuminates Western nations' indifference to sussing out the causes of World Wars and Rwandan-style massacres. The torments experienced by populations on the other sides of hills or years do not warrant attention – even when similar torments threaten to catch us up next week or next year.

Human beings' indifference to the threat of anthropogenic climate change may flow from biologically-predicated myopia rather than oversights that could be remedied by any number of Al Gores giving any number of *Inconvenient Truth* speeches.

The only examples we have of sustained attention to calamitous events involve corporations and politicians advancing profit-taking and hegemony-increasing projects.

The economics machinations and Homeland Security measures emanating from the 9/11 terrorist attack are a good example.

To be sure, many Formal Operationals have little interest in personal aggrandizement and are genuinely concerned about human well-being.

However even these people appear to understand the truncated nature of the Piagetian landscape. On July 1,2005 *Live 8* concerts occurred around the world. The hope was to get millions thinking about poverty and disease and opening their wallets while the tide of empathy and good will was high.

Although no one said so, these concerts targeted Concrete and not Formal Operations individuals. The strategy was not to achieve a public good by appealing to Formal Operations understandings. The plan was an attempt to achieve a useful outcome by providing Concrete Operationals with opportunities to feel good! The only plausible explanation involves an instinctive understanding that most people will not respond to big picture problems without some immediate, tangible reason for doing so — the hallmark of Concrete Operations individuals.

For an encore benefit, *Live 8* audiences got to feel good about themselves because they been tricked into doing something good for people who would not otherwise have crossed their minds!

An impressive roster of musicians, artists and intellectuals continue to invest in such projects. Although they are earnest, lovely people, they seem blissfully (and perhaps carefully) unaware that their careers depend upon the concrete/formal ratio spawning the miseries they sing and pontificate about.

There are parallels between these failures vis-a-vis remote populations and disregard for local well-being more than a day or week into the future. Environmental concerns, resource depletion issues... are on everyone's lips. As well North Americans are experiencing an obesity epidemic while 3rd and 4th world populations suffer from malnutrition. If we ate less and transferred the difference to those experiencing 'food insecurity', we would all be better off. In addition

> There are nearly one billion malnourished peo-
> ple in the world, but the approximately 40 mil-
> lion tonnes of food wasted by US households,
> retailers and food services each year would be
> enough to satisfy the hunger of every one of
> them.[34]

In general, in spite of school-crossing guards, grief counsellors and helicopter mothers, First World claims of concern for the well-being of even heir own children are sounding increasingly hollow. Even if life-style excesses and malnutrition issues are ignored, we would not be out of the woods. Economically, environmentally, psychologically... our circumstances are visibly declining. Yet commentators, climatologists and economists have been predicting this since Thomas Malthus

---

[34] *See more at: http://www.feeding5k.org*

published *An Essay on the Principle of Population* in 1798.

We can, and doubtlessly will, continue to debate how soon the world will run out of oil or how much pollution is survivable, but no *thoughtful* person believes that an endlessly growing population brandishing endlessly growing expectations is sustainable.

I propose that this understanding would be commonplace, and vigorous responses already in place, if most human beings attained Formal Operations.

If our measuring sticks only span inches and our problems are miles wide, we have a non-moralizing explanation for why Cassandra's problem continues to haunt us.

A corollary with implications for inequities and ecological footprints (alluded to by Philip Wylie in *The Magic Animal*)[35] is that Formal Operations people (Wylie referred to them as 'magic animals') can enjoy such rich inner lives that they have only modest interest in wealth and power. Unfortunately, as we have seen, Formal Operations people can also harbour insatiable ambitions – and vantage points from which to pursue them.

However these relationships play out, dividing human beings into (lets say) eighty per cent Concrete Operations people and twenty per cent Formal Operations clarifies the way the world has been working. This proportion has been informing social and cultural events for the 5000 generations or one hundred and fifty thousand years human beings just like us have been knocking around the world.

Sorting populations into leaders and followers occurs in many species, but human beings have been spawning leaders and followers in both subtle and obvious ways.

Several thousand years ago human beings turned an important corner. With cultural repositories compounding differences between cognitive endowments, we started doing something completely unprecedented. We began ourselves

---

[35]Philip Wylie, *Magic Animal* (1968: Pocket Books).

into institutionally-embedded, culturally-transmitted host/parasite relationships.

The 80%/20% Concrete/Formal ratio continues to inform these proceedings. The resulting bigger, higher, faster, wealthier... goals promise to keep human beings locked into a maelstrom until every possibility is exhausted.

This may be in sight. In 2000 AD, 500 human beings were reported to have as much wealth as the poorest fifty per cent. By 2014 AD, this number had 'improved' sufficiently that it only took the assets of 85 of the world's wealthiest human beings to equal the equity of the bottom half of the world's population, something like 3.5 billion.[36]

How did this predicament come to pass? Until perhaps three thousand years ago, relationships between parents and children, leaders and followers, Formal and Concrete Operations populations... enhanced community well-being by equitably distributing the benefits of intelligence, success and experience. Pot-latch ceremonies shared assets across communities – a custom that owed much to the perishable nature of early forms of wealth. Dead animals and food stuffs have short shelf lives. Trading them for community standing and good will made sense.

Bastardized versions of pot-latch still occur. Wealthy individuals endow research projects, academic chairs and community swimming pools. Such distributions enhance communities, but they also legitimize the economic and political processes generating the inequities that make philanthropy necessary in the first place.

This is the important difference between ancient and modern pot-latch. Philanthropists hope to establish legacies even as they benefit communities. (Not all are glory seekers of course. Some donors insist on anonymity and the Nobel Prizes have been an important catalyst of human excellence.) In subsistence cultures, successful hunters enjoy respect and authentication. These rewards encouraged others to conduct

---

[36]http://www.bbc.com/news/magazine-26613682

themselves similarly and community members enjoyed more or less equally enhanced prospects. This wholesome outcome no longer occurs. Modern philanthropists encourage Concrete Operationals to regard wealth, power and inequity as legitimate, benign features of urban life. As well, charitable activities transform rights claims into dependencies and occasions for gratitude.

This reduces the likelihood that Concrete Operationals will see personal economic and political difficulties as problems to be solved.

There is a still deeper problem. Cultural resources are inherently regressive because they are preferentially available to Formal Operationals. This means that mankind's accumulating knowledge, technology, its so-called *human capital*... is adding to the factors sorting people into rich/poor, leader/follower populations. The consequence is that the world is becoming increasingly poisonous for most human beings. Longevity and creature comforts notwithstanding, in the great cities of history and, *a fortiori*, the modern world, the usual person would be better off in virtually any other circumstance.

Regressive cultural resources and inequities mean that Formal Operationals are positioned to acquire wealth and power and trade it among themselves over the heads of the chattering classes. Adding to this *fish in a barrel* predicament, Concrete Operationals seem instinctively disposed to subordinate themselves to anyone claiming to know what is required or where to get it. With this instinct as a resource, all Formal Operationals have to do is provide problems for Concrete Operationals to solve and (promise to) share the fruits of successful solutions.

In urban circumstances this promising is mediated through paid employments for workers and deep discounts for consumers. In previous centuries, share cropping, serfdom, slavery, indentured servitude, the caste system... organized populations along similar lines.

Then and now, some portion of the resulting profit has always been reinvested in infrastructure, circuses and other distractions. The ensuing excitement, reward, pain, danger, need for security... guarantees that most of us are content to hunker down in the cities and towns we call home. We rejoice that leaders and captains of industry have arranged it so that we are never far from home or a weekend, never without work to do and entertainment – and never so satisfied that we are not anxious to get back to work come Monday.

This should be contrasted with life before cultural repositories transformed Concrete/Formal relationships into the modern world. During this period – which probably lasted one hundred thousand years – there was not enough technological, economic or political leverage for small populations to harm anyone more than a few hundred yards away. Future generations were completely shielded from mischief, never mind the Holocaust the International Panel on Climate Change is warning about. During this epoch, Concrete Operationals shared communities with Formal Operationals. Everyone lived identical lives in terms of economic and cultural head starts. With everyone on a level playing field, leaders and followers sorted themselves according to age, experience and genetically-driven endowments – all positive elements for local well-being.

This innocence is gone. We are experiencing a crisis that has nothing to do with nuclear weapons, globalization, global warming and inequities. Many of today's problems can be traced to proceedings institutionalizing and amplifying naturally-occurring Concrete and Formal Operations endowments.

For at least two thousand years, Formal Operationals have been regarding Concrete Operationals as targets of opportunity and as herd animals. The sense of family, clan, tribe and the lack of cultural resources that once combined to harness big picture understandings to community well-being has vanished. As custodians and principal beneficiaries of cultural resources, the cognoscenti, the high priests, the wealthy, the clever... have been acting out conceits and notions of entitlement. Part of this acting out involves people-displacing tools, corporations and institutions whose fruits are also *progressively retained* and whose consequences are (you guessed it!) *regressively distributed*.

Where do these notions of entitlement come from? Researchers recently demonstrated something everyone knows: wealth and power cause recipients to believe that they deserve to be wealthy and powerful - and, indeed, that they deserve even more! This sounds like garden-variety greed but a more useful explanation is possible. During the epoch when human beings lived rough on the ground and Formal Operationals were important elements in community survival, something must have been causing them to go the extra mile or place themselves in harms way. No doubt praise, applause, special places around fires, preferential breeding opportunities... figured in the calculations of both Formal and Concrete Operationals. These calculations are still occurring of course, but they are now amplifying institutionalized, baked-in inequities.[37]

Arguably as well, racism, jingoism and ethnocentrism grow out of the disdain Formal Operationals harbour for their incompetent cousins. Whenever skin colour, language, cultural differences, economic necessities... permit or make possible, contempt flourishes.

Of course, it does not hurt that Concrete Operationals can be counted upon to fall in line and have at one another whenever Dear Leaders bellow "Sic em!"

It is not as if Concrete Operationals can think what else to do now that subsistence activities and domestic problems have been urbanized and monetized.

There may be another link between Formal/Concrete Operationals and bigotry. By definition, Concrete Operationals are 'context-driven' and incapable of sustained bigotry, hatred - or anything else for that matter! Only individuals with the cognitive resources needed to compare and contrast big

---

[37]http://www.nytimes.com/2014/01/20/opinion/krugman-the-undeserving-rich.html?hp&rref=opinion&_r=1

pictures are capable of sustained bigotry.

In other words, systematic, institutionalized, militarized... bigotry and discrimination is beyond Concrete Operations populations. I think this means that systematic, sustained brutality is only possible under the tutelage of Formal Operationals. Of course Concrete Operationals are important in these proceedings. Two hundred millions deaths occurred because of military activities during the 20th century. Concrete Operationals populated every aspect of these undertakings. We functioned as taxpayers, factory workers, consumers and, of course, as soldiers and cannon fodder.[38]

Finally, a striking new feature of 21st century conflict involves suicidal terrorism. Although 1st world populations find such conduct inexplicable, suicidal terrorism can be understood as an extension of Concrete/Formal relationships. Suicidal terrorists invest their lives in 'fell swoops' upon culturally-prescribed targets.

In similar fashion Concrete Operationals submit to military conscriptions and put themselves in harms way whenever required, and otherwise live cheerfully as workers and consumers.... The difference is that the Concrete Operationals fortunate enough to live in secular nations expect to survive from one week to the next. For the most part, we are unwilling to undertake missions wherein they are weaponized and expendable.

They are, however, similarly persuaded that benefits enjoyed week by week make investing one's life lives worthwhile. Terrorists' investments are more focussed and dramatic. They expect correspondingly dramatic rewards in paradise.

---

[38]Small refinements in these proceedings have been occurring along the way. Until a few hundred years ago, 'great leaders' could occasionally be found leading armies into battle, or camped on hills near killing fields. Today – given the size, complexity and logistics of conflicts – battlegrounds are rarely known about in advance, and so the absence of leaders in harms way is rarely noticed.

Vernon Molloy

Terrorists are Concrete Operationals in a hurry.[39] [40] The people helping them correctly position their semtex belts are Formal Operationals with longer-term, larger plans.

For most of mankind's existence, relationships among Formal and Concrete Operationals have been, if not always mutually beneficial, at least survivable. Since the *Industrial Revolution* this has not been the case. Many, if not most, of the problems populations used to have to deal with on a daily basis have been culturally resolved as folk-ways, maxims and best practices. At least in developed nations this is no longer the case. Daily requirements have been automated or outsourced. Water, food, heat, security, entertainment... are piped in and the results flushed away without anyone raising a conscious finger. The Formal Operationals shepherding their cousins into this bright future seem determined to eliminate any remaining consciousness-evoking requirements. Words to watch for: *globalization, efficiency, out-sourcing, middle-class decline...* and, a recent catchphrase among economists and politicians, *deflation.*

Each of these straws in the wind are signalling the imminent return of a rich/poor world. This will be a rich/poor world with a difference however. For the first time most human beings will lack a culture of self-reliance. Even Inner-Directed

---

[39]Whether secular or religious, Concrete Operationals find themselves in a predicament. They must invest their lives in pursuits whose credentials are necessarily inscrutable to them because of the nature of their cognitive apparatus. In 'Virgins? What Virgins?'(*Free Inquiry* 26:1, 2006. 45-6), Ibn Warraq argues that the 72 virgins promised to Muslim martyrs is actually a mistranslation and should read: 'white raisins of crystal clarity'. See also:
http://en.wikipedia.org/wiki/Ibn_Warraq
[40]*Center for Inquiry* (Volume 9 Issue 5, July 2005). Qu'ranic scholar Christoph Luxenberg has tried to demonstrate that many of the obscurities of the Qu'ran disappear if we read certain words as being Syriac and not Arabic. This would include, for example, reinterpreting the promise of virgins in the afterlife as a promise for chilled drinks and good food.

recidivists will be hard-pressed since there are vanishingly few places where subsistence activities are permitted.

There is a light at the end of the tunnel however. History's *Cassandras* and *Chicken Littles* demonstrate that not all Formal Operationals are manipulative and self-serving. Our difficulties may reflect the fact that these benign Formal Operationals have been assuming that all human beings can understand big picture issues if presented clearly or often enough.

What if this is not true? What if most human beings are not, and cannot become, interested in what is occurring on the other sides of hills, or more than a few days in the future?

Although this does not sound promising, it begs two questions. The first is whether the present proportion of Concretes and Formals accurately reflects underlying genetic potentials – a straightforward rendering of the nature/nurture question.

Cultures emphasizing specialized competencies and economic thralldom are more likely to spawn Concrete Operationals than 'inner-directed' populations – to borrow David Riesman's term *The Lonely Crowd*.

In short, it is possible the urbanization, specialization and globalization are creating artificial impediments to Formal Operationalism. These obstacles include:

- centralized economic and political arrangements,
- specialization,
- the demoralizing consequences of urban existence,
- the institutionalization of previously personal responsibilities and prerogatives,
- waning notions of personal potency and responsibility, following the *ought implies can* principle.

We also need to recognize that identifying problems is useless unless repairs are imagined and put into practice. Well-intentioned Formal Operationals need to actualize their understandings in ways analogous to the business plans and corporations brandished by their Machiavellian cousins.

If this could be done, it might turn out that today's

Vernon Molloy

Concrete/Formal ratio is not cast in stone. North America's brief frontier period evoked widespread self-sufficiency and creativity. Unhappily these characteristics vanished as soon as the continent was 'settled sufficiently' for traditional leader/follow relationships to resume. The instinct to tuck in behind leaders remained lurking in the background until opportunities arose to give up the exhausting business of thinking outside of boxes.

I think this implies that Formal Operationals concerned with morality, accountability, sustainability – and alarmed at their own historical record – should invest time and energy nurturing economic and political countervails to imperialism and globalisation.

This was, after all, how ambitious, entrepreneurial... Formal Operationalstransformed millions of villagers and farmers into factory workers, retail clerks and standing armies.

These Formal Operationals were not content to announce the need for more production, more consumption, more loyalty, more defence. They invested their lives and anything they could get their hands on in infrastructure, institutions and factories. They subscribed to the "if you build it, they will come" maxim. They paid Concrete Operationals to 'get er done' every step of the way.

Rewards every step of the way are what makes Concrete Operationals run.

If benign Formal Operationals now recognize that their wholesome, inclusive ambitions require similar treatment, success might yet be possible.

Indeed, it is even possible that more of us might unlock our full Piagetian potential.

Finally, the fact that circumstances are difficult and prospects bleak could be a good thing. These problems are matched by the undeniable fact that Concrete Operationals are good at fixing things and seeing ways forward. Should well-intentioned Formal Operationals begin actualizing the projects they have until now been content to promulgate, the energy and ingenuity of Concrete Operationals might do the rest.

Delusions of Grandeur

Foreword

What does it mean to find one's self alive in a universe that burst into existence 13.8 billion years ago? The following attempts an answer from a reductionist but not a deterministic point of view - a distinction I hope to make clear. Consciousness and self-consciousness encourages persons to think about reality as a storm of objects and entities located in space and passing through time. Thanks to Albert Einstein, we now speak of 4-dimensional space-time instead of a Newtonian 3-dimensional universe passing through time. This change was implicit in Michelson-Morley's 1887 discovery that the speed of light is the same no matter how fast or in what direction observers are travelling. Einstein did not base his theories upon any experiment however – except those carried out in his mind.Certainly specifics about the speed of light are not relevant to his conclusions. Any `fastest possible communication' would lead to identical results. The only difference would be changes to the value of 'C' (the speed light)– and calculations regarding the energy yields of nuclear power plants and hydrogen bombs.

These intuitions suggest a further hypothesis: you and I are events within the Big Bang event that is, of course, still exploding. There are no entities nor objects in this story, only more or less enduring events. You and I know about the value of enduring complex events because we are the result of such events. We have noticing and naming one another and spawning self-awareness by doing so.

By definition, events occur over time and space (they would otherwise be unnoticeable!). Like gravitational influences events ramify endlessly, even though influences fall off exponentially and soon become indistinguishable. Einstein also taught us that the Big Bang event spawned space and time in ways described by General Relativity.[41] These

---

[41]http://math.ucr.edu/home/baez/einstein/einstein.html

proceedings, consequences, influences and ramifications spawned suns, planets, hurricanes and biospheres.

These delights should not distract us from the charm of simple explanations. Whatever is going on is not captured by common sense notions of a world of things and the substances from which things are said to be made. David Hume was right. Only recurring associations can be spoken of. The question: "Do bats cause balls to go in certain trajectories?" becomes: "Does the instrumental value of home runs cause images of bats and balls to behave in reliable ways?"

In other words, the need for causal explanations is as chimerical as the objects and entities they appear to link. Paying attention to what is going on is entertaining and useful. These benefits do not warrant realism's claims. Noticing, naming, discussing... is always about vanished states of affairs. Grumbling that intervals between events and apprehensions are sometimes trivial ignores the primal significance of the fact that they always exist.

Delusions of Grandeur

*There is no need for you to leave the house.
Stay at your table and listen. Don't even listen,
just wait. Don't even wait, be completely quiet
and alone. The world will offer itself to you to
be unmasked; it can't do otherwise; in raptures
it will writhe before you.*

Franz Kafka

I recently observed something every driver has seen - a
squirrel making its run across a road, reversing direction,
reversing again and continuing on. This time the gambit was
successful, in part because I slowed enough to allow the
animal time to `make up its mind'. My travelling companion
had a better description. I had slowed enough to "let the
squirrel decide". This is preferable because what was going on
was the squirrel deciding - not some specialized part of the
squirrel making a decision after consulting information
gleaned by sensory organs, assessed, evaluated, prioritized,
melded with some agenda (to get across the road...) and then
acted upon.

The reason this is preferable is that the alternative is too
complicated. What we observe in road-crossing squirrels is
`decision making' in lock step with local events. We also see
that what counts as *nearby* is determined by sensory organs -
eyes, ears, feelers, olfactory receptors... .

Earthworms and eagles have different theatres of
engagement.

This is worth thinking about because, if this squirrel had been
in the grip of the picture recommended by common sense and
realism, my generosity would not have saved its life.

In Homo sapiens, two renderings of just such managerial
functions are commonplace. The one we should be most
interested in involves ourselves as `persons within' bodies we
think we own, inhabit and ride around. The second involves

analogous functions in institutions, corporations and nations. For example, we believe that corporate undertakings proceed at the behest of managers, administrators, boards of directors, shareholders and citizens.

Since they are human beings, we understand presidents, administrators and citizens as controlled by `inner-selves'.

In this way we concoct a world wherein persons control corporations and nations through a two-stage relationship - persons in bodies controlling corporations by participating in various ways in their activities.

The point is, everywhere we look we imagine we see *persons* controlling some of what is going on. Even when we are not involved at citizens, directors, customers... we take comfort that persons are at the helms of corporations and ships of state. We trust that this common humanity will, sooner or later, prevent corporations and nations from running amok.

This optimism is contradicted by the historical record. More importantly, it depends upon the claim that persons enjoy managerial relationships with their bodies. Even though this claim is fleshed out with gossip about sin/virtue, voluntary/involuntary, who said what... issues, even though this is the claim commerce and justice depend upon for legitimacy, the issue is far from settled.

Leaving aside logical problems, an impressive list of biological, sociological and chemical determinants of human and animal behaviour has already been compiled. As explanations accumulate, the arena left for moral and rational agent talk shrinks. This never seems to give us pause however. We keep moving the 'persons are agents' claim around so it is always outside of whatever is being discussed.

Eventually we will run out of this wiggle room. I think we should grasp the nettle and begin reaping the benefits of an understanding that is not based on primitive *realism* or archaic *common sense*.

Modern Problems, Ancient Perspectives

What has also not been thought about is that non-free will explanations for what human beings get up to renders indifference to the nature of corporate and national intentionality implausible. We often seem to think about cats and dogs as little humans. We refuse the far more plausible hypothesis that nations and corporations are forms of life getting up to stuff that has no external explanation. Of course part of the reason is that we think corporations are constituted and controlled by human beings.

Thus, whenever nations and corporations `behave badly', we believe that such events must be dealt with as failures of the individuals comprising corporations, and the higher up the individual the greater the culpability.

As I write this, September, 2015, the Volkswagon Company is in a great deal of hot water because they engineeered a clever bit of software into their diesel cars. This software knew when it was being interrogated by diagnostic equipment and adjusted engines so they met low emissions standards.

Once on the road however the engines were reconfigured to achieve excellent performance and mileage results – emissions be damned!

Doubtlessly this malfeasance will be analyzed in terms of corrupt executives and moral failings. What will be missing from these investigations is whether there is such a thing as an emergent *Volkswagon entity* fashioning its own intentions, agendas, trickeries... and channeling them through boards of directors, managers, etc.

We have seen such behaviours before, including behaviours during the Holocaust.

Let's suppose that persons turn out to not be in control of their own bodies the way common sense and cultural legacies propose. If so, common-sense feelings of well-being with regards to corporate and nation intentionality are misplaced. (That is to say, we presently believe that corporations and nations have no intentions!) If this is not the cause, and since corporations and nations are immeasurably more potent than individuals, the consequences of getting this wrong could be, and I think have been, serious indeed.

Vernon Molloy

What does it matter if persons are not in control of bodies and corporations the way we have been imagining? A provocative possibility is that human beings have been amalgamating into alien forms of life; and that the resulting corporations and nations have evolved into powerful entities. Events in the 20th and early 21st century certainly look like monsters prowling the world in pursuit of profit and prey. The people comprising these nations and corporations, are often alarmed at what is going on. They sometimes appeal to one another: "Take a different course for God's sake!"

More often than not the protagonists in civil wars and Arab Springs cannot leave off killing one another and must rely upon outside intervention to organize cease fires.

Another danger is more subtle and therefore less vulnerable to charges of anthropomorphism. We regard media presentations, public debates and intellectual undertakings as legitimate responses to problems. Individuals seized with issues such as global warming, HIV/AIDS, the 21st century's rising anti-Semitism... strive to put warnings, statistics and adjurations before the widest possible audience. This strategy - exemplified in America by Al Gore, David Suzuki and Stephen Lewis - assumes the `inner agent' model of personhood. This is the claim that yet more arguments, statistics, and predictions... could one day make a difference.

After all, new data, arguments, presentations... provide persons with opportunities to revisit decisions already taken, or perhaps consider issues for the first time.

However this tautological (meaningless, empty...) claim ought to be regarded with suspicion. The reason it is tautological is that no possible outcome can refute the hypothesis that we are persons making conscious decisions. For example, there is no guarantee that anyone watching Dr. David Suzuki or Sir Nicholas Stern reprising global warming scenarios or Al Gore's "An Inconvenient Truth" will make more `wholesome' decisions. Since nothing determines the sovereign will of persons our only hope is that new statistics, arguments and pleas will result in `better decisions' - without, in any way, determining them.

Even this thin hope flies in the face of history.

The good news is that these failures may not reflect lack of prudence so much as high-toned nonsense about the efficaciousness of consciousness. Let's put the question bluntly. What if conscious moral or rational agents do not exist? What if human beings have been interrupting their natural capacity to make timely responses by substituting endless rounds of analysis and discussion? What if, instead of engaging and actualizing solutions, we have been preaching to one another under the assumption that we are each a sovereign source of moral and rational acts?

What if, while we have been distracting ourselves and one another with such frippery, opportunities have been knocking in vain?

A clue that something is wrong with the common sense view can be found in our inconsistent use of `agent claims'. The claim that personhood is innate and that 'the public' is ultimately responsibility for corporate and national behaviours absolves everyone directly involved – boards of directors, employees, customers and citizens. Individuals can only be guilty of criminal behaviour or treason!

Yet, in every other sense, individuals along corporate chains of command meet legal culpability requirements of, for example, *mens rea* at the time of *actus reus* (a guilty mind at the time of a guilty act). I propose that we take these exculpations seriously. Let's make an assessment of the harm some corporation has caused. If we then subtract however much responsibility individuals comprising the corporation acknowledge, the difference has to be ascribed to the corporation as an intention-generating entity.

One reason this argument will be given short shrift is that two exceptions have been bolted onto the notion that persons are moral and rational agents and ultimately responsible for corporate and national activity. The first is that we love to credit the exemplary conduct of institutions and nations to administrators and leaders. The idea of universal responsibility undermines the superior/subordinate relationships cherished by leaders and followers alike.

A robust sense of distributed responsibility would also challenge the disproportionate wealth and power enjoyed by leaders, who claim to have earned it because they are wellsprings of energy and creativity.

Perhaps more importantly, universal responsibility means followers would no longer get to enjoy perpetual childhood by leveraging deliberate acts of subordination and deference into claims of innocence.

The result is an unwholesome, often toxic brew of irresponsibility, subordination and arrogance. Followers get to be honorary persons, but not moral or rational agents in any way that matters. Leaders get rewards and perquisites with responsibility loopholes.

Thus , a corollary of the standard view - responsibility is integral to what it means to be human - is widely applauded but rarely adopted. David Suzuki and Nicholas Stern and a large contingent of *cognoscenti* and *Cassandras* pursue careers recommending that the public improve their decisions. They see themselves as leaders, asking followers to become better leaders with respect to what their bodies are getting up to.

They appear oblivious that the problems followers suffer from have important roots in the leader-follower relationships their careers depend upon.

The person as agent story has been finessed, massaged and inconsistently applied because human beings cannot afford to be consistently wrong about such an important issue. This would have had such catastrophic results that we would have already been forced to identify and repair our understanding. This is also why - even with sophisticated double-speak stratagems crediting and blaming leaders and villains for corporate and national behaviours — a sense of general culpability remains. The USA is deemed as an evil nation by millions, perhaps billions, of human beings, including many of its own citizens. It is hard to tell whether this means the USA is regarded as a creature with autonomous intentionality, or that it embodies the collective will of its citizens. Doubtlessly some fluid amalgam of both possibilities is in play.

This is a delicate balancing act however. We must negotiate a path between regarding persons as autonomous *choice engines* responsible for what they get up to or as nodes of behaviouristic/deterministic interactions. The latter would leave individuals with nothing to feel good about, or praise and blame themselves and one another for.

Either conclusion would upset the apple cart we are all perched upon. This cart has a few of us in drivers' seats; most of us pulling or pushing; and, it seems, an increasing proportion being thrown under the wheels.

Noam Chomsky - reportedly the most important intellectual alive – has an interesting take on the problem. Chomsky believes in personal freedom and he also believes that every person has a wonderful cognitive potential as we all seem to effortlessly acquire a language capable of what he termed a *torrential output.*

Chomsky also believes that, for post Industrial Revolution Western populations, this potency has been derailed or neutralized. Nefarious individuals, corporations and media interest groups have been managing the media and keeping 'the truth' to themselves. These consortiums have been leveraging wealth and power and 'manufacturing public consent'. Their ambition is simple: (1) advance corporate agendas and (2) generate ever more more wealth for ever fewer people.

Chomsky's solution is to blow the whistle on these proceedings. He does not regard the public as covertly or subconsciously complicit in these deceptions. Chomsky sees public compliance and consent as unwitting, as illicitly manipulated. His remedy — the only plausible, legitimate remedy — is to expose this deception and let a fully-informed public harness their superb consciousness and cognitive

Vernon Molloy

faculties to ameliorate these problems.

Chomsky fully understands how adroitly democratic forms of governance have been manipulated and controverted. In the USA and elsewhere, democracy has become a way to transfer responsibility for what is going on from leaders to followers, from winners to losers, from criminals to victims.

I have always thought Chomsky's critique of miscreant corporations and governments invited an ironic analysis. His indefatigable sense of outrage could be traced to the universal grammar he identified early on in his careet as an academic linguist. According to this hypothesis, human beings possess a remarkable capacity to assimilate and use language. Chomsky speaks of the 'torrential output' of language users - even in linguistically impoverished situations. The fact that individuals with such an amazing capacity for self-expression remain silent in the face of outrageous corporate and political behaviours must signify the presence of deception and charlatanism.

This is why it makes sense to Chomsky that, as soon as this deception is exposed, millions of inherently powerful but temporarily traduced persons will put things right!

A small irony is that Chomsky's indomitable activism may have prolonged public somnolence longer than might have otherwise been the case. Any person with with a sense of alarm over what is going on has a compelling reason for doing nothing. Look at the energy, courage and acumen Noam Chomsky has been investing! Look how things have been getting worse even so!

A supplemental conclusion is that people at the top are too powerful to be deflected - and/or that everyone else is too apathetic to be roused.

A larger ironic possibility is that everyone is standing down because we are all reluctant to put a shoulder to the wheel until we see enough people doing so to make it worth while.

Modern Problems, Ancient Perspectives

A third possibility — one I do not take *that* seriously — is that we are behaving badly and sanctioning toxic outcomes for a reason that dares not speak its name. We could each be solving a existential crisis - our fear of death and non-existence - by doing (or not doing) everything we can to make sure that those who survive us wish they hadn't.

To return to the issue of whether corporations and nations are forms of life, whenever citizens express patriotic feelings for homelands or have some point of view regarding other nations, they have more in mind than a pantheon of leaders and some history. There is something about being a citizen of Canada, the USA, England... that changes and charges populations in ineffable ways. These changes are culturally embedded and transmitted so that 'a people' becomes more than the sum total of present populations.

This is why older people in western nations continue to be wary of Germans and Japanese. They remember the Second World War — the exculpating Nuremberg trials notwithstanding. They remember a sense of something enormously malignant and alien in the world... a presence that had nothing to do with any German or collection of Germans.

Vague unease is as far as we go however. Hard questions: "Could it be that nations and corporations are agents in their own right?" or "Is there something in the German or Japanese air, water, way of life... that changes people irretrievably?" are not asked. To do so would call into question the conceit that human beings are persons continuously choosing what they get up to.

Finally, there are pragmatic reasons for maintaining flexible notions of persons and responsibility. Characterizing nations as intrinsically alive or innately good or evil would make it difficult to resume economic or political relationships after Johnny, or whatever is left of him, comes marching home from the war.

Vernon Molloy

Scapegoating

In spite of contradicting the `axiom of distributed responsibility' – the claim that all persons are moral and rational agents – scapegoating remains the one-size-fits-all defence against moral and rational indictments. Statements claiming that: "I was just doing my job"; "I was obeying the chain of command"; "I was doing what she who must be obeyed demanded"... are only slightly less common than talking about sports and the weather.

Scapegoating is also an excellent deterrent against pangs of conscience or anxieties that the something rotten in Denmark can be tracked back to what the people in Denmark are getting up to.

In America, the first decade of the Third Millennium saw dozens of leaders hauled before courts of law and public opinion. USA President George Bush's lacklustre response to the 9/11 crisis in 2001 continues to be criticized, while others accuse Republicans of over-reacting to terrorism.

In 2005, Mr Bush confessed his government's ineptitude in the aftermath of Hurricane Katrina. The debacle in Iraq was acknowledged in 2006 — a mea culpa that may have reflected the Grand Old Party's assessment of a bleak electoral prospect if confession and reparation was not offered up.

After all, what's the point of Christian fundamentalism if repentance, confession and absolution are not harnessed to political wagons?

A more worrisome implication of 'the axiom of distributed responsibility' may be lurking in politicians' minds. If citizens, workers and consumers ever figure out that they are the ultimate source of wealth and power, this realization could spawn grass roots enfranchisements not yet seen in human affairs!

Better to deflect such possibilities with crocodile tears and suitably awkward confessions as often as the need arises.

Modern Problems, Ancient Perspectives

Scapegoating has an excellent pedigree. The most remarkable example involves the belief that God the Father sent his Son to be sacrificed for the *sins of man*.

This Divine Repudiation of the idea of distributed, innate responsibility continues to have important economic and political benefits. To appreciate this we need to recall that Christianity's more fundamental tenet is that human beings are moral and rational agents. What we get up to is supposed to determine our spiritual and supernatural fate.

Think what a devastating impact this requirement would have had on profit-taking and meritocracies! Something had to be done to head off billions of moral and rational agents looking after one another's well-being!

A fix was not long coming. God sent his only begotten son to be tormented and crucified and thereby absolve the faithful of their sins. With this example in hand there was no need to lead thoughtful, moral lives. All that was required to attain heaven was faith and hope.

As well, a bit of charity has always been welcome. Charity is a wonderful balm for the bruised, marginalized, exploited, impoverished lives of populations living under the aegis of faith and hope. Charity is also a potent dissolver of poverty's character-building potential. Nothing reduces feelings of dignity and self-worth more effectively than needing and receiving hand-outs. Nothing extinguishes pointed questions about what is going on or rights talk as well.

As has also often been noted, religions also lubricate commercial and political machineries by encouraging the belief that present torments are trivial compared to the delights awaiting us in the next. Moreover, stoic endurance and long-suffering is a way of moving up the Divine food chain.

Not only is there no point making a fuss, doing so would be spiritually counterproductive.

Vernon Molloy

These examples are all rooted in the idea that human beings are made up of physical bodies at least occasionally controlled by incarnated or evolved persons.

Even so, even with this existentially-fraught story scaring the be-Jesus into us, had the `axiom of distributed responsibility' been consistently applied human affairs might have proven manageable.

This was not to be however. Instead we concocted a story wherein everyone is responsible for what they get up to, but some are more responsible than others. The gradient of responsibility starts at the bottom and reaches to Heaven. Beings along the way are proportionately responsible according to degree of elevation, with God the most responsible of all.

This dictum can be stretched to any size and shape according to arguments' requirements.

We remind ourselves as well that some human beings really are smarter, more energetic, more deserving... than others. The resulting propensity to doff caps has proven more destructive than the greed, selfishness and cruelty occupying moralists and Cassandras.

During the 20th century, 220 million people perished as combatants or `collateral damage' during two World Wars and dozens of smaller conflagrations.

Sorting populations into leaders and followers continues to be the fundamental strategm preparing populations for slaughter or exploitation:

1. as soldiers executing one another;
2. as workers and consumers struggling to take advantage of one another and their own other halves.

In a thousand ways, the claim that human beings are autonomous moral and rational agents perpetuates confusions and terrifying consequences. Soldiers continue to regard themselves as moral and rational agents because they seem themselves as having 'voluntarily abdicated' decision-making sovereignty during tours of duty. Soldiers under the chain of command see themselves acting out the will of their fellow citizens, channelled through election results and government decisions to go to war or engage in peacekeeping missions.

Citizens see themselves voting for military proceedings because nations A,B,C... have standing armies bristling with terrifying weapons.

In similar fashion workers and consumers see themselves responding to externalities including 'the global economy', outsourcing, automation and the need to remain competitive.

We take comfort that the incremental erosions of local well-being we see occurring are taking place under the aegis and protectipon of conscious human beings everywhere.

Finally, every accommodation made as poor and soon to be poor populations are harried along is stamped with their: *my choice* imprimatur. Because of this constant tweaking of the `agent file', tormented populations retain notions of innate sovereignty no matter how political and economic woes pile up.

In this way victims and losers assume some responsibility for what is happening to them; while their tormentors bank the fruits of righteous moral or rational choices.

My hope is that such examples clear a space to think about the cultural, psychological and economic antecedents determining how our lives are turning out. The issue does not involve seeking justice for past grievances or worrying about spilt milk but whether harms might be avoided in the future.

One question we might ask is simple. Have dictators, Prime Ministers and hubris-addled CEOs been mining the claim: "I am a person in control of my body" in ways that profit them and harm the rest of us?

Is this not the story sanctioning institutions, corporations and nations? Organizations are patterned upon the way we

Vernon Molloy

understand ourselves. We think we are `persons in charge' of our bodies and, through these bodies, corporations and nations.

A more realistic view is that organizations - especially urban organizations - depend upon populations sorted into agent/body, master/slave, strong/weak relationships....

Individuals who have been compromised in these ways are willing, perhaps eager, to lend themselves to whatever projects *organizations* have in mind. In urbanized settings, people need corporations for feelings of identity, direction, purpose — not to mention food, shelter and entertainment.

In such circumstances, we are needier than we were when we enjoyed relatively self-sufficient, community-centred and family-rich lives. We take enormous pride in our nation's exploits. We rejoice in *our athletes'* medals. The dignity of work and a regular pay cheque is claimed with a clear conscience.

Of course, if we happen work for a tobacco corporation and our careers involve killing people, we fall back on our one-size-fits-all explanation: "We were just been doing our job!"

What jobs entail, what their consequences consist of, are beyond the skill sets and post-descriptions of everyone involved.

Moreover, is it not the case that people choose to smoke? Or at least choose to begin smoking?

In every instance, consciences are clear. We are urbanized, specialized, well-fed, entertained and responsibility-free.

What's not to like?

A Clear Conscience

Urban populations, the disappearance of subsistence ways of living, the emergence of specialized employments... mean that everything necessary for corporations and nations to 'come alive' is in place. Specialization and urbanization provide individuals `prepared' to function as administrators, communicators, information gatherers, producers, defenders and clean-up crews. Specialization and urbanization, the absence of subsistence alternatives... , mean an increasing proportion of human beings have little choice save to make themselves available to corporate undertakings and to then vote in every way possible for corporate prosperity. One way or another, the prospects of human beings now depend upon what a few thousand or a few million corporations get up to. An increasing proportion of human beings depends upon them for everything — including externally-triggered conscious episodes courtesy of The Sports Network(TSN) and Reality TV.

More sophisticated palates depend upon talk shows a la Johnny Carson, David Letterman *et al*, where wit and sardonic observations allow audiences to take pleasure in the antics of leaders and followers. These dependencies have been capitalized upon by captains of industry brandishing fiduciary obligations to shareholders. They have been calculating how much they will be able to get away with, and how much of this they will be able to keep for themselves.[42] [43] As statistics demonstrate, things have been going very well.

> *"The US is dominated by a rich and powerful eli-*
> *te." So concludes a recent study by Princeton*
> *University Prof Martin Gilens and Northwestern*
> *University Prof Benjamin I Page.Multivariate*
> *analysis indicates that economic elites and orga-*

---

[42]http://www.bbc.com/news/blogs-echhochambers-27074746
[43]Satirical sketch of corporations and the road ahead:
http://www.upworthy.com/the-most-honest-and-awful-
corporate-ad-i-have-ever-laid-my-eyes-on-no-they-arent-
drunk-i-swear?c=fea

223

Vernon Molloy

> nised groups representing business interests
> have substantial independent impacts on US
> government policy, while average citizens and
> mass-based interest groups have little or no in-
> dependent influence.In English: the wealthy few
> move policy, while the average American has
> little power.

Identifying the beneficiaries of a state of affairs often does little to clarify how this state came to pass. Beneficiaries may look greedy and callous but may have become so because wealth and power came their way. Indeed, this is a useful way to think about equity and power issues. If you and I understand that present inequities have been distilled out of our lives and the lives of others like us, we are well-positioned to do something about them. (Presumably we are also *motivated* - which may be less true than we think.)

However understood, our circumstances should be contrasted with the ironic predicament powerful and wealthy individuals find themselves in. There is a good chance that they have been made greedy, callous and unwholesome by our careless regard for their spiritual well-being. By being inept and foolish, we seduced them into becoming selfish, greedy and wealthy!

Appearances notwithstanding, there are no winners in this story.

A pivotal element in these proceedings is the culturally-embedded conceit that human beings are persons owning and controlling their bodies. The reality is that bodies are complex events occasionally utilizing conscious episodes. These episodes allow more and wider experiences to bear upon problems and inform responses than the instincts, reflex arcs and conditioned responses other forms of life utilize.

Conscious episodes also make complicated responses possible by integrating elements and stages of projects that may take hours or years to complete.

These conscious episodes occur automatically if and only if required. They organize themselves into the picaresque tales

224

we think of as our lives.

Without a shred of evidence — in the face of logical problems — we turned this story upside down thousands of years ago. We regard bodies as *contactors, extensions, tools...*, as resources controlled by persons. The notion of persons owe its existence to conscious episodes, not the other way around. With this conceit in mind, we think of bodies as our means of interacting with the world. We think of ourselves as consciously controlling what our bodies get up to. We imagine ourselves vetoing external proceedings and deflecting harms. We see our bodies inhabiting an actual world. We become realists and common sense proponents.

In this way reality is turned upside down. The bodies and brains that are clearly the source of conscious episodes become *possessions* of the 'faculty of consciousness' and are imagined as *beasts of burden*.

What are conscious episodes? A simple explanation is that they are cognitive events wherein possibilities and dangers are evaluated in automatically-occurring thought experiments. The outcomes — which sometimes include actual responses and sometimes involve further thought experiments — are not the result of decisions made *by consciousness*. They are resolutions that occur *within consciousness*.

Intuitively these proceedings represent a small proportion of the physiological and neurological events constituting our lives. This is not to say that consciousness is not important. Conscious episodes expand and deepen responses. The resulting improved survivability spawned the ability to interpose increasingly sophisticated conscious intervals between external events and responses.

In other words, consciousness has the same aetiology, the same back story, as every evolutionary adaptation.

This is not what we think. Leveraged into claims that persons are not the subjects, beneficiaries or results of experiences... conscious episodes spawned realism, common-sense and and notions of exceptionalism. To give this remarkable story credibility, versions of monotheism eventually emerged — Christianity, Judaism and Islamism. These stories involve versions of *creationism*. However, the central function of monotheism is not to explain the existence of the universe. Monotheism's principal task is to underwrite the claim that there is something special about human beings, that we have a special place and purpose in the universe.

Progress has been made uprooting this nonsense. Darwin's challenge to intelligent design and creationism has been amplified by Richard Dawkins, Sam Harris, Christopher Hitchens and many others. They offer witty and scathing indictments of *Big Fairy* in the sky stories. What remains to be tackled, what will be more difficult to weed out, is the notion that there are *Little Fairies* within each of us, whose equally dubious credentials are not yet even part of the debate.

To be fair, not everyone has been on-side. The Dutch/Jewish philosopher Baruch Spinoza (1632-1677) thought notions of free will were analogous to arrows becoming conscious while in flight - and concluding that they had chosen the target they seemed to be aiming for! The idea of free will as a source of human conduct has no more traction in psychology than it does in chemistry, physics or mathematical equations.

Occasional scepticism proves the 'exceptional rule' however. Although free will claims lack logical credentials, they have been an important factor in human affairs for at least three thousand years. *Big Fairy* monotheism is regularly cited as an important source of conflict and suffering. These harms are small potatoes compared to the consequences of *Little Fairy* myths.

Indeed, the principal function of Big Fairy stories is to make Little Fairy claims plausible.

To take up this story from another perspective, according to Julian Jaynes consciousness is not an automatically occurring faculty distinguishing Homo sapiens from other creatures. Consciousness emerged because of a communication breakdown between the two hemispheres of the bicameral mind. Jaynes believe that this breakdown was noticed and recorded during the 7th century BC in the work of the blind Aeonian poet Homer. On Jaynes' reading, Homer wrote *The*

Iliad using 3rd person grammatical constructions, then adopted a 1st person stance in *The Odyssey*. Jaynes thought that the capacity for self-consciousness reflected in this 1st person point of view demonstrated that a threshold-crossing diminution of once seamless communication between the brain's two hemispheres had taken place.

Although the details are not critical Jaynes thinks a bundle of nerve fibres (the corpos collosum) connecting the hemispheres) and channels `big picture understandings' to the `dominant hemisphere' from the other half of the brain.

In the past, these messages looked and sounded like pronouncements by deities, angels, devils, monsters... projected upon the `awareness canvas' generated by memories and current events via sensory organs. Pre-literate human beings lacked literary or artistic ways to pass information from non-dominant to dominant hemispheres and had to resort to imaginary messengers who typically took on more or less human form and used languages and theatrical performances to get the job done.

This messaging could be thought of as a precursor to consciousness. The virtual theatres or stages involved would eventually `house' the images constituting conscious episodes. Along with their relevance to issues above, the proto-conscious experiences generated when non-dominant hemispheres sent information to dominant hemispheres means the hard problem bedevilling neuroscience and philosophy — why it feels like something to be a person — could have a simple explanation.

Neural events during these communications have to `feel like something' if complex understandings are to be understood as self-evoking and self-integrating. 'Feeling like something' means the organic significance (pain, pleasure...) of possible responses can be probed in thought experiments. If conscious episodes are initiated by internalized cultural resources as well as by local events, more or less constant streams of awareness can result. As Derek Parfit pointed out in *Reasons and Persons*, it is not difficult to understand why such experiences seem like continuous narratives. Since no one is aware of being unaware, awarenesses pick up where they leave off with no apparent interruption.

When I think back to yesterday's events my recollection skips over the intervening night's sleep.

As regards the contents of conscious episodes, introspection discovers that conscious agency plays no part in determining what is going on. Words, sentences, images, intentions, decisions appear unbidden. Creative people talk about consulting muses, of how the characters in novels take control of narratives, of how insights are delivered in dreams or as waking gestalts. This makes sense but only if consciousness is understood as result and not cause.

What leads us to ignore such straightforward explanations in favour of unquestioning belief in objects, artefacts, and creatures? Why do we think we are persons riding bodies through the world as if they were horses? Why do we imagine ourselves having our way with things, creatures and one another?

The answer is that when cognitive and cultural resources became available human beings found it seductive to talk about `persons within' - souls, beings, and selves. In *The Origins of Consciousness...*, Jaynes argued that this awakening had been foreshadowed by a long period - perhaps one hundred and fifty thousand years - during which self-consciousness had little to do with the way life proceeded. Awareness consisted of streaming events, some of which would eventually be promoted into named objects, entities and processes. Before this happened, there were gods and demons everywhere: robust, tangible entities with whom human beings regularly had visceral and occasionally intimate relationships.

On Jayne's account, these entities consisted of images projected upon the `virtual world retina' established by inter-hemisphere cognitive transfers. This is the way big-picture but not yet conscious intuitions and apprehensions are conveyed to the `hands-on' (usually left) brain hemisphere tasked with navigating the world and co-ordinating the bi-laterally symmetrical body halves neurally connected to bi-cameral brains.

During the thousands of generations before self-consciousness became a feature of ordinary lives, `big picture' communications involved hallucinations that seemed as real as real could be. These mirages were ancestors to, and cousins of, the dreams occupying Homo sapiens during rapid eye movement (REM) sleep. The difference is that early human beings did not have reliably self-conscious lives to wake up to. REM sleeps shaded into daily life. Gods, demons, fairies and hobgoblins continued to carry often-lugubrious messages from the furnace room of the brain (Freud spoke of the Dream Factory) to the dominant hemisphere — i.e, to the `machinery division' where responses would be hammered out.

My proposition takes this a step further. The world of common sense objects, creatures and entities is no less imaginary than the gods and demons that once populated the conscious episodes of early human beings and orchestrated their lives. These (phenomenal) objects and entities are the results of reifications similar to those fashioning images out of inkblots and transforming boulders and trees into monsters on dark nights.

Of course, most images are the results of unambiguous proceedings. They appear `rock solid'. They never make figure-ground reversals and so our private `phenomenal worlds', our waking dream of objects and events, seem tangible and real. This is illusory of course. Our perception of a mountain consists of a series of snapshots of a (very) slow moving event. Divine encounters — including sexual encounters with flying saucer crews — are more of the same. The flowing nature of conscious episodes is the result of mutually-invoking, seamlessly melding dispositional representations of experienced events. The innate liveliness of these representations of lively experiences explains how and why they spontaneously integrate into cognitive events, conscious episodes and responses.

229

Vernon Molloy

In the culture-rich post-Homerian world, once seamless communications between the hemispheres of bi-cameral minds transformed into discussions of things, objects, incarnation (birth), death and reincarnation. Supernatural events and creatures continued to be tasked with explaining anything not otherwise accounted for. Jaynes proposed that, as cultural resources, languages evolved and settled communities developed, once spontaneous communication with Gods, demons and familiars began to require rituals, totems and chicken entrails to occur. Driven by rationalism and scepticism - and self-serving opportunism by clever or beautiful people - the horizontal tapestry of gods and demons transformed into hierarchical and eventually monotheistic structures. Communication with these increasingly remote, omniscient and omnipotent beings required shamans, necromancers, oracles, Ouija boards, Tarot cards and – more often than not – collection plates.

Another consequence was a decline in community-centred conversations and independence. Previously mediated by local Gods, fairies and witches, community life collapsed into obeisance to the beautiful, wealthy and powerful individuals. These de facto icons replaced the pantheon of household, community and forest gods. Their sacred images smile at us from magazine covers at grocery store checkouts and smartphone screens.

This is one more reason most human beings now have idolatrous, voyeuristic relationships with leaders, athletes and beautiful people. We hang upon their words. We depend upon them for work to do, for security, for cargo-cult provisioning and round the clock entertainment.

We depend upon them with the patience of newly hatched birds.

Another consequence of moving from Fairies everywhere to one Big Fairy stories is worth thinking about. The loss of forest gods set the stage for monotheism and new forms of human conflict. For the first time populations by the hundreds,

230

thousands, millions... could be organized along ideological lines. Human beings have an instinct to subordinate themselves to anyone presenting as experienced and powerful. This was an excellent strategy until a few thousand years ago. When every human being arrived naked and defenceless and had to run hard just to stay alive, making use of people with experience, strength and resources was a good idea.

Unfortunately the instinct to look for leaders and take direction - that once made survival possible - has not gone away. We continue to seek out and submit to hierarchical systems proclaiming one God, one economic system, one set of values....

Of these institutions, religiosity is probably the most dangerous, especially now that our sense of the Divine includes "the marketplace", "survival of the fittest" and "manifest destiny".

Moreover, whether our allegiances involve Supreme Beings or just the best way of giving one another the business, competing ideologies have no alternative except to do battle. Ecumenical councils rhapsodising about religions getting along because they are only using different names for the same God carries little weight with faithful populations. The faithful know perfectly well that doctrinaire issues cannot be debated. If the logic chopping, hair-splitting intellectuals heading up today's religious institutions are lucky, their arcane mutterings about reconciliation will continue to be ignored.

The alternative is that they will be put to death. Populations serving different Gods know that compromise is impossible. Anyone with a different understanding must be converted or exterminated. The existential alternative is so unspeakable that bomb-belt terrorism or genocide is a legitimate option.

As Christian and secular nations continue to demonstrate, smart bombs, drones, economic sanctions and client states to keep things that go bump in the night safely 'over there', are preferable. However, if these 'civilized measures' fail, we have the BOMB — and we are pretty sure our theocratic (presently

Islamist) adversaries do not. A great deal of energy is being invested to make sure that this continues to be the case.

This is a good idea. The mutually-assured destruction deterrent (MADD) that kept USSR and western nations on short leashes during the Cold War is unlikely to work with people anxious to qualify for a martyrs' reward.

Indeed, quite a few people are worried that Christian and Muslim factions are covertly girding themselves for Armageddon. Fundamentalists on both sides appear to think the weapons now in play — nuclear, chemical, biological, terrorist — could trigger the long-awaited global holocaust that will make all their dreams come true.

I remain guardedly optimistic that this will not happen. I think the wealthy will do everything possible to prevent such a conclusion. They have never had so much skin in the game. They have never had so much to lose.

Let's hope they succeed.

Unfortunately, I don't think most of us will enjoy the alternative they have in mind any more than we would have enjoyed Armageddon.

I recognize that these suggestions are merely sketches. Accordingly I will attempt to link a few of them together. An important suggestion — one that many have made — is that self-consciousness spawns a tangled web of anxieties, greed and hubris. Hubris - a sense that one is innately entitled, exceptional, part of a special class of people... is especially problematic. Hubris is an important reason human beings find it difficult to regard themselves as simply part of the natural order.

The advantages accruing to consciously-abetted vantage points will become manageable if and only if human beings move to a 'flow through', inclusive understanding - i.e., a non realist model of reality.

The fact that it remains important to me to point our the *originality* of this worry is an example of just such hubris. In other words — instead of `nothing held back engagements' like squirrels crossing roads — the arrogance attaching to culturally embedded notions of personhood obstructs experiences that could actually achieve autonomous beings or persons.

This is a great irony. Folklore, fairy tales, sociological projects such as David Riesman's *The Lonely Crowd*... are full of talk about the remarkable individuals, even nations, that can emerge when human beings confront difficulties freed of the need to defend and admire their own excellence.

This ironic state of affairs can be expressed in an equation: the more a person or nation achieves and accomplishes the less likely it is that that person or nation will continue to achieve and accomplish.

Another way of saying this is that nations can become so accomplished that their citizens feel little need to accomplish anything personally. This is what Riesman thought was happening in America in the 1950's. The immigrants settling the New World were refugees from Europe. They had been living *outer-directed* (rigid, rich/poor, aristocratic/serf, Catholic/Protestant) lives. When they landed in America they did as much as possible to recreate these circumstances but lacked the numbers and resources to do so for a hundred years or more. Survival issues, the lack of public infrastructure and governance... generated the need to become *inner-directed*. The creative, energetic results spawned the USA we know today.

These successes also dissolved the need to be inner-directed and — since being inner-directed is a demanding, stressful state we seem inclined to avoid — new world populations became *other-directed* as soon as progress and development allowed.

The resulting collapse into infantilism is how Riesman described North Americans a half century ago: coasting through life, bragging about their nation's accomplishments, watching sports events and other pornographies — and consuming so many corn dogs that seventy per cent would be clinically obese by the 3rd Millennium.

Vernon Molloy

This is not just an American problem. Populations in developed nations have more in common these days than at any point in history. As soon as we could 'afford it', we all travelled down development road so far that even our capacity to live vicariously seems to be drying up. Entertainment and sports events have to be increasingly spectacular to hold our attention. Of course this could be the result of competition among spectacle suppliers. Alternatively, we may have so many options these days that none seem worthwhile.

There could be an even simpler explanation. Developed, urbanized, specialized nations have become as womb-like as money and technology can make possible. This means that the usual person's 'organic vocabulary' — neurological representations of what hot and cold, effort, hunger, friendship... feel like — are no longer being assimilated. Restricted to spectator and consumer experiences, specialized educations and employments, enfeebled by insatiable appetites and relentless convenience... urban populations are becoming infantilized.

If we never have days when we are hot, cold, hungry, tired... if we never experience work and companionship... how can linguistic, visual depictions of vigorous lives evoke empathic feelings? How can tragedies or atrocities elicit responses? How can predictions about, or depictions of, the consequences of global warming or AIDS resonate?

The capacity for internally-sourced self-consciousness is the sine qua non of everything interesting about human beings. Without self-consciousness as a 'receiving entity', recognition of remarkable events (indeed, of any events) ceases to exist. The problem seems to be that, along with making exquisite lives possible, self-consciousness undermines the circumstances responsible for conscious episodes. It does this by setting up `agent within' conceits and *pre-paring* individuals for co-option into corporations and nations. In this regard human beings are indeed multi-taskers! We are capable of simultaneous integrations and incorporations. We can, for example, be dutiful citizens, workers and consumers,

234

Modern Problems, Ancient Perspectives

Catholics or Protestants or Muslims.

(Teasing a bit here! One cannot be a Catholic and a Protestant simultaneously!)

Corporations and nations are tirelessly engaged in self-aggrandizing progress and development projects. The resulting machinations involve promising citizens, workers, shoppers... further consciousness-obliterating conveniences, labour-saving devices and securities.

To appreciate how ironic this is, we need to understand that conscious episodes and self-consciousness are not reliably-occurring evolutionary achievements. Self-consciousness flows from the simultaneous presence of cognitive machineries and cultural resources. This is a chicken-or-egg first issue. Cultural resources exist because historical activities and best practices found ways to record and disseminate information among communities and across generations. What is missing in discussions of commercialization and globalization is recognition that such cultural resources are *necessarily* the fruit of on-the-ground community activities, that they have short shelf lives and must be renewed every generation.

As soon as this fails to happen, human beings fall back to their biological `factory settings'. This can happen with terrible quickness. We are always only one generation away from ways and means of living characterized by Thomas Hobbes as "nasty, brutish and short".

For at least 150,000 years, Homo sapiens have been as capable as you and I of forming complex memories, generating points of view, integrating experiences and noticing recurring events. These capacities existed but, aside from burial customs and cave drawings at such places as Lascaux in south west France 17,000 years ago, there is scant evidence of self-awareness. Only during the last three thousand years have mankind's cultural fires burned brightly enough for us to glimpse ourselves and one another and see beyond *right here, right now* issues.

Without cultural resources lending successive generations a larger and larger leg up, human beings would not have imagined a world of object and entities. We would not have 'capitalized upon' opportunities for profit, power and, occasionally, understanding. We would not have glimpsed the wonders of relativity theory and quantum physics and we would not have any understanding of how and when the universe came into existence.

As we are also seeing, this self-awareness has a dark side. Notions of identity and agent-hood can lead to destructive impulses and responses. We name useful events as objects and entities and then try to possess as many as possible. We attempt to explain their comings and goings — the easy ones with homely explanations, the subtler with `scientific enquiries'. We worry about what identity through change means. We question where objects and entities come from and what happens when they pass out of existence.

These puzzling issues help explain why the notion of persons is so seductive. Our sense of personhood includes the idea that something about us survives across time and through change. This is wonderfully attractive because it opens up the possibility that we might survive death.

This sense of separateness from the vertiginous world (cf., Immanuel Kant's noumenal realm, Plato's Realm of Forms...) reduces the intuition that we are really only eddies in a swirling, flowing reality. I sometimes glimpse that it is possible to let go of self-hood, to stop defending what is already lost and just enjoy the ride.

I am still working on this but one thing is clear. Our sense of uniqueness and separateness rationalizes indifference and greed:

1. Nothing that happens to the world necessarily affects me.
2. It makes sense to grab as much as possible.

As if this was not trouble enough, anxieties associated with separateness and isolation have always been harnessed by gifted, energetic or happily situated (think: Kardashians) individuals. For leaders, would-be leaders and people farmers, existential conundrums mean enhanced opportunities to acquire wealth and power. Most human beings are not really interested in becoming rich — at least if significant investments of time and energy are involved. We do, however, seem fatally inclined to follow anyone with a plan — especially if there will be prizes!

Even if no booty is involved, we pay attention to leaders, media stars, and fabulous athletes.... We like it that there are enough villains and thieves around to warrant police departments, homeland security agencies and standing armies. Villains and thieves also make the rest of us look good. We are soothed by the presence of corporations offering goods and services, and at least promising employments so that they can one day be purchased.

Along with these benefits, excellent corporations and villainous individuals lend direction and purpose to our lives. They define one end of a moral/economic/political gradient. They live large. With their help, you and I are able to imagine that we too are not only human beings but *persons*.

Because of these contributions to our sense of identity and possibility, the famous and infamous are encouraged to harvest as much as they can from us. The more they succeed, the more our lives are reduced, the more exciting the prospect becomes!

Finally: a logical clarification. The events responsible for the contents of conscious episodes have necessarily moved on before awareness occurs. *Awareness is always awareness of* some event (something) that has already occurred.

The ensuing sense that something is going on generates the apparent need to speak of space, time and causality. This brings to mind a debate that occurred between Leibniz and Newton in 1715-1716[44] . Newton believed that absolute space

---

[44](http://www.friesian.com/space.htm)

and time existed. This space and time contained the objects and substances comprising the universe, and that a universal simultaneous present orchestrated events. Against this, Leibniz argued that notions of space and time were illusions generated by perceived spatial relationships among objects and their apparent causal connections: some events preceded others and so were assumed to cause them either entirely or in part.

Immanuel Kant suggested a third possibility: space, time and causality were *a priori* contributions of human mind.

In the proposal I have been sketching, these stories (ontological explanations) overlook an important problem. They talk about images of events as if these images existed in real time in a real, external world. Kant's and Leibniz' suggestions overlook the same problem. Leibniz said

> *"I hold space to be something merely relative, as time is; ...For space denotes, in terms of possibility, an order to things which exist at the same time, considered as existing together."*

My account emphasizes that the need for causal explanations is also illusory. We think we need to explain things only after we imagine them into existence. Causal explanations do important predictive work but have no further significance. In other words, images are 'spatial predictions' achieved by gestalts. Causal explanations are temporal predictions motivated by reliable associations among spatial predictions.

Thus,the space and time in Newton's and Leibniz' models are motivated by the same chimera populating common sense philosophies and realism.

By way of bonus, a process-centred alternative to realism and common sense accounts for the spontaneous, lively character of conscious episodes. This celerity has two sources. Almost everything human beings experience becomes a memory. (How this is achieved is not important for this argument.) What common sense and realism overlook is that memories are not inert. They are representations of *events* — not of inert *things.*

The second source of liveliness involves unresolved tensions in images. Since images involve cognitive activities parcelling and curating sensations, a great deal of cutting away, overlooking, discarding... is involved. As a consequence, images are inexplicable in and of themselves. Explanations must be fashioned bridging gaps between and among them.

To the extent that causal explanations are useful, they reflect proceedings contextualizing the objects and entities we become aware of. Causal explanations are second-order processes bridging among entities and objects imagined into existence. Because they are not crystallized into apparently inert things, causal explanations capture more of the flow of being than the entities and objects they are called upon to explain.

For this reason causal explanations come closer to the pre-reflective lives of squirrels and bicameral human beings. They come closer to reflecting what is going on before consciousness seduced us into realism and common-sense.

With so much on the table, it is not surprising that we resist challenges to realism and common-sense. What could be more fundamental to a sense of well-being than the notion that we are sharing a universe with other creatures and objects? We grudgingly acknowledge that processes cause objects to come into existence, endure for a time as identifiable and re-identifiable entities and then vanish. These anabolic, catabolic (building up, tearing down)... processes remain unwelcome guests at the party we have been throwing.

These catabolic processes must be guarded against with "stitch in time" homilies, oil changes and visits to gymnasiums. We talk about entropic degradation, rusting, wearing out, ageing and death. The objective is always the same: to leave realism and common-sense on the table - even if this means being tormented by 'winds of change' — by the fact that one cannot, as Heraclitus warned, step into the same river twice.

Vernon Molloy

We have a vague premonition that Heraclitus was right somehow but we do not know what to make of it. Obviously always changing water will not stand still to be stepped into even once. The even more unsettling intuition is that we are not the same person from moment to moment either, and cannot step into the same river twice for another reason!

We might therefore ask — if only as a thought experiment — whether the idea of reality as a succession of tormented, thing-laden moments is not mistaken.

Why worry about such questions? Why not leave them for metaphysicians with nothing better to do? The answer is that realism and common sense is the philosophy we have been living by for centuries. Facile realism and impatient common-sense positions human beings to claim exceptionalism for Homo sapiens and to then to claim exceptionalism again and again *within* populations and among nations.

False notions have consequences. Preoccupied with the comings and goings of images, distracted by discussions of origins and fates, we have been comparing and contrasting spilt milk anecdotes and regarding such discussions as intrinsically valuable. Our faint hope is that these discussions are worthwhile because they improve the chance that actual responses will be undertaken further down the conversational road.

Such gossip, such deflections, such deferrals... are as common as grass. The question is whether they are survivable. There are benefits to be gained distilling understandings from experiences. These benefits include tools, techniques and community projects. There are overarching benefits to be gained distilling 'laws of nature' from recurring patterns and central tendencies. (This what the NSA refers to as *metadata*.)

The litmus test is whether such investigations assist or obstruct well-being - with well-being understood in *process* and not *realism/common-sense* terms.

A final thought is about the risk of living in a world of imagined objects and entities. In *Being and Nothingness: an essay in phenomenological ontology* written in 1943, Jean-Paul Sartre described authentic individuals as those with the courage to have goals (projects intending to change being-in-itself or the world of facticity) and to resolutely struggle to achieve them.

In Sartre's view the only time authentic beings cease to strive is at the moment of death - when *pour-soi* (being-for-itself) collapses into *en-soi* (being-in-itself). His point was that people who refuse to dream and struggle are living in what he termed *bad faith*. They are pretending to be dead.

Those who pass their lives gossiping about imaginary objects and the vagaries of leader/follower relationships have much to explain.

Having lived with intimations of my own mortality (and unsolicited observations regarding other shortcomings), I eventually realized that claims of person-hood and agency are themselves forms of death. The reason is simple. Every concept is the corpse of an event or a number of events. Such awarenesses are snapshots or brief videos of a few events along the trajectories of our lives. They often participate in further conscious episodes and can contribute in important ways to understandings.

As we have seen, such experiences can also spawn fantasies that individuals are God-like persons sourcing and implementing un-caused choices.

None of these claims are possible. Persons do not have transcendent, insular or ontologically significant status. Persons are self-imaging, self-imagining fruits of whatever is going on. Persons necessarily lag the processes or events responsible for the conscious episodes generating this sense of being. It does not matter whether this lag is measured in picoseconds or years. Just as the sun could have vanished 8.5 minutes ago with no one the wiser, you or I may have already ceased existing as a viable *organization* although our self-awareness continues for a few milliseconds.

This seems irrelevant because we are accustomed to thinking in terms of `past, present, future'. To repeat what may have been the original challenge to realism, Heraclitus (c. 535 - 475

241

Vernon Molloy

BC) observed that no interval is so short that it cannot be divided again.

The challenge to realism is that the notion of a present interval collapses when examined. When any sum is divided endlessly remainders asymptotically approach Zero.

(Calculus provides a way of summing such divisions — so hares can overtake tortoises mathematically as well as in practice.)

What does this leave us? Human awareness is wide and deep and focal points are needed to integrate the representations constituting consciousness. (Jacques Lacan described this as the hole at the centre of awareness.) Had awareness remained at this level of sophistication, human life would have continued in innocent, pristine ways. Anthropological investigations suggest that this was exactly how matters proceeded for most of Homo sapiens' one hundred and fifty thousand year history. However, accumulating cultural resources eventually combined with existing cognitive endowments and generated points of view.

Before we knew it, these points of view became the proto-persons named and celebrated when birthing events occur. The problem was, sooner or later, every one of these persons died.

What to do? Since we were already in the habit of identifying and naming things, we simply divided these points of view, these persons, into minds and bodies and added a few second tier embellishments: self, soul, entity, essence, noumenal being....

All that was missing was a story associating cultural names (Tom, Dick, Jane, Maxine) with souls. Before long, Tom, Dick, Jane, Maxine... were equipped with corporeal and spiritual essences. The corporeal side became realism. The spiritual side included persons rattling around in heads and owning and controlling bodies.

Finally we had a story we could live with – a story in which supernatural destinies and human exceptionalism seemed to make sense.

Cosmological Aside

> *I remember something... about the ancient Greeks' notion of time: the past is in front of you, discernible in all its detail. It's the future that walks at your heels, unseeable; about to catch you.*[45]

We might also consider the significance of the fact that human beings cannot apprehend themselves for the same reason yardsticks cannot measure themselves. No matter how cognitively well-endowed or technologically sophisticated human beings become, conscious episodes cannot have real-time relationships with their contents.

Awarenesses always involve belated representations of tiny bits of whatever it is that is going on.

The best we can do is infer that relevant events took place a nanosecond or a century before awaremess.

This is also time to notice that you and I cannot have identical experiences of the 'same event' - and not just because of epistemological difficulties. What is going on for each of us is unique because we are 'reporting back' from different points of view. This is another transcendental argument: if we were not reporting from unique vantage points we would not be different persons.

It is not hard to see how thousands of years of such reports spawned culturally-embedded expectations of more to come and a sense that human beings are, in fact, persons authoring activities and projects and receiving appropriate rewards or punishments.

Do such expectations - especially when supplemented with statistical and anecdotal evidence of phenomenal objects, entities, and causal relationships - demonstrate corresponding junctures or partitions in processes underwriting conscious

---

[45]Barbara Quick: Northern Edge, (New York: Donald I. Fine Inc, 1990, p.175)

episodes?

I think the answer has to be no. Any such claim would require explaining how these partitions came to be, and how they came to be organized just the way they are.

The best way, perhaps the only way, to avoid such conundrums is to not talk about the universe as a fait accompli but as a work in process — even if conversationalists hedge their bets with weasel words such as `evolving' or `unfolding', that leave realism's core premise of *material actuality* intact.

During the last two centuries the Newtonian universe has been supplanted by Einstein's relativistic cosmology. Deterministic, either-or, thing-based analyses have given way to quantum mechanics and probabilistic models.

In the secular world, object-centered equations are retained provisionally; even while they are being refined with progressively fine-grained macro and micro investigations and analyses.

This is a `work in process', with entities and objects no longer enjoying pride of place. Modern cosmologies do not really require notions of substances, never mind substances parcelled into things. Such questions as...

- Does the world exist?
- How do I know you exist?
- What is the meaning of causality?
- How can identity and change be reconciled?

are all attempts to understand the origin, interaction and fate of phenomenal objects. These attempts are occurring because human beings occasionally worry about what is going on beneath the events they have identified and named.

Carving objects and entities out of whatever is going on generates phenomena that seem to come into existence, endure for a while and then vanish. The need for brute-force causal explanations is a by-product of taking culturally-abetted imaginary worlds as gospel truth.

Modern Problems, Ancient Perspectives

Sartre's notion of pre-reflective awareness - the sense we sometimes have of footsteps in an adjoining or upstairs room - suggests an analogy. Such episodes become images or apprehensions depending upon whether some organic agenda in the person 'sort of hearing' footsteps causes these sounds to become objects of conscious interest. (I could have used peripheral vision to make this point, but peripheral vision events moving eyeballs is so common that its sense is less dramatic.)

The apparent simultaneity of objects and events: storms, lightening strikes, eclipses, the reliable presence of trees and creatures... comprising the phenomenal world of 'local individuals' should not surprise us. This simultaneity, this apparently-shared present interval, reflects the proximity of relevant processes.

The occupants of vehicles travelling at the same speed and in the same direction on multi-lane highways experience similar (albeit brief) universes of simultaneity. More of the same does not warrant more complicated explanations.

We are being carried along in the current of existence. The fact that we happen to be keeping abreast is why we are able to have conversations.

Vernon Molloy

No Idea Squirrels

A few housekeeping questions: Why are causal - what causes what - questions so interesting? The answer is that paying attention to such associations is how human beings harvest the significance of experiences. This is also how we differ from creatures whose lives are driven by immediate events and physiological states. Other forms of life rely upon camouflage, fecundity, ferocity or strength for survival. Human beings prosper by informing responses from deeper and wider pools of experience.

This is why squirrels crossing roads or birds flying, fish swimming... are aware but not aware that they are aware. Consciousness — the reification of objects, entities, and processes — is not relevant to such adaptive strategies. There is neither need for, nor possibility of, becoming subjects of experience; of having anything like Sartre's *being for itself* experiences. Squirrels have no idea that they are part of a world full of trees, other squirrels and predators.

Feelings of opportunity or alarm on their behalf, that occasionally occur in you and I, occur because images of squirrels, birds, dogs... have taken on a second life in our awareness.

We depend upon animals not being self-aware subjects of experience whenever we enslave them as pets, herd them into abattoirs or cause species to become extinct, apparently at the rate of 200 per day[46]. As magisterial persons riding bodies

[46]According to the UN Environment Programme, the Earth is in the midst of a mass extinction of life. Scientists estimate that 150-200 species of plant, insect, bird and mammal become extinct every 24 hours. This is nearly 1,000 times the "natural" or "background" rate and, say many biologists, is greater than anything the world has experienced since the vanishing of the

around in the world, we seem to regard the extinction of an entire species as equivalent to the death of one human being. Western nations occasionally pass animal cruelty legislation and protest seal hunts; not noticing supermarket shelves groaning under the weight of slaughtered creatures.

Human foetuses can be, and frequently are, aborted because they do not meet 'immigration quotas' into the 'land of the living'. The only stipulation is that the foetus not have developed enough to be viable.

In many nations criminals are executed whenever their crimes are deemed sufficiently heinous that they have forfeited the right to live.

Until recently slavery was commonplace in Canada, Britain and the United States.... Black people were regarded as non-human and women were only recently recognized as persons.

> On Oct. 18, 1929, women are finally declared "persons" under Canadian law. The historic legal victory is due to the persistence of five Alberta women -- Emily Murphy, Nellie McClung, Irene Parlby, Louise McKinney and Henrietta Muir Edwards.[47]

This bigotry is even more devastating in the guise of economic strategies brutalizing 3rd and 4th world lives and undermining well-being in 1st world nations.

Unfortunately, hypocrisy, malevolence and usury are not our most important problems. These behaviours are consequences and not causes except in the sense that they set the stage for more of the same. The question to ask is what lies behind such events and whether repairs are possible. Forensic analysis, reductionism, determinism, scientific inquiries... are only examining the images of birds, squirrels, human beings... in our minds. The plan is to exhume `flight recorders' and figure out what went right or wrong.

---

dinosaurs nearly 65m years ago.
http://www.huffingtonpost.com/2010/08/17/un-environment-programme-_n_684562.html
[47]http://www.cbc.ca/archives/categories/politics/rights-freedoms/general-2/women-become-persons.html

Vernon Molloy

This is often useful, but the data is always limited. Objectified understandings (realism or common-sense) involve looking for simple causes and consequences. Understanding the context of causal claims illuminates them in useful, often surprising ways. Intuitively we understand that objects should be thought of as black boxes containing clues as to what went on during journeys.

Indeed, delving into the contents of black boxes is well-underway. As deterministic or scientific enquiries proceed the way we understand objects becomes more sophisticated on one hand and less certain on the other. Quantum physics certainly has this flavour. Richard Dawkins' discussion of extended phenotypes is an excellent secular example.

We will know when these investigations are complete because there will be no object remaining, only numbers locating events in coordinate systems.

Until we get this done, we risk glossing over, parcelling up or otherwise dismissing the most interesting aspects of experience.

Another harm involves the way objectification and realism clouds our understanding of nations and corporations. We pay attention to the conduct and personalities of leaders. The role of foot soldiers, followers and consumers in the genesis and conduct of leaders is ignored, even though they are the sine qua non of everything going on.

Adolph Hitler would have remained a megalomaniac with a bad haircut had millions of Germans not invested in his fantasies.

More importantly, if `the universe' is thought of not as a creation but as a streaming event, we would have to rethink what moral and rational agency means.

Until we get this done analysing, proselytizing, adjuring one another to do better... cannot recover spilt milk or prevent further losses.

Modern Problems, Ancient Perspectives

A case can be made that brutality, irresponsibility, missed opportunities... are more likely when human beings regard themselves as agents inhabiting a world full of things, entities and events. Separated-out, objectified individuals are inclined to pass their lives acquiring and defending property and possessions.

Indeed, the need to defend ourselves often boils up from acquiring stuff and then being forced to protect it from others with similarly acquisitive urges. I do not suggest that an event-based cosmology would dissolve violence and greed, only that it might make these tendencies a little more manageable.

Replacing realism and common sense with an event-based cosmology would have another benefit. We would be less likely to think of ourselves as Little Gods enjoying collegial relationships with this or that *Big God.*

I am sure you know what I am talking about. I was raised as a Catholic. In spite of my best efforts to eradicate or contain them, I still have religious notions rattling around in my head. The fact is, almost all human beings have been exposed to a God story.

The idea of the Big God we all somehow have privileged access to provides a one-size-fits-all rationalization for enslaving, exploiting, tormenting and exterminating one another.

We need to repair these understandings and we need to rethink the way intimations that `something is rotten in Denmark" are invested. Letters to editors, marches, and learned disquisitions... are messages passing among ghosts. They are useful only if they contribute to better responses. More generally, realizations are valuable if and only if they are translated into responses. How do ghosts manage this? Consciousness is best understood as a series of elaborate, sustained conditioned responses. Conditioned responses involve predictions about where things are headed. These anticipations can guide the throwing of stones to bring down a rabbit. They can initiate the cultivating of soils with a crop in mind. They can encourage trips to gymnasiums because we expect push-ups and jogging to yield strength and health.

By the way, there are more process philosophers per square foot in gymnasiums than anywhere else in the world. On the other hand, the object-laden common sense model explains sports fans, media junkies, ideologues and fanatics rather well. They seem unconcerned that they will never get those hours, weeks, years... back. I think this is because they regard themselves as having already arrived, as *fait accompli.*

This is what happens when we become persuaded that we are Little Gods. Intuitively, Little Gods arrive fully fledged with no requirement to experience, learn, assimilate, reflect or grow. Just by existing, Little Gods qualify as point sources of wisdom, truth and beauty. This is certainly how urbanized, specialized populations regard themselves.

How else to explain the fact that, on February 25, 2014, the issue *de jour* involved the amount of 'screen time' North America's young people are content with?

> *According to a recent study, the average 8- to 10-year-old spends nearly 8 hours a day with a variety of different media, and older children and teenagers* (http://www.psychologytoday.com/basics/adolescence) *spend 11 hours per day. Presence of a television (TV) set in a child's bedroom increases these figures even more, and 71% of children and teenagers report having a TV in their bedroom. Young people now spend more time with media than they do in school — it is the leading activity for children and teenagers other than sleeping* (http://www.psychologytoday.com/basics/sleep).[48]

The palpable alarm one senses in such discussions signals that we may be crossing a threshold with respect to understanding the costs and benefits of social media, smart phones, texting and other disengaged urban activities.

Unhappily, if moralisers and proselytizers have demonstrated

---

[48] *http://www.psychologytoday.com/blog/momma-data/201311/screen-time-gets-time-out-again*

anything over the centuries, it is that passing insights around among ourselves has nothing to do with solving problems. No matter how excellent our deliberations, discussions or speeches, "planning is not planting".

For one hundred and fifty thousands years, human beings prospered — or at least survived — on the merits of cognitive endowments and the ways these endowments contributed to individual and community prosperity. We have yet to demonstrate that we can survive the imaginary selves we went on to concoct; never mind the corporations and nations fashioning themselves using our truncated urban lives as building blocks.

The rest of the story is that corporations, religions, nations... are more like cancers or jellyfish than living beings. They are not aware of themselves and they certainly have no regard for you and I.

Vernon Molloy

Are Corporations Alive?

The search for alien life forms may be overlooking a nearby possibility. To the extent that you and I function as their wings, claws and specialized organs, corporations and nations exist as functional arrangements. Are they alive in more provocative ways?

Since I have been reworking the notion of `living entity' I hope the question no longer seems completely outlandish or entirely metaphorical.

Whether primitive or sophisticated, whether amoeba or *Homo sapien sapien,* creatures consist of symbiotic arrangements of thousands, millions, sometimes billions, of cells engaging in synergistic relationships achieving mutual survival.

Human beings demonstrate what can happen when such synergies cross thresholds of complexity and become capable of conscious episodes.

There are of course important differences between living creatures and corporations. Corporations and nations are assembled utilizing complex beings like you and I in complex ways. This means they can instantly become large and powerful.

Corporations and nations enjoy another advantage. They lack biologically-defined lifespans.

This is not perfect immortality. It simply means that corporations and nations are no more likely to perish tomorrow than today.

Even so this is pretty good immortality, and it introduces an ominous possibility. Although it is possible to regard corporations and nations as forms of life, they are 'organized' so primitively, so parasitically, that they are more like cancers battening upon and consuming the host organisms that make them possible.

Modern Problems, Ancient Perspectives

The process of co-option and assimilation begins as soon as human beings are born.

Nations and corporations are not aggregates of human beings who had already chosen to be Canadian, American, Catholic, Protestant, Hindu or Muslim. We have been indulging a dangerous fantasy.

No matter what vision statements are involved, organizations embody intentions that would not and could not have emerged in their absence.

In chicken/egg/chicken fashion, corporations and nations come into existence by co-opting and organizing human beings and creatures into alien forms of life . Working with already-evolved, already-viable entities, nations and corporations have not been constrained by any need to pursue sustainable, survivable activities.

In other words, corporations and nations are not good at self-preservation. They never went through the checks and balances, the survival of the fittest gauntlets, qualifying and moulding organic forms of life. This is why corporations and nations have no interest in moral and rational issues.

Corporations cannot experience fear or empathy. Existential terrors do not keep them awake at night. This is why we should not be putting all of our eggs in their baskets.

Vernon Molloy

Foreword

I wrote the first version of the Truth Table in 1990, more than twenty-five years ago. This was well before my present understanding of realism and common sense 'materialized'. I have no idea whether these notions boiled up as a by-product of other stuff going on 'down below' or out of the 'externalities' we all spend time digesting.

I have come to understand how and why self-aware episodes spawn notions that the world is actual and tangible and that we are entities situated within this world.

There is no doubt that sorting experiences into categories, partitions, either/or relationships... helps make sense of what is going on. This is just another application of the benefit of parcelling sensations into objects, entities and sets of objects and entities.... Both allow human beings to organize experiences that would otherwise be computationally intractable.

We are similarly hard-edged about the computational consequences of carving point sources of cause/effect relationships out of the Universal Event: good/bad; right/wrong; present/not present; true/false....

Partitioning this enormous, buzzing confusion helps, but this simplifying also set the stage for pernicious us/them divisions and other bigotries. These partitions obstruct nuanced understanding even as they help make languages possible and conversations concise and rich in meaning.

What we must hope for is that these approximations evolve into languages and understandings that are sufficiently sophisticated that partitions can be dispensed with. I have an excellent example. The calculus uses numbers and symbols to capture truths that numbers and symbols cannot express directly.

In *Truth Tables* I apply a simple version of this strategy to relationships, possessions and *The World* wherein these interactions are said to take place.

254

Truth Tables

In every life I am aware of, the world is sorted into three arenas:

- self;
- possessions and responsibilities – home, family, job;
- whatever is left over.

Although this makes sense for species that can be regarded as having families and instinctive responsibilities (i.e., chickens, mammals, human beings, but not frogs and turtles), it is turning out to be toxic for 'modern' human beings.

Part of the problem is that we have the capacity to represent the world to ourselves in our imaginations, to carve these representations into segments, and then act as if the results reflect naturally-occurring divisions.

There is a way to illustrate the problem. If we apply the truth table for an AND GATE – all inputs must be TRUE for the output to be TRUE – an interesting picture emerges. An AND gate (a concept familiar to anyone involved in switching or logic circuitry) can be thought of as a series of valves in a water line. For water to flow, all valves must be open. If one valve is closed the output will be 0.

This is the AND Gate symbol:

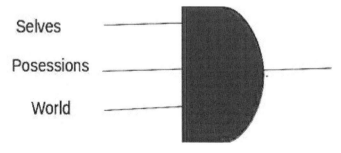

AND gates can have as many "tails" or inputs as one likes. Our model requires three – one for each area of concern. Each input has two possible states: 0 and 1; *false* and *true*. In this account, "1" represents engagement and "0" represents disengagement.

The input-output *truth table* for any 3-tailed AND GATE is straightforward. There are 2^n combinations, where n represents the number of inputs. Thus, 3 inputs means 2 x 2 x 2 = 8 possible combinations. The following sets out these possibilities:

Row #	Self	Stuff	World	Result
1	0	0	0	0
2	1	0	0	0
3	0	1	0	0
4	0	0	1	0
5	0	1	1	0
6	1	0	1	0
7	1	1	0	0
8	1	1	1	1

Row 1 has no relevant human meaning, or perhaps could be taken to describe persons in a 'persistent vegetative state', such as the American woman Terri Schiavo, who died March 31, 2005, fifteen years after suffering brain damage brought on by heart failure.

The next thing to notice is that only Row 8 describes a successful life, i.e., only Row 8 has 1 in the RESULT column.

Objections are possible, not only to this implistic table but to the meaning of the Result column. We might also wonder how individuals could evaluate even 'self-engagement', the simplest of the three arenas. Drug abuse, obesity, steroid use by athletes, criminality... demonstrate that individuals regularly pursue agendas or behaviours to their intellectual, moral or physical detriment.

Modern Problems, Ancient Perspectives

My intuition is that many but not all people merit a 1 in this column.

Truth table advocates (at least the one I know of!) refine the notion of 'paying attention' so that it becomes 'paying useful attention'. Thus, an individual on a sinking boat may be furiously bailing, but he or she is not *usefully engaged* unless water is landing outside of the boat.

In other words, further AND GATE tests on subdivided arenas could eventually determine whether a 0 or a 1 is merited.

To test the usefulness of the Truth Table analogy, we can go through thought experiments and sort our friends, acquaintances (and, of course, ourselves) into the various rows.

Row #	Self	Stuff	World	Result
3	0	1	0	0

Row 3 is the most populous category, at least in 1st world nations. Row 3 includes all those who are careless of both personal well-being and global issues; who focus instead upon acquiring (and sometimes enjoying) possessions.

This is not to suggest that row 3 contains the bulk of the human population. Row 2 describes their lot.

Row #	Self	Stuff	World	Result
2	1	0	0	0

Since more than fifty per cent of human beings have few possessions, their lives are used up securing food, water and shelter and dealing with body waste issues. Such lives cannot have TRUE outcomes and we do not need a Truth Table to demonstrate this. However the Truth Table puts the problem in context and demonstrates something else worth paying attention to. Row 2's 'focus' guarantees that the difficulties fifty per cent of human beings are experiencing will likely continue.

Vernon Molloy

Of course they can legitimately plead extenuating circumstances – *force majeure* to to speak. Even so, the 0 result forced upon them by having to spend all of their time and energy on here and now issues is the point. Failures to address root problems perpetuates and often perpetrates them.

Row #	Self	Stuff	World	Result
4	0	0	1	0

Row 4 describes world-saviours, alarmists, do-gooders and ideologues of all persuasions. Such lives do not deliver wholesome experiences because their personal and circumstantial lives are deficient – and also because these deficits undermine their credibility.

What Row 4 critics (almost always Row 3 people) fail to recognize is how they are similarly incomplete. What is the difference between zealous attention to lawns, picket fences, automobiles... and preoccupation with the arms race, global poverty or pollution? The answer is that acquiring, enjoying and maintaining possessions is universally sanctioned.

Additionally, Row 4 people tend to be wretches who "cannot change their minds and will not chance the subject". If they happen to be good at sounding alarms, they are also alarming. Thus, Row 3 people have many dreasons to dismiss them. The irony is that Row 3 and Row 4 populations often detest one another for identical reasons!

When Row 2 people occur in 1st world nations, i.e., when they are not poor, they can also be painful to be around. Examples include body-builders, hedonists, addicts – and any person with religious convictions.

I had difficulty knowing where to place religious individuals. Since they profess to long for an excellent post-death life-style, they seem to belong in Row 3. However, most regard their lives as tedious preambles to heaven. Concerned with just their souls – charitable works and piousness are best understood as eternal life insurance premiums – they are Row 2 *par excellence*.

Modern Problems, Ancient Perspectives

Row #	Self	Stuff	World	Result
7	1	1	0	0

Row 7 people presented a more interesting challenge. Such individuals rate a 1 in both self and circumstance cells and enjoy comparatively balanced lives. The successes they often enjoy bolster their appreciation of broadly-based ways of living. Physical and mental well-being, energy and imagination... nurture wholesome circumstances – energy efficient homes, organic gardens, good relationships. When these results are coupled with an increasingly plausible scepticism about anyone's ability to usefully engage global problems, the resulting *weltschmerz* easily resists importunities to move to Row 8.

Row #	Self	Stuff	World	Result
8	1	1	1	1

The argument is also made that, if Row 7 people became commonplace, this would repair resource depletion and pollution problems. While thoughtful, expanded self-interest might have saved the day had it rooted up centuries ago, the most optimistic Row 7 scenario will not dissolve modern problems. At the end of the day, the most Row 7 persons could accomplish is to make it as if they had never existed.

This is a step in the right direction, but no longer enough.

Row 7 people also defend themselves by talking about necessary sequences. They observe that one must first attend to survival issues, then move on to creature comfort and family well-being concerns. Only after this has been achieved does it make sense to worry about national and global issues.

Although this makes sense, security issues always involve circumstances beyond one's immediate time and space. If we drive wolves away from our doors, then neglect to close them – or have doors to close in the first place – we will always be in perilous circumstances.

In the end, well-being depends upon wholesome

circumstances – and the broader the wholesome sphere the better. Row 7 people are often successful because they are involved in just this way. Their failure is that they ignore 'the circumstance of their circumstance'. Should this be remedied, i.e., should they now become Row 8 people, they gain the possibility of successful lives.

The fact that we can only say *possibility* is because we have delayed so long that enormous, impediments to well-being have accumulated. These included entrenched inequities, global warming, environmental harms, the cult of leadership and consumerism. Although Row 8 lives are late in arriving and remain thin on the ground, they are the only hope.

- - - -

Row #	Self	Stuff	World	Result
5	0	1	1	0
6	1	0	1	0
7	1	1	0	0

Row 5, 6 & 7 populations are all contenders for the *two out of three* crown. Row 5 individuals are unusual because of their lack of self-hood, their world-engaging activities tend to frustrate them and their lives are not appealing to others.

Row 6 people live in such disarray that they have credibility issues.

Faced with such meagre 'competition' for the best life-style crown, Row 7 individuals often feel superior, condescending and complacent.

Fortunately – an unusual instance of bad news offering hope – it is increasingly difficult to argue for *any* stance save Row 8. Bleak statistics and and ominous portents are everywhere. Five million Canadians depend upon potable ground water to survive. Depending upon whether one lives in an agricultural, industrial or a timber-based economic region, a different brew of hazardous substances is coming out of our taps. Water drawn from lakes and rivers is similarly compromised. Like sunlight, water comes from the world beyond selves and possessions. Both are essential to Row 7 concerns. The conclusion could not be clearer. However successful Row 7 individuals may be in the short term, the posture is flawed because the most important arena is ignored.

If we agree that Row 8 describes the only sustainable relationship of persons and world, this tells us something important. Like stones thrown into a pond, every activity is a point source of influence. Every individual inherits the consequences of not only her activities, but every other person's.

In short, we all live in crucibles generated by our own and other people's lives. Partitioning this seamless reciprocity has been a toxic source of jingoism and ethnocentrism; of willingness to exploit, consume and degrade..., to "saw off the limbs" well-being depends upon.

Finally, if lives can only prosper with I's across the Truth Table, what is the sense of partitioning at all? A further row is needed:

Row #	Self	Stuff	World	Result
8	1	1	1	1

Row # 9	11111111111111111111

In Row 9, partitions are all gone along with the 'result' column. The only variables are selves, possessions and world; and the quality and quantity of these elements is now determined by unimpeded synergies.

These relationships would be so subtle that they often could not be quantified. In other words, the move to Row 8 and finally to Row 9 would be seminal. Just as Row 7 people sometimes argue that their way of life, widely instantiated, would approximate Row 8, it might be thought that Row 8 postures are good enough; that it does not matter whether vestigial partitioning remains.

However, a fully instantiated Row 9 consciousness offers possibilities unavailable to even Row 8 engagements. Row 9 individuals would take pleasure in 'Ducks Unlimited' projects just because ducks are beautiful and enjoy being alive.

A world with lots of ducks is desirable in and of itself, as well as being better than any alternative.

Immortal Creatures

The reason human beings — and species going extinct at the rate of 200 per day[49] — are harmed by truth table partitions is that corresponding divisions do not exist in reality.

The fact that these partitions have both benign and toxic consequences, and that these consequences have become 'local realities' shaping points of view, is part of the human narrative.

On the positive side, languages depend upon naming entities, processes and objects and then minting words representing their apparent interactions.

However, the benefits of naming experiences do not diminish the dangers of mapping fantasies, reifications and other distillations upon what is going on.

This mapping accomplishes me/not me, internal/external categorizations.

In the grip of such pictures, Row 7 people sometimes wonder how long human beings will survive if they continue regarding one another as resources and opportunities and the world as a dumping ground. The fact that such concerns are expressed offers little reason for optimism. Such observations and conversations are doubtlessly *necessary* but they are not necessary and sufficient.

In other words, survivability requires changing how we think about selves, responsibilities and prerogatives. A clue can be

---

[49]Based on their results, the team concluded that the average pre-human extinction rate was 0.1 extinction per million species per year. The current extinction rate is approximately 100 extinctions per million species per year, or 1,000 times higher than natural background rates. They also predict that future rates may be as much as 10,000 times higher. http://www.iflscience.com/plants-and-animals/current-extinction-rate-10-times-worse-previously-thought

263

had by imagining how the world looks to other creatures — and to human beings before we got so smart!

Of course there is no way to do this. The only possibility involves thought experiments dissolving truth table partitions. This is difficult but there is no harm in trying. Pondering dubious credentials and toxic consequences might help us refrain from further partitioning. In addition, to the extent that public harms can be tracked to Truth Table partitions, there is less reason to make scapegoats of present populations. The individuals comprising populations are the vectors and embodiments of harms in motion.

To anticipate another objection, there is no reason to be concerned that Row 9 people will lose 'track of themselves'. Novels and oral tradition narratives are universal cultural achievements because they capture the viewpoint of self-aware beings: me, with or without possessions, families, agendas... against the world, alone in the world..., in some relationship with the world.

This sense of enduring, coherent being has nothing to do with imaginary partitions. Individuals will always regard themselves as struggling with events. The irony is that partitioning experiences to solve problems often makes them worse.

Thus, if the world was not carved into regions, there would be fewer wars, macro-economic events or global phenomena. People would be harder to organize into armies of soldiers, workers and consumers.

The world is a hornets' nest of hard-edged realms — collections of 'self-evident' facts playing one region, one set of economic interests, one faith-addled population... against another. A further danger is that individuals within organizations, corporations, nations... are well-positioned to deny responsibility for everything going on! Every act becomes a response to what other people, especially people over there, are getting up to.

When we all claim to be innocent bystanders or victims we all become one another's scapegoats!

Partitioning the world into enclaves, regions, nations... encourages and ennables us to harvest one another with a globalized economy and multi-national trade deals. It encourages the idea that resources are properly available to anyone planting a flag and figuring out the machineries and machinations made possible by doing so.

There is a great deal of practical truth in this claim — think of the mining, drilling, pumping, scraping and scrapping human beings have accomplished since the industrial revolution! The harm lies in the conceit that these adventures can be accomplished unilaterally — that we can (at least sometimes)rob one another, the world and future generations with impunity.

Deep down we all know better. One reason we are able to continue even so is because our intuitions have been partitioned into Truth Table arenas.

Some will object that we have to pay attention to local issues and that this requires sorting events into objects and entities. The good news is that this does not require abandoning Row 8/Row 9 standpoints. This sorting out is accomplished automatically and effortlessly. Every creature, including every human being, creates and inhabits a sphere of needs and resources. Further organizing the world into *self, possessions* and *world* is unnecessary. Nearby/remote, important/trivial, pleasant/unpleasant... gradations naturally occur.

Of course, legal artefacts involving property, title, ownership, possessions... will continue to exist. They will, however, be peripheral, secondary, helper... functions, not the hinge upon which everything turns.

In this regard it is useful to think of selves, possessions and 'world beyond' in terms of *gestalts* or images. A gestalt results when sensations organize themselves into quasi-entities. Recurring experiences are further distilled into phenomenal objects, and then into *realism* and *common sense* accounts.

If we had stopped 'gestalting' at this point perhaps the 'things' populating common sense would have been okay. However the phenomenal objects (images, gestalts) of daily experience have been collected into meta-objects. The first meta-object is the idea of the self as an enduring entity. The second involves the idea of one's possessions as a unity — the set of objects and entities owned. The final meta-object is the world containing our selves and the things we own.

To function in this capacity, the world object must be understood as an inexhaustible backdrop of resources and possibilities.

These meta-objects, it hardly needs pointing out, correspond to Truth Table arenas. This is one reason Truth Table partition seem natural and unexceptional.

This also illuminates why little progress has been made repairing the way we treat one another. Partitioning experiences into Truth Table gestalts lends each meta-object a cachet of immutability. The resulting sense of personal immortality, or at least durability, encourages the fantasy that we are insulated from what is going on.

A similar sense of permanence and invulnerability attaches to other meta-objects. Thus – although items owned experience 'entropic degradation' by wearing out or breaking down – the meta-objects understood as collections of possessions become trustworthy adjuncts of our imperial, immortal selves.

The importance of these complementary meta-objects is implicit in our efforts to acquire new things, replace broken items and keep everything in good repair.

The remaining meta-object is the world we see ourselves inhabiting. Here, fantasies of the world as obdurate object, rationalize indifference, even in the understanding of professional soothsayers. Dr. David Suzuki travels the world preaching ecological thoughtfulness and exclaiming about environmental footprints — as if he and his audiences were detached from one another and from their own future incarnations. Presumably they have calculated that the environmental consequences of convening such gatherings is neutralized by the good flowing from them.

Modern Problems, Ancient Perspectives

No one has produced evidence that this is true although some have posed the question.

Of the three meta-objects, the only one we think of as problematic is the possession-object. The things we own (H. D. Thoreau would say: "the things that own us") are in such an alarming state that we are forever pruning, painting, cleaning, repairing, replacing... them. Few invest comparable attention in their own physical well-being. Homoeostatic mechanisms, peristalsis and autonomic nervous systems are counted on to keep us alive day-to-day, though perhaps not week-to-week.

As regards the third meta-object, the world seems big enough and resilient enough to not have to worry about. This is what it means to be *the world.*

So there we have it: a set of conceits and images covering everything going on - a set of conceits allowing human beings to assimilate bad news, alarming statistics and global warming signals with aplomb.

Suppose we do some wishful thinking and imagine Truth Table discussions cause a significant proportion of human beings to achieve Row 9 consciousness.

I think this would lead to a wonderful re-purposing of time and energy. The interdependence of world, nature and personal well-being would become clearer. On the premise that "a stitch in time saves nine", a threshold proportion of Row 8/Row 9 lives might avert difficulties not yet identified.

A further benefit is possible. Row 8/Row 9 stances transform wearing out, wearing down issues into reasons for optimism. Only our imaginary selves and the sets of objects we own are cast in stone. In the real world no state of affairs endures because 'everything' is in flux. This leads to maintenance and replacement issues regarding 'our stuff', but it also means that problematic circumstances sometimes dissolve *of their own volition.* The nature of storms includes storms passing.

Row 8/Row 9 stances also imply that problems can sometimes be remedied by judiciously introducing catalysing elements and factors. When things are already 'on the move' (and they always are!) small changes can lead to large results.

Row 8/Row 9 people would also escape the need to periodically upgrade their imaginary renderings. Change, decay, additions, subtractions, new things going bump in the night... must presently be assimilated into meta-objects. This can drive people to despair – in Jean-Paul Sarte's expression, to live in *bad faith,* to refuse to continue.

More commonly, the sense that one is ageing, sickening, declining..., the sense that the world is increasingly dangerous... , urges us to compensate by purchasing more and better things. From the point of view of everyone except Row 8/Row 9 people, this makes sense. The more detailed and luxurious the *possessions* meta-object becomes, the more secure and insulated we feel.

Thousands of years of Truth Table mischief have spawned desperate times and desperate measures. In the aftermath of September 11, 2001, North Americans found themselves living with escalating 'Homeland Security' initiatives and worsening political and economic consequences. On April 5, 2005, the American government announced that Canadians and Mexicans will have to produce passports to cross into the United States. Julian Assange (Wiki-leaks, 2010) and Peter Snowden (2013) leaked troves of classified documents demonstrating that western governments are engaging in what Noam Chomsky calls state terrorism as well as engaging in the mass surveillance of domestic populations.

Of course, no argument, importunity or citing of statistics has ever dismantled even one unhappy circumstance. The most that can be hoped for is some new consensus, some new resolve, among a few people. These results mean nothing if they fade away or are overtaken by events.

A more optimistic possibility requires changes at the Truth Table level. Dissolving the logical and prudential credentials of 'me', 'mine', and 'the world' partitions might accomplish something. We certainly know that dismantling and co-opting lives in the service of this or that –ism: socialism, communism, industrial capitalism... has a frightful track record.

Row8/Row 9 consciousness is the only political and economic experiment that has not been tried. Of course, Row 8/Row 9 lives prevailed for most of mankind's 300,000 years on earth. I think the associated subsistence activities, local economies and equities would flourish again under Truth Table tutelage. Indeed, with the judicious help of new technologies things might go very well indeed.

Certainly human beings' 'lifestyle footprints' would diminish and perhaps become manageable.

To the extent that we no longer understand ourselves in terms of formally-defined spheres of concern and responsibility, partitioned postures and practices would no longer seem necessary. They might seem barbaric.

Finally, Row 8/Row 9 consciousness would understand that political and economic repairs are only possible from the bottom up. This understanding is the only enfranchisement human beings have ever needed. This understanding is the only enfranchisement that has ever been possible.

Vernon Molloy

Foreword

As political and economic events grow increasingly complex, the associated loss of subsistence activities means that more and more of what individuals and communities used to get up to spontaneously must now be organized, supervised and legislatively controlled.

Why the Music Stopped outlines a way of thinking about this aspect of progress and development which attempts to includes the cost of what is being given up.

The question to ask: can progress, development, efficiency... and the well-being of ordinary populations exist simultaneously?

Why The Music Stopped

The law, in its majestic equality, forbids the rich as well as the poor to sleep under bridges, to beg in the streets, and to steal bread.

Anatole France, The Red Lily, 1894, chapter 7.

My assessment is that the bulk of the increase in unemployment since the recession began is attributable to the sharp contraction in economic activity that occurred in the wake of the financial crisis and the continuing shortfall of aggregate demand....

Ben Bernanke, at the Revisiting Monetary Policy in a Low-Inflation Environment Conference, Federal Reserve Bank of Boston, Boston, Massachusetts, October 15, 2010.

On February 18, 1997, Canada's Finance Minister Paul Martin delivered his government's 'stay the course and eliminate the deficit' budget. Pundits and opposition leaders immediately provided the required analysis and bleak predictions.

Modern Problems, Ancient Perspectives

I listened to some of this on CBC radio that evening, while attempting to play Gordon Lightfoot's "Did She Mention My Name?". Perhaps this is what suggested parallels between home-grown music, Canada's public debt and soup kitchens. Many have suggested that I will never be much of a guitar player (I have a partial list) but I started along the C, F, G7 road when there were few alternatives and never had the sense to give up.

I was (and I still am) the oldest of seven children. Our family was steeped in Irish-French bonhomie and subsistence activities like milking cows, hoeing potatoes and bringing in firewood. We valued home-grown music for the same reason moonshine was valued a generation earlier. Neither might have been the best, but both hit the spot. More importantly, both could be enjoyed without getting out a wallet.

It is interesting to ponder the feelings of well-being – bolstered by gardens, goats, a cow or two, preserves in the cellar – this capacity to be self-sustaining must have lent my parents and grandparents.

Such benefits — not to diminish the difficulties involved in subsistence productions — are doubly provocative in the today's world of food banks, charities and working poor.

When I grew up, being poor was nothing anyone hoped for but nothing to sneeze at either. Everyone could grow vegetables, raise animals and cut firewood. Moreover — there being no better motivator than hunger and cold — we all did just that.

Indeed the prosperity Canadians enjoyed during the 20th century grew out of such homely adventures. Communities flourished. Roads, schools, universities and hospitals were built. Universal health care came into existence. We know this because we are still listening to the CBC and going to doctors and hospitals without paying.

However, to be 'up against it' in urban circumstances is another matter. Unlike the people I grew up with, the urban poor today have three possibilities:

1. They must trust that governments will provide a maintenance allowance because they have a right to exist.
2. Failing this, they must depend upon handouts from institutionalized charities, food banks and individuals they come across.
3. They can take up criminal activities or prostitution.

Sporadic attempts to transform welfare claims into workfare obligations (or abolish them altogether) suggest that the poor should anticipate being moved from possibility 1 to possibility 2 or possibility 3.

Conservatives and Republicans claim that there are plenty of jobs in western nations and that what is lacking is initiative. Evidence includes the need to import foreign workers to pick cucumbers and grapes. The underlying issue – urban populations have little experience with or interest in manual labour – becomes an ironic argument for further automation and outsourcing and a moralizing conclusion sanctioning further incursions into family responsibilities and well-being.

When Ontarians learned in 1997 that the *Gaming Control Commission* would licence 36 permanent gambling clubs with a view to generating and additional $180 million for charities, it became clear which direction the wind was blowing.

As 1ˢᵗ world nations embrace conservatism, unemployment rates, incarceration rates and charities... have been rising in lock step.

This correlation is associated by an increasing gap between rich and poor — a fact that is occasionally noted but rarely cited as a factor in faltering economies. I think this is correct. If all wealth was equitably distributed tomorrow and nothing changed in the way business is done and profits distributed, equity problems would immediately start to coalesce.

The most that would be achieved would be a few decades of faux economic vigour.

In other words, there is nothing to be gained by blaming the wealthy for failures of well-being. Equity issues are better understood as middle class and lower class failures to identify and repair political and economic problems. The poor are not making more fuss these days than they ever have. Their days are full because their plates are empty. Getting by is all they have time for.

Therefore there is no reason to hope that the poor will pull the middle class's fat out of the fire because they have figured out how to save their own bacon.

The wealthy will not be riding in to rescue the middle class either. Indeed, now that the wealthy own everything worth having, now that the middle class's profit generating potential has become redundant, now that middle class lifestyles have become the engine of anthropogenic change, the middle class has become a clear and present danger to wealthy well-being.

This means that only middle classers have the resources and motivation to invest in their own survival. What is surprising is that we are so docile. We continue to elect governments promising reactionary, simplistic solutions that have already demonstrated their uselessness. We are told to work harder to become wealthy or at least to maintain your economic status quo. We are told to shop harder for bargains.

Amazingly, no political party has ever offered to help citizens organize themselves into platoons of shoppers with a view to gaining some economic and political leverage, with a view to making competition really work! Even more amazingly, labour unions never seem to notice that they are overlooking an important organizing possibility as close by as their existing membership. Of course, the most remarkable bit of myopia is that you and I have not troubled ourselves to pick this low-hanging fruit.

What have we been thinking?

These failures and oversights may make sense day by day but most people have been experiencing an erosion of purchasing power for decades as good jobs disappear. Ironically this loss of purchasing power has been sanctioning corporations to pursue efficiencies, automation and outsourcing to further

Vernon Molloy

reduce costs and maintain sales volumes.

As we are seeing, eliminating or downsizing *made in North America* jobs set off a race to the bottom. When not scrounging for bargains, we flirt with conservatism, and discard liberalism and socialism. We are told that the public trough, free- loaders and welfare queens are the reason the economic prospect is increasingly gloomy. These are simplistic falsehoods. It is always pleasant to blame problems on the shortcomings and greed of others.

A more plausible and useful explanation is available. There simply is not enough money in middle and lower class pockets to sustain economies large enough to occupy the world's manufacturing capacity. Inequities are therefore a symptom of what is wrong. They do not cause themselves. Any such analysis is flawed and dangers. It is flawed because inequities are *consequences* but these consequences have knock-on sociological and human capital costs and *cause* further inequities.

Simplistic analyses are dangerous because they distract attention from possible repairs.

For example, they encourage middle class populations to blame economic problems on either the greedy wealthy or the inept, lazy, blood-sucking poor who have frittering away tax dollars, monies that would be better spent stimulating economies if left in the hands of businesses and corporations.

These fact-free analyses also set the stage for violent responses by disaffected populations. There is no reason to believe that an American Spring might not rise up!

Another mischievous narrative is blurring an important difference between socialism and charity. Conservatives admire charitable activities because they undermine the idea that people possess rights. Charitable talk transforms such claims into occasions for supererogatory behaviour — wherein the well-to-do get to choose, as Ralph Waldo Emerson observed, whether to give away what they should give back.

In addition, the status quo is shored up when people

understand poverty in terms of personal failures; and inequities as what happens when such failures accumulate and compound. Citizens who depend upon charity are less likely to think about demonstrations, letters to editors or voting socialists into power. They see themselves as supported by hard-working people. Complaining about conservative politics is tantamount to biting the hands feeding them.

Charities have a further toxic consequence. If marginalized populations are seen as responsible for their own poverty those who still have jobs are reassured that they will not be next on the chopping block. Further lay-offs, efficiency improvements, outsourcing announcements... will be regarded as people getting what they deserve until a pink slip arrives at their work station.

What does this have to do with home-grown music? The answer is that there are comparatively few musicians around these days, given the size of our population.

The reason is twofold:

1. There are prodigious musical talents in every community.
2. Corporations have been combing through these virtuosos and packaging their achievements for commercial purposes. The resulting records, CDs, videos, tapes... are distributed as universally as corporations can manage.

So what? We all get to listen to excellent stuff. What does it matter if our musical, literary, entertainment... appetites are satisfied by a small tribe of cognoscenti and a few corporations packaging and delivering their product? The advantages are obvious. It is the downside that is not thought about. The first harm is that fewer individuals are experiencing the pleasures that come from producing music, however amateurishly.

This is not a trivial consequence. My own capacity to enjoy music has been enhanced. My ear has improved, my sense of chord changes and progressions has grown — along with my ability to recognize real musicians!

More importantly, there are parallels between today's depleted reservoir of guitar-pickers and our economic prospect. Once a song has been recorded, it can be reproduced at virtually no cost. Since millions of copies can be sold, it is possible to pay a few performers extraordinary sums, and for producers, promoters and corporations to prosper along with them.

The downside is that the rest of us are reduced to listeners. In fact, listening, watching, applauding, identifying with, purchasing... opportunities have become epidemic.

To be sure, nothing prevents individuals from getting out an instrument and taking a run at a cliff-like learning curve. Under most circumstance however, with wonderful options at every turn, it is clear what will happen. We think: "Why bother? The professionals are so good! Records are so cheap!"

The same process has been occurring in entertainment, sports and literature. The accomplishments of extraordinary people are recorded and reproduced for mass consumption.

There is a critical difference between being occasionally exposed to music, art and entertainment — so that an enlarged sense of possibility results — and being so inundated that there is little need to put an oar in the water.

In *The Globe and Mail*, February 17, 1997, science fiction author Spider Robinson described a young swain who had taken the trouble to inscribe his name and that of his beloved on a side-walk. The problem is, he had written Tood + Janey, which Mr. Robinson took as 'concrete evidence' that "young Todd is unable to spell his own flippin' name".

Again, what does this have to do with soup kitchens, food banks and faltering economies? For at least a century, industry and commerce have been attempting to reproduce the music industry's few producers/many consumers business model. There is, however, an important difference between sound tracks or computer programs — that can be reproduced at almost zero cost — and products requiring significant inputs of material and energy.

The logic is simple. If products and services do not have a human effort component in their manufacture, their production and distribution will inevitably be restricted to individuals owning, organizing, programming and protecting the means of production.

In other words, sophisticated technologies cannot replicate the music industry's zero-cost product. When it comes to basics: automobiles, eggs and housing... , widespread, value-adding employment have to be part of the picture.

Even if products could somehow became free in terms of input costs, i.e., because of some breakthrough such as cold fusion, it is fair to ask why corporations would bring them to market. There would be no profit to be made!

In short, the music industry does not constitute a viable model for the production of tangible goods and services. In the real world, economies of scale, eliminating occupations through automation and intensifying competition with free trade agreements and off-shore labour... mean the erosion of ordinary well-being.

This is not to suggest that productions should be inefficient. However, nothing about Adam Smith's 'invisible hand' balancing supply and demand guarantees that a healthy proportion of the benefits of technologies and efficiencies will get distributed across populations.

An efficient market may or may not result in an equitable, humane world. Historically this responsibility has been left in the hands of wealth-redistributing governments, self-interested consumers and subsistence activities.

The problems seems to be that capitalism, urbanization, global trade agreements and corporations have undermined the capacity of governments and individuals to look after ordinary people. As far as I can tell, it is only a matter of time before the only people shopping will be those owning a piece of automated or off-shore production facilities.

Vernon Molloy

Since this is the direction economies appear to be headed, we should expect the global GNP to shrink until it matches the needs of the twenty or thirty per cent of human beings with money to spend. Whether this downsizing takes two decades or five, the only question remaining is whether middle and lower class populations have the wit and resolve to pry a survivable portion of the benefits of technologies, efficiencies and resource-depleting activities from corporations and politicians.

This does not seem likely. With our permission, politicians continue to 'focus like lasers' upon producers or consumers but never upon persons who happen to be producers and consumers. Conservatives commend micro-economic agendas as if economies consisting of such initiatives could retain enough consuming power to survive. Socialists focus upon consumers, whom they mistake for 'the people that matter.' Both overlook that balancing supply (producers) and demand (consumers) is the only path to sustainability and inclusiveness.

Indeed, focusing upon *individual* and not *producer* or *consumer* well-being might be the only path to rationalized lifestyles and survivability.

The world boasts one example of such an economy. A middle class flourished across North America and Europe after the Industrial Revolution. Things went along famously for perhaps 150 years. Life styles improved incrementally. As long as a balance existed among rural, community and urban elements, an equilibrium existed between progress and thoughtful, measured applications of labour saving devices and life-style opportunities.

Unfortunately this measured progress was merely an interim stage along development road. Economies and ordinary lives flourished during this period. The reason is simple. Although labour saving devices and technologies were increasing productivity, human beings were still involved in the production of goods and services.

As a result, from the end of the Second World War until the

turn of the present century, 1st Worlders enjoyed well-paid and often life-long employment. Because of these employments the benefits of new technologies and resources were distributed across populations.

This halcyon period featured

> • incomes sufficient to purchase goods and services;
> • specialized educations preparing individuals to work in industry and commerce;
> • increasing urbanization;
> • advertising and psychological stratagems blurring the distinction between needs and wants.

Unfortunately, although each new development seemed benign, even exciting, progress and development was setting the stage for collapse. Rather than being the harbinger of wider prosperity, progress and development began eroding the employments that had made the middle class possible. In my recollection — and according to statistics — real wages in North America began to decline during the 1970's.

The proximate cause was urbanization and the commercialization of virtually every aspect of life so that fewer and fewer value adding activities were occurring in homes and communities. The pursuit of convenience transformed domestic responsibilities into commercial and political possibilities.

These encroachments undermined the middle ground between *working* and *consuming* activities. This middle ground is the province of subsistence activities. This middle ground – where people do things for themselves and one another – is the sweet spot where thoughtful people are most likely to develop. This is where individuals are most likely to develop a sense of themselves as both *workers* and *consumers* and not as one and then the other.

This overarching viewpoint is necessary if *working* and *consuming* are not to use up all of our lives and everything in sight. This is the viewpoint needed if human beings are to become persons with a wholesome wildness and

Vernon Molloy

unpredictability about them.

At the risk of repeating myself: if human beings believe that personhood is a birthright achieved through ensoulment or extraordinary evolutionary achievement... the likelihood of persons turning up is vanishingly small.

You may object that the middle ground was wonderfully broad before the Industrial Revolution — if middle ground means a large gap between rich and poor and where subsistence opportunities were thick on the ground. You point out that this did not prevent the modern world from emerging. You observe that the persons/individuals ratio has always been depressing.

Both observations seem true enough but pre-Industrial Revolution populations also suffered from a lack of cultural resources and they eked out a livelihood with primitive technologies and a great deal of labour. These are also obstacles to personhood on a par with urbanization (although perhaps not with smartphones).

The middle ground I have in mind was an unintended benefit of the Industrial Revolution: the emergence of a neither rich nor poor way of life. This unprecedented, now vanished, state of affairs was the sweet spot we should have hung onto. This middle ground could have catalysed subsistence activities and community resources and prevented corporations from rushing into every corner of every life.

Instead we collapsed into abject dependencies. Corporations now get whatever they want by threatening further people-displacing progress and development measures.

Robotic possibilities, globalization, multinationals, outsourcing..., have altered the balance of power across bargaining tables. This is the reason real wages in First World economies began to shrink in the 1970's. This is why the prospects of emerging nations are being obliterated as they replicate our few rich/many poor predicament.

Modern Problems, Ancient Perspectives

If these immolations proceed slowly and carefully enough middle class populations may fade from history in a politically-manageable diminution of expectations. The luminous future the Industrial Revolution made possible will vanish with no one to mourn its passing. Newly unemployed specialists will retire to television sets and computer screens, ear buds at the ready should another trip to the food bank become necessary.

In other words — although the planet is predicted to host 10 billion human beings by 2050 — only a small percentage should expect a life worth living. We have been clutching a viper to our breasts. There is nothing in capitalism's business plan *requiring* the distribution of the benefits of 'progress and development' across populations.

More importantly — as we all experience whenever someone asks us to give up something or take on some new responsibility — something within us recoils when equitable distribution talk begins. I hope that this is because urban consciousness alternates between *worker* and *consumer* standpoints and rarely from the point of view of a person who works and consumes but has an overarching human life of her own.

This is certainly how I remember the my young life. Unfortunately my generation took our wonderful lives for granted and never asked whether we were selling our souls for a chance to watch Ed Sullivan. In our defence, the problems we were buying into only recently became unmistakeable. When subsistence activities still occurred on farms and in communities, when wants and needs had not all been translated into goods and services and then outsourced or automated, workers could almost always be re-employed in new ventures.

This is no longer true. For an increasing proportion of human beings, the idea of skilled labour has become an anachronism. Manufacturing and information-processing tasks are being 'analysed to bits' and translated into computer-mediated procedures. For a few more decades, a significant proportion

Vernon Molloy

of human beings will find low-grade employment in call centres and automated factories. The complexity and responsibility of work will continue to diminish. As tasks and responsibilities get simpler, wages will shrink. If we object, they will shrink faster still.

If you remember how things used to be, this would be a good time to call your friends and discuss what to do. When the music people used to make faded away, mere silence did not take its place. Every person today has more music, entertainment, sports events... at his or her beck and call than any previous generation. The downside is that there are fewer home-grown musicians, fewer comedians, fewer athletes... on a *per capita* basis.

The disappearance of home-grown musicians, moonshine and self-sustaining communities signifies a more important problem. This has nothing to do with yard sales, Mall crawls, spectator sports or media events. It has everything to do with the loss of a middle way of life. The people I grew up with were happy to extricate themselves from back-breaking labour but had not been completely seduced.

The sounds we hear today: the slamming of factory doors, the explosions in marketplaces, the shriek of incoming missiles... are music to the ears of the corporations rushing into the vacuum created when we stopped making music of our own.

The score they have in mind involves whatever is left of us.

Time in Cities

I have been rooting through old files because I remembered writing something about an unexpected consequence of being urbanized. The question was whether being urbanized and organized predisposes people to becoming more urbanized and organized.

If so, as seems likely, would this progression spontaneously conclude at some level or would it keep going until something external forced a halt?

A related question involves the consequences of living in an organized state of social, political and economic existence.

I am most interested in the dark side of watches and calendars, especially the consequences of sorting human lives into weeks.

During this 'research' I came across a couple of items written in the 1980's. I know this because the pages had been typed on an IBM Selectric typewriter — an obsolete technology even when I got my hands on it, but one that seemed marvellous to me.

I have reproduced these pages more less as I found them. They anticipate much of what I am on about in this book. I was chagrined at first to see how little progress I had made; then realized that this is as it should be.

Neither you nor I author the ideas constituting our awarenesses. They boil up from non-conscious proceedings within and among us.

We are simply the first awarenesses generated.

In my case these proceedings have continued to stew away – with occasional fresh ingredients including efforts to understand my failures to interest you in such exciting notions.

Vernon Molloy

Death

Death is everything we did not experience.
Death is everything we will not experience.
We are the space between *did not* and *will not*.
Death occurs when this space vanishes.

I have no idea how you feel about this.
I have no idea how I feel about this.
I know we make notes on calendars.

Sneaking Away

Is it possible that we embrace declining health in middle and old age because death would be too much to bear if it came upon us while we are vigorous? The anticipated struggle... or even just the fright and pain... may be thought to be lessened in this way.

Is it possible that this is why we cut life-lines rather than enduring and damning the consequences? Is a peaceful death not a common ambition? — ideally one that comes while we are asleep? Might we not have some vague sense that our chances are enhanced if we experience *beforehand* the anaesthesia of declining vigour?

We certainly take to armchairs with unseemly alacrity. We un-gird our loins as soon as possible. God is in his Heaven preparing a place for us. Matters will proceed wonderfully if only we keep the faith, if only we do not make a fuss.

In this context it is worth mentioning a few aspects and assumptions of urbanized life that seem to me to covertly promote self-immolation.

1. God is a technology to end all technologies. Priests, ministers and sycophants are technicians delivering the goods. God will adjust his natural order on our behalf – if we catch his attention and present ourselves in ways warranting intervention.

2. In the meantime our ambition to experience as little stress, physical discomfort or effort as possible... makes us willing to disengage, to hand over responsibilities to leaders and corporations. .

3. In cities, movers and shakers are ecstatic about how these characteristics help their projects succeed.

4. Carefully and slowly they have been institutionalizing new areas of responsibility.[50] Grief counsellors, pet

---

[50]   http://www.seriouslysmartkingston.com

Vernon Molloy

psychologists and medical marijuana are already just a phone call away.

Perception of Time in Cities

What I am now certain I am beseeching them to feel is that of itself longevity is utterly without redeeming qualities, that one has to live the contributive, the passionate life, and that this can be done as well in twenty-six... as in a hundred and twenty-six years, done in no longer than it takes a man to determine whether the answer is yea or nay.

Frederick Exely[51]

Modern calendars mar the sweet simplicity of our lives by reminding us that each day that passes is the anniversary of some perfectly uninteresting event.

Oscar Wilde

The quiet dream of men and women has always been to extend lifespans beyond the three score and ten years prescribed either by God or evolutionary calculations. It has not escaped our notice that many creatures live longer than we do – tortoises, sturgeon and elephants come to mind, and that some trees survive a thousand years.

Doubtlessly few of us would trade places with any of these, but longevity counts for something. Moreover – since we cannot really grasp what it means to be a bat or a sturgeon or a tree – we are not sure that we are not being short-changed. For all we know other forms of life could be having rich lives flying or swimming about - or watching the seasons from rooted vantage points.

If this is not the case – and we know that youth is wasted upon the young – is not superb longevity wasted upon vegetative and, at best, dimly conscious forms of life?

To make matter worse, most human beings only survived twenty five or so years during the 200 millennia they inhabited

---

[51]Frederick Exely, A Fan's Notes (Washington Square Press,1968) p. 352.

Vernon Molloy

the world. During this enormous span, only the vigorous, resilient or lucky lived a full life-span. This is why it takes a lot to do us in. The resistance and vigour required of individuals saddled with a slow and cumbersome reproductive strategy has much to do with our rich lives.

Living longer than strictly required to reproduce, especially for species relying upon quality rather than quantity of offspring, invites open-ended solutions. Some think this is why human beings live twice as long as might be expected, long enough to become *grandparents* and thus serve as cultural repositories and proto-schools.

As well, there has been a substantial increase in the proportion of human beings living our their full lifespans. This has to do with improved hygiene, lots of food diet and medical advances.

Paradoxically however - this is what I want to talk about - an unexpected shortening of subjective life-time has occurred. In other words, 'centralization' (the processes leading to cities and longer lives) has been shrinking our sense of being alive and knowing it.

There suggests another possibility. Centralization's success in lengthening life may only represent a portion of the elongation available – and the principal obstacle to this exciting possibility is centralization itself!

How can such claims be advanced? My answer involves distinguishing subjective time from raw statements of number of years lived. We need only ask whether we would choose 400 years of comatose life over 40 years in a normal mix of consciousness and sleep to get a sense of the issue.

My worry is that centralization is inducing varieties and degrees of somnolence. The consequence is that our conscious lives are being reduced, perhaps drastically reduced, compared to what they could be.

Let me begin by describing one practice shrinking both the number and the duration of conscious episodes. In cities the passage of years is no longer marked by the march of seasons

288

but by calendars. Calendars acknowledge months and years but they are principally occupied with weeks. The week is the time unit par excellence of the modern world. It is *the week* that shuttles tirelessly in and out, sewing billions of lives into homogeneous patterns. The week ignores natural divisions of time. Weeks are identical one with the other. They are unaffected by spring rains, summer sun and winter cold. The world is glimpsed through the week's interstices: Monday, Tuesday, Wednesday... , or at the appropriate weekend time.

Natural units of time... days, seasons, young, adult, old... are also insulated from urban consciousness by increasingly detailed infrastructure. We live under the auspices of central heating, trucked-in products, abundant and unchanging supermarket offerings. Nature has been bulldozed into submission, pushed beyond peripheries; admitted provisionally in the guise of exotic creatures in zoos or as pets. Beyond these exceptions the world is regarded as a resource and dumping ground; a destination for family outings or a value-adding context for cottage investments.

(In 2014 several national parks in Canada will begin supplying Wi-Fi hot spots!)

Even so, these partitionings and co-opting are innocuous compared to the estrangement accomplished by the invention of 'the week' – a cunning, completely arbitrary parcelling-out of what is going on.

Why are weeks so insidious? A week is long enough to accommodate the needs of commerce and industry, long enough as an uninterrupted work schedule to be efficient, yet short enough that weekends are never far away. This proximity rivets urban populations upon here and now issues.

Just as destructively, so many weeks always seem to remain ahead of us that we are careless of all of them; as one who has limitless money scarcely notices or enjoys her wealth.

A heightened awareness of the passage of time, such as occurred when humans lived in the context of seasons and years, would mitigate this dangerous conceit. The regular in-

and-out of weeks weaves a comfortable fabric we slide beneath... to perhaps emerge at the end and wonder – "Where has my life gone?"

Do you wonder at the magnitude of this loss? Who does not remember their childhood, when summer vacations seemed to last forever? The loss of opportunities to have new experiences explains some of the quickening of adult life, but technically-abetted convenience and homogeneity are important factors. Adults have not lost the capacity to live deeply. Now and then we all have days yielding new memories. If you remember only a few such days last year, those were the days when you were alive and knew it. Almost certainly the remainder were passed in the service of some nation, some corporation, some profitable enterprise.

By our own accounting, these days were passed in somnolence, in semi-consciousness.

> *Lost yesterday, somewhere between sunrise and sunset, two golden*
> *hours, each with sixty diamond minutes.*
> *No reward is offered for they are*
> *gone forever.*
>
> Horace Mann

We should do do whatever it takes to increase the number of conscious days we enjoy. If we cannot wind this clock back, it matters little what else is accomplished. This is why urbanization is a terrifying factor in human affairs. To live in cities is to be fully exposed to the myopia-engendering influence of weeks. It is to be removed from the ebb and flow of the seasons that once enlivened our days, reminded us of how brief life really is and sometimes elevated our thoughts from here and now issues.

To be urbanized is to be divorced from community life, from barn raising projects, threshing bees and wood splitting parties. I apologize for these antediluvian examples but Santa Claus parades, Gay Pride demonstrations, Terry Fox Marathons and Ontario's Highway of Heroes are the only other examples of community activity I am aware of.

Modern Problems, Ancient Perspectives

They have more to do with the lack of community life than than anything else.

Perhaps the suggestion that urban circumstances harm subjective lives needs further motivation. We commonly believe that cities offer variety, dash and verve, a panorama of sophisticated entertainment and social opportunities. A moment's reflection challenges such notions. If a choice must be made,the sinewy demands of rural living is preferable to urban circumstances, but that is not what I am proposing.

I think an adroit rural/urban mix is the best possible setting for vigorous lives and rich consciousness.

The 'broad margin' to life admired by Henry Thoreau separates individuals sufficiently that we are sometimes glad to see one another. In cities the logistics of moving people, cars, foodstuffs... dictate identical solutions. Most human beings experience one another in the context of free ways, traffic congestion, supermarkets, fast food outlets, parking meters and anonymity. Urban lives are replete with advertising, political rhetoric and "opportunities" for vicarious living and voyeurism. Smart phones transform gatherings into half-duplex torments. Like it or not, we spend time listening in on one-sided conversations. We must watch out for people coming down stairs, crossing streets or traffic lanes while talking to or texting one another.

Out of self-defence we grow aloof and guarded: states of mind made necessary and possible by faceless multitudes, anonymous streets and high-rise apartments. When every place is like every other place, there are no places to speak of.

At the same time, city life is full of energy and variety. The energy is frenetic and direction-less, the variety superficial and crass. Who would have imagined that millions of human beings at the the vanguard of progress, development and civilized life would settle for reality TV and Corn Dogs?

Of course we should have seen this coming. In the thousand channel universe, media productions are necessarily repetitive and banal. Audiences are fragmented because there are countless equally vacuous ways to invest evenings and weekends. If one is a morning person, Jerry Springer offers up caricatures designed to make even your and my accomplishments seem exceptional.

The sports establishment works the other end of the achievement continuum. Sports fans have more entertainment options than they can shake a hockey stick at. Sports events: hockey, baseball, football ... remain seasonal events although the demarcations are becoming blurred. Perhaps this is because associating sports activities with otherwise irrelevant seasons refreshes our interest in "He scores, he shoots!" dramas.

Sports events also instruct the hoi polloi ('the many') that even exceptional individuals lose more frequently than they win; that the real test is whether one has what it takes to be a sport about losing. These are valuable moral lessons as populations watch their prospects decline while winners (the *hoi oligoi* or 'the few') whistle their way to banks.

In the meantime we have not been resting on our self-immolation laurels. We have been pursuing vicarious living and voyeurism as if our lives depended on it. Time spent in front of televisions, computer screens and smart phones reached 11 hours a day in Canada in 2013. Along with direct consequences including obesity and rewired neural circuitry a corresponding diminution of family and community life must be occurring. Only a few seem worried about this.

Of course we could all be emailing, texting and Face-booking one another about these problems with no one the wiser!

Pundits worry about declining empathy quotients and capacity to pay attention to non-verbal social cues. There is evidence that our brains are being rewired to accommodate new technologies and that the capacity to pay sustained attention — i.e., read a novel — is eroding even in adults who once enjoyed doing so.

No less importantly, our sense of what counts as worth paying attention to appears to be atrophying. Increasingly banal, lewd or violent productions are able to - or perhaps are needed to - keep the commercial ball in the air.

Along with these consequences the content of public discourse appears to be 'trending down'. Opinion polls corrupt democratic proceedings by giving pundits opportunities to gossip about who is ahead instead of discussing issues. Polls also encourage politicians to be vague, slippery and ambiguous because they need to be able to change direction if poll results are not encouraging.

More generally, meaningful conversations about what is going on should be on every endangered species list. We can be so quickly informed with *Wikipedia* and *Google Search* at our service that nothing warrants conscious attention. We can inform ourselves as soon as any need arises — but such needs never rise up from within these days.

I think this is what Henry David Thoreau had in mind when he wrote that individuals should only read one issue of one newspaper in their lifetime. They should then spend time thinking about what was reported and - it goes without saying - doing something about it.

The need to respond to respond to events with internally conceived thoughts and projects has been replaced with Google Search *availability*. If anyone actually does enough research to become agitated, the need to wait for corroboration tomorrow still allows a good night's sleep.

> *Society everywhere is in conspiracy against the manhood of every one of its members.*

> R. W. Emerson

Economic encroachments would be reduced if we reminded ourselves of an "apodeictic principle" – a statement wearing its truth on its face. The lives of creatures, including human creatures, should remain as available as possible for their own use. They should not be slaughtered for the fun of it,

293

transmogrified into pets or driven into extinction as collateral damage of business plans.

Similarly the productive activities of human beings should not be harnessed to the building of pyramids, bigger and better cities, or the generation of profit for corporations or individuals. Our lives, work, dreams and fears... should not be harnessed to legislators' desires for herd animals servicing the status quo.

Yet this is what is going on. A news item March 19, 2014 observed that 45 individuals have much wealth among them as half the human population[52] .

Even so it would be a mistake to identify the wealthy as responsible for what is going on. We must look beyond those convening and profiting from inequities. Such people exist because of what you and I get up to — and, more importantly, because of what we fail to get up to.

You are probably objecting that *rich get richer, poor get poorer* proceedings have to be involved in inequities. This is correct but only if we restrict our analyses to present moments. Today's inequities emerged over generations. Each step along the way seemed unexceptional, perhaps promising, perhaps inevitable... to our parents and grandparents. We know what this feels like. The economic and political developments in our own lives have seemed natural, harmless or inexorable to us as well.

The moral, the principle, the homily... is simple. We inherited the consequences of our ancestors' failures to hang on to the value of their work, just as our children and grandchildren will inherit our narrow dreams. The fact that these consequences look like poverty for most and wealth for fewer and fewer must no longer distract us from Pogo's famous statement: "We have met the enemy and he is us![53]

This is all actually good news. If we understand inequities as

---

[52]http://www.bbc.com/news/magazine-26613682
[53]http://upload.wikimedia.org/wikipedia/en/thumb/4/49/Pogo_- Earth_Day_1971_poster.jpg/360px-Pogo_-_Earth_Day_1971_poster.jpg

legacy consequences of our narrow lives and the narrow lives of our parents and grandparents we immediately see what must be done.

Vernon Molloy

Bling la Dish vs. Bangladesh

The *hoi oligoi* (the wealthy, powerful beneficiaries of apathy, scapegoating and gossiping aka the 1%) are glad to be blamed for what is going on. They may not often think about where their good fortune and excellent fortunes come from but they intuitively understand that as long as they are being blamed, their future is secure.

In other words, as long as you and I continue to believe the problem is that a small population has been *taking too much,* we will continue overlook the real issue is that we have been *giving too much*!

The only possible solution to inequity involves cutting off the flow of value, the blood supply, that has been spawning cancerous individuals, corporations and nations.

By elevating a few to God-like status and forcing them to become autonomically greedy, the rest of us have been tormenting rich and poor alike for at least as long as records have been kept.

However, until the Industrial Revolution, these proceedings were survivable. Human beings lacked the technological prowess to generate anthropogenic threats. We did not have bombs capable of destroying everything alive a dozen times. The Industrial Revolution transformed an exploitative, brutal but survivable state of affairs into something far worse.

As well the middle class emerged and catalysed a second transformation – the Information or Digital Revolution complete with smart technologies and geopolitics threatening not only the middle class but poor people everywhere.

Now that subsistence activities have been vanquished and populations herded into urban cul de sacs the end game can begin. To be centralized and urbanized is to live in the most dangerous circumstance possible. No matter how drab lives become, no matter how ominous the 'effluents of affluence' or pervasive the beggaring, cities grow by promising to solve the very problems they created by coming into existence.

As well, just by existing, cities offer to solve the existential issues religious institutions and aristocracies have been milking for thousands of years. Perpetual progress, increasingly well-appointed homes, Olympic Games... answer "Who am I?" "What is life for?" questions.

Of course not every anxious moment will be deflected. Not to worry: dividing time into weeks renders any remaining misgiving manageable. Who among us is willing to admit that he or she cannot keep it together until the weekend?

Vernon Molloy

Threats to Consciousness

What is not much thought about is that urbanization's principal charm — its ability to generate thousands of competing solutions for a few dozen problems — is offset by its inability to solve problems created by doing so.

The most important of these problems is that, along with setting the stage for pollution, climate change and militarism, urbanization has been outsourcing the need to generate conscious episodes from internal resources, memories and cognitive events.

In other words, as progress and development explores roads leading who knows where, people are finding that they have less to think about and less to think with. Their singular remaining responsibility is to earn enough to acquire or upgrade products they have been instructed to purchase and whose longevity has been engineered to last for months and not for years.

Even the incidence and quality of conscious episodes while working is under attack. Work experiences are banal and repetitive, increasingly under the control of inspectors, regulators, legislations, software systems - and increasingly likely to be automated out of existence.[54]

The remaining consciousness-involving activities: leisure pursuits, vacations, weekends... involve primal needs for food, shelter and entertainment. Just in case time and money remains, commercial blandishments, diet plans, exercise and lovelorn advice... torment us day and night.

Ironically, this tormenting is being integrated into what is going one. Nuisance telemarketers reassure us that most of our affairs are being conducted in legitimate ways. The

---

[54]http://www.bbc.com/news/business-32837071

298

Vernon Molloy

monies we earn and spent authenticate the corporations and governments that make earning and spending money not only necessary but possible.

This works no matter what work is involved! Factory farms, abattoirs, genetically-modified foods, fracking, anthropogenic change... are all accommodated.

The guards at Auschwitz went home every night to families and domestic lives; to evenings that repaired their souls sufficiently that they could soldier on.

In similar ways, wages paid to urban employees are a cost of doing business — not just in the obvious sense, but because wages paid constitutes a backdrop against which commerce seems wholesome and inevitable. People must be getting something out of what is going on. In 1st World nations what we have been getting is the wherewithal to purchase lovely lives.

The fact that this getting often involves giving people 'over there' the business in ways that impoverish them makes the Faustian bargain even more seductive.

Dividing lifetimes into seven-day slices further underwrites our sense that the world is rational. Five days of work justifies two days of personal time. (It used to take six, leaving Sunday for church. This is seen as more proof that we are making progress!) The pleasures and opportunities experienced during these weekends authenticate progress and development agendas. 'Earning a break' and 'taking a break' fifty two times a year reassures us that so investing our lives makes sense.

When these proceedings run smoothly, lives shuttle through a seemingly bottomless bank of seven day cycles, until retirement or illness interrupt languid dreams.

Even when old or sick however we rarely ask whether our lives have been wisely invested. If worries occur we remind ourselves that we have had rich lives — even if we cannot remember much about them!

Retirees do not ponder what is going on or what it all means – much less ask whether they themselves have any explaining to do.

This shallowness has risks of its own of course. Now that retirees can do whatever they wish, they often find that few wishes occur to them. They wander the concession roads of vanished lives. They take coffee with people they once worked with. Some remember the wars they fought in, that seem to them to prove they once had fortitude and virility but really only prove they once knew 'sic em'!

They go on vacations. They wait to die.

These 'golden years' were purchased with lifetimes of work whose fruits have gone we know not where. (Talk about inequities and obscene wealth does not cause us to connect dots!) What we are experiencing is that a lifetime spent at some specialized task is poor preparation for a few final years of glorious self-realization. This is not a trivial issue. Old age is when opportunities to be active and purposeful are most important. When there is less love to make, when dreams and possibilities no longer come easily, opportunities to be relevant and useful should be part of every personal, family and community plan.

In the past these possibilities occurred naturally and had benefits all around. Oldsters shared experiences and skills with young people in families and in communities. This was built into the way the world worked. Old people did not spend their time exclusively with other old people, perhaps hoping for dementia, senescence or cancer to take the sting away.

The communities and extended families that once made old people relevant have been replaced with pensions, senior citizen warrens and something we rarely think about - the pace of progress and development.

Modern Problems, Ancient Perspectives

Indeed, the accelerating rate of progress may be our most insidious threat. The experiences older people once brought to dinner tables and work experiences are no longer relevant to their children's lives, never mind their grandchildren's.

We are progressing so rapidly that experiences, opinions and skills from even a decade ago can now feel antiquated to the person whose experiences they are. This complements another Industrial Revolution invention. *Occupational specialization* reduces the relevance of anything you and I might have to say to anyone outside of our areas of expertise.

Of course, governments and corporations are well-served by these consequences. People who cannot communicate are divided and conquered. They can be organized, herded and farmed .

An even more draconian problem may be on the horizon. Old people are not only becoming *persona non grata* in terms of cultural relevance, they risk being identified as economic millstones.

- Oldsters are no longer involved in passing cultural resources from one generation to the next. In pre-Industrial Revolution economies grandparents freed up parents to pursue subsistence activities. Women harvested small animals, fruits and vegetables. Men passed their days running down large animals. This division of labour meant there were two sustenance streams supporting families and communities.

- One theory about why Neanderthals perished is that both Neanderthal men and women pursued the 'large game' strategies. This placed both at risk. Infants either had to be left behind or brought along 'on the hunt' – both perilous circumstances. To be sure, Neanderthals had survived for close to 400,000 years but this single income strategy may have meant they were unable to cope with, for example, climate change or possibly the advent of *Homo sapiens*.

- Although human beings arguably owe their survival to

Vernon Molloy

'income diversification' we do not seem understand its importance. After the Industrial Revolution community and family based subsistence-activities were systematically replaced with 'labour saving' alternatives. The quid pro quo included diminished independence, lost self-sufficiency and increased exposure to exploitation.

- How did this counter-intuitive change gain so much acceptance so quickly? Part of the answer is ironic. The existence of grandparents allowed both parents to start turning up at factories! The fact of grand parenting set the stage for understanding subsistence activities as primitive and unsophisticated.

- In a mere two centuries these changes cooked up a fine kettle of fish. Entrepreneurs, corporations and governments encouraged these proceedings because they realized that subsistence activities were not create wealth, power or governance opportunities.

- Indeed, they probably recognized that new technologies meant community-based subsistence activities could threaten hierarchical arrangements. What could be more dangerous to a rich/poor world than a pool of self-reliant individuals armed with new tools and a keen interest in doing things for themselves and one another? They might realize that wage employments were survivable, perhaps even desirable, but only if they financed new subsistence possibilities!

- In Industrial Revolution economies men replaced running down large animals with 'getting jobs'. In both cases the results are dragged back to relevant communities. These raw materials, these carcasses, these sacks of flour and sugar, these bolts of cloth and cords of wood... catalysed value-adding work in families and communities. Grandparents were involved of course, women and children, and possibly by the five per cent of human beings who find themselves homosexually oriented. These arrangements and ratios could have evolved as a family and community-based reproductive strategy under the heading of *inclusive fitness*. These relationships were synergistic and complementary. Everyone became a little wiser day by day; and if things were going well everyone became a little wealthier. No one became rich in this story however. If anyone expressed an unseemly interest in or proclivity for becoming rich, a trip to the woodshed straightened them out.

- In the past, with grandparents transmitting subsistence skills to next generations, human beings enjoyed equitable relationships with one another. This state of affairs endured for thousands of years. The problem is, subsistence activities can be onerous and demanding, and human beings are naturally interested in easy solutions. By helping adults opt for industrial and commercial replacements for subsistence activities, grandparents facilitated the emergence of the global economy, wall-to-wall profit-taking, and politicians' smiling faces on every wall and television screen.

- As these proceedings matured corporations and governments turned upon the grandparenting that made them possible. Grandparenting became an unprofitable, untaxable, intrinsically seditious activity - a problem to be solved.

- Now that kindergartens, nursery schools and licensed day-care facilities are up and running, now that palliative care units and euthanasia clinics are just around the corner, grandparents can go the way of the Dodo bird.

If grandparenting has been outsourced and grandparents rendered superfluous, what's next? Now that old people's contributions to family and community life have been eliminated they have no economic or cultural function. They have become unnecessary the way the human appendix is regarded as a *vestigial organ* – serving no useful function and prone to infection.

Put another way, old people, retired people, unemployed people, disabled people... are consumers and nothing but. They are points sources of inflation. As long as they have money and assets they continue to *demand* goods and services. Old people (and other malingerers) are not generating goods or services to compensate for goods and services they consume. This capacity to consume value when when the capacity to generate value no longer exists is inflationary.

We all recognize that inflation must be managed. Economic vigour and stability requires that nations (or consortium's of nations) balance supply and demand elements so that they enjoy inflation rates in the 2%-3% range.

Old people (and other groups past their best before date) make this balancing more difficult. Modern economies would be well served if oldsters embraced timely conclusions so their assets could be put to balanced use.

An unpleasant notion occurred to me several years ago. I started wondering how long it would be before evidence that 'old solutions' were in play would start turning up.

Then I realized that such evidence would be subtle and mixed in with other explanations. Once this was clear I began seeing that solutions to the problem of old people were well underway:

- Old age homes and the dismissal of grandparenting implicit in urbanization and mobile nuclear families are already well-established;

- Garden-variety abuses of old people can be explained in terms of greed, the demands of city life and the loss of bonding opportunities implicit in the loss of extended families and communities;

- 'Old people' solutions need not involve indictable conspiracies. A strategy with a proven track record involves corporations and governments *not choosing* to implement repairs, solutions and countervails.

This last solution has both logical and Divine credentials. Logically it is more difficult to blame someone for not doing something than for what they actually get up to. Similarly it is easier to forgive one's self for not doing something.

In terms of Divine sanction, the Ten Commandments are either direct "Thou halt not... do x" statements, or can be readily converted into such statements. There is no comparable list of things human beings should get up to, beyond the amorphous, easily-overlooked "Do unto others..." Golden Rule.

This means it is possible to lead a technically moral life by assiduously, consistently, conscientiously... doing nothing.

With these elements in place, oldsters and other marginal groups can be hurried into oblivion simply by not interrupting economic and psychological proceedings undermining their mental and physical health.

The life-shortening consequences of institutionalizing and medicalizing old age are widely acknowledged.

Time for a somewhat happier thought. Today's epidemiological bulge of oldsters may be enjoying a 'stay of execution' because they are inadvertently helping post-Industrial Revolution economies transition from a three-tier (upper, middle, lower) society to a more environmentally-friendly rich/poor world.

By being points sources of inflation, oldsters help nations harvest the benefits of automation and globalization in politically manageable ways. In other words, the nature of progress and development is itself evolving. The agenda no longer involves making work easier and lives better because doing so is profitable. The project now focusses upon downsizing or replacing workers. This can be immediately profitable, but its more important, long-term goal is to secure historical profit-taking, i.e. assets in wealthy hands.

Progress have always had regressive consequences because it

involves obsoleting old ways and means of doing things. These changes generate new employment opportunities. If these employments are roughly equal in number and quality to those obsoleted then the benefits of new techniques and technologies transfer to general populations.

The problem is, this wholesome proportion is not guaranteed, has never been legislatively enshrined, and shortfalls have been apparent for at least a century.

Offsetting this, significant subsistence activities have until recently been occurring in rural communities, towns and even cities. This bottom-up stream of value from families, communities, cottage industries and underground economies have been shielding communities and mainstream economies from the regressive consequences of progress and development. However, a corner was turned around the middle of the 20th century. The ratio and quality of replacement employments began to dramatically decline. This was partially due to the intelligence being incorporated in new technologies and software programs. At the same time, subsistence activities drained away to the point that the usual person's ability to produce anything at all from personal, family or community resources fell to zero.

It is frequently observed that modern technologies could feed the world and eliminate poverty and disease. The fact that this is not happening tells us is that capitalism has no mechanism for actualizing wholesome possibilities and equitably distributing wealth. .

On the other hand, urbanization and the decline of subsistence activities has been sanctioning corporations to pursue 'bigger is better' business plans. As a consequence corporations waste countless billions of your and my money fighting among themselves to see who gets to plough our fields and harvest our dreams.

When automation and outsourcing started visibly drying up good jobs and shrinking the wages of those remaining, when free trade agreements and globalization placed every worker in competition with every other worker, consumer demand started to contract – compared to the demand that would have occurred had the proportion of good jobs remained constant. This led to calls for still more progress and development, still more automation and outsourcing, as corporations and retailers attempted to source cheap good and services poorly employed workers could afford.

Western economies are coming to the end of this race to the bottom. This is why talk about the beleaguered middle-class is included in every politicians' platforms and talking points.

This is why every politician assiduously avoids discussing what would have to be done to fix the problem. No repairs are possible until 'progress and development', the engine that made the middle class possible, is recognized as inexorably dismantling its creation.

Applying progress as medicine when the disease is progress i cannot work. Anyone who talks this way is up to no good.

To return to the good news story, the present crop of oldsters in western nations is functioning as a buffer protecting global economies from deflating too rapidly or too soon. Since they are no longer active on the supply side, oldsters' purchases contribute to demand-pull inflation. This has been offsetting the deflationary consequences of lost and downgraded employments associated with technological developments and globalization.

To appreciate the importance of this factor we need to remember another hypothetical: the deflationary consequences of goods and services coming into the market without human involvement or at least without expensive human involvement. An increasing proportion of world GNP is coming from emerging nations and automated machines that never take a break or do any shopping.

In other words, if an artificial level of demand was not in play and creating an offsetting inflationary pressure, western economies would already be experiencing deflation. (Many are on the tipping point!)[55]

When this bulge of old people works its way through western nations, the underlying supply/demand imbalance will be fully exposed. The 'duffer buffer' masking the consequences of automation and outsourcing will vanish within a decade or two, let's say by 2030.

Although it might not seem to matter whether old people spend money themselves or hand it over straight away, doling out resources over a decade or two is a more sustained countervail than the measures impatient heirs and right-to-die ideologues likely have in mind. A reliably inflating economy — economists recommend something like two per cent — enjoys positive feedback while deflating economies are associated with depressions. Part of the reason is intuitive. If money will buy more next month or next year I may put off some purchasing. Deflating economies are also problematic for lenders and borrowers who must rejig financial instruments since borrowers will repay debts with increasingly valuable money[56] [57] [58].

Low inflation rates - and of course deflation – also have regressive consequences. Investors do not have to pay tax on income that goes in part to restore purchasing power. A low or no inflation climate means earned incomes must assume a larger share of public expenditures, transferring these costs from upper to middle and lower class populations.

Beginning in 1990, Japan spent more than a decade trying to extricate itself from a deflating economy. Economists have coined a wonderful term for this: *reflating.* This is akin to trying to get a tire to hold air without fixing the leak that

---

[55]http://knowledge.wharton.upenn.edu/article/europes-deflation-problem-is-everyones-problem/
[56]http://krugman.blogs.nytimes.com/2010/08/02/why-is-deflation-bad/?_php=true&_type=blogs&_r=0
[57]http://www.forbes.com/sites/saranyakapur/2013/01/25/japans-new-fiscal-policy-explained-and-why-it-matters/
[58]http://topdocumentaryfilms.com/how-economic-machine-works/

caused it to go flat in the first place.

But what if a deflating economy is also just what the doctor ordered to resolve pollution and resource depletion issues? A bout of global deflation might be welcome news. Now that the world's wealthy no longer need to extract profit from middle and lower class comerce they may be thinking outside of the box.

What if mankind's only survivable option requires global deflation?

Although this might seem counter-intuitive, becoming still wealthier is irrational if you are part of a population that already owns everything. Indeed, becoming wealthier is logically impossible! The only prospect that makes sense involves organizing a future wherein being wealthy continues to mean something. This includes a world with sun, fresh air, lovely beaches... and may require that most human beings become so poor that we cannot consume or pollute much.

As the present bulge of old people passes through, western economies' underlying deflation will be unmasked and may trigger just such a meltdown. For most of us this will be bad news – although perhaps the best we can hope for. If business as usual means even more anthropogenic change, the poor will be even more exposed to flooding, droughts, storms and civil unrest.

Even so, reconciling ourselves to a future that includes only ten per cent of human beings with a life worth having is a moral outrage even Hitler could not have envisaged.

I think this is true even if the individuals involved recognize that they will be among those turned away from Eden.

So let's get to work!

We can begin by recognizing a simple truth. More efficient workforces or machines cannot solve the problems facing us. A blizzard of efficient workforces and machines spawned them.

Vernon Molloy

So what to do? Socialist governments failed to solve problems of initiative, responsibility and equitable distribution. Experiments in Russia, China, Cuba, Venezuela... foundered on the shoals of corruption at the top and indifference and irresponsibility elsewhere. Capitalism – at least as practised in modern nations by present-day corporations – has enterprise and vigour to spare, but suffers from even more inequitable wealth and power distributions. Dr. Kai Nielson (Philosophy Department, University of Alberta) observed that capitalist countries are only interested in equalizing opportunities to compete to be unequal.

These problems cannot be tracked back to the machinations of rich and powerful individuals – who keep turning up no matter how carefully they are legislatively circumscribed. Rich and powerful people will keep turning up until the rest of us recognize that they are being spawned by our narrow, ineffectual and therefore vulnerable spheres of engagement.

An even narrower agenda can be identified in the antics of oldsters winding down their lives in urban environs. Their despicable strategy often centres upon dying as broke as possible, sometimes with the help of reverse mortgages.

To be fair, many parents and grandparents hope to pass on something to their children and grandchildren. However it is not clear how or why this generosity is less greedy than straightforward hedonism and self-indulgence.

If one's life-style ambitions expand to include family members and family members only, the resulting in-groups can seem more legitimately greedy and involuted than egregiously selfish individuals.

No one I know expresses active interest in retaining or resurrecting a world resembling the one they grew up in.

As we have seen, urban oldsters' final "Have a nice day!" salutation may be lending a deceptive balance to economies already collapsing into deflation. If so, human beings' first and probably last middle-class experiment could be vanishing before our eyes.

310

Modern Problems, Ancient Perspectives

Yet it is interesting to think how much has been accomplished in a few hundred years! Middle-class economies spawned technologies and and political machines capable of supporting a small population of human beings in splendid fashion. In addition, just by existing, western middle class populations seduced billions into crowding into cities and rendering themselves as hapless as fish in barrels.

From the point of view of the world's wealthy, the need to wind the global economy down is clear. The necessary machines, urban cultures and global economy are in place and running as smoothly as could be hoped for. Any difficulties encountered, any Arab Springs, any Islamic State contretemps, any global banking fiascos... make what is going on seem authentic and spontaneous.

All that remains is for the wealthy to stand clear; to look innocent and surprised — and express dismay when things start going really badly, by which they mean really well.

Co-opting oldsters into community-obliterating stratagems is ironic for another reason. Like subsistence economies, old people have always been potential sources of trouble for 'the establishment'. Old people have deep wells of experience. They often have assets and sometimes harbour the dangerous notion that they have nothing to lose.

Oldsters threaten apple carts for another reason. The sight of old people struggling through infirmity and disease underscores the hollowness of working like horses so we can spend like asses. Old age is when human beings are most likely to think about how they should have hung onto the value of all those years of work – and most likely to want to pass just such suggestions along to anyone willing to listen.

This is when human beings are most likely to conect handing over our lives and labours 'to the man' with so many being so poor and so few so rich!

To guard against such realizations, western nations have found it useful to provide old age security programs and other reassurances to urban populations. These programs are touted as evidence of a caring society. There is truth in this of course, but pension plans are also a pat upon urban heads. What is being said is: "Relax – you're doing splendid work. Things are going handsomely and your future is secure."

The most seductive machination involves organizing our lives into *weeks*. Think of it! A typical fifty years working lifetime means 2600 work weeks. This is a large number. With so many weeks awaiting us we seem to be swimming in an ocean of time. There is no reason to be concerned about how any one week is invested; which means there is no reason to be concerned about how they are all invested.

Lulled into sleep in this way, people scarcely glance up to see whether their lives are being well used or where the whole contraption is headed. Corporate coffers are filled by farming diligent workers and sharp-eyed consumers. The rich grow richer. Nations become powerful and belligerent in lock-step with the neediness of citizens increasingly willing to do whatever it takes to keep the ball rolling.

We live experimentally, mostly in the dark; each generation breaks its eggshell with the same haste and assurance as the last, dreams the same dreams, or others just as absurd, and if it hears anything of what former men have learned by experience, it corrects their maxims by its first impressions, and rushes down any untrodden path which it finds alluring, to die in its own way, or become wise too late and to no purpose.

George Santayana

I suggested earlier a few ways the natural order is kept out of the consciousness of urban populations. This does not mean that there are no seasons in urban lives. On the contrary, cultural proscriptions, government pronouncements, socialistic programs, the requirements of industry and religion... establish "proper schedules" for lifetimes. This might seem contrary to what has been argued. Signposts marking life's passages[59] could rouse somnolent citizens and prompt awkward questions. Apparently the risk is worth taking. Economies and public order are advantaged if an orderly progression from birth to death occurs. As well, there does not seem to be much danger that citizens will start thinking outside the box. The young have too much spring in their step to waste time upon issues appropriate to "fall guys". Later on, after they have invested decades in status quo living, there will be growing pressure to not question life-path "decisions".

As well, as progress and development proceeds, the plausibility of questioning anything declines. The absence of alternative employments, often the absence of employments of any kind, simplifies 'which way shall I go' decisions.

'Career constraints' have always been part of life. Accidents of birth and time, caste systems, feudal arrangements, rich/poor divides... locate and define the arenas lives play out on.

What is bleakly interesting is that such constraints are increasing. What is the point of moving from City A to City B if architecture, employment prospects and entertainment possibilities are identical? Although we still believe in the Horatio Alger myth (any person can become president) the problems socially and geographically mobile populations once posed to hegemonic interests are being dissolved. This is one of the more insidious consequence of urbanization and globalization. We are all of the same caste. There are no places worth going to. There are no economic ladders to climb.

Now that democracy is everywhere there are no revolutions to think about.

The seasons of human lives - rural or urban - are well known. They are:

1. Infancy/Childhood
2. Youth
3. Young maturity

---

[59]I borrow this term from Gail Sheehy

4. Middle maturity
5. Late maturity
6. Old age.

Obviously, a good deal of this occurs naturally. We are born, mature physically and psychologically and eventually die. The intervals between these stages, and their behavioural markers, are regarded as immutable and given. Through enculturation, each person becomes both a repository and vector of expectations establishing 'appropriate behaviours'. These behaviours are celebrated or grumbled about in literature and music and embodied in institutions.

There are schools for youngsters, sports activities for individuals in their second and third decades. Old age pensions and retirement homes kick in a few decades later.

Institutions, prohibitions, licences and commercial activities service these expectations. We vote, drink, drive and go to war at certain ages. We assume adult responsibilities and prerogatives at certain ages and are allowed, even encouraged, to set them aside upon retirement. There is scarcely a moment when every aspect of our lives is not prescribed and proscribed, permitted or forbidden.

This is why we smile at youthful excesses and do as much as possible to prevent the young from taking themselves seriously. Child prodigies and savants are celebrated by adults for being *old souls,* and despised by their peers for the same reason.

What we do not ask is to what extent these expectations produce the results they claim to acknowledge. The young expect "old" behaviours of parents and vice-versa. These are, to some extent, self-fulfilling prophecies. It seems to me that such conditionings are more prominent and efficacious in urban circumstances than in rural. Professional athletes are often too old beyond thirty years of age. Movie stars are scrutinized for wrinkles and evidence of cosmetic surgery and global sales of cosmetic products are expected to reach 105 billion in 2016[60] .

Human beings are so suggestible that few avoid mutually-induced hypnotic states of mind. We are harried along by one another's expectations. We are, as David Riesman warned against, *Other Directeds.*

There are four results:

1. The economic, political and cultural programs of centralized life are hypnotic and comprehensive. They profoundly contract the subjective lives of urban populations.

2. In cities circumstances and options are homogeneous and increasingly identical for everyone.

3. A intuitive possibility is that longevity is influenced by how long individuals expect to live. This is known to be true in the prognosis of the critically ill. The will to live is an important factor determining outcomes. Why should our general will-to-live not have similarly profound effects? I do not suggest that potential life span can be altered by psychological states of mind... only that achieved spans can be shortened. We often notice how quickly people die after retirement (civil servants survive an average of three years). Conversely we sometimes remark about how durable some people seem to be – generally those who remain active beyond the habits of their fellows.

   Could it be that these people simply do not believe that 60 or 65 is the end of the road and adjust their life-spans accordingly?

   The point is, as the Other-Directedness of urban life increases, it seems plausible to suggest that life stage conditioning would become an increasingly potent determinant of health and longevity.

   (Of course you are correct: this is nothing more than

---

[60]http://brandongaille.com/26-cosmetics-industry-statistics-and-trends/

an intuition. I recommend it anyway! What do you have to lose?)

4. We can expand 3) by stating its corollary: If people were not exposed to stage of life expectations "deciding" when youthful zeal ended would be more a matter of physiological limits than psychological conditioning.

Many will be object that it is not plausible that human beings could suffer diminished subjective lives... much less number of years lived... no matter how pervasive urban machinations become.

To counter this it may be useful to remember that urbanization makes extensive use of two human characteristics. The first is common to all forms of life. The second is a feature of urbanization not yet mentioned.

Both involve memories.

We know that every creature must respond to events quickly to avoid danger or seize opportunities. Part of this cognitive machinery making this possible works by ignoring repetitive stimuli after an initial period of attention. The phenomenon is called *habituation* and is common to all forms of life.

The relevant problem is that this defence affords no protection against encroachments that proceed slowly and incrementally. If we survive a toxic, dangerous or usurious state of affairs for more than a few moments our cognitive system labels it benign and pays no further attention. In this way toxic states can emerge so long as they do so slowly enough that *habituation* masks encroachments and incursions.

A frog can be boiled alive without becoming alarmed so long as the temperature is raised slowly.

Recent revelations about government surveillance of other governments and domestic populations (in the USA, *The Homeland Security Act* passed in 2002) are excellent examples of habituation in action. These encroachments have already become part of the backdrop against which further encroachments will be measured.

After a few moments, states of affairs become the lens through which further changes to states of affairs are viewed.

Habituation has a helper function that has also been co-opted by *urbanizers*. Like many creatures, human beings have built-in measures to prevent familiar circumstances from 'shutting down' consciousness. All else being equal, many creatures, and certainly human beings, seek out stimulation after a period of nothing going on requiring conscious attention.

Unfortunately this defence is unable to judge the quality of experiences and is therefore *promiscuous*. (How could new experiences be judged pro-actively?)

What seems to be occurring is that the individuals and corporations servicing urban populations are now providing not only food and shelter but stimulation.

This cunning work has made media-driven, technologically-abetted voyeurism the core of billions of lives. Professional sports, reality TV, social media... can all be understood as mechanisms supplying novelty to jaded populations.

Even though these presentations are not interesting in any way that matters, they are novel enough, flashy enough... to evade habituation responses and garner enough eyeball time to keep commercial balls in the air. We have no defence against counterfeit novelty.

An adaptation that once helped human beings survive has been turned against us.

The need for stimulation also explains why urban populations tolerate intellectually vacuous but commercially useful entertainments - the form of stimulation without content. This could also explain why we fail to respond to alarming economic and ecological signals. Facile, banal, vacuous... productions become increasingly acceptable when alternative sources of stimulation are demanding, alarming or laden with responsibilities.

A more subtle consequence of urbanizations involves the loss of Inner-Directed persons. The importance of this loss becomes apparent when the nature and function of subjective lives is considered. Internally-sourced subjective experiences occur when memories combine with local events or conversations. Memories are not inert representations of experience. They are distilled experiences and retain the active nature of the events generating them. This means they invoke and evoke one another automatically and generate conscious episodes based upon lives lived, local events and conversations. These episodes can also participate in new conscious events and source new understandings and memories.

This is why we should be concerned about the invidious consequences of urban life. To realize rich inner lives persons must have expectations of themselves as initiators of action. They must see themselves as enduring subjects of experience, as centres towards which information streams and as loci from which understandings and intentions emanate.

Many variables facilitate or impede these proceedings. Destructive influences are known to include repressive societal experiences: the presence of what Dr. R. D. Laing termed the "schizophrenogenic family"; traumatic childhood events; courses of experience leading to poor self-confidence and naturally occurring variations in assertiveness.

My suggestion is that the "degree of centralization" constitutes an important additional factor. In *The Lonely Crowd*[61] , David Riesman differentiated societies into three characteriological types: Other-Directed, Outer-Directed, and Inner-Directed. Briefly, Outer-Directed societies tend to occur in "old, poor countries", with rigid stratifications, social mores and detailed folk-ways defining behaviours. The caste system of India is such a society.

---

[61] *David Riesman, The Lonely Crowd* (1961: Yale University Press).

318

Modern Problems, Ancient Perspectives

Other-Directed was Riesman's term for 1st world nations' post-Industrial Revolution urban culture. People depend upon the purveyors of consumer goods and governments for notions of identity, value and fulfilment. Only the *Inner-Directed* person in Riesman's three part classification enjoys autonomous life. Riesman's example was the frontiersman who emerged during the settling of the United States. Out of necessity, such individuals developed a capacity for self-reliance and self-government. The USA owes much to the original immigrants who arrived in the New World with cultural resources and not much else and were forced to put these resources of languages, skills and expectations to work.

In the 1950's Riesman thought Inner-Directed recidivists could still to be found in America although he thought their numbers had been depleted; ironically as a result of the economic and technological achievements and urbanization Inner-Directeds had carved out of The New World.

Intuitively, Inner-Directed individuals are more likely to enjoy internally-sourced subjective lives. Benefits include the delights of self-prescribed tasks and a sense of well-being rising from self-reliance. Inner-directed persons are less likely to suffer contraction of subjective lifetime, even when they find themselves in centralized circumstances!

I propose (perhaps as a research topic) that Inner-Directeds live longer than other characteriological types. Indeed this possibility has been investigated. An article entitled "Why Bosses Live Longer" in the Toronto Star, December 8, 1990 suggests that a critical factor seems to be whether one is "in control of one's life".

> Something is killing the great lower classes of the modern world, grinding them down before their time. The statistics show it's also killing the middle classes, who live longer than the poor but not as long as the rich. You die younger than your boss, but (if it's any consolation) he dies younger than his boss.

Corporations and governments are ambivalent at best about the existence – never mind the cultivation – of Inner-

319

Directeds. Socialistic initiatives, obscurantism, jargonism; specialized educations; the licensing of plumbing, electrical work and auto mechanics... imply that the usual person is incompetent to perform even simple tasks without training.

Even pigs have been caught up in these proceedings. Historians have suggested that pigs were officially labelled as unfit for human consumption in both Jewish and Muslim cultures for a simple reason. Pigs were such a prolific, important food source that the power brokers of ancient times worried about controlling their restive populations. If families and communities could simply head off whenever it suited them, their retinue of pigs dutifully following along, how could God's work get done? The answer was not long coming. Pigs are vectors of Satanic mischief. They eat the faces of unattended children. When priests exorcise demon-infested human beings, ousted demons seek refuge in the closest pig.

Like the foxbats thought to be the reservoir species for the Ebola virus, pigs symbolize subsistence-activity threats to hegemonic arrangements. This is the reason they were condemned in both Jewish and Muslim nations.

(At the end of this book I describe a more wholesome reservoir species possibility.)

As a result of these prohibitions, now expanded to include Granny's cookies and raw milk, a growing proportion of human beings are suffering from insecurity, anxiety and feelings of inferiority. These problems have become so widespread that self-help gurus can find profitable niches repairing anxiety and personality deficits that rarely occurred when families and communities enjoyed a healthy proportion of subsistence activities.

The moral is simple. No society can survive without a threshold proportion of Inner-Directed people and subsistence activities. What is this proportion? We presently seem to be striving for a nice equilibrium between docility and self-expectation. Psychological well-being is reckoned to include functional – but not problematic – levels of initiative and personality.

One must be integrated to be a productive employee but not so integrated as to be productively self-employed. What productive now means involves working on corporate or national projects conceived by Inner-Directeds who continue to turn up in spite of the best efforts of corporations, politicians and educators.

This arrangement works for captains of industry and politicians but leaves much to be desired for the rest of us. Robert Lindner has offered a description of the well-adjusted urbanized person.[62]

> In conversation with analysands, analysts, and the so-called "well analyzed"I have been shocked to learn that they have felt themselves to have achieved their analytic goals when they became placid, accepting, undisturbed by the condition of man and the world, uncaring for the fate of their fellows and able without guilt or strain to pursue wholly selfish goals... and pride is taken in having approached or attained the resignation of barnyard fowl.

Although we continue to fantasize that governments strive for the greatest good for the greatest number of citizens, this is clearly not the case among the rapacious, powerful, armed-to-the-teeth nations prowling the planet.

Even within nations,evidence of mutual solicitude or empathy is ambiguous. What statistics seem to demonstrate is that social and economic arrangements have only passing interest in ordinary well-being. Governments and corporations are more interested in organizing workers and consumers with increasing GNP's or trouble-free regularity in mind. If workers and consumers enjoy some quality of life along the way, this is well and good and perhaps a defensible cost of doing

---

[62]Robert Lidner, *The Revolutionist's Handbook* (New York: Grove Press Inc., 1971)p. 111.

business.

The need for Inner-Directedness is not pedantic moralizing. History is full of examples of what happens when citizens are dependent to the point that they have no choice save to support economic and military aggressions: middle-class + rich vs. the poor; wealthy vs. the middle class... and, more obviously, international conflicts wherein the line between economic and military activities is blurred.

As well, governments appear to be waging war against their own citizens (see: A Solzhenitsyn, The Gulag Archipelago)[63] . Subtler aggressions have become business as usual: the contempt evinced by corporations purveying sometimes deadly, usually needlessly expensive and deliberately short-lived products.

The emergence of a larger proportion of Inner-Directeds would repair many of these problems. Indeed it is arguable that a lack of Inner-Directeds allowed these problems to come into existence in the first place! Nations with a healthy ratio of self-sufficient citizens would not look anything like what is going on. Without any sense that they can conceive and actualize projects personally, individuals have a correspondingly diminished sense of a personal future. They do not understand themselves as individuals for whom memories and cultural resources have utility or practical application.

In the absence of such expectations, only information labelled as important by institutions: schools, churches, employers, governments... becomes data to be remembered. When such individuals are out of an institutional context (away from work, away from their church or mosque, away from shopping malls...) their disjointed, partitioned... experiences and memories are unable to generate internally-sourced conscious episodes.

---

[63]A. Solzenitzen, *The Gulag Archipelago* (New York: Harper & Row, 1974)

Modern Problems, Ancient Perspectives

The explanation is simple. Since such individuals are not functioning as Inner-Directeds during cultural excursions or other experiences, the resulting memories have limited ability to invoke one another and generate internally-sourced subjective experiences.

In other words, as cities transform populations from Inner-Directeds to Other-Directeds, people become de facto memory banks and appendages for institutions, corporations and governments. Individual cognitive capacities become the assets and data banks of external systems. The only issues actively engaged are those brought to attention by outside events — questions in text books assigned by teachers, problems encountered in work places, goods and services on commercially-orchestrated bucket lists....

At the end of the day, all such experiences will be able to be tracked to external events triggering internally located but otherwise discrete and disconnected memories, anxieties and needs.

The consequence is that our conscious episodes – the only way we have of knowing we are alive – are increasingly dependent upon externalities: music, food, fan-based voyeurism, weekends, vacations and, of course, corporations and governments.

This means individuals can be integrated into institutional, corporate and national organizations with little or nothing remaining. Their primal self-preservation instincts are now harnessed to the protection of the institutions and organizations they constitute.

The resulting capacity for monstrous commitment is underscored by the antics of ideologues, zealots and bomb-belt terrorists.

The result is moral and intellectual paralysis punctuated occasionally with demonstrations and riots. Unemployed, marginalized or simply Other-Directed, it never occurs to urban populations that their circumstances are the cumulative results of historical working and consuming decisions. These circumstances now include automation, global trade agreements, outsourcing, and carefully-engineered product life-cycles.[64]

These problems will only be solved if we start thinking about ourselves in whole person terms. We presently regard ourselves as workers part of the time and consumers the rest. We rarely think of ourselves as persons who are both workers and consumers because the conscious episodes of urban individuals are always sourced in one activity or the other.

Only Inner-Directed populations have the wherewithal to become persons.

The importance of whole person understanding is impossible to exaggerate.

I have an example. For more than a century trade unions played an important role in improving wages and working conditions in western nations. What is significant is that trade unions never got around to organizing their members' consuming needs with a view to doing some group bargaining with suppliers and retailers on their behalf.

This extension of the union mandate would have complemented wage and working condition achievements in wonderful ways. Such groups could have invited suppliers to quote on members' recurring needs. They could have established mutually-beneficial relationships with local businesses and industries.

Such an expanded unionism could have included the retired, the unemployed and the non-unionised in spectacular bargaining initiatives.

Sized-up and made relevant by organizing consumers as well as workers, unionism could have boycotted, or threatened to boycott, corporations whenever outsourcing, downsizing or automation projects threatened local employments,

---

[64]http://www.bbc.com/news/magazine-26669971

324

communities and families.

A good deal of lip service is paid to the importance of competition in the market place. Nothing sharpens competition faster than having consumers approaching retailers and corporations in groups of 10, 100, 1000.... The fact that loyalty discounts already exist in the market place (Canadian Tire money and credit cards, signal that merchants like the advantage of servicing de facto groups but want to remain in the drivers' seat.

Another repair – obvious to Inner-Directed sensibilities – would be for a political party to campaign on replacing percentage-driven remuneration adjustments with one-size-fits-all settlements.

In this story every employee gets the same increase – $500.00 or $5000.00 – whenever a contract is renegotiated. This would preserve workplace equity and avoid the compounding calculations ballooning wages year-over-year and dramatically separating top from bottom.[65]

A thoughtful political party would go one step further and advocate frozen remuneration schedules. Think of the benefits! The only way to 'get ahead' in such circumstances would be to pay attention to getting better value for one's money. This could translate into durable products and less expensive ways to promote and distribute them.

The names of the threats confronting us are as familiar as our own: nuclear, chemical, pollution, global warming, resource depletion.... The issue is not whether these threats are here or merely imminent. The issue is where they are coming from. I hope I have persuaded you that these threats are *derivative*. They are rooted in the progress and development projects gutting subjective lives and economic independence in both developed and emerging nations.

With billions already disenfranchised and moribund in urban barns, corporations and institutions are rushing in to

---

[65]I sent these notions along to Canada's Green Party a few years ago.

Vernon Molloy

complete this terrible business. In the last half-century alone corporations have been skewing political events and elections so nations take up internecine struggles. They have been promoting addictive, disease and obesity-infected life-style addictions.

Common sense, humanity, justice, self-preservation... are rarely encouraged by those who see themselves orchestrating the paths nations take. They think nations require citizens properly organized and disposed to provide tax dollars and patriotism for God and Country.

Of course these understakings and characteristics are termed jingoism, bigotry and fanaticism when opponents are in view.

In such circumstances the idea that modern problems flow from too few Inner-Directeds on one hand and too many Other-Directeds on the other is unlikely to cross many minds.

To further confuse matters, Other-Directeds are often attractive individuals. After all, putting on a pretty face is their principal ambition. Other-Directeds can also enjoy fulsome relationships with families, peers and neighbours.

What is important to recognize is that – to the extent that they are Other-Directed – these individuals are unable to participate in mutually-nurturing communities. They are unable to work towards well-being – their own or anyone else's – even a month or a year in the future. Overwhelming concern for what is going on right here right now is as good as it gets! On the surface this looks like selfishness and greed. However *selfishness* and *greed* are scapegoating concepts that do not suggest a way forward. Understanding these characteristics as consequences of lost Inner-Directedness is more useful.

With this in mind we see why communities must contain persons growing more persons. In other words communities must contain a threshold proportion of individuals capable of generating ideas, values and conscious episodes out of internal resources.

Modern Problems, Ancient Perspectives

What we must also recognize is that such communities must be economically self-subsisting to a wholesome degree.

The reason is simple. When not engaged as workers or consumers Other-Directeds only think about homes, families and friends, and they only think about them within spheres encompassing a few days and a few kilometres.

This is not a moral indictment. These are not *consciously chosen* priorities. They happen whenever human beings get the chance to leave off being persons; and they certainly happen when human beings find themselves in urban wombs.

This means that the storied Inner-Directeds of North America's pioneer days were not engaging social or moral issues in ways we are failing to equal. The conscious lives of cowboys, settlers, lumberjacks, factory workers... were generated by local challenges, resources and events.

The same is true of every human beings. Conscious lives are generated by what is going on around us and by what is being asked of us.

The difference is that every previous generation spent a good deal of time performing subsistence activities. These activities had an important feature. They involved conceiving and carrying out projects with whatever resources happen to be at hand (think: MacGyver!)[66] . Such experiences build up expectations that individuals are persons – moral and rational agents capable of organizing and actualizing projects using consciousness.

I think it is fair to say that this usually fruitful, occcasionally dangerous fantasy has disappeared in today's cities. It has been replaced a sad tale of human beings partitioned into workers and then, later on, into consumers.

Instead of reviewing these circumstances and asking whether the Faustian urban bargain was a good idea, we seem to be growing increasingly arrogant.

- We claim to be more sophisticated about moral and

---

[66]http://www.macgyveronline.com/

ethical issues than any generation before us or elsewhere. We believe we consummate our responsibility to insights if we share them with others.

- Sharing insights used to be cumbersome. Conversations, gossip and telephone calls were involved. Producing essays or books required sustained effort and then there was the business of getting them published and sometimes read.

- The result was that, every once and a while, we would get impatient and act on them ourselves!

- Now that the INTERNET has arrived, we all get to publish insights. This means that we can get rid of them effortlessly. Since no one reads them – unless to make a scathing, probably scatological comment – the INTERNET functions as an infinitely capacious dumping ground for pesky conscious episodes, just in case any pop up.

- Of course now that Inner-Directed conscious episodes are withering away, the risk of anyone reading, let alone writing, more than a few hundred words on any topic no longer threatens anyone.

Whatever the explanation the result is pandemonium. Billions of people are watching their lives swirl from crisis to crisis with the indomitable indifference of barnyard fowl. A few stalwart individuals in "positions of authority" are trying to avert a thousand disasters.

Arguably, their occasional successes may be spawning greater dangers. If they are seen as making headway this is probably interpreted as sanctioning still more urbanization, specialization and globalization.

People such as David Suzuki and Noam Chomsky may mean that our eventual denouement will be even more catastrophic.

One almost wishes the progress and development train had derailed a century ago when the conclusion might have been survivable.

The Great Wars of the 20th century taught us little. Rather than thinking about the origins of internecine violence, we debited them to a handful of madmen and accelerated the processes spawning even larger cohorts for even more megalomaniacal Hitlers and Kim Jong-uns.

The "peace" the world has enjoyed since did not flow from new reservoirs of wisdom and tolerance. The Russian economy could not compete with American capitalism or the nominally communistic, Chinese economy.

Replicating Western-style capitalism was the answer. Enter *perestroika* (economic reconstruction) and *glasnost* (openness).[67]

In a few decades, suitably laundered capitalistic ingredients transformed the Russian proletariat into rough versions of American workers and consumers.

They are already reliably productive wealth generators. They have already become Other-Directeds like you and me.

If this outcome was back of mind in the USSR's movers and shakers in the 1980's, the prospect is frightening indeed. This

---

[67] *Perestroika refers to the reconstruction of the political and economic system established by the Communist Party. Politically, contested elections were introduced to reflect the democratic practices of Western society and allow citizens to have a slight say in government. Economically, Perestroika called for de-monopolization and some semi-private businesses to function, ending the price controls established by the government for the past seven decades. The goal was to create a semi-free market system, reflecting successful capitalist practices in the economies of Germany, Japan, and the United States. Unfortunately, such an economy took time to thrive, and people found themselves stuck in a worn-out economy, which led to long-lines, strikes, and civil unrest. http://www.coldwar.org/articles/80s/glasnostandperestroika.asp*

would suggest that the rich and powerful are beginning to consciously regard urban populations the way farmers regard barnyard animals.

Moreover - to the extent that human beings are urbanized, dependent and Other-Directed - the question of whether investigative reporters, David Suzukis and Noam Chomskys... ferret out the news that we are being manipulated and traduced may not matter.

Such concerns are simply outside the conscious episodes occurring within Other-Directeds. The mythical, autonomous persons we imagine ourselves might be interested in such information. Half-witted workers have more pressing agendas; as do half-witted consumers.

Now that we are *industrialized creatures,* now that we are no longer self-subsisting to any degree, we are either workers or consumers every moment of every day. Our conscious experiences are triggered by corporations and politicians who know what buttons to push to get what response.

Every farmer worth her salt block develops just such a vocabulary: "Co boss, Co boss; Here piggy piggy, Here chicky, chicky...."

This explains why the threat of nuclear destruction, the reality of compromised life-styles, food, water and ecological crises... remain non issues.

It is not that we turn away from or ignore such issues. They simply never cross our minds.

For Other-Directeds the litmus test is always whether responding to Al Gore, the IPCC, the Club of Rome, the threat of nuclear Armageddon... involves a lifestyle change or an enlarged sphere of responsibility.

In short, solving political and economic problems is something middle and lower class populations are going to have to achieve. The beneficiaries of what is going on are not going to stop. They are not going to respond to moral arguments or pleas to cease and desist.

They are, however, delighted that such pleas continue and keep an ear to the ground so as to notice any ominous silence. Wealthy apple carts will only be at risk if a new genre of agitator turns up. The people organizing marches and demonstrations are only reassuring the one percenters they imagine themselves confronting.

The agitators needed to solve today's difficulties are not going to waste time banging pots – even if 'the establishment' encourages such behaviour with rubber bullets and tear gas canisters.

What is required involves resurrecting family and community lives, subsistence and local economies, until at least twenty-five per cent of our needs flow from local economies.

Until this is done no repair is possible. As soon as this is done, nothing further will be required.

Finally, it is the nature of governments to govern. The more they get to do the more they yearn to do. Corporations are legally obligated to endure, grow larger and pass profits to shareholders. This is why governments and corporations are equally interested in reliable citizens, employees and customers. This is why Inner-Directed persons and subsistence activities are anathema; even though Inner-Directedness has to be what is meant by *persons;* even though promoting Inner-Directedness is the official reason democracy is valued and promoted.

Contrary to appearances and gossip, corporations and nations are not inert structures persons conjure into existence and perhaps unwisely instruct. Corporations and nations are best understood as parasitic quasi forms of life. They are cancers. They feed off of living arrangements that have let their guard down, that suffer from faulty immune systems or, more likely, that have no defence against these alien creatures.

There is another question to ask: where are the energetic,

331

talented individuals that keep turning up in families? What became of the sons and daughters who might have been expected to defend their communities, parents and grandparents against corporate threats? The answer is that the best and brightest migrated to cities and became part of the problem!

No doubt, they did so innocently, dreaming of careers, of becoming businessmen, administrators, academics – of succeeding.

Perhaps they do not realize how much modern success is counted in terms of other people's losses. No one can know what is in anyone's mind as they take up a position with leaders, managers and apologists.

We know what they have been getting up to however. They have been capitalizing upon, organizing, harvesting and often obliterating the activities and circumstances that made them possible.

In double-entry, zero-sum economies, wealthy lives are funded by debits from thousands or millions of small accounts. When leaders and managers proliferate – and when have they not? – small accounts risk becoming no-accounts.

Now that the world is subsistence activity free, the increasingly abject state of marginalized populations is being used to justify further incursions. If people must be provided for, looked after and kept under surveillance, let's spare no expense setting up the necessary machineries!

Does it matter that these costs contribute to their further undoing?

Faced with such malignant intentions it is hard to see where solutions could be found. One possibility – perhaps the only possibility – is that people are not malicious so much as thoughtless. Maliciousness emerges when thoughtless people coalesce into corporations and nations.

This thoughtlessness reaches its apogee when the people

constituting *corporations and nations* see themselves as innocent bystanders or victims and one another as villains.

A more thoughtful calculus is needed. When nations and corporations harvest domesticated populations, profits are apportioned among those visibly responsible. When deficits or harms are distributed, the calculation is turned on its head.

Here is the equation: profits to leaders; harms to followers.

If we somehow repaired this hypocrisy, perhaps by achieving the twenty five per cent subsistence rule, who knows what could be accomplished?

To be sure, we will not undo in a year what it took centuries to create. All that can be hoped for is a movement away from dependency and economic thralldom. Naturally-occurring subsistence living and communities are gone, perhaps forever. This does not mean that new versions could not be retrieved and invented. Urban crowding, mutual need, social media... all provide opportunities to organize the unemployed and marginally employed into local economies where they perform value -adding work for themselves and one another.

Indeed massive urbanization opens up community possibilities that did not exist a century ago. Nothing prevents individuals from organizing into groups of 100 or 1000 and doing some serious bargaining with retailers. Smartphone apps could allow shoppers to coalesce into platoons on the fly and approach delighted retailers with offers to purchase - if the discount offered warrants their fickle attention!

Bidding wars could break out among retailers hoping to attract the platoons of shoppers marching through shopping centres, smartphones at the ready ready to receive and vote upon the latest bids!

Urban populations could also arm themselves with wristwatches showing the current week as a fraction of the weeks remaining in each life. If we assume three score and ten years, each week would flash up every morning as some

Vernon Molloy

number over 3640.

Finally – more seriously – we must include enough culture, technology and urbanization in our communities to keep nations and corporations alive – but not so much that they spin out of control.

This will be difficult. The alternative far more so.

Euler's Identity and Realism
$e^{j\pi}+1=0$

Euler's identity is regarded as one of the most beautiful mathematical equations ever achieved.

According to Prof David Percy from the Institute of Mathematics and its Applications (http://www.ima.org.uk/):

> ... *"It is simple to look at and yet incredibly profound, it comprises the five most important mathematical constants - zero (additive identity), one (multiplicative identity), e and pi (the two most common transcendental numbers) and i (fundamental imaginary number).*

> *"It also comprises the three most basic arithmetic operations - addition, multiplication and exponentiation.*

> *"Given that e, pi and i are incredibly complicated and seemingly unrelated numbers, it is amazing that they are linked by this concise formula*

If, as I suspect, a process model eventually replaces realism — the notion of objects and entities in a presently-existing material world — these objects and entities will then be understood as reifications, gestalts, images... concocted by human beings (and other creatures)for reasons involving computational efficiency and success.

You ask: success for or as what? What we will also then be talking about are narratives featuring reliably enduring, coherent processes; the way we now talk about clouds that sometimes look like monsters or people and that sometimes spawn hurricanes that warrant attention and even names 'of their own'.

- - - -

Vernon Molloy

As realists we believe that object and entities exist separately from one another. They come into (and pass out of) existence by way of midwifery processes: stellar and organic evolution, conception, birth, death....

If realism turns out not to be true, realizations should already be occurring on the front lines of research and understanding.

I think this is the case. For almost a century physicists have been talking about various cosmologies, relativity and quantum physics.

Albert Einstein sidestepped both realism and process cosmology alternatives by talking about *local simultaneity* - exceptions to the special and general theory of relativity that allowed Newtonian physics to apply wherever awarenesses occur but nowhere that awarenesses had not yet seized upon and *realized*.

This was the issue Alfred North Whitehead *took* exception to. The cosmology contained in *Process and Reality* approached the question of being from the bottom up rather than from the top down or the outside in.

It is interesting to think about mathematics in similar terms. My understanding of mathematics is rudimentary at best so what follows is nothing more than an intuitively-motivated conjecture.

Here is the identity again:

$$e^{i\pi}+1=0$$

What we need is a definition of terms:

> *e* represents the natural logarithm of continuous growth and is irrational (cannot be expressed as a fraction).

> *i* represents the imaginary number obtained by taking the square root of -1. This is also the number obtained by taking a derivative, i.e., the slope of a tangent to any curved surface. Although derivatives are approximated in practical situations with non-imaginary numbers, if the process was taken to its conclusion (i.e., to infinity)

i would result.

π is the irrational number obtained by dividing the diameter into the circumference of any circle.

What does this have to do with realism? On the standard view, numbers were invented when human beings encountered the need for and then devised ways to count recurring objects and entities.

The assumption has always been that these were *found objects* but a simpler explanation is possible. Counting strategies could have emerged to keep track of imaginary objects human beings were comparing and contrasting, imaginary objects distilled by cognitive processes yielding *reifications, gestalts* or *images.*

From the point of view of individual beings, nothing changes. The difference involves the status of things. There are no actual things in a presently existing material world — there are approximations, derivatives, predictions, expectations... .

Since we are talking about imaginary objects and entities distilled out of recurring events — for example, discussing the location of stones in a stream so community members can cross without getting wet — the fact that human beings invented numbers is a poor basis for realist claims.

It is said that we use base 10 numbers because this is how many fingers we have.

Arithmetic systems did not have 0 until someone thought about subtracting 1 from 1. The notion of negative numbers quickly followed. Then - by performing addition, subtraction, multiplication and division upon the results - the *real number line* swam into view; a veritable zoo of possibilities with, for example, an infinite set of numbers between 0 and 1 as well as infinite sets of odd and even (smaller and smaller) numbers.

What does this mean? I suggest that when human beings began distilling notions of objects out of 'object free reality' we imported something of reality's flowing nature along with the apparently countable results underwriting realism and common sense.

Vernon Molloy

Thus — even though we can add, subtract multiply and divide numbers — sometimes we come up with rational results and sometimes not, as is the case with the symbols in Euler's identity.

It is these pesky irrational, imaginary, transcendental... numbers that blow the whistle on what we are up to. These numbers share 'DNA evidence' of their genesis as approximations, as crude partitions imposed upon what is going on by awarenesses like you and I. You and I have reasons for doing what we do, but these reasons are far removed from the deep, beautiful, undivided nature of what is going on.

$$e^{i\pi}+1=0$$

If we look at Euler's identity, all the interesting stuff is occurring in the first term. The elements of this term are either irrational or imaginary. The identity tells us that if we take the results of this computation and add 1 the result is: 0

Interestingly, the same result occurs if $e^{i\pi}$ is replaced with -1. What could this signify? The thing that occurs to me is that the number 1 could be thought of as a consequence of fishing information from the stream of being, fashioning the distilled results into phenomenal objects, discovering that these images can be tallied and added to and subtracted from one another.

Presumably -1 represents undoing this mischief .

In other words, Euler's identity could be a reminder that *realism-based* arithmetic does not withstand close scrutiny; and a therapy reinstating a flow-based model of reality where 0 = 0.

Diverging or Converging?

Suppose we set questions about realism and common sense aside and agree that objects and entities are carved out, worked-up but still evolving parts of a material universe.

I think we would still have to agree that this universe is changing day-by-day and perhaps even moment-by-moment.

In other words, the distinction between an object-based and a process metaphysics comes down to a debate over whether changes occur the way rivers flow or in lurching, step-by-step increments.

No matter which story is fastened upon, the universe is not the same from moment to moment - if only because we could not otherwise be having a conversation!

This leaves two possibilities. The universe is either becoming larger or smaller, more or less complex, or - in entropic terms - contains more or less information.

The second law of thermodynamics tells us all we need to know:

> Entropy may also be viewed as a physical measure of the lack of physical information about the microscopic details of the motion and configuration of a system, when only the macroscopic states are known.... This is why entropy increases in natural processes - the increase tells how much extra microscopic information is needed to distinguish the final macroscopically specified state from the initial macroscopically specified state.

An excellent explanation has been provided by Richard Feynman.

> So we now have to talk about what we mean by disorder and what we mean by order. ...Suppose we divide the space into little volume elements. If we have black and white molecules, how many ways could we distribute them

339

> *among the volume elements so that white is on one side and black is on the other? On the other hand, how many ways could we distribute them with no restriction on which goes where? Clearly, there are many more ways to arrange them in the latter case. We measure "disorder" by the number of ways that the insides can be arranged, so that from the outside it looks the same. The logarithm of that number of ways is the entropy. The number of ways in the separated case is less, so the entropy is less, or the "disorder" is less.*[68]

I bring these ideas up because they challenge the notion that persons sometimes choose what they get up to; that consciousness is the 'choice engine' making this possible; and - more importantly - that only conscious entities are able to do this and that therefore only conscious entities are responsible for what they do.

We already agree that persons are not responsible unless they are conscious before and during relevant acts. While we are children, while we are asleep, in a fugue state, having a psychotic episode..., we are not culpable and do not exist as moral and rational beings.

This premise is contained in a common dictum: unconscious persons and animals *behave ;* conscious persons *act.*

What does this have to do with entropy? The idea of consciously choosing and responsibility implies awareness of relevant facts.

The problem is that, according to the principle of entropy, information is being constantly lost at the microscopic level. This increasing disorder must be compensated for with increasingly detailed explanations and equations. The rate of entropic degradation cannot be part of real-time conscious episodes.

Even if they could be brought into awareness,this awareness would still lag my relevant states of affairs. (We saw this

---

[68]http://www.panspermia.com/seconlaw.htm

earlier: Awareness is always *awareness of...* something.)

The other possibilities referred to cannot be part of anyone's awareness either. They include more or less complex, larger or smaller, universes.

All of these proceedings can be organized under *diverging* or *converging*.

What would questions about responsibility look like in either circumstance?

The thing to notice is that both *diverging* and *converging* universes proceed outside of the realm of possible conscious episodes. Converging or diverging proceedings are the backdrop against which such episodes occur. And once again conscious episodes do not and cannot have real time relationships with what is going on. They always lag the events responsible for their content.

Awareness is always awareness of... some event.

The even more interesting observation is that a diverging or a converging universe would amplify or diminish the consequences of 'choices made' and 'actions taken'.

Since these amplifications or diminutions are outside of anyone's possible consciousness, we have a reductio ad absurdum.

The notion of 'consciously choosing' is an oxymoron.

Gordon Molloy's Corvette

My brother Gordon lived from Oct 29, 1950 to Dec 9, 2011.

He always knew houses were wombs for cute things.

He eventually learned that Corvettes are not cute.

On November 23, 2014, while walking from my house project to a nearby workshop for something, I was pleasantly interrupted. Two of my nieces pulled into the barnyard – two of the three on the cover of the e-pub version of this book.

They arrived with husbands and children, husbands proud as peacocks and three boys young and full of energy.

This was an unexpected pleasure. Hardly any one drops in these days. My version of Socrates' "torment the comfortable" project appears to have become common knowledge.

Modern Problems, Ancient Perspectives

Alternatively – and probably – it could be that I am just regarded as another old guy who cannot join in the fun – and cannot stop pointing at the horizon one moment and the ground we are standing on the next.

The visit was pleasant for another reason. Christmas was approaching and, for once, I was prepared. I had taken to carrying around a bag of gift DVD's. These DVDs contained more than a hundred 'short introductions' to philosophical and scientific topics commissioned by Oxford University.

I have been handing these treasures to anyone I think might be interested.

I know this is not ethical and this worries me. I know that if I had laboured on a book that was being distributed in ways that did not profit me I would be ambivalent.

Even so I have concluded that not sharing these treasures – which I acquired via *Napster,* a now illegal file-sharing website – would be worse than the alternative.

Because of my facile generosity these authors get to live in a world wherein more people enjoy their insights than would otherwise have been the case.

As well, people I hand their treasures to might one day buy something on their own recognizance.

Of course these are rationalizations! What can I say? Desperate times call for desperate measures!

In any event, after pleasantries had been serviced, I passed along my DVDs, one per niece, one for the missing cover girl and one for an absent nephew we thought might be interested.

More small talk. Once again I brought up the question of what to do about the 1968 Corvette that I had been storing at the farm for thirty years.

The Corvette belonged to my now deceased brother Gordon and had spent twenty years in the barn.

Vernon Molloy

My brother's dream had been to restore it.

During these twenty years, the most Gordon ever managed was to come along each year in July or August and drive the Corvette up and down the lane.

This accomplished, the potentially-handsome steed was returned to the barn and fresh plansmade for its resurrection.

Beers were consumed. Good times – I thought they would never end.

I wish I had paid more attention.

The plans never came to fruition and the road trips eventually petered out. Perhaps they reminded Gordon of trips he was not taking, of adventures he was not experiencing.

When this became clear, a cement floor project required moving the Corvette into the barnyard.

I remember hoping that exposing the Corvette to the elements this way would get the project moving.

Another ten years passed. Suddenly – Gordon had been in vigorous health – my brother 'passed' in 2011.

The Corvette endures however. I migrated it to a hill a hundred yards north of the barn. I joked that I wanted it on higher ground in case the melting polar ice came this far up the Great lakes.

In the summer sumacs shield the Corvette from prying eyes.

In the winter its truth is clear for anyone to see.

An uneasy discussion followed. I said I wanted the Corvette to have a happier fate than mouldering away in a field. I also wanted the Corvette gone. I don't need it to jog my memories. My memories jog me all the time.

My nieces wanted a tour of the house project.

Modern Problems, Ancient Perspectives

I had been hoping this would not be necessary. Such excursions involve exclamatory talk about this or that convenience feature, this or that colour scheme, this or that life-style possibility.

I find such conversations embarrassing and terrifying. They remind me that I should be making better use of my time. They are terrifying because they demonstrate that my failures are so commonplace that they seem perfectly natural.

They are embarrassing for another reason. I have outlived a younger brother and sister. I find myself joking about being reluctant to fill my gas tank or purchase green bananas.

The truth is, I find the idea of anyone spending time and money trying to get more comfortable than they already are disgusting.

I know that I should be trying to make amends – not for what I have been doing as much as for what I have been failing to get up to!

This does not feel like altruism or moral excellence to me – it feels like self-preservation. The fact that I will probably not live long enough to take the full measure of harms we have been sowing does not dissolve my feelings of alarm.

Moreover, whenever I look at people who share my 'best before date', it is clear that the more comfort we strive for and achieve the more discomfort and decrepitude we experience.

"Shoes will have to come off!" I warned, still hoping to put off the inevitable. "No problem!" I was assured. Indeed my nieces clearly approved of my sense of responsibility, not realizing that no such rule applied when I was alone.

We trooped in, nieces, husbands, lads... and undertook a preliminary inspection. After perfunctory congratulations, husbands and lads escaped outside: to ponder hunting possibilities perhaps, to keep an eye out for interlopers, or – I like to think – to consider what house projects signify and entail.

Inside the house the real work began.

Vernon Molloy

My nieces examined the project from top to bottom. They discussed possibilities and merits. They pondered colour schemes, kitchen layouts, lighting and plumbing technologies.... I was not involved in these conversations except that, once and a while, I was asked whether I had done something myself or hired its achievement.

As I listened two things became clear. The first was that my 'house builder' usefulness was being evaluated.

I instinctively knew that the results of this investigation would determine the treatment their respective husbands would enjoy for some time.

Fortunately for their husbands, I had little difficulty persuading my nieces that I was not up to much. (They were already inclined to that opinion.)

The more pressing business involved the two of them sorting out had the best grasp of aesthetics, the best understanding of available products....

They were competing to determine which of them was best equipped to 'conceive a house' and transform it into a home.

After the house had been sussed out and the sisters had settled whatever they were negotiating, a lull occurred.

I took the opportunity to again bring up the Corvette issue.

To my surprise, a proposition resulted. I could move the Corvette to Gordon's property (now Gordon's children's property) if I helped the family build a garage.

"Holy Cow!" I thought.

"Are you serious?" I said.

They were serious.

"What about one of those tarpaulin car garages?" I suggested frantically. "They're inexpensive and do not require a building permit. We could get the Corvette under cover while you figure out what to do with it."

346

"Absolutely not! Those things are ugly, ugly, ugly!"

"Well I'm not able to help you build a garage. Does this mean the Corvette stays where it is?"

"Uncle Vernon, that's up to you!"

"Holy Cow!" I thought.

Then a light went on. I asked: "There is something that has always puzzled me. Why did Gordon not take the Corvette home in the first place? He had everything he needed to do most of the work."

"Uncle Vernon, I thought you knew. Mom never knew the Corvette belonged to Dad.

She thought it was your project. She thought Dad was going over once and a while to lend you a hand."

Vernon Molloy

Growing Persons

Although I have been taking a sceptical line regarding the claim that consciousness makes decisions and that persons come into existence every time a birth occurs, this does not mean I think persons are impossible or even improbable. My suggestion is that the number of persons is not the number population figures imply. There have been millions of persons. We know some of their names as well as we know our own.

Indeed, the plentiful existence of persons in times past is the reason we have languages to communicate with and names to go by.

To put this another way, every newborn is a potential person. Deficits in the way we conduct our affairs can be summed in a simple ratio: the number of persons/the number of people has never achieved 1:1.

Intuitively, morally, ethically, prudentially... our obligations to ourselves and to one another involve bringing this ratio as close to 1:1 as possible. This is merely a clumsy version of the *Golden Rule.* Its merit is the way it combines moral, ethical and prudential issues and provides a way to think about and intuitively quantify how matters are proceeding.

I suggested earlier why people who become wealthy and powerful almost always develop corresponding degrees of arrogance and hubris. As we are seeing, these consequences are insatiable. What we have not noticed is that the multitudes whose lives have been harnessed and harvested to fund the wealthy and powerful develop corresponding feelings of inadequacy and worthlessness.

In other words, both parties to this wretched business become parodies of human beings instead of fully-fledged persons. The fact that neither understand this is part of the predicament.

The conceit lubricating these proceedings is the idea that consciousness is a decision-making faculty. This claim takes two forms. The most familiar stipulates that conscious decision-making occurs *ex nihilo* or out of nothing. In this story we think that our choices occur in a magic realm outside of causal relationships or determinism.

Persons choosing or willing choices (including activities putting choices into play) bring events into existence that would not otherwise have taken place. This is why we believe only conscious persons 'in possession of their faculties' can author actions and be responsible for them.

There is another sense in which consciousness is seen as making decisions. In this account - increasingly popular amongst those watching *The Nature of Things* and *National Geographic* - individuals research facts, current events, wants and needs... and make decisions with these in mind.

Once again the premise is that consciousness evaluates relevant facts and underwrites the claim that persons are praiseworthy or blameable authors of ideas and actions.This connects choices with circumstances and histories, while positioning consciousness in an overarching, magisterial, *causality-defeating* role.

As far as I can understand, this wiggle room attempt does not succeed. Whether choices are ex nihilo or research-based, consciousness is still regarded as the 'agent within'. Conscious still sets the stage for seeing ourselves as Godlike creatures operating outside of causality.

The alternative I have in mind is that human brains are not Divine endowments or evolutionary achievements capable of consciousness, which somehow then "takes control" of cognitive processes. Brains: your's, mine, the central nervous systems of other creatures... are better understood as *cognitive digesters.*

Cognitive digesters operate the same homely way alimentary systems function. Information comes in, stews around, gets dissassembled into useful elements and is then incorporated into new thoughts, insights, resolutions and, sometimes, dreadful by-products.

Like bodies, the brains of organisms embody genetic

information achieved by evolutionary proceedings. This genetic information is further shuffled by sexual reproduction machineries, further improving heterogeneity so populations can test a wider range of possible adaptations (different sized beaks or brains) and respond to a wider range of habitat changes.

The results include a cognitive blank slate element whose capaciousness varies from species to species. What you and I think of as activities or behaviours are what happens when these capacities are informed and tested in local event crucibles.

The results of these proceedings - the so-called survival of the fittest – are what individual narratives look like to those in the grip of common sense or realism.

If we stand further back it is possible to glimpse that the narratives we think of as species are formed out and informed by the narratives think of as the individual lives of species members.

In other words, 'individuals' can be regarded as the thoughts of organisms we think of as species. In this story whiskers, eyes, ears, human beings' conscious episodes... are probes exploring possible futures.

By constantly putting 'individuals' at risk, possibilities are evaluated and adaptations spawned by sexual reproduction and mutations are tested. In this story, successes or failures (births, deaths) signify species 'actively pursuing' possibilities or avoiding cul-de-sacs.

You and I can be similarly understood. We are thoughts and actions undertaken by *Homo sapiens sapiens*. Our sense of robust actuality is simply part of a proper testing regimen. I think this is worth thinking about in the context of modern problems because it invites us to climb down from our high horses before we really hurt ourselves.

Modern Problems, Ancient Perspectives

To continue a little further along this path, we know that a great deal of human brain development occurs after birth. An obvious reason involves the small radius of human birth canals.

Inter-species differences are striking:

> *The rat cortex reaches approximately 90% of its adult weight by pnd (post natal day) 20, the typical age of weaning in rodents. In humans, brain weight reaches a similar plateau by 2–3 years of age (Dekaban et al., 1987; Dobbing and Sands, 1973, 1979). Thus, based on brain weights alone, pnd 20 in rats appears to correspond to a 2–3 year old human child.*[69]

Another reason involves the important role of post-natal environments in cognitive development. This allows brains to mature in ways that reflect not only Homo sapiens' evolutionary history but local events and cultural achievements.

The best example involves the effortless way children absorb languages and folk-ways. The result is that, when conscious episodes begin after three or four years of growth and interaction with families and communities, the neurological groundwork has been laid in rich ways that reflect local circumstances.

This is why new human beings take to their surroundings the way ducks take to water. This is why we become Canadians, Americans, Aboriginals, Hindus, Muslim, Catholics, Protestants....

On the other hand, atheists, agnostics, sceptics... must renew their numbers every generation. These wretches rarely form institutions. They do not tithe or tax. They have nothing to offer except the astringent, unreliable delights curiosity delivers. They have no inducements or threats on a par with Heaven or Damnation and Eternal Punishment.

More importantly they do not offer simple recipes guaranteeing feelings of identity, importance, entitlement and

---

[69] http://www.ncbi.nlm.nih.gov/pmc/articles/PMC3737272/

rectitude.

Three converging streams (genetics + culture + local events) spawn notions of personhood. These notions encourage us to think of ourselves as entities acting *ex nihilo* - of, at least occasionally, transcending causality and becoming *Little Gods*.

You and I know how this works. We see ourselves as authors, editors and managers of theatrical productions starring ourselves. We see others as involved or complicit in some of these narratives. Most of the time we see others as audiences for our displays of derring do and tales of woe.

Now comes a tricky part. In order to keep the fantasy alive - the notion that we live in an external world and choose to do or not do stuff – we need to think of ourselves as Little Gods operating outside of causality and determinism. At the same time we have to find ways of deflecting the responsibilities such an account implies.

Since we are nothing if not facile, we have contrived a thousand ways to have this cake and eat it too.

We do this impossible think all the time. We think of ourselves as *moral and rational* agents and as *innocent bystanders* or *victims* simultaneously. We talk up determinism or behaviourism whenever unwelcome responsibilities are on the table. Whenever praise, promotions or *Little God* status are up for grabs, we remember that we are incarnated souls, or that we possess an evolution-achieved consciousness capable of taking and acting upon decisions.

The alternative I propose features a less distracting metaphor. Human brains are *digesters* decomposing and recomposing the legacies, cultural resources and experiences comprising our lives.

These resources, cultural legacies and events are constantly melding and generating cognitive events in ways analogous to intestinal tract proceedings . Conscious episodes are among these results. These episodes involve *insights* generated by mutually-digesting experiences triggered by internal or external events.

Most of the time I do not think of these proceedings in terms of flatulence but the parallels are provocative and instructive:

- both have unseen origins;
- both rise up without having been consciously summoned;
- both offer feelings of closure when uttered.

This digester model solves a number of puzzles. Logically insights, flashes of inspiration, feelings of alarm or purpose... cannot determine their own content or the course of conversations or activities.

This does not mean that conscious episodes are unimportant. Their functions include elongating stimulus-response events so that broader spheres of experiences and ruminations improve outcomes.

In this way conscious episodes make coherent, sustained responses possible. They create the possibility of co-ordinated responses involving dozens, hundreds, millions... of people. The means that the capacity for conscious episodes makes nuclear bombs, solar-powered airplanes and cities possible.

This is not the same as saying that consciousness conceived, imagined or sanctioned any of these proceedings.

Conscious episodes also mean human beings can fly around *future terrains* cognitive digesters imagine into existence as effortlessly as birds take wing and fish swim. (Such experiences are sometimes referred to as *flights of fancy.*)

Conscious episodes also distinguish human beings from other forms of life. However, to adopt an important logical notion, conscious episodes are *necessary* but not *sufficient* to explain what human beings get up to.

This simple statement changes everything. This simple statement means that everything presently understood as morality, responsibility and prudence will have to be rethought.

Vernon Molloy

The cognitive digester model underscores another important idea. Conscious episodes are generated by the same events responsible for their content. This is why there is never a mismatch between the scope of a conscious episode and the ideas and images, the *semantic content...,* therein. Perfectly sized conscious episodes are imagined into existence by the same processes imagining their contents. This is why every idea, thought, urge, conclusion... seems perfectly plausible and perfectly constituted. This is why hubris, arrogance and 'pig headedness' are universal problems. They are not, however, moral or rational failings. They reflect human beings' 'factory settings'.

The sense we have of an actual world includes a sense of space and notions of past, present and future. How can these common-sense experiences be explained in non-realism terms?

This question has enjoyed a great deal of philosophical attention for thousands of years. My abbreviated suggestion is our sense of time and space flows from the (semantic) content of conscious episodes. When we construct images or predictions we also and necessarily construct the logical or subjective space needed to contain them.

This is reminiscent of the debate between Leibniz and Newton, when they argued over whether space and time existed independently of the contents of space and time. Newton thought that space and time existed whether the universe contained objects or not. Leibniz thought objects and entities existed but that our sense of time and space was *relatavistic* – it grew out of noticing relationships among objects and then noticing that they endured. They could be 'looked at' and then 'looked at' a second time an hour or a day later.

My proposal is simpler. Human beings imagine objects and entities into existence. As soon as these images float into view a corresponding space-time geometry springs up and provides context and backdrop. When these images fade, the geometry disappears as well.

Modern Problems, Ancient Perspectives

Space, time, objects, entities... have no other existence.

More importantly, the contents of conscious episodes consist of predictions about what will happen if possibilities are pursued. These predictions take the form of sensuous *insights*. This explanation dissolves long-standing puzzles about the nature and origin of consciousness. Consciousness is a feature of elongated stimulus-response capabilities. Consciousness is an integrated, emergent, straightforward manifestation of an adaptive strategy pursued by all forms of life.

In short, the world looks and feels like something because

1. memories involved in the generation of conscious episodes contain the flavour and energy of events represented; and
2. looking and feeling like something is an efficient, way to 'test' responses in 'thought experiments'.

Your and my sense of a world stuffed with objects, entities and events are 'privately achieved' predictions of what is going to happen to each of us more or less immediately.

The fact that cultural resources and languages allow us to talk to one another about experiences and useful commonalities does not demonstrate the existence of a corresponding, externally-existing reality.

In political and economic terms, the point is that conscious episodes do not function the way common-sense supposes. Consciousness does not make or take decisions, although it is frequently 'involved' the way blackboards facilitate solving equations or producing lists.

This is why brains are usefully understood as stomachs or digesters and not as intrinsically-active machineries operating upon stored data. In the digester model experiences are internalized the way food is ingested. Every human being embodies an idiosyncratic collection of stored experiences ruminating upon its contents and local events in unique ways.

In this story brains are crucibles wherein representations of experience digest one another's significance and generate insights. (The body keeps the stew pot at an optimum temperature of 98.6 degrees F.)

When all goes well, understandings, urges, sentences, sometimes whole books... flash up. Over time, these illuminations, these *insights*, can generate notions of selves. These conceits can then become so narcicistic that they attempt to take credit for everything that has been happening, even for everything that has been causing them.

The stew pot metaphor is improved if we recall that memories are not inert, passive sources of sustenance, energy or information. As suggested in the dispositional model discussion, memories are lively in their own right. They are lively because they embody lively events. This innate liveliness explains how memories are able to initiate, energize and guide cognitive activities. This is why resolutions, thoughts, sentences, conclusions... are reported as occurring, spontaneously.

This is why there is no requirement for consciousness to initiate or orchestrate cognitive events, or even be involved.

However, conscious episodes have consequences. The most important involves a sense of space and time sufficient to contain the events, objects and entities populating subjective lives and providing the rationale for realist claims.

This backdrop also illuminates the cultural context against which *person talk* occurs. Conscious episodes sometimes participate in knock-on mental events. The resulting *awareness of awareness* sometimes leads to notions of objects, entities and selves,

----

What is also important is that cognitive events often participate in 'self-funded' ruminations without further inputs. The results may or may not result in conversations. We sometimes debate among ourselves, perform music and/or go camping. Of course, such ruminations can lead to 'actual responses' of interest to religious people or law enforcement agencies. If this happens, proximate conscious episodes will be held responsible.

Moralisers and gossip-mongers notwithstanding – and with David Hume's advice about confusing *association* with *causality* in mind – this is nonsense. How can this or that conscious episode along a stream of conscious episodes signify that a person is responsible for this or that act? Why not indict the episode or string of episodes just before the episode before the court?

Would a dozen, a hundred – indeed the sum total of a person's conscious experiences – not be a more plausible candidate for villain or her?

In the leaps of faith every one of us gets up to thousands of times a day, such questions are deflected with talk of a *faculty of consciousness.*

 This accomplished, the only further requirement is that individuals be of sound mind (*compos mentis).* Presto! We have persons that can be praised or blamed.

As every lawyer knows, demonstrating that an indicted person was not of sound mind (*non compos mentis*) at some relevant juncture is an excellent defence.

Indeed, such a finding is better than being found innocent of a particular crime. Such persons are *universally innocent.* They are innocent because they are incapable of *acting.* They have the moral status of animals. Such persons may be lethally dangerous but they cannot be held responsible.

This is the slender thread upon which the justice system and economic meritocracies depend.

At the same time, there is evidence that we understand deep down that realist, moral, rational agent... stories are not true. We speak of 'gut feelings'. Artists report that they are only transcribing information boiling up from within. We wonder where slips of tongues, spoonerisms and dreams come from.

Vernon Molloy

We certainlyknow that conversations proceed at such breakneck pace that we only aware of our words as they come out of our mouths.

The stew pot metaphor is improved when we notice that 'cognitive digesters' have 'turn around' times of milliseconds; and, conversely, that some human ruminations rumble along for years.

Another benefit is that the digester model explains conscious episodes as emergent phenomena. This avoids pesky *infinite regress* problems encountered trying to understand what *consciousness* could be consulting while 'deciding things'. If your and my consciousness is not 'consulting anything' and therefore making choices 'freely', how could these outcomes be relevant or even survivable? On the other hand, if consciousness is consulting stuff, awkward questions turn up: where are these resources located? How are they stored? How is 'consciously consulting' administered and what mechanisms are involved?

I have no awareness of researching or pondering facts of the matter before thoughts and conclusions pop up. After this occurs I sometimes become aware of reacting to their quality, admissibility, provocative nature... but these awarenesses also pop up or coalesce fully formed.

True enough, some thoughts and conclusions are so worrisome that they are held back or even vetoed - but the reasons they are worrisome or vetoed are not part of awareness either.

None of these proceedings and experiences support claims that consciousness does stuff or is efficacious in the way common-sense, the justice system and moral pronouncements require.

More importantly, dissolving the claim that consciousness confers Godlike status means human beings are more likely to turn into the persons we have been imagining ourselves to be as a birthright.

There are no guarantees, but 'lack of guarantee' is an important ingredient in every 'cook up a person' recipe.

Modern Problems, Ancient Perspectives

Anyone persevering this far knows that I do not claim to have discovered even one new truth.

I have been arguing that some common-sense claims are incoherent. For the most part, this involves reducing the number of elements in explanations as far as possible - as recommended by the *Law of Parsimony* or *Occam's Razor*.

I sometimes attempt *transcendental* arguments - a grand word that only means asking whether notions (i.e., about God's plan for Man or the efficaciousness of consciousness) are internally coherent or compatible with simultaneously-held claims.

Transcendental arguments have the great merit of challenging positions from within. I remember my mother pointing out that I should not be concerned about someone staring at me in church. Her logic was that if I had not been staring at the person I was complaining about, I would not have noticed the injury I was experiencing.

Whenever such incoherence can be demonstrated, the notions involved are *within* persons. Caught in such traps, individuals must discard some cherished claim, axiom or factoid... or retreat into talk of manifest destiny or the inscrutability of God's plan.

Not surprisingly, 'God's Plan' rejoinders happen more often than not. If internally-conflicted individuals are further pressed, violence is likely to ensue - as history continues to demonstrate in conflicts between Israel and Palestine, Russia and the Ukraine, Shia and Sunni Muslims....

These consequences might be more manageable if the claim that persons are moral and rational agents is replaced with the idea that brains are 'experience digesters' and nothing but.

In this story what differentiates species is the capaciousness of stew pots and the relative importance of sensory inputs. Eagles depend upon visual acuity. Bats and dolphins garner auditory information. Human beings require grandparents, communities and, lately, Google Search.

In human beings the notion of consciousness choosing is replaced with the idea of digesters generating *private insights* dramatizing possible responses a moment or a month in the future. These dramatizations featire a sense of what possible responses will feel and look like as a convenient, computationally-efficient way of evaluating them.

These subjective, internal experiences of possible responses appear to us as glimpses of an externally-existing world. If communities and languages exist, predictions and possible responses will be wrought into community and cultural resources and gossiped about.

Common elements will be promoted into named objects, entities and persons.

Eventually the persons doing this promoting and naming, *this reifying*, perceive and promote themselves into Little God status. They come to see themselves as entities with free will and the capacity to initiate actions that have no other explanation.

After aeons replete with Forest Gods, Greek Gods, Roman Gods, Norse Gods... talk about this or that one Big God erupted. The function of this One Big God is to make otherwise ludicrous talk of Little Gods plausible.

We are well down this road. Billions of cognitive digesters are now strutting around brandishing homilies and threats.

If these 'infected 'I's' cannot be repaired by philosophers administering transcendental remedies they often 'have no choice' except giving up 'actually talking' -- or taking up more draconian solutions.

The problem is 'actually talking' requires minds that have not yet baked all the conclusions they think they need and switched their digesters off. 'Actually talking' requires curiosity and interest in what is going. 'Actually talking' is the defining characteristic of young people.

Unhappily, the curiosity that makes actually talking possible has been quantized, co-opted, wrought into Gross National Products, social media start-ups and "Idle No More!" demonstrations. Curiosity poses awkward questions: "Why does the emperor have no clothes?" "What is really going on?"

> *Fanaticism is the enemy, not faith. It always is. But only a fool would deny that faith has been the seedbed of fanaticism in mankind's long and sorry struggle for the light. That's why, when the non-religious commit acts of shocking cruelty and intolerance, as they often have and will again, it is normal for us to say that they have made a religion of their politics, or that they are in the grip of a blinding and inhumane dogma.*
>
> *Andrew Goopnik Jan 13, 2015* [70]

Actual conversations have additional merits. They are a way of retaining - and possibly regaining - childlike curiosity, of having a young outlook no matter how old.

To the extent that we lack curiosity – often because some Big God claim has rooted up in our lives - we have little choice except to abandon discourse. *Little God* claims cannot be risked in conversations. They must be hidden behind Big God claims which, in turn, must be defended by any means necessary.

These days there are almost as many Little God claims as people. Little God claims include the fantasy that we own, inhabit and ride *our bodies* around upon an *actual world*.

These claims are so seductive that surprising numbers of human beings are prepared to blow themselves to smithereens if they can take a few infidels with them. Terrorists seek out such opportunities. The moderately faithful watch anxiously from the sidelines. They express consternation of excesses even as their faithful postures legitimate the Bible or the Koran proselytizers and jihadists claim to be closely following.

---

[70]http://www.bbc.com/news/magazine-30746910

Vernon Molloy

How many slain infidels does it take to make a bomb-belt investment worthwhile? Is one sufficient? Does it matter whether victims are powerful or insignificant? Are children fair game? How are infidels identified? Does anyone claiming a relationship with a God other than my God qualify for conversion or execution?

These questions have already been answered millions of times. In 2014, kidnappings and grotesque executions made headlines under the aegis of the Islamic State or ISIL. Secondary questions are also being sorted out. What is to be done with atheists or agnostics who do not make Big God claims? They are infidels by definition, but perhaps more tolerable than theists on the other side of lines in the sand. Atheists have not sworn allegiance to a Big God other than the Big God of my dreams.

In fairness, most human beings are not really interested in fundamental issues of any kind. Like beds, our minds are made up and only require occasional tidying.

What we do not notice are the many ways our faithful, disciplined, dutiful... lives underwrite and sanction extremism, terrorism and bigotry. Mainstream Muslims have been repudiating terrorism since 9/ll, even as they act out the scriptures fundamentalists see themselves taking to proper conclusions.

The complicity of Christian populations in global violence is more subtle. For the most part, Christians see themselves as having nothing to apologize for - even as their corporations chew up resources and distant lives and their weaponized drones seek out enemies with hardly any collateral damage.

Faithful populations in secular nations are also capable of vigorous efforts. One of my diversions involves proselytizers (usually Jehovah's Witnesses) who keep turning up at my door. An apparently inexhaustible supply are willing to spend evenings and weekends pointing out the road to salvation to anyone willing to listen.

The proportion of people 'willing to listen' must be large

enough to make these efforts worthwhile - which is a bit surprising since, as soon as a conversion results, willingness to listen vanishes. Subsequent invitations to convert to another faith will be given short shrift and, if pressed, elicit violent responses.[71]

This is, after all, what it means to be faithful.

What is significant is that the urge to tuck in behind god-like people (and eventually this or that Big God) seems to have been part of the human story from the moment the capacity for consciousness emerged. In *The Birth of Religion, National Geographic* (June, 2011), Charles. C Mann describes possibly the world's first monumental religious structure, constructed almost 12000 years ago by hunters and gatherers.

> *At the time of Göbekli Tepe's construction much of the human race lived in small nomadic bands that survived by foraging for plants and hunting wild animals. Construction of the site would have required more people coming together in one place than had likely occurred before. Amazingly, the temple's builders were able to cut, shape, and transport 16-ton stones hundreds of feet despite having no wheels or beasts of burden. The pilgrims who came to Göbekli Tepe lived in a world without writing, metal, or potte-*

---

[71]Jehovah's Witnesses have another reason to knock on doors - and perhaps hope that their efforts will be futile. They believe that God is waiting until a suitable proportion of mankind has been given an opportunity to embrace salvation before pulling the Armageddon switch.

Why does this matter? If a Jehovah's Witness happens to be alive when the Apocalypse occurs he or she will transition into the Millennium (the thousand year period of peaceful life on earth with Satan safely locked away) without having to go through the messy business of dying and being ressurected. No one knows what this proportion is or how close missionaries are to achieving it.
The next door knocked upon, the next earnest invitation repudiated, might do the trick!

*ry; to those approaching the temple from be-
low, its pillars must have loomed overhead like
rigid giants, the animals on the stones shivering
in the firelight—emissaries from a spiritual world that the human mind may have only begun to
envision.[72]*

Modern descendants of such people - including my Saturday
missionaries - deserve a soupçon of respect. They have ideas
they invest time and energy in.

The rest of us could learn from their example.

---

[72]

http://ngm.nationalgeographic.com/print/2011/06/gobekli-
tepe/mann-text

Before them are dozens of massive stone pillars arranged into
a set of rings, one mashed up against the next. Known as
Göbekli Tepe (pronounced Guh-behk-LEE TEH-peh), the site is
vaguely reminiscent of Stonehenge, except that Göbekli Tepe
was built much earlier and is made not from roughly hewn
blocks but from cleanly carved limestone pillars splashed with
bas-reliefs of animals—a cavalcade of gazelles, snakes, foxes,
scorpions, and ferocious wild boars. The assemblage was built
some 11,600 years ago, seven millennia before the Great
Pyramid of Giza. It contains the oldest known temple. Indeed,
Göbekli Tepe is the oldest known example of monumental
architecture—the first structure human beings put together
that was bigger and more complicated than a hut. When these
pillars were erected, so far as we know, nothing of comparable
scale existed in the world.

"These people were foragers," Schmidt says, people who
gathered plants and hunted wild animals. "Our picture of
foragers was always just small, mobile groups, a few dozen
people. They cannot make big permanent structures, we
thought, because they must move around to follow the
resources. They can't maintain a separate class of priests and
craft workers, because they can't carry around all the extra
supplies to feed them. Then here is Göbekli Tepe, and they
obviously did that."

This does not mean that what they are up to is not full of mischief. After a few moments letting my polite emissaries explain how I should conduct myself I interrupt to suggest that the God they are talking about could not possibly wish to have his *Plan for Man* sabotaged by people like them telling people like me about it.

The reason is *apodeictic, self-evident* - dare I say *transcendental?* On religions' fundamental premise a reasonable question is: Why would God have created the universe if not to provide human beings (and similarly-endowed creatures anywhere in the universe) opportunities to live ingenuously on their own merits?

Does this not suggest that God wants beings capable of moral and spiritual existence to *not know* of his purpose, plan and hopes? How could any kind of interesting spirituality develop if potential moral agents are distracted, seduced, terrified... by notions of Heaven or Hell?

Crass, self-serving calculations - greed for Heaven/terror of Hell versus secular temptations - cannot be what God had in mind when he invented or created the universe!

Follow-up questions are possible:
1. Does the Bible not describe Satan as a wonderfully-clever fallen angel determined to thwart God's plan? What could be more cunning, more devilish, than doing so by spilling God's Divine Beans?
2. Who did you say you were working for?

Enough cheap fun! Beyond a wholesome 'lack of guarantee' - i.e., not having Bibles or Korans to bash one another with - what would improve the chances of persons emerging from raw human beings?

I have been suggesting a healthy proportion of subsistence activities in personal, family and community lives.

As well, recognizing that consciousness is an occasional, fragile and episodic achievement may be the most important understanding human beings can have. Understanding conscious episodes as events with cultural and community elements is another way of saying that they occur within human brains but are not generated by brains alone.

In other words, human brains are *necessary* but not *sufficient* for conscious episodes to occcur.

Why turns on getting this right? If consciousness is neither a God-given nor an evolved faculty, if conscious episodes include elements generated by what Sigmund Freud referred to as *dream factories,* then the conscious episodes associated with subsistence activities reflect these origins as surely as those experienced by *workers* and *shoppers* reflect their partitioned lives.

Only subsistence activities generate overarching *supply/demand* or potentially whole person awarenesses.

If human beings are not incarnated souls or do not possess innate moral or rational agency, then the difference between subsistence activities and modern employments cannot be overstated. Subsistence activities become the only source of whole person, family, community... standpoints likely to perceive exploitive, frivolous and spurious commercial activities as harmful.

1. Such activities will be seen as siphoning the value of work performed for the benefit of a small population of wealthy individuals.
2. In environmental footprint terms, populations engaging in subsistence activities are more likely to husband resources consumed and pollution generated because personal, family and community well-being are factors in conscious episodes.

The disappearance of subsistence activities and loss of whole person viewpoints explains a great deal. Growing inequities, dysfunctional societies and international turmoil notwithstanding, few seem to consider that how we earn our living could be an important factor in modern problems.

Wealth and power could not accumulate in so few hands if most human beings were not anxious – or at least willing – to lead domesticated, comfortable, *rarely conscious* lives.

When urbanized populations are no longer able to ignore problems we opt for simplistic solutions. These solutions rarely work but they invariably reinforce and deepen hegemonic relationships responsible for problems in the first place.

For the most part, we appeal to the wealthy and powerful to fix the inequities that make their excellent lives possible.

This has not been going well. On January 19, 2015 Oxfam International reported that

> *...The world's richest people saw their share of global wealth jump to 48 per cent last year from 44 per cent in 2009.*[73]

This proportion is expected to reach 50% by 2016. In spite of relentless failures we continue to march up and down to get attention and respect. We bang our pots while 'they' rejoice that we still have not figured out where our problems are coming from.

In First World nations, thoughtful people occasionally attempt to elevate public consciousness by sharing some magnificent understanding. When these measures fail, they lapse into silence. A few become criminals, suicide-bombers, Jihadists... and a few young women have been proffering their reproductive organs to nascent Islamic State warriors.

A kind of bleak logic can be discerned in these proceedings. Now that a small proportion of human beings own everything, now that the rest of us have nothing to lose, our only apparent move is to cause the wealthy as much grief as possible.

If we destroy one another in the process, what does it matter? Canada's Stephen Lewis, delivering the November 21, 2014 Symons Lecture, made reference to Tutsi children shot by their parents rather than being left to be butchered by their

---

[73]http://www.thestar.com/news/world/2015/01/19/richest-1-will-own-more-than-half-the-worlds-wealth-by-next-year-study.html

Hutu adversaries.[74]

Fortunately this bleak history and prospect need not mean that some human beings are innately greedy and manipulative and the rest myopic and unable to defend themselves. It could mean that urbaniz populations see economic events from the standpoint of either *workers* or *consumers* and never as individuals apprehending themselves simultaneously as workers and consumers.

This suggests an exciting possibility! Retrieving subsistence activities and inventing new ones could be a way to engage economic and political problems. Urbanization, industrialization, progress and development... may be spiralling out of control because of the disappearance of subsistence activities, families and communities.

These losses are problematic in their own right. They entail the loss of overarching perspectives only subsistence activities can generate. These perspectives never completely protected populations from manipulation and exploitation, but they were better than nothing!

When we understand that conscious episodes are generated by what is going on in lives, in concert with stored experiences and internalized cultural resources, a great deal becomes clear. We suddenly understand why lives alternating between

---

[74]The Rwandan Genocide was a genocidal mass slaughter of Tutsi and moderate Hutu in Rwanda by members of the Hutu majority. During the approximate 100-day period from April 7, 1994, to mid-July, an estimated 500,000–1,000,000 Rwandans were killed,[1] constituting as much as 20% of the country's total population and 70% of the Tutsi then living in Rwanda. The genocide was planned by members of the core political elite known as the akazu, many of whom occupied positions at top levels of the national government. Perpetrators came from the ranks of the Rwandan army, the National Police (gendarmerie), government-backed militias including the Interahamwe and Impuzamugambi, and the Hutu civilian population.
http://en.wikipedia.org/wiki/Rwandan_Genocide

worker and *consumer* activities, suffer from half-witted understandings.

As history continues to demonstrate, people in the grip of half-witted understandings can be readily organized into mobs, corporations and nations. Indeed, they often spontaneously organize into collectives, corporations and systemic bigotries.

In the final analysis, details of who has been organizing economic and political machinations do not matter. What is important is that the loss of subsistence-activities means *workers* can be tricked into targeting *consumers* and vice-versa. Urbanized workers think of consumers as resources and markets. Consumers regard workers as incompetent, lazy feather-bedders. They automatically support progress and development initiatives: automation, out-sourcing, global free trade agreements... because they understand well-being in half-witted ways. They never ponder what their purchasing decisions will mean in terms of domestic employment. This is why Big Box stores, malls and liquidation centres are filled with shoppers pawing through products from sweat shops and pollution-spewing factories 'over there'. This is why local suppliers and legacy retailers are abandoned as if nothing turned upon their disappearance.

For their part, workers seek wage increases as if they would not have to pay for increasing wages in their alter-ego consumer lives.

Equally remarkable examples of self-immolation occur at the macroeconomic level. Corporations and nations outsource and automate the employments consumers and citizens depend upon as customers and tax payers.

In spite of gathering evidence of middle class rot in First World nations, there is little recognition that progress and development initiatives have regressive consequences. These consequences almost always outweigh short-term advantages for most people. Only those designing, implementing and owning new technologies or global trade agreements reliably benefit from 'bottom line' improvements.

Urbanized, specialized, economically-dependent... populations pursue economic activities as if they were at war intra-nationally and internationally – and even with their other halves! Consumers overlook that their comfortable lives depend upon exploiting Third World populations and using up resources as if tomorrow does not matter. Corporations spend billions of (customer) dollars as if it was important that the public sees another picture of an automobile, lawn mower or pound of ground beef.

These advertising costs reduce the amount consumers can purchase.

As an aside: I have been urging Canada's Green Party to talk about removing advertising costs from the list of allowed business expenses in their platform. If advertising must be done, costs should come out of business profits rather than consumers' wallets.

In the meantime, advertising costs, and the costs of other arbitrary or superfluous economic activities, are effectively being stolen from emerging nation workers, who must sell the work they do into bloated, self-congratulatory, frivolously-competitive distribution systems.

In fairness, Third World populations are complicit in this race to the bottom. They too have been embracing magic thinking and cargo-cult fantasies. They too have been rushing into ever-larger, cities. Even with First World predicaments to warn them, they have been abandoning subsistence activities and communities that could have kept them out of the clutches of the American Dream.

Although these conclusions seem intuitive to me, I recognize that intuitions can be dangerous and seductive. Thoughts, premonitions and conclusions always seem perfect to persons 'having them' - the way newborns seem *miracles of conception* to parents.

Modern Problems, Ancient Perspectives

Fortunately, western nations have been conducting a sociological and economic experiment demonstrating the importance of subsistence activities.

Around three hundred years ago three events began that would change the world. Each would have had a substantial impact on its own. Together they spawned an epidemic of industrialization and globalization some think has pushed the biosphere beyond sustainability. More optimistic pundits think a fifty year survivability window remains.

These events include:

1. Industrial Revolution machineries;
2. the discovery of the New World;
3. the development of fossil fuel technologies.

These stories have been told many times. I would like to describe a fourth narrative.

The social and economic resources and circumstances of pre-Industrial Revolution populations played an important role in the Industrial Revolution. They provided a population of individuals able to undertake physically demanding work, endure onerous working conditions and (usually) survive the hazards of working with primitive machines. These individuals were resourceful and hard-working because subsistence activities required j such skills and 'get her done' attitudes.

The importance of this factor can be glimpsed if we think about the impossibility of starting an industrial revolution using the work ethic and life-style expectations of today's First World populations. Western nations now import *Temporary Foreign Workers* to work on farms and in fast-food outlets because locals are unwilling, and often physically unable, to perform such tasks.[75]

At the same time, the rigours and shortfalls of subsistence living made 'better life' promises of industrial proselytizers doubly attractive. In short, industrial revolutionists inherited everything needed to get the show underway:

- the discovery of fossil fuels and ways to harvest them;

---

[75]http://www.cic.gc.ca/english/hire/worker.asp

Vernon Molloy

- a new continent to explore and exploit;
- unprecedented levels of literacy made possible by Gutenberg's printing press;
- rounding out this picture, manufacturing and transporting goods could be achieved by steam-powered factories, ships and trains.
- Finally, and most importantly, there was a large population of individuals with useful combinations of *Outer-Directedness* and *Inner-Directedness*.

This state of affairs was described in David Riesman's *The Lonely Crowd*.[76] Populations in Europe and Great Britain at the time of the Industrial Revolution were *Outer-Directed*[77] the way non-urban populations in China and India continue to be today. In Outer-Directed societies, each generation internalizes a sense of hierarchical responsibilities and prerogatives. Individuals are born, more or less permanently, wherever fate dictates. Social mobility - the idea that anyone could become president! - is never thought of. Cultural resources and *mother tongues* are absorbed and, almost always, religions fleshed out with grand institutions, rituals and costumes.

In western nations, Catholic and Protestant versions of Christianity have been fractious bedfellows for centuries. In eastern nations variants of the Islamic faith, primarily *Sunni* or *Shia,* orchestrate domestic populations into implacable, mutual hatreds. The only thing they are able to agree upon is that Western nations are hives of infidels that should, in ascending order, be shunned, converted or obliterated.

Statistics for India, the world's second largest nation,

_____

[76]http://en.wikipedia.org/wiki/The_Lonely_Crowd

The Lonely Crowd is a 1950 sociological analysis by David Riesman, Nathan Glazer, and Reuel Denney. It is considered, along with *White Collar: The American Middle Classes*, written by Riesman's friend and colleague, C. Wright Mills, a landmark study of American character.[
[77]Sometimes referred to as *Tradition Directed.*

demonstrate that hardly anyone escapes religiosity's siren call:

> The largest religion in India is Hinduism. ...At
> the time of the 2001 census, 80.5% of Indians
> were Hindus. India's second religion is Islam –
> 13.4% of Indians are Muslim. Other major reli-
> gious groups in India are Christians (2.3%), Sik-
> hs (1.9%), Buddhists (0.8%) and Jains (0.4%).[78]

What is not immediately obvious is that Outer-Directed or traditional populations lead more nuanced lives than these statistics suggest. Outer-Directed lives required a core of Inner-Directedness to survive. What is interesting - what Riesman was already observing in the 1950's in America's move to Other-Directed forms of life - is that Inner-Directedness is not valued by individuals or by the institutions, corporations and nations they constitute.

Indeed, it seems that the need for Inner-Directedness is universally regarded as a problem to be solved. Moreover, efforts to 'solve' this problem has been an important source of cultural activity, invention, progress and development.

The point I wish to make is that, when Outer-Directedness defined nations, widely distributed Inner-Directedness was also informing conscious episodes and cultural, economic and political narratives based upon these episodes.

Although there is no non-intuitive way to demonstrate this, I propose that the need for Inner-Directedness in Outer Directed societies has been a stabilizing, mitigating, moderating... factor in history.

With subsistence activities generating whole person perspectives, talk of persons, souls, immanent beings, moral and rational choices... could amount to more than hollow anthropomorphisms.

Linking subsistence activities with personhood helps us

---

[78]http://worldpopulationreview.com/countries/india-population/

understand many problems. In merely two hundred years, the Industrial Revolution transformed most of the world's Outer-Directed populations into urbanized Other-Directeds.

This matters because nations and corporations constituted by Other-Directeds soon come to depend upon being able to orchestrate the working and consuming activities of populations. They have no use for Inner-Directeds or homely subsistence activities. They see subsistence activities as annoying, superfluous, antiquated, perhaps even subversive.

Coupled with human beings' apparently instinctive aversion to circumstances demanding self-reliance, initiative and responsibility, the move from Inner-Directed to Other-Directed cultures progressed quickly. Even in communities where subsistence activities remain a fact of life - in Canada's aboriginal populations for example - the perceived value of such activities has vanished.

Indigenous populations have been traumatized and seduced by mythical lives portrayed on television screens, movies and magazines. They want nothing more than to give up homely, demanding, demeaning self-subsisting activities and join Other-Directeds in *Hog Heaven*.

Of course people living in urban circumstances know that the fantasies portrayed in commercials, on television and in the movies are not to be taken seriously. People watching from a distance have no such understanding. This is worth thinking about for another reason. Urban populations may be insulated from hedonistic despair by post-modern cynicism but they pay a hefty price for this analgesia. They have become sardonically indifferent to anything and anyone beyond a few friends and a few days. here are *outliers* of course, busily writing letters to editors and declaiming endlessly to anyone willing to listen to them. This is also ironic. The protests of earnest activists enable mainstream urbanites to rationalize their own circumscribed spheres of engagement. There are people sounding the alarm so all is well. Alternatively, there are people sounding the alarm and they are clearly wasting their time. Either outcome guarantees that future exhortations will fall on increasingly stony ground.

In fairness, the number of restive individuals on the low end of the rich/poor spectrum does seem to be increasing. Unhappily the scope and subtlety of their critiques remain *concerning.*

(I use this annoying word – occasionally heard on the CBC – because it somehow manages to diminish any issue it draws attention to. This watering-down occurs outside of awareness and is an interesting of *cognitive digester* function.)

However the principal source of activism is not poverty in and of itself. Activists are individuals who have not completely migrated from *Inner Directed* to *Other Directed* lives. This population alone remains capable of internally-sourced conscious episodes. This population alone remains capable of insights from which judgements and condemnations are possible.

Like Canada's Aboriginals, these individuals are on the outside looking in because they still exist *on the inside looking out*. They compare the sense they have that their lives are worth living with those portrayed by *Hog Heaven* proselytizers.

Along with activism, these individuals are prone to apathy, despair, rage, and suicide.

In the same way, the rise of global terrorism reflects the emergence of Other-Directed populations and associated elimination – or at least devaluation – of subsistence possibilities. The loss of Inner-Directedness has psychological and political consequences. Second-generation urbanites may not have the experiential basis to notice or mourn the loss of subsistence possibilities. They may very well count this loss as progress. However the collapse of autonomous economic activities means the depletion of personhood – or, to use an increasingly archaic word, the loss of one's soul.

The result is that - whether eking out an existence in cities or struggling to survive on margins or fringes - billions of Other Directeds are frantic for someone, anyone, to lead them anywhere.

—

In the grip of this picture, few seem interested in doing the one thing that could help: retrieving and inventing subsistence lifestyles. Doing things for ourselves and one another is so old school! We have not understood - perhaps can no longer understand - that giving up subsistence activities means giving up conscious episodes wherein one's entire being, one's family, one's community, one's *person*... swim into view.

The loss of subsistence activities and Inner-Directedness also diminishes the robustness of *personal narratives:* a sense of self rising from within instead of being initiated, sanctioned, mandated... from outside by external agencies.

Thus, cognitive digesters full of messages from corporations, the Kardashians and antics on TSN, we do not understand a terrifying truth. In merely two hundred years the Industrial Revolution transformed - perhaps transmogrified is a better word - a grand possibility into a horrifying reality. The reason is simple. For the first time human beings can be gathered under one heading: *Other-Directed*.

To appreciate the enormity of this change, pre-industrial revolution populations were Outer or Tradition-Directed but retained subsistence-activity skills, resources and socializing expectations. During this epoch, most conscious episodes grew out of individual, family and community activities. They proceeded in autonomous Inner-Directed ways, albeit within bounds prescribed by overarching cultures and folk-ways. David Riesman emphasized the stabilizing and perpetuating role of Outer-Directed elements in Old World societies. As far as I know, he did not talk about the subsistence activities simultaneously generating self-reliance and personhood within individuals, families and communities.

Perhaps Riesman thought core Inner-Directedness was so deeply integrated into human cultures that it did not require mentioning. Perhaps he was seized with a view that continues to distract us: the view that consciousness is innate and infallible, a faculty that occurs no matter what and which therefore stands on guard against complete Other-

Directedness.

It is also true that a core of Inner-Directedness was an efficient way of organizing populations that did not have corporations and technologies anxious to monetize the homeliest details of life. Such Inner-Directedness still exists in China and India - even among newly-minted urbanites from farms and villages. Of course there is reason to believe that their second and third urban generations will not have the same sense of self-hood and mutual responsibility. Like us they will become quasi-persons depending upon corporations, governments, smartphones, the INTERNET... for everything - including information about what should be on their shopping lists!

They too will discover that, should such information not be forthcoming, or should unemployment prevent shopping lists from being filled, other avenues will be pursued.

Western nations already report second and third generation city-dwellers unable to resist the siren call of violent solutions when robust notions of entitlement are thwarted.

Thankfully most urbanites are too engaged with TSN and NetFlicks, Tweeting and texting to do much acting out. Their days are are so filled with externally-sourced conscious episodes that crossing streets can be an adventure.

Of course, if the power goes off or the INTERNET goes down for more than a few hours, Other-Directeds would boil out of high-rises, basement apartments and rooming houses and lurch into the light of day. This is worth thinking about: A Zombie Apocalypse is only a day away!

The Industrial Revolution changed the way the rich and poor regard one another. During the centuries leading up to the 1800s ruling classes were content to leave individuals, families and communities to fend for themselves.

Of course there were no free lunches - even when individuals are growing and preparing their own sandwiches! The business of defending nations, maintaining roads and protecting assets has always been expensive. Such costs must be passed along to the people whose activities sourced the assets and infrastructure in the first place.

In 'days of yore' trickle-down responsibilities included share-cropping arrangements and, later on, rents as public or common lands were surveyed, carved into properties and bequeathed to fortunate individuals. In one form or another, taxes have always been collected on behalf of aristocrats and Royalty. Tithes have always been collected on behalf of whatever God happened to adorn national pecking orders.

In addition - not surprisingly with such benefits coming their way - the *hoi polloi* have always been required to perform military duties whenever their dear leaders deemed them necessary.

Relentless hegemony, usury, exploitation... is not how the world seems to populations being conscripted, downsized, outsourced or obsoleted. Economic problems and military duties are instead understood as happening to individuals, communities and nations. They are caused by external events. The sense of what counts as external is dictated by the scope and proximity of problems. Individual issues flow from family and community shortcomings. Community problems result from provincial or federal failures. National issues have international origins.

Few ask whether half-witted working and consuming activities could be part of all of these problems.

There are, of course, plenty of hindsight analyses of the shortcomings of Richard Nixon, Neville Chamberlain, the George Bush presidents.... Such explorations of greed and hubris encourage people to perceive political and economic problems as visited upon them; i.e. to see themselves as innocent bystanders or victims.

Granted, the fact that nations are organized into hierarchies and meritocracies makes it easy to perceive troubles as originating *up there* or *over there.*

There is often a good deal of truth in these perceptions. Every nation is a factor in the way the world works. However - to repeat a point made earlier - there is an important difference between *necessary* and *necessary and sufficient.* No nation brings about international events unilaterally. Although it was a principal catalyst and protagonist, Germany did not spawn the First and Second World Wars in a vacuum.

What would recognizing the distinction between *necessary* and *necessary and sufficient* accomplish? If nations cannot unilaterally spawn political or economic events, they cannot unilaterally extinguish them either. Thus, when problems require protagonists to simultaneously cease and desist - and each regards the other as the *necessary and sufficient* cause of the problem - there can be no solution beyond complete capitulation or mutual destruction.

Ironically, although nations cannot unilaterally abandon aggressive circumstances, people sometimes can. A famous example of 'peace breaking out' - the Christmas Truce - occurred during the First World War:

> The Germans started it. First with carols, then with a white flag. And then, unthinkably, on Christmas Eve 1914, one of the strangest events in military history unfolded when 100,000 soldiers on the Western Front laid aside their arms, their orders and their prejudices and embraced. They told jokes, they swapped rations and, near the tiny Walloon village of Ploegsteert in southern Belgium, they played a famous game of football. [79]

Regrettably the idea did not catch on. The next cessation of hostilities would take another four years.

An current example of intractable violence is the Israeli/Palestine conflict. Each nation regards the other as the necessary and sufficient explanation for what is going on. Each claims the moral high ground. Each has persuasive arguments.

---

[79]http://www.telegraph.co.uk/sponsored/travel/first-world-war-centenary/10942667/christmas-truce-1914.html

The moral is, if one slices across any circumstance at different points in time or from different vantage points, the same data points can support different accounts of what is going on. The solution is to recognize that no individual or nation is necessary and sufficient to explain anything going on, but that every nation and every individual is complicit. There are no innocent bystanders. We are all victims or beneficiaries

----

More importantly, individuals and nations who overlook the distinction between *necessary* and *necessary and sufficient* tend to understand problems in terms of *externalities* - as originating *over there, as* being someone else's fault. Local complicity in the origin or escalation of difficulties rarely occurs to citizens or leaders. Anyone introducing such considerations is likely to be considered unpatriotic and perhaps seditious.

The moral is that not understanding the difference between *necessary* and *necessary and sufficient* often condemns individuals and nations to endless, needless strife. In the grip of this picture, individuals and nations are free to blame one another for whatever is going forever. In 'all or nothing' calculations the idea that all protagonists are *partially responsible* never occurs to anyone. We only do black and white: if you are not totally at fault with respect to some issue, then I must be. Since I know this is not so, I must have at thee!

You come to the same conclusion using the same logic.

We are, at least, consistent because the same all-or-nothing calculus is used when assigning credit. When things are going well, cheques are cashed and praise accepted with scarcely a thought for all those whose lives, efforts and prospects contributed to excellent outcomes. We are even more dismissive of distant populations and future generations harmed by, for example, burning as much fossil fuel as possible as soon as possible to keep the good times rolling.

Crying *victimhood* is legitimate and important when doing so reflects what is going on. Fires need to be put out and toxic activities need to be apprehended. However, when problems reflect nations', communities', individuals'... historical sanctions and complicities, pointing to external factors as complete explanations eliminates nearby opportunities to begin putting things right.

In August 2014, in the midst of the another round of shelling by Palestinians and Hamas and counterstrike by Israel (of course, many put the cause and effect relationship the other way around), US President Obama observed:

> *"It is amazing to see what Israel has become over the last several decades," ..."To have scratched out of rock this incredibly vibrant, incredibly successful, wealthy and powerful country is a testament to the ingenuity, energy and vision of the Jewish people."*

Mutatis mutandis, the same could be said of America. The New World was colonized out of the same population moving into cities and manning Industrial Revolution machines. These colonists included individuals who had failed to find a place in Europe's industrializing cities - perhaps because factory life did not appeal to them. Australia received many European convicts - some of whom who may have harboured especially robust Inner-Directed habits!

> *During the late 18th and 19th centuries, large numbers of convicts were transported to the various Australian penal colonies by the British government. One of the primary reasons for the British settlement of Australia was the establishment of a penal colony to alleviate pressure on their overburdened correctional facilities. Over the 80 years more than 165,000 convicts were transported to Australia.[80]*

Whatever its proportion and origin, Inner-Directedness was an important characteristic of individuals colonizing the New World. In its beginning the New World lacked the institutions

---

[80]http://en.wikipedia.org/wiki/Convicts_in_Australia

and cultural practices constituting Outer-Directed societies. This meant the colonists' core Inner-Directedness had to expand to meet the challenges of settling a continent, 'managing' indigenous populations and generally having a good time.

For two hundred years these colonists demonstrated the vigour and creativity human beings are capable of in the absence of leaders, governments, churches and corporations.

They were also demonstrating something we ought to find alarming. Folklore and political rhetoric notwithstanding, human beings do not seem to really enjoy circumstances wherein all-day, every-day Inner-Directedness is required. At a primal level such circumstances probably signify that all is not well. The need to be Inner-Directed, to be perpetually on guard and alert... means borders have not been secured, larders have not been stocked... to the point that we can relax enough to let externalities dictate what happens next.

Our instinct seems to be to replace the need for Inner-Directedness with leaders, governments and corporate machinations.

In other words, urbanization and specialization can be understood as flowing from instinctive efforts to escape the need to be Inner-Directed. The need to be actively and consciously engaged with what is going on is 'understood' (in a non conscious way!) as signifying that individuals and families have not gotten things tidied up and secured.

An important problem is emerging from these proceedings. The resulting externalities – nations, institutions, corporations – are developing increasingly robust intentions and agendas that have nothing to do with the agendas of the individuals constituting them. These non-human agendas emanate from institutions, corporations and nations. They flow through human beings, transforming populations into leaders and followers, rich and poor, us and them....

As institutions, corporations and nations continue to evolve, further possibilities swim into the conscious episodes of politicians and executives. The world is proceeding along paths simultaneously suggested and made possible by the emergence or evolution of non-human forms of life.

Along with day-by-day consequences for populations, corporate and national agendas continue to mould the capacity for intentionality of future governments, institutions and corporations. Nuclear power and nuclear weapons have already affected everything going on politically and economically and these are early days. The capacity to genetically modify plants and animals is changing what we eat and will soon change what food looks like. The INTERNET is morphing into the 'internet of things' where refrigerators have IP addresses and computers look like wrist watches and hats.

These antics, and the increasingly strident demands of proselytizers and supreme leaders, dramatize what human beings will put up with if the quid pro quo includes laying down the burden of Inner-Directedness.

Our instinct is to find recipes, best practices, leaders, ideologies... that allow us to avoid subsistence activities and torment of conscious episodes.

This was well and good when our best strategy involved tucking in behind anyone claiming to know where food, water and safety.

The problem is instincts have no means of switching themselves off. Circumstances wherein human beings could safely let their guard down from time to time have become circumstances wherein persons are being institutionalized, outsourced, monetized and obliterated.

Final Thoughts

The idea of trafficking people provides a way to think about modern economies. The obliteration of subsistence possibilities among urban populations means entrepreneurs - whether individuals or corporations - are best understood as traffickers.

The reality is that all, or almost all, goods and services are now transacted - not only intranationally and internationally among individuals and corporations - but *within* human beings. The lack of subsistence possibilities partitions individuals into workers and consumers. Even banal activities: brewing coffee, making sandwiches..., almost everything beyond breathing and brushing teeth, have been commodified and monetized.

This state of affairs did not exist until recently. It does not – indeed cannot - exist in other species.

Since urbanized, specialized individuals rarely produce anything that they consume directly, everything needed must be purchased with monies from paid employment or investments.

In other words, urban populations are penned-in, encorcled, helpless... economic chattels. Urban populations are completely exposed to coercion, manipulation and exploitation.

The individuals, corporations and nations organizing and profiting from this state of affairs are best understood as traffickers.

The sort of trafficking we are taking about involves a lot of accounting. The accounting equation at the heart of capitalist economies is: Assets = Liabilities + Capital. This equation is suprrisingly rich in meaning. The key concept is *equality*. Any amount can be entered on either side of the equal sign and a corresponding sum springs into existence on the other.

Along with Generally Accepted Accounting Principles (GAAP),

formalized profit-taking and taxation, this equality raises the possibility of spawning new forms of life *ex nihilo.*

The nations and corporations I have been referring to came into existence even more naked that you and I were when we arrived. Newborn corporations have neither assets, liabilities nor capital. They demonstrate the simplest possible balance sheet equality: $0 = 0$.

This innocence does not last long. These place-holders are fleshed out with private or public investments in the form of share purchases or other equity inputs. These investments become assets balanced by corresponding liabilities to shareholders and so on.

This powerful device transformed human and non-human life by making a new kind of (virtual) life, industrial economies and globalization possible.

While admiring what we have wrought and imagining that it flows from ingenuity and enterprise – and sometimes greed and lust power – we have been overlooking something important. Wherever wealth exists, it signifies the existence of corresponding debt obligations among individuals, corporations and nations.

The money sloshing about in the global economy (something like 60 trillion US dollars in 2014) is balanced by the ability of those possessing this money to command the lives of others.

There are advantages to this arrangement. Huge projects can be capitalized and the process of capitalizing them creates debt obligations guaranteeing that there will always be people anxious to do the work. Another way of saying this is to recognize that the volume of money in circulation represents the disappearance of subsistence activities and transactions involving chickens, gardens, blacksmith shops, unpasteurized milk and water that has not been bottled.

If it ever becomes the case that human beings must purchase air to breathe the world GNP will become significantly larger and the volume of money in circulation will increase sufficiently to accommodate these new transactions. I hope it is clear that this would not constitute progress – even if a bottle of air looks like a boon to individuals gasping for breath.

An identical equation applies to power relationships – whether expressed in Divine/human or Aristocrat/serf terms. Whenever we imagine Gods into existence, and especially when we start talking about Big Gods, we diminish or obliterate subsistence-style spiritual and moral activities.

A dreadful question is again haunting the world: is anti-Semitism genetically embedded in populations? Does anti-Semitism reflect some sort of non-conscious recognition of the intellectual superiority of Jewish people? Can anti-Semitism be explained in cultural terms alone?

These questions are important because a new wave of anti-Semitism is crossing Europe and North America and adding new urgency to middle east issues where anti-Semitism is, culturally and constitutionally, business as usual.

One basis for inferring that Ashkenazi Jews have high intelligence is their prevalence in intellectually demanding fields.

> While only about 3% of the U.S. population is of full Ashkenazi Jewish descent,[2] 27% of United States Nobel prize winners in the 20th century, [2][3] 25% of Fields Medal winners,[4] 25% of ACM Turing Award winners,[2] 6 out of the 19 world chess champions, and a quarter of Westinghouse Science Talent Search winners have either full or partial Ashkenazi Jewish ance-stry.[81]

Can these statistics be explained as the result of selection pressures akin to the evolution of drug-resistant diseases because of the promiscuous use of antibiotics in medicine and farming? Have complementary selection pressures - including military events slaughtering the best males in non Jewish

----

[81]http://en.wikipedia.org/wiki/Ashkenazi_Jewish_intelligence

populations - been contributing to these results?

The article suggests other possibilities:

Wealthy Jews had several more children per family than poor Jews. So, genes for cognitive traits such as verbal and mathematical talent, which make a person successful in the few fields where Jews could work, were favoured; genes for irrelevant traits, such as spatio-visual abilities, were supported by less selective pressure than in the general population. As well

> *Ashkenazi Jews suffer from a number of congenital diseases and mutations at higher rates than most other ethnic groups; these include Tay-Sachs, Gaucher's disease, Bloom's syndrome, and Fanconi anaemia, and mutations at BRCA1 and BRCA2. These mutations' effects cluster in only a few metabolic pathways, suggesting that they arise from selective pressure rather than genetic drift. One cluster of these diseases affects sphingolipid storage, a secondary effect of which is increased growth of axons and dendrites. At least one of the diseases in this cluster, torsion dystonia, has been found anecdotally to correlate with exceptionally high IQ. Another cluster disrupts DNA repair, an extremely dangerous sort of mutation which is lethal in homozygotes.*

The authors speculate that these mutations give a cognitive benefit to heterozygotes by reducing inhibitions to neural growth, a benefit that would not outweigh its high costs except in an environment where it was strongly rewarded.

In addition, a radical new form of intelligence-diminishing selection pressures may be operating in First World nations. If intelligence can be correlated with middle-class success, the middle class appears to be engaging not only in economic self-immolation but self-administered genocide! Middle class populations are not reproducing sufficiently to sustain their numbers either in absolute terms or in proportion to domestic or international poor populations. In Canada, only aboriginal populations are growing 'natively'.

On the global economic front, the world appears to be dividing into two zones: developed nations with a collapsing middle class and emerging middle class populations elsewhere.

While the middle class is expanding in emerging and developing countries, in rich countries it is shrinking and feels incapable of sustaining, much less expanding, its middle-class lifestyle.

> The rising expectations of the expanding middle class in developing countries contrast with the stagnating living standards of a shrinking middle class in OECD countries. Today both middle classes are awakening. Each with its own specificities, will these middle classes be agents of change?[82]

I suggest that the middle class populations emerging in developing nations will not be positive 'agents of change'. They will instead function as *conduits* facilitating a second wave of technologically-abetted regressive development. The consequences will obliterate their hopes in a few decades instead of the century it took in western nations.

As these proceedings evolve, hard-pressed populations in each region will identify one another as 'agents of change' responsible for local predicaments.

These analyses will continue to delight wealthy populations everywhere. Middle class populations in western nations are already blaming anybody but themselves for problems flowing from the regressive consequences of half-witted progress, development and globalization.

For at least a half-century, interest has been growing in democratic forms of governance. The reasons are not hard to

---

[82] http://www.oecdobserver.org/news/fullstory.php/aid/3681/An_emerging_middle_class.html

discern. Democratic nations formally acknowledge that leader-follower relationships are provisional and provide orderly processes for replacing governments. Of course, all nations are ultimately democratic - as revolutions periodically remind leaders.

The problem is, revolutions are chaotic. The wrong people are sometimes killed. Property is often destroyed and investments lost.

Accordingly, individuals at the top of the world's hegemonic relationships have plenty of reasons to plump for democracy. One reason that can never be spoken about is that governments, corporations and the wealthy have come to realize that majority rule does not threaten wealthy minorities.

This is especially true these days. Urbanized, specialized and dependent citizens have little choice except to vote for the status quo and lots of it.

In addition, democratic capitalism has proven to be the most profitable way to organize populations. Democracies are immune to revolutionary antics. No matter how egregious inequalities become, what would democracy replace itself with?

This is why even dictators hold toy elections. North Korea's Kim Jong-un travels about with a throng of goose-stepping followers clapping as if their lives depended upon it. "Wait a minute!" You are saying. "Their lives do depend upon it!"

You are right of course. However, rather than crowing about our lives, we might ask how different First World lives really are.

We do a lot of idolatrizing.

In addition to these benefits, rulers in democratic nations enjoy an advantage dictators can only dream of. Elections cleanse citizens' moral palates and nations' moral slates. They renew the legitimacy of nations that have offended the world

Vernon Molloy

with violent transgressions. This allows miscreant nations such as Germany and Japan to resume seats at bargaining tables and political conversations.

Domestically, elections mean governments can claim to represent a fresh expression of the will of the people. Elections provide politicians and candidates with opportunities to confess one another's sins.

The most subtle benefit goes to the wealthy. Along with economic vigour and stability, wealthy individuals are also absolved of responsibility for regressive practices. Elections provide a one-size-fits-all amnesty. Voters absolve the miscreant, greedy,incompetent... leaders they spawn and depend upon by assuming responsibility for their transgressions and shortcomings.

This, at least, is as it should be!

In summary, proper democracies make scapegoats of voters and citizens while appearing to empower them. Like Catholics sanctified by periodic confession and absolution, elections refresh government mandates and sanction new people at public troughs.

All that is necessary is that each new batch of politicians give voters the business in ways that do not get them indicted before the next election.

Then they - or someone very like them - will 'move the nation forward' along trajectories well-defined by this remarkable contraption and its equally remarkable contrivances.

Recent additions to democracy's bag of tricks include opinion polls, super pacs, talking points, attack ads and refining slippery answers. These antics have nothing to do with probity or the quality of political discourse. Their purposes include avoiding hot-button issues and identifying wheels that could profit from some greasing.

More Final Thoughts

Two centuries of most reluctant Inner-Directedness among North America's colonists and settlers led to:

- The American Revolution and the Declaration of Independence[83] ;

- The American Civil War and the abolition of slavery would not have occurred without the robust notions of persons and inalienable rights only Inner-Directed populations are capable of generating.

- The USA, indeed much of the western world, has been enjoying technological development and economic vigour. This success appear tos be waning in lock-step with urbanization, progress and development.

- Why would this be so? One possibility is that ease and comfort leads to indolence and indifference. A more interesting possibility is that human beings have an instinctive desire to extricate themselves from circumstances requiring Inner-Directedness. Any state of arousal requiring conscious attention suggests that something alarming is occurring.

- The instinct to hand-off responsibilities to elders and surrogates is toxic in the context of cultural resources and gradients of wealth and power.

- Mankind's most important failure is the failure to invest cultural achievements in projects diminishing the need to idenfify and submit to leaders. Cultural achievements could have allowed human beings to acquire best practices and improve self-sufficiency without exposing themselves to mischief.

- The proclivity of leaders to develop notions of entitlement could be a complementary *quid pro quo* instinct to encourage them to put themselves in

---

[83]http://www.archives.gov/exhibits/charters/print_friendly.html?page=declaration_transcript_content.html&title=NARA%20|%20The%20Declaration%20of%20Independence%3A%20A%20Transcription

harms way and protect and promote kin groups.

- In other words, human beings have two complementary instincts:

  1. to promote one's self to the front;
  2. to stand back and let others take the point.

- Which instinct prevails in any given circumstance will be resolved by many factors but it makes sense that human beings would instinctively identify their fittest individuals and encourage them to take up dangerous challenges.

This could explain our inexhaustible fascination with athletic accomplishments and competitions. In primal circumstances these sortings out would have been matters of life and death – not only for protagonists but for their communities or kin groups.

- The dispositional explanation of consciousness clarifies what it means to say that something is axiomatic, apodeictic or true. To take a familiar example, we have registered what counts as *harmonious* by encoding the characteristics of human ears as musical scales. We did not prescribe this however, we noticed and formalized a feature of community experiences.

In a similar way, what counts as an axiomatic truth may be genetically encoded. Axiomatic truths are simply statements that sound true. Thus the statement: a straight line is the shortest distance between two points just sounds right. The three notes comprising a C chord sound right.

These examples provide a glimpse into the nature and origin of instincts. Some predictions are so important and frequently useful that they have been embodied genetically. Some sound patterns are pleasing and some are discordant. These discriminations became part of our genotype as music co-evolved as communication medium and mnemonic strategy.

Modern Problems, Ancient Perspectives

- This suggests a cheap test demonstrating how much of daily experience is orchestrated outside of consciousness . All one has to do is read the lyrics of popular songs without musical accompaniment.

  Many are unendurable and most trivial.

- The take-away is that our values and priorities are generated outside of awareness and then become the so-called semantic content of conscious episodes. The rest of the story is that these conscious episodes can be sourced from within, or they can have external elements. This proportions establishing this internal:external ratio are also unknowable. The reason is that these proportions are part of the machineries generating awareness. They are unknowable for the same reason yardsticks cannot measure themselves.

- I think we can extrapolate this. The sources of everything we get up to lie beyond possible awareness. Whether human beings or squirrels, the cognitive mechanisms involved feature more or less elongated stimulus-response capabilities. These elongations range through conditioned responses, instrumental learning and other possibilities not yet catalogued.

- In the case of Homo sapiens sapiens, these elongations can become so capacious that a new possibility emerges. The ability to have conscious episodes creates the possibility of awarenesses becoming aware of previous episodes. This means human beings can experience themselves experiencing! We can remember conscious episodes involving identical places or persons. We can remember ourselves!

- These magical proceedings have been compounding and reinvesting conscious episodes for thousands of years. These proceedings catalysed the enlightenment, the Renaissance and the Industrial Revolution. They are the proximate cause of our latest claim to fame: the anthropogenic era.

- These remarkable 'returns on investment' demonstrate the capacity of culturally-enabled conscious episodes to achieve progress and development.

- Not all is gold that glitters however. These results also now include a radical diminution of most human beings' prospect – a poignant outcome when so much seems possible.

We should be worried about this but it is too soon to be dismayed. What we have been getting up to, especially during the last few hundred years, may only reflect the consequences of being partitioned into half-witted workers and consumers.

There are, of course, other reasons human beings sort themselves into rich and poor populations, and I have been suggesting that the way men and women relate to one another is a hitherto unindicted factor. One factor that is not open to debate is that cultural resources are not equally available to new generations. Secular reasons include financial, legal and political mechanisms transferring wealth and power from one generation to the next over the heads of most people.

As well, some individuals are simply better equipped to take advantage of cultural resources. This has always been the case and nothing can be done about it.

Another new factor involves the disappearance of subsistence lifestyles, families and communities. (This factor is closely linked to the male/female dynamic just mentioned.) This means that everyone is completely exposed to economic Ponzi schemes.

Taken all together, these consequences could be a deal breaker. No other species has contrived circumstances wherein next generations inherit such tilted playing fields. This corollary of progress and development reduces the capacity of our species to adapt to changing circumstances. It does this by reducing the ability of an increasing proportion of human beings to compete economically.

The incidental fact that middle class populations appear to be engaging in self-administered genocide by not reproducing sufficiently to maintain their numbers adds an unexpected, ironic twist to what is going on.

By way of aside, there is evidence that a long-standing association between higher education and low fertility is reversing among wealthy women:

> ...A yawning inequality gap may help explain why fertility rates among highly educated women are rising. ...the growing divide between rich and poor in American society has created two groups of women: those who can afford to buy help to raise their children and run their homes and those who are willing to supply such services at affordable prices.[84]

These proceedings illustrate a few consequences of dissolving naturally-occurring, naturally-regenerating equities. Human beings used to arrive naked in the world, neither richer nor poorer than anyone else. Their only possible advantage involved genetic endowments. These endowments would not have occurred had previous generations lived in circumstances where a small proportion owned everything the eye could see!

It is also interesting to think about what is going on in terms of *speciation*. Speciation usually occurs when populations find themselves in geographically isolated areas and evolve separately until they can no longer successfully reproduce.

This isolation need not be geographic however. Human beings could segregate into rich/poor population pools and evolve into two or more species.

Of course there are more pressing problems. Even if speciation is occurring no one will notice it happening. Since

---

[84]http://www.theguardian.com/lifeandstyle/2014/oct/25/women-wealth-childcare-family-babies-study

conscious episodes will always be generated by cognitive digesters stewing up local events and producing *insights* incrementally-changing circumstances will always seem as right as rain.

They will always seem natural and wholesome. Some of Kim Jong-un's goose-stepping cheer-leaders doubtlessly imagine that they are living in the best of times.

Human beings constantly and effortlessly adapt to changing circumstances if the rate of change is slow enough. We 'move through' childhood, adolescence, adulthood and old age. Ambitions, priorities and dreams change with circumstances. Faces in mirror are is always the face tjeu should be even if they only vaguely resembles young progenitors.

In the same way, the advantaged or lucky quickly believe wealth, power and luxury is nothing more than their due. With equal alacrity, the poor are persuaded that they deserve to not get what they are not getting.

In similar fashion – no matter how dire circumstances become – women and men continue to distract one another from big picture issues as they struggle in circumstances inherited from similarl- distracted parents and grandparents.

Women continue to provide men with tasks to perform. Men continue to take up these challenges because doing so provides feelings of identity and purpose. Indeed these benefits are so intoxicating and reassuring that men keep inviting ever more challenging nest-building, luxury-acquiring tasks.

Women appear endlessly willing to play this game. They have an impossible benchmark and an inexhaustible guilt . No conceivable level of comfort and security approaches that provided by wombs. No conceivable external womb would not profit from a bit of improvement.

The resulting domestic projects also provide men with a chance to do something Sigmund Freud talked about: to crawl into a womb-like world - *and feel good for having done the heavy lifting* that made doing so possible!

Modern Problems, Ancient Perspectives

As far as I can tell, men who do not attach themselves to a woman (or a succession of women) have little idea about what to do with their lives, beyond getting lost in the woods, boasting about exploits and squabbling.

Women come 'factory-equipped' with feelings of purpose and identity. They take up projects involving safe, comfortable spaces. They do whatever they can to fill these spaces with babies – or at least with cute things.

Women adorn themselves for reasons complementing their interest in attractive homes. The primary reason is to attract suitable males and keep children warm and safe. I have been told that women also compete with one another the way dogs mark territories.

Whatever reasons are involved, women strive to create womb-like circumstances for children and a few significant others. We should all applaud this because the human race would not have survived otherwise. Human beings are born prematurely and complete much of their development outside of the womb.

An important reason for our premature birthing involves the need to stimulate and optimize Big Brain growth. According to Chomskian linguists, every human being has a genetically-endowed language faculty whose switches are set in various ways by language communities. This allows children to effortlessly acquire mother-tongue languages and cultures.

The resulting standpoints cause individuals to view one another and 'the world' from particular vantage points.

These standpoints leverage our capacity for conscious episodes into cultural achievements including institutions, corporations and nations. These organizations, whose existence is as real as any of the other events we imagin into phenomenal existence, have been co-opting and incorporating creatures like you and I for thousands of years.

They have been having an orgy lately, gorging on a half-witted

workers, consumers and citizens.

Because a proportion of human beings retain childlike curiosity no matter what their circumstances, new insights, devices, technologies and stratagems keep occurring within corporations and nations. Some of these insights become new machineries harvesting resources and producing goods and services. Some become remarkable cultural achievements and lend a patina of legitimacy and wholesomeness to toxic proceedings.

Something else that is alarming is going on. As low-hanging resources and pollution sinks are exhausted, as manufacturing becomes expensive because of environmental limits or political responses such as carbon taxes, there is good reason to believe these nations and corporations will turn upon one another in vicious attempts to keep wheels turning and growth rates sustained.

The wealthy will regard these initiatives as wholesome and life-affirming because they are reducing human beings aggregate environmental footprint.

As this end game plays out, the fifty per cent of human beings on $2.00 a day life-styles will become eighty per cent.

With these prospects in view, the need to uproot the conscious agent myth becomes urgent. A related obstacle is the belief that consciousness functions as a kind of guardian angel, an automatically-occurring, perpetually-operating countervail to stupidity, greed and brutality.

Consciousness is not our guardian angel. In fact, consciousness does not exist – only conscious episodes automatically stitching together into seemingly seamless experiences. These experiences are the medium within which corporations and nations hatch. They are communication channels and portals incorporating workers, consumers and citizens into unholy forms of life.

Finally, the notion that consciousness is the seat of

moral/rational agency has been distracting us from the harms of centralization, specialization and fanciful gadgets. Never before have human beings had the capacity to recreate the Garden of Eden for everyone. Never before have we been so far removed from doing so.

Having spent many hours in social and family settings hoping to come across people keen to discuss what is going on, I have been dismayed by the relentless silence. Of course one hears and reads of Cassandras sounding alarms but I rarely come across any.

What is more dismaying than my conversational failures is the lack of spontaneous interest in non-trivial matters. Instead there seems to be an aggressive silence after anyone says something politically provocative. This is not *silent silence* either. After a momentary pause the chattering and nuzzling, the stroking and admiring of minute concerns, resumes with renewed vigour.

There are endless recipes worth sharing, any number of places where bargains can be found!

Does this fascination with minutiae somehow reassure us that all is well: that we have achieved security; that barbarians are not at the gate, and the proof is that we can be frivolous and get away with it?

If so there may be a way to put a positive spin on my experiences. The cognitive digesters of the people I have been buttonholing must be paying *unconscious* attention to what is going on. This means that their cognitive proceedings are being informed subliminally. How else could they respond so unerringly with minutiae?

Thus gossiping and shopping offer two existential components. The fact that we are able to successfully pass our days in banal ways means things can't be too bad. Then the fact that we are able to co-opt one another's time with persiflage is reassuring.

Surely we can't all be wrong that it is safe to be frivolous!

399

There is, of course, a more ominous possibility. Big picture concerns may lie beyond the spheres of engagement most human beings are capable of.

If most human beings are Concrete Operationals then they will always be the mercy of Formal Operationals. Nothing can be done about this. This probably means that nothing that can be done about the way things are going.

However – and this is what I think – some combination of genetic and circumstantial explanations are in play.

There may even be a way to test this hypothesis. We can simply watch to see whether our growing problems: global warming, rising inequities, new rounds of anti-Semitism, nuclear proliferation... lead to in further trivializations of public and private discourse.

Although this would be a bleak outcome, it leaves room for optimism. It would imply that the usual person's cognitive digesters is capacious enough to contain troubling information, ruminate about it and then take *deflective action*.

In this story, our myopic lives do not mean we are bred in the bone Concrete Operationals. They can instead be tracked back to a deliberate – but still non-conscious – averting of eyes.

This could even explain the proliferation of the INTERNET, social media and smartphone technologies. The need to assuage deep-running anxieties may explain their *stunning* successes!

Towering Problems

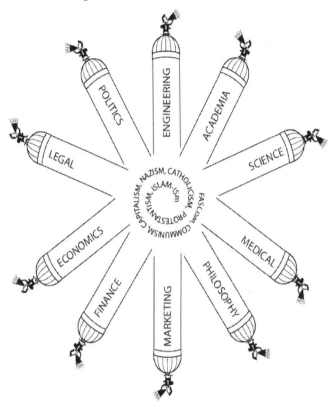

Another problem sets todays difficulties apart. Every academic, scientific and technological discipline boasts impressive bodies of research, analyses and argumentation. These resources exist in the minds of *cognoscenti,* in cultural repositories and in peer-reviewed journals, conference proceedings and books.

These papers, articles and books follow a pattern. Authors set out some problem or topic, summarize what is known and what they hope to demonstrate. A thesis is developed by way

401

of footnoted facts, arguments, and expert opinions.

An important part of this process involves peer-reviewing articles and papers before publication and their often continuous critiquing afterwards.

Thus, to name a few of my favourites, Albert Einstein, Ludwig Wittgenstein and Henry David Thoreau... continue to be responded to long after publication. An important aspect of these proceedings involves bibliographies their situating articles, papers and books in the idiom and *generally accepted problems* of various disciplines.

These practices have much to recommend them. People interested in issues can follow relevant arguments to their heart's content. Careful examinations and critical reviews refine and develop understandings in rigorous ways.

This is well and good. These proceedings have a dark side however. Individuals unable or unwilling to invest years of study - usually by acquiring academic credentials - find that anything they have to say will be dismissed by both professionals and the public-at-large.

This may not seem much of a loss. A more subtle consequence is that individuals also come to understand their own opinions, and the opinions of anyone they know, as also without merit.

To be sure, most of us acquire skills and knowledge sufficient to 'earn a living'. In my case, this consisted of installing and repairing traffic control systems, a subset of electronics involving electro-mechanical devices and printed circuit boards with discrete components: transistors, capacitors, inductors, diodes, resistors....

Twenty or so years ago the development of integrated circuits containing thousands of components rendered my knowledge and troubleshooting skills redundant. If a piece of electronic equipment fails these days all that is required – indeed all that is possible – involves identifying and replacing a defective module. Increasingly, these modules do their own troubleshooting. Diagnostics are performed by software programmes. Some devices contain tell-tales or flags identifying signalling malfunctions and – in mission critical applications – automatically-deploying redundant systems.

Obsolete skills and career dead ends are not the important problems associated with occupational specialization. During my lifetime no one ever asked me what I thought about something going on outside of my sphere of competence. If I volunteered an opinion – and I often did – it was ignored or indulged according to the temperament of the person I was talking to.

If my interlocutor happened to possess relevant professional credentials, the best I could hope for was patronizing bemusement.

For the most part, this seemed natural and proper. I had my work to do and was being paid to do it. My obligations were restricted to doing my job and minding my business. It was just assumed that I would respect the boundaries defining other people's duties. Indeed – since I worked in a union environment – this expectation was spelled out in post descriptions.

What proportion of human beings understand their lives in such terms? I think something like 90%. The quid pro quo is that this 90% (pick whatever percentage makes sense) gets to enjoy followership, life-long infantilism and perpetual innocence.

What does innocence mean in this context?   This is one of the most important questions we need to think about. According to the dictum: *Ought implies Can,* individuals can only be expected to do something if it is reasonably possible for them to do so. The problem is, specialization, urbanization, the loss of subsistence capabilities... mean that less and less falls within the usual person's purview.

Specialization also shrinks the likelihood of individuals taking advantage of cultural resources or new technologies. The reason is that specialization diminishes perceived requirements to inform ourselves or make judgements about

Vernon Molloy

proceedings outside of spheres of competence.

The psychological and economic consequences of these contracting spheres of competence and engagement feed back into daily lives and urge ever more focussed skills and spheres of responsibility.

Another consequence of specialization is the need to organize and supervise workers so useful productions occur. These costs must be subtracted from the economies of scale and efficiencies attending specialized proficiencies.

Micro-economic and macro-economic balance sheets overlook other costs of the way we do business. I will not belabour this beyond suggesting that historical decisions to abandon subsistence activities and community productions reflect micro-economic calculations by individuals who soon become their own victims. They also reflect more sophisticated calculations by individuals who hope to get in on the victimizing.

When I went to public school in the 1950's there were small, often one-room, schools on every concession road in rural Ontario. Parents did did whatever it took to get their children to school but usually left them to find their way home at the end of the day. In my case this involved a three mile (five kilometre) walk. There were no school buses or crossing guards. There was bullying of course, but it happened in the light of day and teachers and fellow students could and would intervene.

To take up another modern problem, I do not recall a single obese student at public school and only a few at Madoc High School. The moral is that, when pondering whether to make improvements to the way we live, there is a tendency to overlook elements in circumstances that work so well they never participate in conscious episodes.

I think this is an ironic, unindicted problem in the way the world works. Best practices rarely inform the cost/benefit calculations promoting progress and development projects. I think this illuminates why subsistence activities, families and communities were abandoned as soon as 'commercial opportunities' came along. The lovely, wholesome features of the way we were living were working so well we never had to think about them. Their importance and value never crossed our minds! This is why we traded them away so cavalierly for for a ride to promise land.

An even more subtle problem is having its way with us. Assigning responsibilities according to focused skills and understandings is a slippery slope. By shrinking or eliminating conscious episodes each step along this path prepares the way for the next contraction.

Thus, in Canada's federal election in 2015, national child care programmes became a litmus test of political thinking. Proportional voting and guaranteed annual incomes also become topical. I think there are two reasons for this. The first is that proportional voting attempts to distribute perceived responsibility for what is going on more widely across the electorate. (An enlarged enfranchisement no longer worries the wealthy and powerful because democratic proceedings have proven eminently manageable.)

The second motivation is that economic and geopolitical problems are looming on the horizon. In such circumstances, stability and public order are best served by having as many citizens as possible functioning as scapegoats.

A similar analysis suggests why guaranteed annual incomes have become political talking points. The reality is, globalization and free trade agreements make such programs impossible. Not only are domestic economies no longer able to support them, there is a good chance that they have been prohibited by free trade agreements. The argument is that they would give corporations in such nations an unfair competitive advantage.

This being so, debating whether a guaranteed annual income is now a good idea deflects suspicion that political parties have been complicit in proceedings that have already made them impossible.

More generally, specialized competencies amount to a one-size-fits-all way to evade pesky conscious episodes. Cultures predicated upon urbanization, specialization and Outer-Directedness pass responsibility for global events to leaders and savants. In some circles even conceiving children has been monetized and occurs *in vitro*. Healthy eggs are harvested when women are starting careers and doing so is more important than starting families.

These contractions, deflectings and abdications are why subsistence activities, families and communities have become antediluvian notions. They are the reasons the names of leaders, savants, athletes and entertainers are more familiar to us than our own.

When personal or local responsibilities are handed off to corporations and governments, two realities are overlooked. The first is that wealthy individuals inevitably develop a sense of entitlement and superiority. This sense of entitlement, recommends still more progress and development.

The second is that, if human beings really were the moral and rational creatures common sense proposes, our history of usury, slavery and internecine violence would surely have led us to discard or at least rethink idolatrous proceedings. Yet we continue to regard these arrangements as natural, wholesome and, in some sense, inevitable. Leadership qualities are admired. Corporations and governments offer courses to employees interested in getting ahead. The idea of getting ahead always involves moving into a leadership role.

I have not come across a single individual or article applauding *followership.* Followership is not a desirable career path. Followers lack ambition and are unwilling to be all they can be. They are *people* but not really *persons* - even though followers' characteristics: loyalty, fealty and patriotism... get good grades.

The hypocrisy behind these contortions is that rich people require poor people, and the more the better. Leaders require followers, in similar proportions.

The reason this hypocrisy is universal is simple. As soon as individuals become rich or powerful, they become dismissive of governed populations. They come to believe that poverty reflects failures of initiative and not top-down exploitations. They conclude that the excellent lives enjoyed by wealthy people reflect the excellent choices they make as moral and rational agents. They think poverty reflects wilfully inept or lazy choices.

Dastardly or criminal lives are similarly analyzed. Anyone who worries about antecedents or extenuating circumstances is guilty of *sociology*.

The lives of winners and losers, leaders and followers, appropriately reward and punish excellent and dubious choices. The USA is the wealthiest nation in the world. If I have this right, they also have more people incarcerated than all other nations combined.

Along with being oxymoronic, apologists' for this state of affairs overlook that leader/follower proceedings are archaic, antediluvian, primitive... forms of life. They hearken back to the period when human beings lacked cultural and intellectual resources and had no choice except to tuck in behind anyone offering to lead them anywhere.

This instinct to idolatrize and submit to authority is part of the 'hard wiring' Canada's Chief of Defence Staff Thomas Lawson referred to as an element in sexual harassment in the military.[85]

In an era lacking social media and 'hooking up' communication channels, in an era when 'reproductive opportunities' were probably few and far between,

---

[85]In an interview with CBC News Tuesday night, General Lawson told host Peter Mansbridge that sexual harassment in the Canadian Armed Forces is a result of men's "biological wiring."
http://www.cbc.ca/news/politics/gen-tom-lawson-current-defence-chief-to-step-down-later-this-year-1.2979941

Vernon Molloy

opportunistic sexual behaviour might have been essential to species survival.

The emergence of cultural resources allowed human beings, for the most part, to move past the hard-wired sexual proclivities General Lawson alludes to. I do not recall General Lawson making this connection but the sub-text of what he was saying is that instinctive proclivities are closer to the surface in the charged circumstances military personnel find themselves in or training to be in.

Recognizing this has to be part of any solution to such behaviour.

What is interesting is that there has been no comparable repudiation of a more far more dangerous instinct: our continued idolatrization of leader/follower relationships.

Both behaviours are bastardizations of possibilities cultural resources make available to human beings.

General Lawson should be applauded. The fact that his efforts landed him in hot water is also auspicious. General Lawson reminded us that we have factory settings that orchestrate what we get up to unless neutralized or overridden culturally.

I look forward to the day when leader/follower relationships receive the same censure as abusive sexual relationships.

Both involve powerful people fucking helpless people. The sense of this now vulgar expression hearkens back to its Anglo-Saxon root, which had farmers going out every day to fuck their fields: cultivating them with a view to inseminating and harvesting new life.

The second consequence of the *ought implies can* dictum is subtler. People at the top of professional and academic fields have little credibility with their counterparts in other disciplines. What a conundrum! If professionals cannot make useful observations outside of their disciplines, how can they make judgements about the overarching industrial, technological, political, military... capacities these specialities give rise to?

The paradox is instructive: the more powerful and sophisticated human enterprises become the less likely anyone will even attempt to understand what is going on.

This is not something we seem to worry about. Academics, doctors, engineers, scientists... recognize the difficulty of keeping up-to-date in their fields. Focused arenas of knowledge and responsibility offer relief.

In tandem with the urban specialization that trains and licences people to perform small tasks as often as possible, the world is now comprised of human beings who consider themselves disenfranchised in terms of understanding what is going on. We regard ourselves as victims or bystanders.

The well-educated lead amazing lives in silos of information and expertise. They enjoy respectful relationships with one another. The only thing they share is a bleak estimation of the rest of us: a blend of condescending dismissal and patronizing concern.

They acknowledge that 'the rest of us' are the source of wealth, power, research grants..., but then remember that we share in fruits of their research and ingenuity. Our lights come on, our computers work, our magic carpet cars take us effortlessly wherever we want to go.

The fact that we only want to go round and round in circles is not their problem.

For the first time in history most human beings have been identified, catalogued and accounted for. For the first time, most of us are regarded the way farmers think about cattle, pigs and chickens in barns and fields.

This may be the best we can hope for. It is difficult to imagine an alternative. Even so imagining an alternative is a matter of life and death. Sorting populations into *cognoscenti* and *domestic populations* has spawned technologies and industries that are impoverishing most human beings.

Along the way they are disenfranchising wealthy and poor alike from understanding, much less taking responsibility, for what is going on.

In my view, this relationship should be rethought if not *reversed.* The work ordinary lives perform, the products and services they consume, the taxes they pay... are the life-blood governments and corporations.

Moreover, followers' expectations of themselves and one another are powerful determinants of what will happen. Thus, the further down *progress road* we travel the more natural and desirable next steps seem to be. Further along development road means narrower skills, greater dependencies and reduced ability to notice what is happening, much less judge whether it constitutes progress.

The predicament is being compounded by global democraticization. Democracies have wonderful benefits for elite populations. They absolve the wealthy of responsibility for the machinations their lives depend upon. Democracies transform *noblesse oblige* 'insights' into supererogatory opportunities. Endowments, Bill and Melissa Gates foundations... legitimize and rationalize the hierarchical, hegemonic, rich/poor relationships that make charities necessary.

I saved the best for last. There are no innocent people in these proceedings; and your and my complicity points to where we can being repairing problems. The commercial and industrial activities cultural resources, urbanization and specialization make possible are embraced by urban populations. Black Fridays, Christmas Seasons, Boxing Day sales... sanction further commercial and industrial investments. These successes sanction corporations and nations to do whatever is necessary to keep economies growing.

We have a tiger by the tail and dare not let go of – even though we have a bad feeling about how things are turning out. Two or three per cent GNP growth per year is considered a safe minimum. Every three months (every quarter) nations take their economic temperature. If the growth rate is less than the preceding quarter's this is termed a *contraction, disinflation* or *recession.* Recessions that continue for two or more quarters are termed *Depressions*.

This is important because depressed economies risk *deflation* - a circumstance wherein units of currency have more purchasing power year over year. This happened during the Great Depression in the 1930's and in Japan in the late 1990s. [86] Deflating economies can spiral downward and fiscal and monetary tools become ineffectual. Contracts and debts must be settled with increasingly valuable money. Purchases tend to be put off because goods and services will be cheaper next week or next year. Underground economies flourish because institutions are no longer seen as the path to a secure future.

These consequences and considerations are only relevant to those with assets and investments. The impoverished do not worry whether economies are experiencing inflation or deflation. Like cattle and chickens, they are occupied trying to stay alive. They have little interest in whether farmers' houses are luxurious or burning down.

This myopia – natural and inevitable when talking about cattle and chickens – has not been serving us well. The crisis of economic and environmental sustainability is rounding upon human beings whether they are rich or poor, leaders or followers. This is why recalling what happens to cattle and chickens when overseers' prospects take a turn for the worse is useful. The issues being decided include whether assets will be sold, culled or continue being milked.

The parallels have been unmistakeable for decades: factories

---

[86]Japan has suffered from long-lasting but mild deflation since the latter half of the 1990s.... After reaching 11.6 percent in the first half of the 1970s, annual average CPI inflation rates declined, becoming around zero or slightly negative from the middle of the 1990s. A similar trend can be observed for inflation rates calculated from the GDP deflator, although they tend to be somewhat weaker than CPI inflation...
https://www.boj.or.jp/en/research/wps_rev/wps_2012/data/wp12e06.pdf

are constructed, dismantled, automated or outsourced... according to considerations far beyond workers' and consumers' spheres of awareness and responsibility.

Of course there are differences between human beings and farm animals, even if we have been overlooking them. Locked into tiny worlds animals are unable to defend themselves because they are congenitally unable to understand what is happening or where it is coming from.

The difference is that our lives do not have to run this way. The torments we have endured and visited upon one another over the centuries have happened because we tricked or seduced ourselves into not paying attention to what our farmers were getting up to.

The fact that we could not wait to be tricked and seduced means that we should not waste time blaming others. Of course we should be ashamed of ourselves. However this complicity is good news. As soon as we figure out where our problems are coming from, *as soon as we recognize that we are the problem*, we can get to work figuring out new ways to get to work!

In case more motivation is needed, the world's growing population continues to call for economic and technological development. Unfortunately, 'progress and development' need not mean improved lives, or at least permanently improved lives for most of us. If anything, 'business as usual' has been making us poor, fat, and dysfunctional. How can more of the strategy have a different result?

In spite of this example, Third World populations appear equally naive about American President Kennedy's 1963 homily: "A rising tide lifts all boats". It was already clear that this optimism applied only to those with boats already in the water. The yachts dominating modern harbours certainly make it clear that most of us are "not wanted on the voyage".

The fact that emerging nations are doing everything they can to join the First World on development road is disappointing for for another reason. Third Worlders have the benefit of our example. They have 'research data' western populations did not have when the Industrial Revolution was getting underway. What they overlook - what western populations continue to deny - is that the middle-class was a radical departure from the rich/poor cultures dominating history. This should have told us that rich/poor forms of life reflect human beings' 'factory settings'.

Instead post-Industrial Revolution populations continue to assume that human beings are finally getting it right and that economic well-being will keep enlarging until every boat has been floated.

The reality is that increasingly powerful economic forces continue to shape all of our lives. Some have familiar names like greed and avarice. The most important involve male/female subordinations and our inclination to sort ourselves into leader/follower hierarchies. The results are coming fast. They include not only an unexpectedly short-lived middle class in First World nations, but a middle class unwittingly serving as a laboratory and incubator for still more people-displacing technologies.

Now that specialization, urbanization and globalization have been accomplished - now that most forms of subsistence living have been rooted out - the middle-class population that made of this possible is redundant and dispensable. The skills and employments that spawned the middle class possible have been automated or outsourced. Urbanized, domesticated and now completely dependent people have no move to make. There are no places left for us to move to. We have no Inner-Directedness to build upon if such places existed.

The irony is that the middle class populations cannot really object to this crisis. Resource depletion, pollution and climate change problems mean human beings must find ways to tread more lightly.

How can this be achieved with emerging nations clamouring

to emulate western consumerism? [87] The world might support five hundred million wealthy people - if the rest of us make do with $2.00 *per diem* life-styles![88]

So there we have it. Unless you and I figure out how to live modestly and sustainably – in ways that contain a critical proportion of the value of our work for our own use – we must take comfort that the wealthy are doing all they can to avert disaster.

By scooping up as much of our lives as possible they are preventing us from making the world uninhabitable.

---

[87]http://www.nytimes.com/2015/01/28/world/asia/obama-ends-visit-with-challenge-to-india-on-climate-change.html?hp&action=click&pgtype=Homepage&module=second-column-region&region=top-news&WT.nav=top-news&_r=0
[88]http://www.bbc.com/news/magazine-30949796

Spring Hope in the Dread of Winter

I originally thought to name this final chapter *The Fleming/Thomson Hiatus* in honour of two individuals I recently worked with on a house-building project.

After consulting with one of them I learned that being included was okay but not if it involved being associated with the other.

This did not surprise me. I had observed how combative these two became whenever they were together. Both were hard-working, skilled and resourceful. Both could see how to proceed whenever a problem arose. The problem they could not resolve - could not even be tricked into discussing - was that neither was the slightest bit interested in deferring to the other.

After a few months of bickering the difficulty was resolved in the only civilized way possible – one of them downed tools and walked away.

I should say that both of these individuals passed Immanuel Kant's universalizability test with flying colours: a world comprised of such people is not only imaginable, it would be prosperous and interesting.

This cannot be said of an increasing proportion of human beings. It is impossible to imagine a pleasant, sustainable world composed of managers, engineers, unionists, accountants, professors or soldiers.

In addition, anyone whose central tendency can be described with a word ending in -ism almost certainly fails Mr. Kant's test. Communists, capitalists, Catholics, Hindus, Muslims... come to mind.

Mr. Thompson, Mr. Fleming - and other Inner-Directeds I have had the fortune to know - helped me understand many of the issues discussed in this book.

Vernon Molloy

I will repay them by suggesting why they embody an important possibility, perhaps the only one remaining.

First, a bit of history:

I often find myself deferring to people who present themselves as skilled at some task at hand – even when I could carry off the work myself. This seems to involve an automatically-occurring adjustment of my sense of competence and responsibility. I find myself waiting for direction from whatever expert happens to be on site.

This does not mean that I consciously defer, or even that I am conscious of deferring. I just suddenly find myself unable to see a way forward. I wait to be instructed - just as I sense people waiting upon me when roles are reversed and I become the momentarily-relevant expert.

Why should this be so? I think the answer can be tracked back to our primal beginnings. As well, I think it reflects our flawed understanding of the nature and function of consciousness. We do not *choose* to become leaders or followers. This sorting out occurs spontaneously and organizes human beings into leader/follower hierarchies whenever groups occur.

Some of this could be explained as learned, conditioned or pragmatic behaviours. However such explanations do not explain the ubiquitousness of hierarchies or how they got started in the first place.

More importantly, these learned behaviours – and rational/moral conscious *choices* – cannot explain why human beings remain willing to slaughter one another *en masse* whenever credible leaders – and institutions comprised of credible leaders – stipulate that this should happen.

Similarly, learned behaviours cannot explain why we continue to believe progress and development will soon deliver Heaven on Earth when most lives increasingly resemble scenes from Dante's *Inferno* or a dystopian novel.

These outcomes cannot be explained by pointing to malignant leaders or corporate malfeasance. Something instinctive must be going on. I propose that current events and Toynbee's historical narratives flow from instinctive procedures tirelessly sorting populations into leader/follower groups of various sizes, agendas and temperaments.

Sorting human beings into networks of leaders and followers was once essential to survival. The problem is, the instinct to do so has been appropriating cultural and technological achievements into increasingly toxic organizations.

Rich stores of information and miraculous technologies now link individuals, communities and nations in ways unimaginable even fifty years ago.

These resources – and their technological and industrial concomitants – not only render leader/follower relationships unnecessary they make them unsurvivable. Kant's universalizability test explains why: a world organized into leaders and followers is a world Hell-bent for elections, and a world Hell-bound in general.

Alternatively, an interesting, sustainable world comprised of Inner-Directed persons is conceivable. Of course there would be lots of squabbling and projects involving large groups might never get off of the ground.

I would be okay with that.

Culturally-enabled leader/follower relationships are toxic for another reason. Becoming wealthy or achieving leadership status invariably means becoming arrogant, greedy and self-serving.[89]

In the good old days – when leaders had nothing to gain from taking the point and putting themselves in harms way except opportunities to feel good about themselves – sorting human beings in this way was an excellent strategy

The rest of the story is that followers are corrupted in complementary ways. They tuck in behind leaders. They applaud, wheedle, whine and fawn. They perform tricks, retrieve sticks and demonstrate that they know "Sic em!"

---

[89]http://www.bbc.com/news/magazine-31761576

Followers eagerly put themselves in harms way for a *Greater Good*, a *Greater God*, a chance for a ride on a *Highway of Heroes*, a promise of Paradise ripe with impatient virgins and free of impatient wives.

No matter how dreadful wars become, no matter how terrifying threats of nuclear or biological devastation, anthropogenic change… grow, we have yet to question the relevance or survivability of leader/follower relationships. Arnold Toynbee's analysis of the rise and fall of civilizations includes a mechanism of internal decay and collapse involving "creative minorities":[90]

> *Toynbee does not see the breakdown of civilizations as caused by loss of control over the physical environment, by loss of control over the human environment, or by attacks from outside. Rather, it comes from the deterioration of the "Creative Minority", which eventually ceases to be creative and degenerates into merely a "Dominant Minority" - which forces the majority to obey without meriting obedience. He argues that creative minorities deteriorate due to a worship of their "former self", by which they become prideful and fail adequately to address the next challenge they face.*

Mutually-corrupting leader/follower relationships expand this mechanism so that it becomes *dyadic*. Like chickens and eggs, leaders and followers reliably perpetuate one another. Unfortunately they are also reliably self-destructing.

Creative minorities (leaders) do not wrestle, trick or seduce followers into obedience. Leaders and followers bring one another into existence the way the double-entry bookkeeping system spawns assets and liabilities out of nothing and provides mechanisms for keeping them in balance.

Toynbee's 'creative minorities' exist alongside subordinates whose deficits of engagement and spirit precisely balance the '

---

[90]http://en.wikipedia.org/wiki/A_Study_of_History#Genesis

418

arrogance and hubris of leaders.

This suggests a way human beings could extricate themselves from Toynbee's cycle of civilizations coming into existence, decaying because 'creative minorities' become dominant and then corrupt. When they become corrupt enough that they can no longer perform their reassuring leader function they are thrown out and the cycle begins again.

Cultural achievements made it possible to evolve beyond this dreary torment. Properly invested, cultural resources could expand subsistence activities, vitalize local economies and enlarge the proportion of human beings developing into persons.

In this narrative, scientific and technological developments would be automatically harnessed to small-footprint ways and means of living.

Along with stabilizing and rationalizing central economies, these technologies and best practices could have been adopted by Third World nations. This would be far less destructive path than the witches' brew multinational corporations and free trade agreements have been forcing upon them. First World nations would have benefited as well. They would be enjoying economies whose vigour and stability was not predicated upon subordination, exploitation and corruption. They would be enjoying a more peaceful world.

Instead of going down this lovely path, leader/follower relationships have been feasting upon cultural achievements. Individuals who might have grown into persons have been partitioned into workers and consumers. The resulting half-wits have instead been organized into nations, corporations, ethnicities, interest groups and sects.

The ensuing fractiousness and requirements for supervision and organization are interpreted as calling for more 'progress and development', more legislation and surveillance and 'peace and security' initiatives.

Vernon Molloy

Few notice that this race to the bottom makes no sense because events are thought about day-by-day rather than over months, years or decades. Anyone pointing this out is shouted down or ignored. This has nothing to do with moral turpitude or myopia of victims. The instincts spawning leader/follower relationships operate unconsciously.

We also fail to understand that conscious episodes do not make judgements or choose yes or no. Conscious episodes are passive the way communication media and blackboards only function to transmit conversations and record results.

To be sure, conscious episodes generate spheres of awareness. There *apperceptions* have been seducing individuals into seeing themselves as consciously doing stuff, as contesting for leadership roles – or as encouraging others to do so.

An old joke is that soldiers do not *volunteer* for dangerous or onerous missions – volunteers are those who fail to step back smartly. I think we glimpse this going on from time to time. I have noticed myself myself deferring to self-anointed leaders, most recently Mr. Thomson and Mr. Fleming. I am sure they notice as well. This reinforces their already robust sense of competence and importance – and the complementary notion that I might be useful if carefully instructed and monitored.

The rest of the story is that I find myself agreeing with these estimations. This is not the end of my perfidy. I am vaguely pleased that my perceived incompetence encourages them to assume responsibilities.

It is not much of a stretch to see how human beings might cultivate perceptions of incompetence and neediness as a way of inveigling 'warriors and hunters' into putting themselves in harms way.

To put this in context, the Province of Ontario recently renamed a stretch of the MacDonald-Cartier highway:

> *On August 24, 2007, the MTO announced that the stretch of Highway 401 between Glen Miller Road in Trenton and the intersection of the Don*

420

Valley Parkway and Highway 404 in Toronto would bear the additional name Highway of Heroes in honour of Canadian soldiers who have died. This length of the highway is often travelled by a convoy of vehicles carrying a fallen soldier's body... from CFB Trenton to the coroner's office at the Centre for Forensic Sciences in Toronto. Since 2002... crowds have lined the overpasses to pay their respects as convoys pass.[91]

What a remarkable stratagem! By providing opportunities to flex patriotic muscles, the Canadian government has found a way to involve citizens in a war they might otherwise grumble about, Citizens get 'real time' opportunities to 'give something back' to corpses taking their last ride.

Young people are encouraged to visit recruiting offices and replenish vacated 'hero holes'.

We can be sure that similar proceedings are occurring everywhere. When the nations involved are allies there is talk of loyalty, courage, patriotism and duty. When they are on the other side of whatever line in the sand happens to be in vogue, the talk is about conscription, indoctrination, brainwashing and radicalization.

Everywhere we look blandishments, enticements, seductions, emergent pecking orders... are transforming human beings into factions, sects, corporations and nations. Under the aegis of leader/follower relationships, economic, political and military processes are advancing towards unknown or terrifying conclusions.

As the Fleming/Thomson hiatus demonstrates, it is hard to see an alternative. If their squabbling means anything it must be that people who do not meld into leader/follower relationships lead fraught lives. They drive one another off to gain credibility and breathing room.

---

[91]http://en.wikipedia.org/wiki/Ontario_Highway_401#Highway_of_Heroes

Vernon Molloy

Outer-Directeds and Other-Directeds have a easier time of it. They sort selves, families, groups and communities into leader/follower relationships and lead nicely-ordered lives.

There is, however, an important difference between Outer-Directeds and Other-Directeds. Whether living as leaders or followers, Outer-Directeds retain a core of Inner-Directed resourcefulness. However, unlike Fleming/Thomson recidivists, they take no pleasure in being so constituted. They interpret their own resourcefulness as signalling the need to solve more problems, fill larders, secure borders... until the need for pesky conscious episodes becomes manageably small.

What is worth repeating is that these sortings occur outside of consciousness. Instincts rarely require conscious episodes to get going, although awarenesses are often involved as events proceed. To take a familiar example, men and women form romantic relationships based on unconscious responses and instinctive assessments, then experience plenty of conscious episodes as relationships proceed.

There is another deep-running reason we are reluctant to blow the whistle on ourselves. Even considering the possibility that leader/follower hierarchies are instinctive would make it difficult to claim that they make moral or rational sense, or that leadership qualities or achievements warrant large incomes and fame.

Another signal is that we never talk about the importance of followership. Schools never offer courses preparing one to be a follower. To be a follower is kin to being a loser.

The idea that followership is the *sine qua non* of leadership never crosses our minds. Even so I think we understand intuitively that, without followers and losers, leaders and winners could not exist. However, discussing this would come uncomfortably close to acknowledging grass-roots complicity in all kinds of mischief, including our now global economic dependency, that often seems to shade into infantalism .

The question of what would be an optimum leader/follower

ratio is never discussed either[92] . Our sense is that more leaders would be a good thing; although we acknowledge that followers will always outnumber leaders.

The symmetry between leader/follower winner/loser ratios is one of several elephants in urban barns. Leaders and winners ride in style. The rest of us bring fodder to beasts, walk behind them with shovels and try to avoid being trampled.

This state of affairs is the consequence of historical failures to replace leader/follower relationships with subsistence activities and communities.

With these thoughts in mind, professional sports can be understood as having a more interesting function than pornographic titillation and vicarious participation opportunities. Human beings seem endlessly interested in identifying the fastest and strongest members in relevant communities. In the primal world this made sense. Survival depended upon identifying such individuals, training them up and encouraging them to take point duty and man the ramparts.

> *No free-time activity or interest comes close to the amount of engagement or number of people who are sports fans. And that interest is mostly stable. For 20 years, 85 to 90 percent of Americans have had some interest and 28 to 32 percent have had avid interest in sports. In 2013, 88 percent are fans and 31 percent are avid fans. While the percent of Americans following sports has remained constant, the number of fans has grown along with the overall population from roughly 189 million to 219 million people (ages 12 and older).[93]*

In other words – although usually thought of as entertainment

---

[92]http://journal.frontiersin.org/article/10.3389/fnhum.2014.00363/full

[93]http://www.sportsbusinessdaily.com/Journal/Issues/2014/01/06/Research-and-Ratings/Up-Next.aspx

with little more than national or community pride on the line – the relationship between athletes and fans is an instinctively-driven version of choosing sides and letting the games begin.

Like fear of heights, snakes and spiders… fandom hearkens back to an epoch when such behaviours were the *sine qua non of* survival.

The leader/follower arrangements controlling human life can be seen as primal stand-ins for cultural resources. Until a few thousand years ago 'cultural resources were thin on the ground. They consisted of memories and skills in short-lived adults' minds. These memories and associated oral traditions were the only repositories of wisdom and best practices for thousands of years.

This is why music and artistic/mnemonic devices are profoundly interesting to human beings. Cultural resources, languages, books, technologies, the INTERNET… mean we can now move – could have already moved in fact! – beyond leader/follower arrangements.

Of course, there is no guarantee that cultural resources will ever be used this way. The problem involves the instinct to sort ourselves into leader/follower arrangements. No matter how rich our cultural achievements this primal relationship governs what we get up to.

If anything, matters are getting worse. Every generation struggles to survive leaders with increasingly sophisticated tools at their disposal. Leaders today brandish slogans praising democracy as they take control of more and more of what is going on. Followers occasionally express outrage but, for the most part, appear content to lead child-like lives in vast urban barns.

Although instinctual programming goes a long way towards explaining these proceedings, it is not the entire story. An important factor involves the elimination of subsistence possibilities and associated erosion of *wildness quotients*. Everywhere one looks, families, communities, private lives…

are being domesticated and monetized under the banner of progress and development, comfort and security.

This bastardization of culture's most interesting promise – a world free of half-witted leaders and followers – is almost complete. Instead of improving the human beings/persons proportion we have been melding into dinosauric undertakings: corporations, nations, military organizations... with a small percentage of human beings owning and apparently controlling everything.

Of course this is not what is really going on. A few million human beings now pass their days fantasizing about being in charge while the rest of us chuckle that we have tricked them into doing the heavy lifting. After all, no matter how poor and bedraggled we become, we get to inhabit warm urban barns and live as children. What's not to like?

"Not much springy stuff here!" you are probably saying. I do not have a good feeling either. Even so a small possibility exists in the *Fleming/Thomson Hiatus.* Although the numbers are dwindling such people can still be found everywhere. (How else could I have come across so many?) They are, of course, quarrelsome, intractable and prickly. Trying to organize Inner-Directeds is like trying to herd cats.

These are precisely the qualities needed to address what must be done!

Unfortunately, persuading Inner-Directeds to harness themselves to externally-mandated tasks is difficult. Fleming/Thomson individuals (almost always male) pass their days looking for tasks that do not involve factory regimens or Tim Horton hair nets. They mostly spend time looking for a woman, or a succession of women, willing to give them something to do.

I say *succession* because Inner-Directeds are not good at taking instructions from women either and lead lives best described as serial monogamies. Fleming/Thomson types also experience fraught economic lives. Resourceful and skilled, they do not worry about investments, nest eggs or rainy days.

They rarely take advantage of other people which is the way most of us acquire wealth. Their vehicles and houses tend to be neglected because they can always fix them if something actually breaks.

Careers or businesses are limited to tasks that can be undertaken single-handedly.

If an employment involves institutions or corporations, if more than one person is required to 'get er done', squabbling about how to proceed usually makes the experience unpleasant for everyone concerned.

So what is the way forward? Whenever I get the opportunity I raise arguments I hope my Fleming/Thompson friends find provocative. I point out that they are the remnants of the once-robust population of Inner-Directeds that colonized the new world – the population David Riesman thought was already dwindling in the 1950s.

Like Inner-Directeds across history, their problems have a *transcendental* source. Being proudly independent, Inner-Directeds refuse to join or form organizations. There are no clubs or organizations for individuals who refuse to join clubs. There are no political parties representing those who find politicians distasteful.

This is unfortunate because it means Inner-Directeds have always failed to represent themselves, their understandings, their values... politically or economically.

The rest of us have no such reluctance. We form protest groups, associations and corporations every chance we get. We organize hierarchies of leaders and followers. We elect governments as soon and as often as we can!

Not surprisingly, these governments and corporations have been concocting legislations further constraining, licensing, inspecting and taxing... subsistence activities. Governments and corporations have a similarly jaundiced view of Inner-Directeds. They mutter about underground economies. Worries about unpasteurized milk, overcooked cookies, undercooked cookies, cookies lacking GMOs and TRANSFATS...

wrinkle official brows and elevate sclerotic risks in corporate boardrooms.

The result is that Inner-Directeds are increasingly marginalized. They are regarded – they often regard themselves! – as antediluvian recidivists, as cowboys without horses and with nary a cow in sight.

Moreover, no matter how many tools and skills they possess, no matter how impressive their half-ton trucks, they know deep down that there is nothing they can do about what is happening to them!

Actually there are lots of things they could do, but they all involve getting together and discussing possibilities. They all involve occasionally giving up bickering and posturing.

The only possibility I can think of – the only way forward – involves Inner-Directeds giving up their hope that some eagle-eyed women will discern how good they are at building 'wombs with a view' and make them an offer.

I have noticed something else. Fleming/Thomson people have opinions about everything. These opinions are advanced eagerly and defended vigorously. If they do not have an opinion because an issue has just came up, they will construct one on the spot, advance it eagerly and defend it vigorously.

This is also an obstacle to what we need to get up to. In addition to your and my feelings of perfection whenever a thought or memory crosses our minds, Fleming/Thomson individuals suffer from a double-helping of rectitude. They have contempt for individuals requiring guidance or external life-support systems.

On the other hand, if they come across individuals who are also Inner-Directeds with half-tons of their own, an even more primal competition comes into play. More than Other-Directeds and Outer-Directeds, Inner-Directeds regard each and every understanding and opinion they have as perfect.

In the language of the digester metaphor, Inner-Directeds are cognitively *constipated* in that they are full of themselves . The

427

fact that they are not half-witted rarely rescues them from rational and moral paralysis. Their facile opinions, the fact that few of us are able to confront them, means they get away with not being really interested in big-picture issues or discussions.

When large issues are on the table, Inner-Directeds dismiss people *en masse* rather than one by one.

However understood, Inner-Directeds are being obliterated. They have not been able to defend the subsistence activities, families and communities that are their natural habitat. The truth is, they do not seem to have not been trying to do so.

This does not augur well. If Inner-Directeds – with their tool boxes, skill sets and 'do it myself' attitudes – are unable to defend themselves what chance do you and I have?

The erosion of subsistence possibilities and activities – the reason Fleming/Thomson people are on the endangered species list – is an important factor in today's political and economic problems. Fleming/Thomson individuals are like canaries in mines. Their fate tells us that something analogous to oxygen is being depleted in urban life. Most human beings are capable of Inner-Directedness if sufficiently pressed – a "When the going gets tough, the tough get going!" story. Unfortunately most of us do not like "doing what we want to do" all of the time. The responsibility is nerve-wracking and anxiety-provoking.... Whenever a conscious episode rises up we are seized with the need to put that aspect of our circumstance in order.

Putting fires out, getting a wood pile together, killing rats in pantries, filling these pantries with preserves... is almost always a good idea. The problem is, our big brains and cultural achievements mean we can mount increasingly powerful responses. After immediate problems are solved, we look around for permanent solutions so we will not be bothered again.

This is why labour saving, convenience and security technologies are always in vogue. This is why Canadians figured out how to heat their homes with firewood piped from

Alberta. This is why human beings seek out 'promising leaders' and make them offers they are unable to refuse.

As soon as these leaders and heroes sign on – North Korea's Kim Jong-un makes it clear that we are not that discriminating – the rest of us get to lay 'need to be Inner-Directed' burden down.

These proceedings became doubly seductive after the Industrial Revolution. Urban wombs became so accommodating that even poor people could live and die as if they had never been born. With food trucked in, waste products flushed or trucked away, houses heated and cooled homeostatically... nothing had to be thought about beyond doing 'one's job'.

Whether we are young, old, retired, unemployed or off-work, entertainment is now available twenty four hours a day. Advertisements telling us what to wear, where to go, who to vote for... are as relentless as mosquitoes.

Polls and questionnaires reassure us that we are in charge of what is going on by constantly asking what we think about what is going on.

To be sure, even with all of this support, anxious moments sometimes occur. Not to worry! The weekend is almost here. A shopping trip will dissolve doubts and refresh our sense that all is well.

This is not perfect of course. The more vigorously disgruntled among us will sometimes demonstrate their metal (mettle?) by marching up and down, banging pots and gesticulating. Some block highways on holiday weekends and set tires on fire to underscore that they also mean business.

These ' antics do not worry anyone. Leaders are reassured that the status quo will continue because of this fresh evidence that followers wish it so. Followers rejoice in their capacity to promote proper people into leadership roles. We want to object to what is going on but to do so in ways that

Vernon Molloy

leave apple carts upright. If this were not the case how could followers have had such a long history of selecting leaders reliably capable of wretched outcomes?

I am being facetious of course. There is nothing magical about identifying suitably corrupt leaders. Being promoted to a *leadership* role invariably corrupts individuals. There is little need to worry that excellent leaders will rise to the top and do something useful before quick-witted followers put an end to them! (Granted, there have been close calls: Christ, Ghandi, perhaps John Kennedy....)

In addition, leaders who seem reliably corrupt at the outset (i.e., who identify social problems in terms of *us vs. them* instead of *us creating them*) sometimes wiggle about sufficiently that they are difficult to assess. After repudiating the Nation of Islam in favour of the Sunni Muslim faith in 1964 (an act which led to his assassination in February 1965 by three disgruntled former colleagues) Malcolm X observed:

> *I did many things as a [Black] Muslim that I'm sorry for now. I was a zombie then—like all [Black] Muslims—I was hypnotized, pointed in a certain direction and told to march. Well, I guess a man's entitled to make a fool of himself if he's ready to pay the cost. It cost me 12 years.* [94]

So there you have it: my arguments on the table. You will note that there is not a truth-claim among them. Nor am I interested in making another demonstration that the 'emperor has no clothes'. My ambition is more provocative. I propose that talk about emperors (including notions that human beings automatically turn into persons) is anthropomorphic self-deification.

This is not a truth claim. This is a challenge to a truth claim so commonplace that it appears axiomatic.

For thousands of years we have been seeing ourselves as captains of our ships, owning and controlling bodies we

[94]http://en.wikipedia.org/wiki/Malcolm_X

inhabit and ride around in. These days we are urban cowboys driving splendidly efficient, low-emission contraptions.

In previous generations we had to make do with motorcycles, sailing ships and honest-to-God horses.

Changing the mode of conveyance does not change the logic. We have always thought of ourselves as cowboys riding our bodies across the world.

We have always been all hat no cow.

The idea that consciousness is the seat of agency, that realism regarding the phenomenal world makes sense, is an important obstacle to repairing the problems these claims have been spawning.

The difficulty is to challenge these conceit without making repeating them in sneakier ways. My ambition has been to characterize what is 'really going on' without muddying the water.

Acquiring a point of view that understands points of view as useful sophistries is still a point of view.

"Why bother?" You ask.

Along with fun and excitement, uprooting confusions makes one alert to sophistries and wishful thinking. Recognizing that ontological claims are always false because they always refer to vanished states of affairs does not prevent some claims from being recognized as more outlandish than others.

How can claims be rank-ordered in terms of danger? This is difficult – but dangerous notions often signal their presence by annointing themselves with words ending in ...ism: communism, capitalism, Catholicism, fascism, globalism....

This is not a perfect test but it is better than nothing.

To sum up, the engine propelling human beings towards the abyss can be described in a few words. Human beings instinctively organize themselves into hierarchies. These arrangements occur more or less automatically and make good use of cultural repositories and *Homo sapiens sapiens'* capacious brains.

These capacious brains, coupled with music, songs, poetry, mnenomic devices and oral traditions... , have been spawning cultural resources that could have mitigated the need for leader/follower arrangements.

Cultural repositories consist of information about ways and means to survive and prosper. These resources did not and do not have to be harnessed to projects subordinating the many to the few.

This is important to think about for a second reason. Leaders invariably become greedy, ugly human beings. Followers invariably become puerile subordinates willing to do whatever greedy ugly people tell them to do.

It does not have to be this way. Cultural repositories are 'external memories' making important or sublime experiences available to communities and succeeding generations.

They can also be harnessed to mad, megalomaniacal undertakings comprised of corrupted leaders and followers. My favourite example is North Korea's Kim Jong-un and his retinue of terrified admirers, but history is full of human beings goose-stepping towards oblivion.

Rather than replacing or mitigating the need for hegemonic relationships, cultural resources have made them more pervasive and toxic. Technologies, including money, legal institutions and police forces now keep the peace and protect asset. They increase leaders' ability to industrialize everything in sight. They increase the likelihood the rest of us will applaud and vote **yes** every step of the way.

As industrialization proceeded, subsistence cultures were replaced with commodities and services flowing from corporations, institutions and governments. Subsistence activities that resisted commercialization were identified as dangerous. Thus the education and socialization of children; the preparation of food for public consumption, the keeping of backyard chickens... were institutionalized, frowned upon or forbidden altogether.

To borrow a word programmers use for functional but dated coding practices – other rogue activities were *deprecated* as obsolete or anachronistic.

Not surprisingly the sternest censure was reserved for *underground economies.* In Canada snitch lines have been set up. Carpenters, plumbers, electricians... suspected of working for cash can be reported. Revenue Canada will take your call day or night. You don't have to give *your* name but it helps if you have *someone's* name to share!

As a consequence, the economic resilience and democratic vigour flowing from a healthy proportion of self-reliant individuals, communities and local economies vanished during the 20th century.

We did not notice this for many reasons, some already touched on. One of the more interesting is that subsistence activities occur without anyone having to conceive, convene or implement them. Whether one is a human being, a squirrel or a whale, the need to engage in subsistence activities is like breathing, digesting, defecating, finding food, avoiding danger.... The ability to engage in subsistence activity is what it means to be alive.

In the case of human beings, conscious episodes are often involved in responses to particular needs. The problem is, best practices usually occur without conscious attention and so their benefits do not come to mind when contemplating what to do next.

As a consequence, when the Industrial Revolutionists came calling, all subsistence economy populations thought about was the difficult, labour-intensive, uncertain nature of the activities they had been depending upon.

They had no awareness of what they were giving up when they embraced urban solutions to the difficulties that had been constituting their conscious lives.

Even so, until perhaps fifty years ago, subsistence activities in Canada and other western nations remained so commonplace that governments and corporations deemed them worth dismantling or capitalizing upon. Until this occurred there were plenty of Inner-Directedd whose skills and work habits could have turned progress and development initiatives into wholesome outcomes – if anyone had noticed what was happening!

Unfortunately these erosions and encroachments occurred insidiously and perhaps surreptitiously enough that few demurred. Consciously-abetted or not, subsistence activities, families and communities were obliterated slowly and hardly anyone noticed. Instead of asking important questions, the hens among us passed weeks, months, years... clucking over advertisements and bickering over who possessed the best nest.

As Mr Fleming and Mr. Thomson have been demonstrating, the roosters – who might have been expected to sound the most strident cacophony possible – passed their days comparing trucks and quarrelling over who was best equipped to build yet another 'womb with a view' for yonder comely lass!

These difficulties can be summarized in a sentence. Now that subsistence activities have disappeared, now that leader/follower arrangements are everywhere, there are fewer and fewer *persons* to be found.

As long as subsistence activities were occurring, as long as some human beings had both producing and consuming activities in view *simultaneously*, there was a chance they would grow into persons with a bit of *wildness,* a bit or unpredictability and creativity.

In spite of, and because of, cultural resources and technological prowess, we machined ourselves into component parts and formed into monster corporations and monstrous nations.

Modern Problems, Ancient Perspectives

Since then we have been more or less eagerly identifying with whatever crosses their minds.

For the first time, human activity can all be organized under the aegis, the yoke, the umbrella of leader/follower arrangements, corporatiions and nations.

The reality that makes this truly terrifying is that these corporations and nations possess powerful technologies and dreadful weapons. Economic and political globalization means the world exists in a state of perpetual, universal conflict.

This theatre of war includes every corner of every nation. Islamic State, Boko Haram, Hezebollah, drone weapons, smart bombs, nuclear weapons, suicide bombers... have become global realities. This state of affairs, which includes politicians talking up terrorism for terrorist reasons of their own, has not been spawned by the conscious decisions of morally-corrupt individuals. Morally-corrupt individuals are the faces, the GUIs... the public face of unconscious proceedings. They serve as focal points, mediums and conduits for toxic events.

The fact that they identify themselves as *agents responsible* , paves the way to identifying you and I as targets, as resources, and perhaps as infidels in need of sanctioning up to and including beheading.

Another fantasy is that problems can be resolved or dissolved by consciousness-raising efforts. Our difficulties are boiling up from what is going on within us. These proceedings 'help themselves' to conscious episodes whenever doing so links neural events so that big pictures and big projects are envisaged and can be sustained for moments or years.

This means that solving 'big picture' and 'big project' issues involves improving the quality or variety of ingredients in digesters in the hopes that they inform future outcomes in wholesome ways.

A good deal of this used to be accomplished by way of

subsistence activities, responsibilities and possibilities.[95] This was never perfect of course. Human beings have always been capable of mistreating and slaughtering one another if sufficiently charismatic ass-holes said that this should happen.

Even so, until recently, most human beings spent most of their lives pursuing activities that did not require and did not finance the systematic destruction of everything in sight.

This is how I remember life in a farming community near Ivanhoe, Ontario. We had wonderful times. We generated enough value that we grew grow up big, strong and foolish but not enough that we became fat, lazy and sick. The beautiful thing was that, after the people involved took their share of the fruits of their work, there was not much left to finance and corrupt a rich and powerful one per cent.

My hope is that the arguments I have presented persuade a few people to take a sceptical look at *common sense* and *realism* and a second look at the importance of subsistence activities. I have no big-picture replacement for realism. If any such understanding crosses my mind, I promise to keep it to myself!

The trick is to hang onto curiosity and humility, which happen to be two sides of the same coin.

> *The presence of those seeking the truth is infinitely to be preferred to the presence of those who think they've found it.*

Terry Pratchet (1948-2015)

We are all curious while young, which is good because the learning curve is steep and arrogance would be fatal. If all goes well, some of this curiosity remains. Unhappily this does not seem to often happen. Most of the time we find a perch along some leader/follower hierarchy.

---

[95]But see:
http://www.nytimes.com/2011/10/09/books/review/the-better-angels-of-our-nature-by-steven-pinker-book-review.html?pagewanted=all&_r=0

Modern Problems, Ancient Perspectives

This was okay when human beings were the endangered species and survival depended upon finding experienced adults and persuading them to allow us to tag along, or at least to not strangle us.

It is not okay now that human beings have become the principal cause of endangered species and our own worst enemy.

Vernon Molloy

My Last Card

Since I can't count on people reading these notions and wrestling themselves onto a sustainable path, I am going to put the my last card on the table.

A substantial population of rag-tag, dishevelled, belligerent salt-of-the-earth types – described above as the Fleming/Thomson impasse, snarl, imbroglio... – can still to be found in towns and rural areas across North America. I am told that such individuals exist in emerging nations as well, probably in larger proportions.

My intuition is that these numbers are shrinking everywhere. I do not see much evidence of Inner-Directedness in cities; and smart technologies are making every place an urban place. Even when specialization and urbanization are not yet occurring the INTERNET and smartphones are reducing rural populations to peering and peeping through store windows.

However, no matter how bedraggled and diminished, these Inner-Directeds represent an important possibility. They are best understood as a reservoir species keeping the possibility of persons alive while the rest of us sort ourselves into *half witted* transmogrifications of human beings.

As far as I can tell, Inner-Directeds have no idea of how important they are; even though they each think they are more important than anyone they know.

As well, just in case I have not made it abundantly clear, I regard women as intrinsically, instinctively, magnificently... Inner-Directed. I think this even though, on the surface, women appear Outer-Directed. They spend an amazing amount of time searching for bargains for the important people in their lives, for products to make nests more comfortable and – if resources remain – a few gewgaws to make themselves look better.

Women are Inner-Directed for many reasons:

  • Women do not give a damn about where these

438

bargains, embellishments and gewgaws come from. They do not give a damn about costs to the planet or whether individuals were harmed in their production. The only thing they require is that unsavoury events along supply chains occur behind closed doors or *over there.*

The fact that a small proportion of women are volubly worried about such issues proves the point. Rachael Carson, Naomi Klein, Linda McQuaig, Michele Lansdsberg... are exceptions that prove the rule. They stand out against a backdrop of women fully engaged building and feathering nests.

- Women spontaneously and tirelessly nurture a few children, a few friends and often a few pets. These behaviours well up from unconscious sources. They have nothing to do with socialization, education, political blandishments or corporate advertisements. Corporate blandishments and advertisements exist because women pay attention to them.

- Women often complain that the world is full of glass-ceilings and abusive and misogynistic men. What I have yet to hear discussed – what I have yet to successfully introduce as a topic of conversation – is whether women are complicit in these problems.

- Whether problems occur at the community, national or global level, women perceive them from insular, self-contained vantage points. As long as domestic projects are not being compromised, even local community issues are ignored.

- If troubles come closer still, women see themselves and their circle of important people as bystanders or victims.

This sense of aggrieved, insular innocence flows naturally from Inner-Directed points of view. Significantly, similar complaints are frequently expressed by Fleming/Thomson individuals.

The story works better for women:

- Women are often abused.
- Women are the *bearers and nurturers of life.*

My next suggestion is so outrageous that I tremble to write it down. I suggest that women have been complicit in all of the cataclysms of history. With every fibre of their being, women have been sanctioning processes leading to economic and political problems, to anthropogenic change, to psychologically and physiologically compromised children and to abusive relationships.

I am not actually claiming to be courageous. The truth is, I know that I have no reason to worry. I know this because I have attempted to raise this issue with dozens of women.

The most I have ever managed to provoke are raised eyebrows and indulgent dismissals before conversations turn to more urgent matters.

This is what bred-in-the bone Inner-Directedness looks like. This sense of certitude and indifference puts the antics of Fleming/Thomson individuals to shame!

In other words, a profound myopia characterizes Inner-Directedness. In women this manifests as indifference about where gewgaws and nest-building embellishments come from. Women and Fleming/Thomson individuals are similarly uninterested in issues a week or a year removed. This makes sense from an evolutionary perspective. Until a few thousand years ago, paying attention to immediate issues was essential to surviva. Even then the typical life-span was one-half or one-third of what it is today.

Those days are gone. They are probably gone forever. We extricated ourselves from pressing problems we were more or less equipped to manage to find ourselves in depressing circumstances with unfathomable boundaries. An important reason involves human beings' failures to extricate themselves from leader/follower arrangements as cultural resources made larger spheres of subsistence activities possible.

These failures – and the associated indifference of men and women to the cumulative big-picture consequences of their domestic projects – is a central ingredient in the so-called anthropogenic era. Women have always been muttering to themselves about which domestic project should come next. For thousands of years men have been competing to see who gets to help out with whatever they have in mind.

This close attention to reproductive matters and nest building projects once made human survival possible. It is now our greatest threat.

Members of the Fleming/Thomson group do not care about big picture issues for another reason. They have little interest in becoming either leaders or followers. Their pride is that they do things without anyone telling them to. Because they see themselves as self-starters and self-sufficient, because they are uncommonly able to look after themselves, they pay little attention to what is going on beyond the projects they take up.

These projects almost always involve boyish enthusiasms – bigger trucks, bragging about hunting and fishing exploits, physical contests.... In other words, unless taken on as a domestic adjunct, Inner-Directed males pass their days comparing tools and testing one another's mettle.

The parallel with female Inner-Directeds is striking. Both are indifferent to the political, corporate and environmental consequences of the only agenda they have, until now, been able to agree upon.

This agenda includes:

- womb-building projects – houses, apartments, cottages, travel trailers, slums and flying toilets;
- gathering houses and apartments into cities to maximize security, comfort and convenience;
- establishing police services and military resources competent to contain urban fractiousness and defend hapless citizens crowded into cities.

Even with these consequences in mind, it remains true that

women's focus upon nurturing continues to be the *sine qua non* of survival. Therefore any repairs must build upon this reality.

Even with men lending a hand domestically, the heavy reproductive lifting continues to be done by women. Women know this, stay at home dads and day-care programmes notwithstanding. Women know that they and they alone sustain life, in the womb and afterwards.

This is why women are like squirrels leaping fearlessly from branch to branch. They cannot afford a moment's uncertainty about what they are doing or where they are headed. This sense of certitude, this ineluctable Inner-Directedness, is why I can suggest that women have been complicit in spawning Hell on Earth and not earn an iota of interest or indignation.

Women know that men cannot be trusted. They know male opinions are worthless when it comes to issues that really matter.

Problems resulting from this state of affairs share three elements:

1. The nurturing activities of human couples have become the stock-in-trade of nations, corporations and institutions.
    These activities need not involve actually reproducing, as Western populations experimenting with pet ownership and self-administered genocide are demonstrating.
2. The people and institutions doing this nurturing possess tools and technologies amplifying nest-building projects far beyond what is good for children, and far beyond sustainability.
3. The third element involves nations and corporations feasting upon the value nest-building pairs are capable of generating. They have been harvesting women's insatiable interest in creature comforts and men's equally inexorable desire to demonstrate nest-building credentials and insinuate themselves into cosy pictures.

I said 'most men' because Fleming/Thomson Inner-Directeds do not seem to be included in mainstream economic and political proceedings. They rarely become leaders and are never happy in followership roles.

This innate intractability is the light at the end of the tunnel. If Inner-Directed women could be persuaded to take a fresh look at nearby Fleming/Thomson types wonderful possibilities could start turning up.

I sometimes dream that the arguments sketched above could repair many problems. I am especially optimistic about the benefits of dissolving the conscious agent myth!

At the same time I know that the chance of this happening because of a few unwelcome and obscure arguments is small.

Accordingly the possibility of a well-placed, potentially powerful solution is good news indeed. To paraphrase Konrad Lorenz's comment: *Man is the missing link between apes and human beings,* I propose that Inner-Directedness of the Fleming/Thomson variety is the missing link between human beings and persons.

Accordingly I appeal to women and to members of the Fleming/Thomson group:

- Take off your High Hats.
- Climb down from your High Horses.
- Stop fussing about a few favourite people. Stop blaming a tawdry stable of villains for stuff going wrong.
- Stop bickering about who can build the best 'Womb with a View'.

You have bigger fish to fry.

A few suggestions:

- The first thing necessary is a way for Inner-Directeds to identify one another. Of course most Inner-Directeds are women and eminently discernible.

443

However Inner-Directeds of the Fleming/Thomson variety, usually bedraggled males, can be hard to pick out.

This is an issue because people who retain a bit of wildness are a valuable resource – but only if they find ways to co-ordinate their activities into useful responses to institutions, corporations and governments.

- In practical terms this means resurrecting local economies and communities, the natural habitat of Inner-Directeds. This will require all of the skills, tools and half-ton trucks Fleming/Thomson types have at their disposal – and a good deal of luck besides.

On its face this is not much of a plan. However an enormous pool of potential help is nearby. Fifty per cent of human beings are Inner-Directed women!

The fact that neither women nor Fleming/Thomson types recognize their common Inner-Directedness makes the possibility even more exciting. Perhaps all that is needed, even at this stage in the game, is for these Inner-Directeds to join forces and catalyse a *devolution.* If subsistence living, families and communities ever consciously root up, the idea could spread like wildfire!

After all, distributed-living technologies now exist that had not been dreamed of fifty years ago. The INTERNET and social media could co-ordinate producing and marketing goods and services locally. Solar and wind energy options, fuel-cells and lithium battery technologies make distributed, decentralized communities possible.

To the extent that these resources are thoughtfully deployed, communities could still extricate themselves from thralldom.

Is this likely to happen? I am guardedly optimistic. We have learned a great deal about what happens to economies and civil society when the equilibriums and countervails inherent in subsistence living are obliterated.

- A symbol would help Fleming/Thomson individuals and women identify one another. This image (see below) should be suitable to put on half-ton trucks, T-shirts and tool boxes – and perhaps even serve as a flag for a new political party!

- What a party this would be! Meetings would never be held, platforms would never be struck or candidates fielded.

- Such a party would improve democratic outcomes every day of every year. Think about it! A party of individuals congenitally unable to join an organization could become the *Latent Political Force (LPF)* party.

- Every political party needs a slogan. Politicians often talk about *revolutionary change.* Sometimes they mean what they say and *REVOLUTIONS* occur. This has never been a good idea. Revolutionary wheels have moved many times and they always conclude with a 'new few' at the top, a new crop of survivors at the bottom and countless lives ground up, ground down and ground away.

- In keeping with their sinewy, recalcitrant nature, members of the Latent Political Force party would reject this exhausted, noisome business.

  The LPF slogan expresses an idea whose time has come: *DEVOLUTION*

The LPF slogan also underscores a truth democratic populations have lost track of. What people get up to between elections determines how lives and nations proceed. The vigour and scale of self-sufficiency, the proportion of livelihoods achieved by subsistence activities..., represent what people really think of governments and corporations.

Democratic elections have become tawdry reality shows distracting citizens from the only enfranchisement that matters – the possibility of saying no to corporations, no to progress and development... and developing ways and means of making this repudiation mean something.

Replacing corrupt or ineffectual politicians with individuals who will be corrupted in turn because they have been elected is a recipe for disaster. The way to achieve wholesome democracies is to make sure citizens have ways and means of sanctioning central economies by participating in (voting for) local alternatives and subsistence activities.

This sanctioning would not require anything approaching 100% withdrawal. Moving from complete dependence to 10% or 20% *local sourcing* would send a strong message.

Moreover, once the idea of subsistence activities as a new form of political enfranchisement roots up, once technologies start being developed with community-building possibilities in mind, who knows what the future could hold!

Think of your favourite politician, then imagine him or her with a suitable frown on his or her visage!

My example is Daryl Kramp, Canada's member of Parliament for Prince Edward-Hastings:

Clearly these images need work. (Mr. Kramp remains smiling.)

Modern Problems, Ancient Perspectives

They were harvested from the INTERNET (in fact from Mr. Kramp's website) and have poor resolutions. I was worried about this and contacted Mr. Kramp's constituency office to see if they would send along something better.

After waiting a few weeks I realized that *poor resolution* was an excellent rendering, not only of the subject but of issues that have us by the throat.

I will conclude with something exciting. Recently I came across a symbol Inner-Directeds could use to identify one another. This image, based on the work of American psychologist Joseph Jastrow (1863-1944), is a veritable 'moving picture' that switches from duck to rabbit, rabbit to duck... as you watch.

This restlessness illustrates a claim made earlier. What we think of as objects composed or carved out of elements mined from the material world are better understood as guesses or predictions based on experiences. Jastrow's duck-rabbit demonstrates that what appear to be tangible objects are the results of cognitive events triggered by information streaming from internal and external events.

This means that the processes responsible for conscious episodes are more nuanced than we think. The alternative I have been sketching is that objects imagined into existence are not renditions of actual objects in an external world. They are *predictions* about how events will unfold, predictions informed by our respective, private experiences and physiological states.

Hungry people generate more food images out of ambiguous stimuli than well-fed people.

Modern Problems, Ancient Perspectives

With regards to the Jastrow image, conscious episodes are *involved* when rabbits switch to ducks and ducks become rabbits. However consciousness is not choosing when these switches occur or what the results will look like.

As far as we know, only human beings have sufficiently capacious brains to not only generate the conscious episodes that make Jastrow's switching images work but to have enough temporal depth to allow them to be seen working!

To return to the business at hand, I propose that whether persons eventually hatch out of raw human beings depends upon whether individual narratives retain enough childlike curiosity to experience images in the raw.

Whenever we take images too seriously we risk collapsing into realism, common sense, doctrinaire views and self-idolatrization. We risk strutting about with leaders' hats on or, more likely, tucking in behind some such individual, hoping he or she does not notice our treachery.

Jastrow's duck/rabbit performs another service. The symbol reminds us that – just because the images populating common-sense never shift around – the simplest, most elegant and plausible story is still that they are also imaginary.

This restiveness, this unwillingness to be pinned down, is why Jastrow's duck/rabbit could be an excellent symbol for women, for Fleming/Thomson individuals – and possibly for the quicksilver LPF party. Because they refuse to become leaders or followers women and Fleming/Thomson individuals retain the possibility of becoming *persons.*

Let me attempt a definition: a person is any human being capable of creating value where none existed, using a combination of internal and external resources. Women have this capacity from birth. When men are involved the picture is less optimistic. However the same calculation applies. Persons have an element of unpredictability reflecting the inscrutable nature of internal cognitive processes; and the value they generate must be greater than the value they suck up.

Vernon Molloy

Albert Einstein was such a person. Adolph Hitler was not.

Intuitively, individuals are more likely to transform into persons in the context of subsistence life-styles and communities. The reason is simple. To the extent that individuals understand what it going on holistically and wholesomely, to the extent that they see themselves as workers and consumers simultaneously, they are positioned to see the world and one another in inclusive, empathic ways.

This capacity to be inclusive and empathic belongs to women as a birthright. The problem is that their empathic circles rarely extend beyond a few people. Men have relatively little automatically-occurring empathic capacity. This is one reason they instinctively hold women in high regard.

This is also why primitive and insecure men attempt to secure 'their women' from lustful eyes; or, if they have a secure perch in some institution, to brandish, flaunt or abuse them.

The other reason for fraught male/female relationships is that women can give birth and men cannot. Women are the creators of life, or at least its principal conduit. Men cannot come close to this potency – no matter how powerful their trucks, no matter how they bristle with tools, no matter how skilled they become in their use.

Here's the picture I see:

- 50% of human beings are women. Every woman is Inner-Directed. Nothing can be done about this. Nothing should be done about this – even though corporations promoting *in vitro* fertilization and frozen egg technologies are sniffing around.

- Somewhere between 5% and 10% of male human beings are Inner-Directed, no matter what their circumstances. They are not as vigorously Inner-Directed as women. They tend to lead disordered lives, especially if they do not establish a relationship with a woman.

- This population of Inner-Directeds thrives in the

context of subsistence activities, families and communities. If substance activities are not occurring, for example because of urbanization and specialization, Fleming/Thomson Inner-Directeds do what they can to keep the possibility alive.

They do what they do under the radar. They do not always take out building permits. They do not report all of their income and rarely organize receipts by the month.

Fleming/Thomson Inner-Directeds are reservoir persons. We all know a few. We often have them on speed-dial.

- What is more important than their uncommon resourcefulness and utility is the quality of their awarenesses. For example, Inner-Directeds – and I think only Inner-Directeds – occasionally integrate sustainability issues and empathic concerns in what they get up to. This should be contrasted with the half-witted conscious episodes occurring in leaders and followers and producers and consumers.

- The remaining 40% – 45% of men are hard-wired to sort themselves into leader/follower arrangements.

- They are also hard-wired to seek out women and offer their nest-building services.

- How did this come to pass? Perhaps 10,000 years ago human beings figured out that sex had procreational as well as recreational utility. As soon as this understanding spread, hunters and gatherers settled down. They invented communities and agriculture. They did this because they suddenly realized that they needed to keep an eye on one another and do some serious nest building.

The resulting *agrarian* culture formally sanctioned men to seek out women willing to take them on as helpers. Their quid pro quo was a sense of purpose, identity and a bit of existential relief.

As well, men gained opportunities to help out with

nurturing responsibilities. They leveraged this foot-in-the-door into sometimes iron-clad guarantees that they would get exclusive rights to participate in reproductive events getting domestic balls rolling.

In spite of its charms, this Faustian bargain is the most dangerous element in human beings' cultural inventory. Although highly empathic within small spheres, women seem incapable of worrying about what is going on more than a few hours or a few miles away from where they live.

The men they take on as domestic adjuncts have even smaller spheres of engagement. Indeed, this is a make-or-break requirement during employment interviews in back rooms and back seats.

The consequences are coming fast and furious. Once men realized that they could steal a sense of purpose and identity from women, once they tasted domesticity's delights, a new rendering of Hell on Earth rooted up.

Last year's accommodations are no longer sufficient! More importantly, there is no reason to hope that the 'progress project' will ever come to a halt because enough has been accomplished.

This means that today's problems are not due to greedy corporations, corrupt politicians or megalomaniacs. They flow from the fact that men and women see the world from complementary, half-witted viewpoints. Each sanctions and goads the other into ever more luxurious, ever more accommodating projects.

These projects are chortled over by the corporations capitalizing them and harvesting fortunes.

No conceivable threat will ever cause women to say: "That's enough lads! Thanks very much! Let's pause until we figure out how how much comfort we really need. Let's think about survivable ways to get it."

I can report that any male proposing any such understanding will be given short shrift indeed.

Modern Problems, Ancient Perspectives

Just in case this is not motivation enough, a 'green solution' appears to be crossing the horizon. The world's wealthy have an incentive – and they now possess the needed technological and political machineries – to render the rest of us so poor that mankind's aggregate footprint becomes sustainable.

Ironically, unless men and women start talking to one another and coming up with alternatives, this is the best we can hope for. Having air to breathe and water to drink is worth something.

I hope I have persuaded you that one such alternative involves local economies and subsistence activities.

If human beings are to survive globalization and technological development, we must organize corresponding *localizations*. The 'rest of us' must achieve local economies generating 20%, 30%, perhaps 50%... of what we need.

There is only one chance of this happening. The world's Fleming/Thomson types must join forces with women and become catalysts for local communities and subsistence forms of life.

Is this likely to happen? I am not sure. I know that Mr. Fleming's and Mr. Thomson's ancestors functioned as reservoir populations keeping the possibility of persons alive through the collapse of many civilizations[96].

If they pull our fat out of the fire one more time, perhaps we will finally get it right.

---

[96]The number historian Arnold Toynbee believes can be identified is 19:
http://en.wikipedia.org/wiki/Arnold_J._Toynbee

Vernon Molloy

Afterword:

I have other projects you might find interesting.

- *The Backlander Project* should be finished in 2016. This book includes arguments for economic and political decentralization and describes subsistence strategies including expanding labour unionism to include consumers as complementary bargaining entities.

- *The Colour of Angels* is a discussion of religiosity, atheism and agnosticism from a *transcendental* perspective — a way of thinking that asks whether belief systems are or can be internally coherent.

  - Transcendental arguments work especially well with religious issues because they do not depend upon external evidence or critiques.
  - Tenets, axioms and 'received truths' can often be shown to be mutually incompatible.

- This presents an interesting challenge. Even if Divine Sources are claimed as a foundation, faith-based lives still require an internally-coherent core language if doctrines are to be comprehensible and communicated to other people and new generations.

I have been thinking about evolution as manifesting the fundamental theorem of calculus. Every creatures is a calculus machine. Lives consist of acting upon derivatives based upon integrations. The consciousness human beings are capable creates the possibility of second, third... order derivates depending upon the 'cognitive capaciousness' of individuals. The connection is with the "Concrete Problem" discussion above

http://www.backlander.ca contains material and arguments relevant to all of these projects. I have example database projects facilitating communities, subsistence activities, local economies and group shopping.

454

Modern Problems, Ancient Perspectives

If you would like to be informed if anything comes of these projects email: *ivanhoe@sympatico.ca* or write me at 1579 Hollowview Road, R. R. # 2, Stirling, Ontario K0K 3E0

Index

Alphabetical Index

48077045R00250

Made in the USA
Charleston, SC
23 October 2015